To Matt,

With thanks for in strengthening Anglo-

& every best wish,

[signature]

Savile Club
6.6.11

D1321248

MY LIFE OF CRIME

MY LIFE OF CRIME

Cases and Causes

Sir Ivan Lawrence QC

Book Guild Publishing
Sussex, England

To my beloved Gloria and Rachel.

And to my many close friends, legal and political colleagues and members of my family, who have played such important parts in my life yet I have not been able to mention in this book; they know who they are, and will understand and forgive me.

And to my publishers Carol and Joanna at Book Guild without whose help and encouragement this book would not have been published. James Morton's 'True Crime' books have been invaluable in jogging my memory.

The flaws and failings are all mine.

Contents

Foreword

This book is a gem. It recounts the life and career of Sir Ivan Lawrence. And what a life it has been and, happily, still is.

Almost 50 years as a barrister and 23 as a Member of Parliament, Ivan Lawrence has taken part in some of the most notorious criminal trials of our era and some of its most tumultuous political controversies as well. He tells his story with gusto and humour, and the reader will not be disappointed.

The criminal trials brought him into contact with many of the most famous, and infamous, criminals of the age – the Krays, the Richardsons, Mad Frankie Fraser and very many others all make an appearance.

Very early in his career he defended the Kray twins on a blackmail charge. They were acquitted. Later, in May 1968, he represented Ronald Kray when he was accused, with others, of the murder of George Cornell at the Blind Beggar Public House in Whitechapel, and then the murders of Jack 'the Hat' McVitie and of 'Mad Axeman' Frank Mitchell. He appealed his client's convictions all the way up to the House of Lords.

Later trials included those of mass murderer Denis Nilsen and of Russell Bishop, wrongly accused of the Babes in the Wood murder in 1986.

Accounts of the earlier trials are replete with instances of police malpractice often aided by the fact that there was, at the time, no tape recording of interviews the police conducted with those suspected of committing an offence.

This was something that Sir Ivan himself, as a Member of Parliament, did much to remedy. And the book is a brilliant account of the trials and tribulations of life as a backbench MP. We are taken through the torturous route to selection for a winnable seat, the thrills and spills of elections and the many demands and satisfactions of life in Parliament when you've got there.

The campaign for the introduction of tape recording police interviews was only one of the many causes in the course of which Sir Ivan was able to bring his practical experience as a barrister to bear on the lawmaking issues facing the House of Commons.

And the book is, above all, a testimony to the ability of people like Ivan Lawrence to combine two careers, one in Parliament and one outside, to the great benefit of both and of the country as a whole. No one reading this book would dare suggest that either career suffered. Both Sir Ivan's constituents and his clients obtained full value from his services.

Yet it is now becoming more and more difficult, and in the case of practising barristers virtually impossible, to continue an outside career with a seat in the House of Commons.

Sir Ivan is one of the very last of a dying breed. And we will all be the poorer as a consequence.

Michael Howard,
Lord Howard of Lympne, QC
Leader of the Conservative Party 2003–2005, Home Secretary 1993–1997.

Preface

Why bother to read the memoir of a less-than-famous MP and criminal lawyer? A fair question, so may I tell you why I have written this book?

In the past fifty years I have been privileged to play a small part in politics, particularly during the momentous Thatcher years, and in the law, engaged in some really fascinating criminal trials, like those of the Krays and Denis Nilsen. Members of Parliament make laws and create crimes, so they ought to realise what effect those laws will have on people. The inter-linking of these two careers will be of interest to anyone curious about how Britain operates. But there is a very important difference between the political and the legal advocate which may be one reason why, contrary to mythology, there are so few practising lawyers in Parliament. The political advocate speaks of his, or her, own beliefs and causes, and to be effective, must do so with passion. The lawyer advocate speaks for someone else, his client, and to be at his most effective he must do so analytically and without passion.

I hope that my family, friends, those whose lives I may have touched along the way, and the general reader, might enjoy remembering some of the cases and causes in which I have been an advocate. Moreover, I believe that those of us who have been fortunate enough to have made something of our lives, despite expectations to the contrary, ought to pass on some of our experiences, and with them the message of hope and encouragement, to others who may want to follow down the same path. Someone asked Sir Isaac Newton how he could see so far ahead. 'Because,' he answered, 'I stand on the shoulders of Galileo.' We all have something to learn from others and the wheel does not always need to be reinvented. And those entering careers in the law and politics have the right to expect guidance and encouragement from those who have been there before them, to help them to choose what to attempt and what to avoid. They might also learn that you do not have to be brilliant to make a difference and contribute to the happiness of others in the community or to live a happy and useful life.

One of the greatest American judges, Oliver Wendell Holmes, famously said in a Memorial Day Address: 'I think that, as life is action and passion, it is required of a man that he should share the passion and action of his time, at peril of being judged not to have lived.' It must be for others to say whether these following episodes of action and passion in which I have played a part have been interesting enough to share with my reader. It has, alas, been necessary for me to say something about myself and my upbringing in order to set the context and for this I apologise.

I must also be honest and say that I hope that when I have gone, I may have left, if not something as big as a footprint, at least a very small toe-mark in the sand.

1

My Family and Earliest Years

'Begin at the beginning,' the King said gravely, 'and go on till you come to the end: then stop.'

(Lewis Carroll: *Alice in Wonderland*)

1936 was a year of momentous events. King George V died, Nazi Germany re-occupied the Rhineland, the Arabs in Palestine revolted against British rule, Italy invaded and annexed Ethiopia, the *Queen Mary* made her maiden voyage across the Atlantic, the Spanish Civil War began, the Olympic Games were held in Berlin, the BBC launched its first television service, and President Franklin Roosevelt was re-elected on a landslide. For my parents, a few days after the abdication of King Edward VIII, there was my birth. The event very nearly took place in Woolworths, where my mother was Christmas shopping when she went into labour. The shock of my birth and infancy must have been considerable, for I remained an only child.

Our families had been surprised that my mild-tempered father, Israel (known as Leslie), a short, dark-haired, dapper and attractive man with a neat moustache, who had been the part-time choirmaster at Middle Street Synagogue in Brighton, and who often wore spats to work as an electrician, should have married my mother. That they had a child was, for some reason, an even greater surprise. This may have been because my dear mother, Sarah (known as Sadie), a very pleasing-looking brown-haired girl, was much less mild-tempered. In fact her father had actually warned my father against the marriage. She was also very strong-willed. After my father had fallen off his motorcycle several times, she made him leave it at the nearby garage for good. She would make him hand over his pay packet every Thursday night, bank it, and give him pocket money. A hard-working shorthand typist, she eventually set up and ran one of the first secretarial employment bureaux in Britain. She was very bright, and one of my treasures is a *Complete Works of Shakespeare* given

1

to her in March 1920 for 'good conduct and good work' at school prize day by Mr Joseph Lyons, the magnate of an empire of tea, tea shops, ice cream and Corner Houses.

She was devoted to the family and was a most caring mother. After the war she would walk to my boarding school every Wednesday, with fresh eggs for my tea which father must have obtained on the black market. She was also ridiculously frugal. To save money she would get off the number 35 bus at the bottom of Montpelier Road, where we lived, and walk the three hundred yards up a steep hill laden with shopping bags, rather than pay an extra penny for the ride to the next bus stop that was more or less outside our house. The wartime generation saved where they could.

It is one of the strange paradoxes of my financially careful mother's life that she developed a passion for greyhound racing in her thirties and, in her later years, became a regular player of roulette and blackjack at the Brighton Metropole casino, prepared to lose hundreds of pounds in an evening. For her, looking after the pennies did not necessarily mean that the pounds would look after themselves. My father shared these enthusiasms, though with more restraint. Sadly my dear parents are no longer playing at the casino tables which, in their old age, became so much a part of their lives. I have had inscribed above their graves the words that they used to hear most often from the croupier: '*Rien ne va plus*'. I think that they would have enjoyed that.

Forebears

My mother's parents were Romanian immigrants who had met, while escaping a pogrom at the turn of the century, on a boat to Britain. They spoke yiddish at home and were, as immigrants often are, obsessive in admiration of their new country. Their deep affection for the British Royal Family was expressed by buying every outsize volume of *Royalty in Procession*, *Royalty at Weddings and Christenings* and *Royalty at Tiger and Elephant Shoots* that they could lay their hands on. They set up a tailoring business at 248 Old Kent Road in South London and had four daughters, Fay, Bee, Rosie and Sadie, and a son, Alan. He grew up to become a West End bandleader, club manager and man of property. Auntie Fay became the mother of my cousin Alma Cogan, the top British pop singer of the Fifties and Sixties, 'the girl with the laugh in her voice' – and of her sister, actress Sandra Caron. My grandparents were bombed out of Old Kent Road in 1940. They moved to Shepherds Bush where, in 1941, they were also bombed out, and moved to join their daughters in Brighton where, in 1942, they were bombed out yet again. They died a decade later – of natural causes.

My father's grandparents, on his father's side, were from Vilna in Russia. They had also fled to Britain to escape a pogrom in the late nineteenth century. His grandparents on his mother's side were from Italy and South Africa. My father's parents were British, and my grandfather fought in the British army in the trenches of Flanders in the First World War. The family became tailors and furriers and settled in Stroud. My father was born in Bristol. He had two brothers, Wilfred and Sidney, and a sister Pauline. Pauline is still, thankfully, with us and Sidney lived until recently, to the age of almost 89. That he survived at all past his twenties was almost miraculous, so I must tell my reader about him.

Group Captain Peter Townsend, Princess Margaret's paramour, was, until his death in 1998, a good friend of Uncle Sid. In his book *The Postman of Nagasaki*, 25 pages are devoted to parts of my uncle's amazing life. When the Second World War ended, Sidney was the sole survivor of a Royal Air Force squadron that had been wiped out on the island of Java. For several years he was a prisoner of war in Japanese prison camps. He escaped. He was found, brought back to camp and tortured. His accounts are horrific and amazing, and I tried to persuade him to write them down, but I do not think he ever did so. You can hear some of them, which he was prevailed upon to tape-record, at the Imperial War Museum. Then, as if he had not experienced horrors enough, on 9 August 1945 he was in Nagasaki when the atomic bomb exploded above his head – and he lived!

He had been on a Mitsubishi working party, clearing debris from an earlier bombing. The other prisoners in his group had moved round to the front of a small hill ahead of him. When the bomb exploded, Sid threw himself down and must have been protected from the blast by the mound. When it was all over, he picked himself up and went in search of his friends. They were the other side of the mound – they were just bones. How could anyone have been so close to that blast and that radiation, and lived? Seventy thousand people died, and Japan surrendered six days later – perhaps saving millions more lives. When he was repatriated to England, Sid was in a terrible physical and mental state. My mother looked after him and, he swore, saved his life. Until his death, he lived with Pearl in a charming flat on Hove seafront. And that is another story.

Pearl had married Sidney in 1940, a few weeks before he left for the Far East. He says that the thought of her waiting for his return sustained him throughout his appalling ordeals. When he returned to Britain he found that she, believing he was dead, had married someone else. Sidney met a girl called Irene, married again, and had a son. Irene died in 1986. When I next saw Sidney he was living in Hove with his first love and first wife, Pearl. They had each lived their separate lives without contact, then met up again by chance and decided to live together for the rest of their days.

Sidney practised his Orthodox Judaism, for he said that his belief helped him in his hours of greatest need. Although suffering from throat cancer and leukaemia, both held mercifully in check for a number of years – his doctor assured him this was due to the amount of plutonium in his body – he would lead the Sabbath morning service at the Middle Street Synagogue, which has had no Rabbi since the previous incumbent, Rabbi Fabricant passed away. 'Fabbi' used to tell me that he had a son interested in politics whom he would like me to meet, and so we did. In time his son, Michael Fabricant, became Tory MP for Lichfield and my next constituency neighbour.

When the VJ day celebrations took place, on a Saturday in June 1995, I was invited to the cathedral service at Lichfield as one of the MPs in the diocese. But Uncle Sidney was leading a service of thanksgiving at Middle Street Synagogue, and I wanted to be with him to pay my respects. I was torn, so my wife Gloria and I decided to split the engagements. She attended the service at Lichfield Cathedral; I attended the service at the Brighton synagogue. After the Brighton service the congregation adjourned for luncheon in the Fabricant Room, which adjoins the synagogue.

'Where is Michael Fabricant?' congregants asked. 'At this very moment,' I was able to answer, 'he will be sitting with my wife in a front row at Lichfield Cathedral.' Rabbi Fabricant would have been delighted.

My father left school at fourteen, and enlisted in the Merchant Navy. He rose to the heights of purser's assistant on RMS *Olympic*, as it plied its 'Blue Riband' way across the Atlantic to and from New York. He had stories to tell about himself and Tallulah Bankhead, the silent-movie star. He made himself invaluable on the ship as friend and helper to

Jews who were fleeing Central Europe for America before the war, and who could speak only yiddish. He was the kind of storyteller who was so good at weaving together fact and fiction that we were never quite sure which was which. When, towards the end of his life, as he felt his strength ebbing away, he dictated some of his experiences onto tape. Sadly I have not yet found time to listen and transcribe them: perhaps there will be another book!

My mother, fed up with my father's travelling, had made him set up in business as an electrician, from a shop in Brighton. He was very clever with his hands, and no mechanical task ever seemed to be beyond him. Some time before direction indicators appeared on cars, he designed an imitation hand at the end of a metal arm which, on the throw of a switch on the dashboard, would spring up and indicate the direction in which the driver was proposing to turn. Proudly he showed his invention to others, but sadly never thought to get it patented.

When I was young, I used to go with my father to the homes of his customers, when he was installing and mending their electrics. I was required to hand him his tools, but I was easily bored, and always yawning. Once, while daydreaming, I forgot where I was, and put my foot through a ceiling, bringing down a shower of debris upon a dining-room table below. That may have taught me to be careful where I put my feet later in life.

Dad was very charming, especially to the ladies, and was much in demand, though mother expected me to go with him in school holidays – in case he got too charming. When the war came, he worked at the great factory of Allen West in Lewes Road, on the construction of the radar location equipment that helped to save Britain from invasion. It was a priority war effort and my father was never allowed to join up for active fighting service, though not for want of trying.

He enlisted in the army and was sent for officer selection. He was brought back to Allen West by men in grey suits dispatched to fetch him, because his war work was considered to be more important than anything he was likely to achieve on active duty. He disagreed. He enlisted in the Royal Air Force, and was again brought back by the men in grey suits. Finally he tried the Royal Navy, but the same thing happened. He had to make do by joining the Home Guard. I used to play with my father's helmet, Sten gun (unloaded), and other military equipment, including our gas masks, which hung in his tool cupboard. He spent the war at Allen West where he became a shop steward in the Amalgamated Engineering Union, and then was elected regional president.

'Les could always get things done for us,' I was later told by one who worked with him, 'because he never took "no" for an answer.' I think he learnt that from my mother; and I must have inherited that trait from both of them.

After the war my father manufactured brushes for builders and decorators with his uncle Julius, from a factory, now a porn shop, in Surrey Street in Brighton. He was also the firm's salesman. When I was eight or nine, I used to go with him in my school holidays, when he sold the brushes and chamois leathers. As he went from shop to shop, in towns and suburbs all over southern England, I would sometimes nip into a shop my father had told me he was going to visit, and tell the shopkeeper that I was helping my dad to sell brushes and chamois leathers. When he arrived to do the business, he would be met with: 'I'm so sorry, Mr Lawrence, you're too late. We've just bought two dozen brushes and a gross of chamois leathers from this young man!' That is where I learnt the art of cold-calling for a sale, which might have turned me into a secondhand car salesman, but in fact gave me the self-confidence to become a politician – and also to stand up to judges in court.

In later years, my father became a property negotiator, worked for a time as a salesman for Michael Winner's father, owned some houses of his own, managed one or two old people's homes for friends and family, and became a name at Lloyds. He was never wealthy and, unhappily, the 1980s Lloyds asbestos crash, together, I suspect, with my mother's gaming losses, meant that practically all that I inherited in the end was the family house in Brighton with its four sublet flats.

When I was born, my parents were living in Norton Road, Hove. This would be of little interest to anyone except for an extraordinary coincidence. Forty-two years later, my wife and I were staying with friends in Beverly Hills in California. One evening they gave a dinner party, at which two of the guests were Alice and Alan Gardener, who used to tour the world for artefacts with which to stock their antique shop in one of the Hollywood boulevards. Next day we went to visit their shop. At the entrance was a 'lucky dip' basket in which I saw some parchment tied, in the British legal fashion, with pink tape. Being curious, I opened it up. It was the title deed, dated 1884, to the very houses next door to where I had been born in Norton Road, Hove! The odds against such a coincidence must surely be greater than winning the National Lottery – about which more later.

Another of the dinner guests was the astronaut Scott Carpenter. He told us that, as he hurtled through space, he could not keep the thought from his mind that every part of his capsule had been manufactured and installed by the lowest bidder!

I have vivid memories of my childhood in Brighton. I was sturdy and wilful, so my family called me 'Butch.' At two years of age I was pushing other children, often fully clothed, into the paddling pool on the seafront by the West Pier. I had another joking activity: if I pulled away strongly enough from grown-ups taking me for a walk, my arm would dislocate and frighten the life out of them. As a small child I was very inquisitive. I had seen my father put plugs into sockets causing lights and radios to come on, and I longed to be like him, a person who could make things happen. At the age of two I stood on a chair, took a key from the Yale lock, plunged it into an electric wall socket and was shocked – literally – to see it melt in my little hand. I went off electricity, but the desire to make things happen has stayed with me all my life.

I first ran away when my mother left me strapped in my pram, as mothers had little fear of doing in those days, outside Plummer Roddis, the department store at the bottom of Montpelier Road where we lived. I must have un-strapped myself, for I can hardly believe that any passer-by would have done it in response to a request from very little me, though the task cannot have been easy for me to accomplish on my own. I must then, with astonishing precocity, have asked a kindly grown-up to take me across the busy and dangerous Western Road. That done, I would have run 300 yards up the hill to my home, at number 73. When my distraught mother arrived an hour later, fearing the worst and trailing the local constabulary behind her, I explained that I had got tired of waiting. I was three years old.

To forestall any developing tendency to impatience, I was issued with a nanny. She lived just down the road and came in daily to look after me. It is a little surprising to recall that even working-class families had nannies in those days. Several of my aunts and uncles had maids and one had a chauffeur/handyman. With hundreds of thousands of men and women 'in service' – considered to be a very respectable occupation – there can have been very little unemployment.

Schooldays

I have many memories of the war – the air-raid sirens, the blackouts, the 'closed for the duration' sign on the local shoe shop. My father being on war work and in the Home Guard, and my mother being a secretary by day and fire-watcher by night, I was sent off to board at St Anne's Kindergarten School in Norfolk Road – all of 200 yards from my home. There I was machine gunned.

In August 1942 a Messerschmitt fighter was shot down by the seafront defences, and crashed on the edge of St Anne's Wells Park just behind us. The siren must have gone off, and I have no doubt that Miss Townsend, the headmistress, called us in from the school garden in which some of us were playing. But I have always been slow to answer calls from officialdom. The pilot, probably too low to use his parachute, had decided to meet his end gloriously, with all guns blazing. To this day I can remember the gravel being churned up by his machine-gun shells only feet away from where I continued to play in the garden. Later we all went to see where the plane had crashed: it had, tragically, demolished a house with an entire family inside it.

On another occasion, as I was on my way to have the mastoid I was developing in my ear treated at the Ear, Nose and Throat Hospital, another German fighter was shot down over the town. I saw the pilot's body, dismembered by shells, coming slowly down on a parachute into St Nicholas's churchyard a few yards from me. I remember, too, being on a seafront bus when the British army blew up part of Brighton's West and Palace Piers. This was to make things difficult for any invading Germans who might choose to arrive by pier rather than by the beach, upon which concrete tank traps had been laid for them.

When my parents could take a week off for a summer holiday, we used to go and stay on Mr Brown's farm, ten miles outside Brighton, at Barcombe Mills. There, on one occasion, I watched with a child's wonder two Hurricane fighters bravely positioning themselves to nudge a 'doodle-bug' (V1) off course, until it crashed into the field next to the riverbank into which my father had pulled our small rowing boat for shelter. In the evening we watched the glow in the distance, as London burned after a blitz.

As a child I was quite musical, inheriting the modest musical genes of my extended family. My mother could play the piano a little, and used to turn the pages for Auntie Fay (cousin Alma's mother), at the piano of the Trocadero silent-movie house at the Elephant and Castle. In the annual music festival at Brighton's Dome, where my school was a contestant, I played 'The Pirate King', and we won first prize in our class. I was then all of five years old. Ten years later, during the 1951 Festival of Britain, my school put on a production of German's *Merrie*

England. I sang in the girls' chorus and pulled the entire front row into the orchestra pit on dress rehearsal night. I have never been asked to sing since.

I also started to learn the piano, and my mother bought an Eavestaff original 'mini-piano' with a lovely dark-green veneer, and a soft but deeply rich musical tone, from Auntie Bee. It was the sister piano to one owned by Auntie Fay. Fifty-two years later my mother, living alone at the age of 85 at our home in Montpelier Road, sat down to watch *Home and Away* in the dining room. She must have lit a cigarette, had a heart attack, and died on the spot. As she fell she dropped the cigarette, and the room went up in flames around her. It was horrible. About the only piece of furniture that could be salvaged was the piano. Although the veneer had been quite badly burnt, I thought I should have it renovated for memory's sake. It now fits beautifully into my daughter Rachel's flat and she, a talented pianist, now plays it.

A few years ago, while reading cousin Sandra Caron's biography of her sister Alma, Rachel noticed that Paul McCartney had composed 'Yesterday' on Auntie Fay's piano. She telephoned me excitedly, in the early hours of the morning, for reassurance that she had inherited that priceless piano. I had, alas, to tell her that she had not inherited Auntie Fay's piano – only Auntie Bee's!

When I was seven, my parents tried to get me into Brighton College, the public school, but they were told that the school already had its full quota of Jews. I do not remember anyone thinking that this was an infringement of my civil liberties or discrimination against Jews. It just never occurred to anyone in Britain at that time: we all knew our place. So I took an examination and passed into Brighton Hove and Sussex Grammar School for Boys in Dyke Road, Hove. This splendid educational institution has been the alma mater of Aubrey Beardsley (the famous illustrator), C.B. Cochran (the musical-comedy impresario), Professor S.T. Bindoff (the historian), Walter Adams (the Principal of the London School of Economics) and a notable succession of famous musicians, politicians, lawyers, sportsmen, generals, admirals and successful businessmen. A short time ago, out of the Royal Navy's 32 admirals, four were old boys of this school: how many other grammar schools of our great seafaring nation can boast such an achievement?

In 1912 the school left its premises in Buckingham Road for what was a greenfield site on the borders of Brighton and Hove, where Dyke Road meets the Old Shoreham Road. The new occupant of the old site was to be the Sussex Maternity Hospital. Because the school motto had been set into a stone block as part of the arch of the building's entrance, it was too difficult to remove. Nothing could have been more appropriate for the building's new occupants, for the motto was *Absque Labore Nihil* – nothing without labour! It was in that hospital that I was born twenty-four years later. I remained at the Grammar School for eleven years, a length of time I share only with Michael Till, the former Dean of Winchester, whose father had, not altogether appropriately for his son's future career, opened the first Brighton casino at the Hotel Metropole – the casino at which my parents were to become regulars.

Perhaps because I was an only child, I enjoyed my school years and the company of other children, although they were not without their moments of pain. Until I reached the age of eleven, I used to make the twenty-minute walk to school every day from Montpelier Road on my own: in those days no one thought that it was a dangerous thing for a child to do. It was on my arrival at school that problems occurred. The reigning bullies of the day often snatched my school cap and followed up with a fusillade of fists and feet, accompanied by shouts of 'here's the dirty Jew boy'. It was, after all, at the end of the war that a lot of people seemed, oddly, to think might never have happened but for the Jews. I was not particularly frail or skinny, and arms whirling like a dervish, I usually gave as good as I got. On one occasion Mr Pewtress, the PT master who had played cricket for Lancashire, separated me from my tormentor, and took us both off to the gym. He made us put on boxing gloves. With one inelegant but vicious swipe I knocked my opponent off balance and he crashed against the wall-bars, unhappily putting him out of school for many weeks. This must have done wonders for my playground 'cred', for I cannot recall anyone ever really hurting me after that. From that day to this, I do not think I have ever landed a physical blow on anyone else, elegantly or otherwise. It did perhaps teach me that you have to be prepared to stand up to the bullies in life.

There were days when, walking to school, I would catch up with a much bigger and older boy, Fenton Bresler (who later became the well-known *Daily Express* legal columnist), and he would provide protection for me from possible aggressors. Strangely, I do not remember these incidents spoiling the relationship that I had with my attackers once the school day started. We still sat happily enough with each other in class, and played football together in the playground during the breaks. No aggro, no resentment, just nasty little schoolboys doing what nasty schoolboys of seven do, I suppose.

During the war many of our teachers were women. When the war ended their places were taken by their husbands, returning warriors who had taught at school before the war. These were men whose terrifying experiences on the real battlefront made them less tolerant of childishness, even from children.

'If you don't play ball with me, I won't play ball with you, and you'll find yourself batting on a sticky wicket, by golly,' said the very stern and white-moustachioed English master, Captain Alexander. He meant it. Another, Major 'Rastus' Randall, used to blow a gasket every time I handed in an essay, which, as I recall, was not all that often. Our Welsh physics master, Mr 'Stooge' Williams, was another teacher on a short fuse, and was given to either taking a rubber Bunsen burner hose to my hand, or wildly throwing the wooden blackboard cleaner at me, which would sometimes miss and hit someone or something else – and that would make him even angrier. Mr Woolven, the woodwork master, preferred words to actions: 'Don't waste this wood, sonny,' he would say, 'it doesn't grow on trees.'

I am sure that I must have been insufferable for my 'dumb insolence' as a schoolboy, for I was more often to be found outside than inside the classroom and made to stand facing the wall in the corridor. To this day I can draw the wallpaper designs and remember the details of the pictures on the walls: Van Dyke's 'Jan Arnolfini and his wife', Rembrandt's 'L'Homme de Casque d'Or', Vermeer's 'The Girl with the Pearl Earring' and a view of a small bridge over a Dutch canal, which I have always meant to visit one day. It gave me an enduring love of great paintings.

My parents used to say, of my bad school reports, that it was more important for me to be good than to do good work. How I must have disappointed them. I was caned regularly, by Mr R.J. Milton, the junior school headmaster. He was a gentleman, for he always shook hands after the action, and used to congratulate me on taking the punishment so well. Contrary to modern thinking that has outlawed such practices as inhumane, I am certain that it did me far more good than harm. I recall one proud moment when Mr W.A. Barron, the school headmaster, an enormous man with Simon Rattle-like grey hair, assessed my term's work, and congratulated me on the decided improvement in my behaviour – as indicated by no beatings and only twenty detentions. I went home with my head held high. I went on to become president of the school Old Boys Association, details of which can be found, for other old boys and interested parties, on our web site.

In 1948, the school decided to have boarders, and I enlisted enthusiastically. At first there were only 38 of us in the new Marshall

House – known, like both my later Oxford college and my still later place of work, as 'the House'. In time our number grew to over a hundred. The new headmaster was Harry Brogden, whom we all immediately liked because he had played soccer for Wolverhampton Wanderers. He lived in another part of the school building with his wife Wendy, who went on to live well into her nineties. They, the two housemasters, Mr E.S. Dickinson and Mr Stephen Pratt, and Matron, ate their meals with us, and we inevitably became a more closely knit unit than did the day-boys in their houses. The 'esprit de corps' and pride in being small Marshall House impelled us to collective victories in work, sport and music that I am certain our individual raw material would never have otherwise attained. It was also due, of course, to the strict allocation of time for work, the closeness to the cricket nets and other sporting facilities where we could practise whenever we had free time, the continual encouragement of the house-masters and, very importantly, the absence of such irritating and unnecessary distractions as girls and television.

I was in the 'A' stream at school, played soccer and cricket for the House (and sometimes for the school), was scout patrol leader of the Peewits, played the fife in the Corps of Drums, and trained and conducted the House choir in the school music competition every year. I enjoyed my boarding school years very much. I had no really close school friends, although 55 year later I was still playing squash on Sundays with one friend, Robert Blundell (a Guildford GP and former mayor and alderman of that town), who had been a House prefect, school goalkeeper and English schools discus, shot and javelin champion. Alert to the medical possibilities, he always brought his resuscitator to squash – just in case I overdid it. Very sadly it was his own playing days that recently ended with a terrible stroke, though not while playing squash.

My unsatisfactory school conduct stopped in the fourth form, although my term reports still contained such gems as: 'much promise: no fulfilment', 'not so good as he thinks he is', and in a sixth-form English comment on my essay on the early Milton by the unforgettable Jack Smithies: 'Presumptuous, supercilious, superficial and impudent. The first requisite of the student of English literature is a strong stomach: the second is intellectual humility.'

I was, by nature, rather erratic. On one athletic occasion I might sprint 100 yards in 10.5 seconds and 220 yards in 25 seconds (both excellent schoolboy achievements in those days), but on the next occasion I would take 12 seconds for the one and 30 seconds for the other. I might on one musical occasion play a piano piece flawlessly, and on the next occasion fail to hit one note correctly. In my school fourth year I came top in both history and physics and had to make a choice between science and the arts. I chose the arts, and often wonder, of course, what I might have achieved had I chosen science. I got to Oxford with a very good state scholarship, in the days when such scholarships were few and far between, yet I nearly failed my degree. I am no longer erratic, simply, I feel sure, because I have learnt the importance of hard work, targeted application and consistency.

I was also by nature quite placid and laid-back, like my father, and not adventurous enough to like roller-skating, switchback railways at the fairgrounds, or riding on motorcycles. I only asserted myself to the rather limited extent of being, I believe, the first at school to sport a 'crewcut', to wear long trousers in my class, and to tie my school tie with a 'Windsor knot.' But what did always get me going was any suggestion that I might not be good enough at something. When my English master, Mr Randall, said that my knowledge of the subject in the sixth form was 'pitiful,' I made sure that I got a distinction in my scholarship paper. When I asked my sixth-form economics master Mr Shrewsbury if, like the others, I could go to university, he said: 'Come on, Lawrence, let's not be silly...' so I drove myself to win distinctions at advanced and scholarship level economics. When the Head told me that more time in the sixth form would serve little useful purpose, and I should, perhaps, consider becoming something useful like a probation officer, I left school and won my state scholarship and Oxford entrance examinations from the Royal Air Force. I was certainly contrary and must have loved the challenges. Challenge still brings out the best in me. It must be the reason why I love the Bar and politics so much, for in both those careers challenges are constant and considerable.

A world of change

The years since my boyhood have brought so many changes in the way we live our lives that often we seem now to be in another world. In those days – before interplanetary travel, global warming, the mapped human genome, in-vitro fertilisation, stem-cell treatments, computers, the internet, mobile phones, police officers permanently in flak-jackets, human rights, women's equality, anti-biotics, drinking water at three pounds a bottle, and Harry Potter – life was so very different. Before colour television in every home, with its perpetual diet of sport, soaps, competitions, foul-mouthed stand-up comedians, latest and oldest films, and the limitless flood of information on the internet and in our newspapers, we had more time to read, to think and to do things, and there was less pressure on us to make choices. There were also far fewer distractions. Refrigerators were for the wealthy: my family had ice-boxes which were refilled weekly by a door-to-door salesman. We had outside lavatories, telephones were a luxury, and hardly anyone had television. The radio went off at midnight, unless you could get Jack Jackson on Radio Luxemburg. Mass international travel, with package tours and discounted flights in jet planes from a myriad airports, was as yet undreamt of. There were no motorways. The nation spent its holidays at Brighton, Blackpool, Margate and Southend. Cars were black, hardly ever needed to be locked, let alone alarmed, and there were so few of them that there were no parking meters or congestion charges. There was never any difficulty parking or driving into towns. But there were queues everywhere: at bus stops, at railway stations (where trains were still mainly steam-driven), in the food shops, at street telephone boxes, and at the cinema. Children always wore school uniforms. I remember receiving a 'detention', thereby having to miss a needle cricket match against our rival Varndean Grammar School, because Mr Berrey, the geography master, had seen me take off my school cap as I got onto a bus – at the age of 17!

Most people had a weekly bath night, women had one 'hair' night a week, and women and girls wore corsets, so that heavy petting after meeting a girl at a public dance was not only frowned upon, it was practically impossible. There was, of course, no equal pay for women, whose place was considered to be in the home. Few women were in parliament or the professions other than teaching, and the contraceptive pill had not yet been invented. Many young people had bad teeth (probably from the wartime concentrated orange juice children were forced to drink), and most adults had false teeth fixed to a plate which they removed when they went to bed – giving rise to the old joke: 'Your teeth are like stars, they come out at night'. A visit to the dentist was frightening. If a filling became necessary the tooth would be repaired, not with a high-speed drill after a local anaesthetic, but by the painful and forceful application of a pick, followed by the insertion of a plug of cancer-inducing amalgam. It was even fashionable for women to have all their teeth out, to avoid pain and unsightliness later in life. Everyone smoked cigarettes, and I was brought up in a perpetual fug of foul air.

As the years hurtle by, it is getting more and more difficult to remember what our lives were like in that world without digital cameras, mobile phones, i-pods, personal computers, e-mail, or the internet, when one of the major frustrations of daily life was to press button B in the street telephone boxes to get your two pennies back, only to find that the damned thing had not been emptied recently and had therefore jammed.

Behaviour in public was also very different. Nothing more than chaste kissing was allowed on the cinema screens, two people – even married couples – could not be shown to be in bed together, and sexual activity of any kind was censored. Paradoxically, when men and women danced in public they were expected to hold each other close, which was obviously far more sexually stimulating than the bodily separation of dancing today. In those days there was also theatre censorship to remove vulgarity. Today, expletives seem to have become not only acceptable, in the cinema, the theatre, and on television, but an indispensable part of ordinary everyday conversation.

A 'joint' was meat for Sunday lunch; 'chips' we ate with fish; a 'mouse' was chased by, and was food for, the cat; 'grass' grew in fields and meadows; a 'hard drive' was a batsman's stroke at a cricket match; 'coke' was what we put in the coal cellar; a 'partner' was one's business colleague; and people who were 'gay' were just jolly good company.

2

National Service and University

'Rejoice, O young man in thy youth.'
(Ecclesiastes)

While awaiting my call-up for National Service, I went to work as a labourer on the building site that was to become Crawley New Town. There I unloaded bricks from the backs of lorries, carried hundredweight sacks of cement on my back, swept houses after the plasterers, 'chippies' and 'sparks' had finished their ill-supervised and therefore often shoddy work, carried bricks in a hod up and down ladders, drove a dumper truck filled with sand, and was put in charge of a cement mixer. I also learnt that if you worked too fast, you worked yourself out of a job! I made myself so popular – or perhaps it was just that my mates, who had to work for a living, were frightened of losing their jobs – that I was deputed to speak for the men, to the bosses, about their unsatisfactory wages and conditions. I did this so successfully that I was elected a Transport and General Workers Union shop steward, and would have taken up the position – yes and probably voted Labour too – but for the arrival of my call-up papers.

These summoned me first to RAF Cardington in Bedfordshire. On this site, zeppelin airships had been built, and from there the ill-fated R101 had set out in 1935 on its voyage to India, crashing during a storm at Beauvais in France and killing all 48 officers and men on board. After the preliminaries, I went on to do my square-bashing at RAF Hednesford in Staffordshire.

I was not a very promising recruit, and Drill-Sergeant Page had it in for me on the parade square. 'You look like a sack of potatoes, Lawrence', and 'If you don't do better than this, I will back-flight you so far that you will be in the air force before Pontius was a pilot', or, as I fumbled to get my bayonet into its holster, whilst holding myself erect and looking straight ahead, 'You would find it soon enough if it had hair round it,

17

you horrible little worm' were among his more repeatable utterances. Thus acclaimed, I had next to choose my occupation for the remainder of my National Service.

Since I am lacking in physical courage, and heights give me queasy feelings below the waist, I have no idea why I ever wanted to become a fighter pilot and to fly Gloucester Meteors and Lightnings. But I did apply for the job, and was forthwith dispatched to RAF Hornchurch. There I was one of only two, out of over a hundred applicants, who passed the preliminary aptitude tests, coming first, as I recall, in finger dexterity. But I never became a fighter pilot because I failed a second medical examination – early childhood ear maladies having left me with perforated eardrums.

Forty years on, another of those strange coincidences occurred in my life. I kept having colds that then went to my chest. My GP said that I might have an allergy, and referred me to the ear, nose and throat consultant at St Georges Hospital (pre-Lanesborough Hotel) at Hyde Park Corner. I told my examiner about my early years of constant earache and near mastoid, from which, incidentally, I had been saved by having my tonsils removed. He asked if those miseries had had any lasting effect upon me. I said no apart, that was, from causing me to fail my attempt to fly jets, because I was told that sudden changes of altitude would burst my perforated eardrums. He asked where I was told such rot.

'RAF Hornchurch,' I replied. He asked when that was. '1955,' I answered. He asked the month: I told him October. Was it the beginning of the month or the end? I told him the end. He asked if it was a woman doctor who had failed me, and I did indeed recall that my examiner had been a woman.

'May I tell you something extraordinary,' he said. 'I took over from that woman medical officer at RAF Hornchurch at the end of October 1955, and discovered that she had this crazy idea that sudden changes of altitude in a jet would burst perforated eardrums. I reversed as many of her decisions as I could find, because we were losing good potential pilots.'

To think that the whole course of my life might have been different! As a pilot, had I lived through the training (as, very sadly, one or two of my school-friends did not), I would probably have signed on for longer than my two years' National Service. I might eventually have flown with BOAC. I might have become a civil airline instructor. I might have been active in the British Airline Pilots Association. I might have ended up like … Norman Tebbit.

Back in 1955 they told me that I could fly propeller planes with Transport Command, provided I signed on for three years. I told them I was only interested in flying fast and solo, and declined the offer. Instead I took up trade as a wireless operator, and went for training to RAF Compton Bassett in Wiltshire – a bleak posting where I do not remember the sun ever shining. To avoid drilling and rifles, to which I had taken an intense dislike in the Combined Cadet Force at school, I used to escape to the Education Section on the camp, and pretend that I was studying. Eventually they called my bluff. I had then to decide between being disciplined for skiving, or being looked up to on the camp as a man of intelligence and purpose. I did not hesitate. I had kept all my sixth-form notes and coming to them again for revision, after a gap in schooling of six months, must have given me fresh vitality. *Daily Mirror* leader-type journalese had been forbidden at school, where we were taught to write longer, tailored sentences, but I thought that an examiner might prefer that style to the stilted text school pupils normally produced, so I wrote short pithy sentences. It certainly paid off. The great Lord Denning, in his judgements and books I was later to learn, did the same thing.

I also had some luck. I was made to take the Oxford and Cambridge Scholarship 'Use of English' paper while sitting in the prefabricated Education Section, with its paper-thin walls, a drill-sergeant bawling on the parade square, jets screaming past overhead, WAAFs shrieking and giggling in the next room, and the loudspeakers whining on with 'Tannoy testing. Tannoy testing'. Totally unable to concentrate, I happened to notice that one of the essay titles on offer was 'Noise'. I remembered a childhood rhyme I had once learnt. 'What sort of noise annoys a noisy oyster? Oh it is a noisy noise annoys a noisy oyster.' With that quotation, I began to write. I thought that the examiner might want to hear about the dreadful cacophany of unbelievable noises that were making it quite impossible for me to concentrate enough to compose an essay. I got quite carried away with this theme. We were expected to write two essays in three hours, but I only wrote one. Amazingly, it secured a distinction. Equally amazingly, I did well in the other subjects for which less imagination and a little more knowledge and learning were required.

At about the same time I came top in my wireless operator's course tests. That won me a posting to RAF Mountbatten, Headquarters 19 Group (Coastal Command), on a wind-blown promontory in Plymouth Sound. It was idyllic. It had been the RAF station to which my namesake, Lawrence of Arabia, had sought seclusion as Aircraftsman Shaw, after leading the Arab army to victory against the Turks. He was still remembered by some of the civilian wireless operators working at the station. That great Lawrence had seen the first flying boats arrive at the station: this rather lesser Lawrence was, thirty years later, to see the last of them leave. That Lawrence would ride from RAF Mountbatten via Tavistock, on the Brough Superior SS100 motorcycle that eventually killed him, to have dinner with the first woman MP, Lady Astor, at her home in Plymouth. This Lawrence would ride the new ferry across Plymouth Sound, for snacks, walks and dances with two delightful young ladies, Ethnee (a naval officer) and Betty (a beautician). Sometimes, on my days off, I would go to sit in the public gallery of Plymouth Magistrates Court, and marvelled at the way some people lived their lives. On other days I would go to watch the jury trials at Plymouth Assizes. Thus it was that in that historic city the first seeds of my interest in criminal law took root. Then the Suez war broke out; or rather, as Prime Minister Anthony Eden put it, 'We are not at war with Egypt. We are in a state of armed conflict.'

Malta

I telephoned my parents to tell them that I had been sent to the Mediterranean battlefront, to fight for Queen and Country. My mother sounded confused. She kept trying to tell me that I had just won a state scholarship. I did not believe it: I kept telling her that there must have been some mistake. On 6 June 1956 I flew, in an Aquila Airlines passenger jet, to the beautiful island of Malta, marvelling at how safe it was to take off and land on water. Some years later, that very same airliner crashed while taking off from Southampton; after banking, it dived into the Isle of Wight, killing 39 passengers and crew.

In hot and sultry Malta GC, my base station was RAF Siggiewi, known to us all as 'Siggy-wiggy.' It lay just past the end of the Lucca airfield runway, from where our attacking land-based bombers were to fly. Since I was practically the only wireless operator with any actual experience of land-to-aircraft communication, I was immediately made an instructor. I found myself able to teach everyone everything I knew about wireless operating, in about two weeks. I was then directed to a new job, working with that contradition in terms – military intelligence – on ciphers, in a dark sparsely furnished claustrophobic underground room somewhere in Valetta.

I was to work with two commissioned officers. One told me he was a squadron leader, who had every intention of finishing the war as a wing commander. The other was a flight lieutenant, who intended to finish the war as a squadron leader. I told them that my more modest ambition was to be allowed to work in civilian clothes, because it would be too embarrassing for my adorable Maltese girlfriend, Rachelle, who was usually squired by majors and lieutenant-commanders, to be seen promenading on the seafront with someone in the uniform of a mere senior aircraftsman, to which heady height I had by then risen. The pact was sealed. I doubt not that our small team was brilliantly successful if, sadly, the war itself was not. I hope that mine was not the only ambition achieved.

After evenings with my girlfriend's delightful family in Valetta, I would catch the last bus back to the village from which my station took its name. I had a mile to walk back to camp, along an unlit country lane, followed by a pack of wild dogs, which would gather silently in the dark and move in with menace behind me. Fortunately, they never attacked me, and when the pack of dogs grew too large and menacing, the Motor Transport Department at the camp would take corrective action, culling them against farm walls. This scary walk on dark and moonlit nights, clutching a Coca Cola bottle very tightly in each hand, was the bravest action of my entire military service.

Just before Christmas, and the war being eight weeks over, I could not help noticing that my friends at Siggiewi were disappearing. I went to see the CO.

'Where is everyone?' I asked.

'Going back home to Blighty for Christmas,' he replied.

'Well, what about me?' I asked.

'No,' he answered. 'We're not sending you back because we need you for the station soccer team.'

What? I threw a tantrum. I had absolutely no desire to play any more soccer in Malta: the ground was as hard as rock, and besides, my talent for the game was very limited. I informed my commanding officer that it was most unfair to keep me there now that the war was over. I insisted that I could do more for my country back home – a persuasive argument, apparently, for I was allowed to leave, just in time for my twenty-first birthday.

I had had so much fun in Malta, that I could not bring myself to apply for the General Service medal which I was told would be mine, having served the required length of time in a combat zone. In fact there was only one event in my six and a half months on the island that might conceivably have warranted a medal: that was when I saved Britain from a Third World War.

It happened thus. I was on supervision duty, one afternoon in the first week of November, when one of the operators received over their radio a message from the lead ship in the flotilla advancing from Malta to Port Said and addressed to the Commander in Chief, Mediterranean Fleet. It was a 'flash' message, so urgent that there was no time to put it into code. It reported unidentified submarines across their path, and sought permission to depth-charge them. I processed both this message and the very immediate, and doubtless panic-stricken, 'flash' reply. It ordered: 'Imperative no depth charges be dropped: repeat imperative no depth charge.' The submarines turned out to be nothing less than the United States Eighth Fleet, deployed on the orders of President Eisenhower for the purpose of obstructing Sir Anthony Eden's prosecution of the Suez war! Thus unimpeded, the fleet carried on to Port Said, discharging its marines and helicopters to join the Anglo-French force which had landed at the Suez Canal the day before. One of the fighters, from the British aircraft carrier, tragically shot up British marines by mistake as they were marching up to Port Said. In all six hundred Egyptians were killed in hand-to hand fighting, twenty-six English and French troops died and 160 men were wounded. The American Secretary of State, Foster Dulles, forced us to a cease-fire and humiliating withdrawal by threatening to allow the run on the pound, which had just begun, to continue if we did not withdraw. The whole thing was a dreadful disaster for Eden and Britain, with the Egyptian President Nasser claiming victory.

The incident of the submarines seems to have been one of the little-known events of the war. Perhaps, if I had been dozing or sitting reading a book in the lavatory when the first signal had arrived, as so easily might have happened, we might have blown the Americans out of the water, and there could have been another kind of war. No one offered me a medal for being efficient, alert and awake – or even said thank you for averting a war.

Back to Mountbatten

I was posted back to RAF Mountbatten where I served out the remaining nine months of my National Service. I did not have to complete the full two years, because I went up to Oxford in September.

When I eventually got the written confirmation that it really was me who had won the state scholarship, I asked my ex-headmaster, Harry Brogden, who had earlier so seriously misjudged my academic potential, which colleges at Oxford I should apply to. He suggested those that had been attended by masters at the school – St Peter's Hall, Lincoln, Jesus and Exeter. I had never heard of any of them, and when I applied, none of them wished to hear any more from me. This was, of course, another challenge. I decided to show them. I wrote to the colleges that I had heard of because they were the grandest and most famous – Balliol, Magdalen and Christ Church. These all, to my amazement, showed some interest in me, and indeed the first two invited me to sit their open scholarship examinations – which I duly did. I passed the written papers for each, and was invited to a final oral interview for both. Unfortunately, both invitations happened to be for the same day, and at the same time. Also on the same day and time, Christ Church invited me to apply for a commoner's entrance. I could not possibly do all three. I decided that however much luck I had had so far, my chances of winning one of the handful of open scholarships or exhibitions at the most sought-after colleges in the most sought-after university in Britain, without the examination tuition given to my competitors from the nation's finest public schools, was negligible. I was in danger of losing everything: such challenges were too great for me. My chance for a common entrance at Christ Church, on the other hand, though still extremely slim, seemed more realistic. So I sent an apology to Balliol and Magdalen, withdrew from their interviews, and accepted the Christ Church examination and interview instead.

The written part over, I was led into a room where sat a committee whose members happened to be among the most renowned academics, writers and theologians in the country. Only later did I learn who my interrogators had been: the historian Hugh Trevor-Roper (later Lord Dacre, who famously misidentified a forgery as being Hitler's true diary); the celebrated poet W.H. Auden; J.I.M. Stewart (alias the popular detective novelist Michael Innes); Canon Lowe (the Dean of Christ Church); Robert Blake (later Lord Blake, the distinguished historical biographer of Disraeli); my tutor to be, the great E.H. 'Teddy' Burn (now a senior consultant with the leading City solicitors Clifford Chance); and Professors Driver, Simpson and Mascall (the leading clerics who were then engaged upon no less a labour than the writing of the twentieth-century Church of England authorised version of the Bible).

My interview seemed to me to be a complete disaster. These great men were certainly very friendly, laughing kindly at everything I said, even when it was not funny. But they asked none of the obvious questions I had been expecting – like why I wanted to study law. I returned to RAF Mountbatten, tired and angry with myself for not taking my chances with Balliol and Magdalen, and fell asleep on duty, by a ticker-tape machine covering the flight schedules I was supposed to be monitoring. I awoke hours later to find myself buried in miles of unread tape. Deep in the pile, almost the last piece I came upon, was a memo from Christ Church. It offered me a place as a commoner for the following September. It was so utterly unexpected, that I became emotional. I was the first person in my family ever to receive a formal education and to go to any university, let alone Oxford. I was also the first person from Brighton Grammar School to go to Christ Church. Even then, I nearly did not make it, for I might have been court-martialled.

What happened was this. RAF Mountbatten's established marine wireless operator also played soccer for Third Division Plymouth Argyle. A needle match fell on a Saturday when, as luck would have it, a massive NATO exercise in the English Channel had been planned. RAF Mountbatten was to provide the lead patrol boat to guide the Southern Command naval fleet into the area of operations in the Atlantic. Although I had never been aboard either a pinnace fast patrol boat or a target-towing launch, I offered to take my friend's place – another challenge – and got him to remind me of the practical rudiments of maritime radio-telegraphy direction finding.

We set out in rough seas but, alas, I was no sailor – certainly not at those speeds. Repeatedly throwing up, confused and quite inadequate to the task, I must have subtracted 180 degrees when I should have added them. We never did meet up with the NATO fleet, because we must have been going in the wrong direction. It may be that no one ever met up with anyone. No one ever told me. Miraculously nothing dreadful seemed to have happened to me or to the British fleet. Perhaps I have blotted further detailed recollection from my memory, as I have often tended to do with events I would rather not remember. The criminals I defend seem to make a habit of doing the same thing: they go into complete denial, which may explain why they sound so convincing in conference with their lawyers, and sometimes to the juries trying them.

As my time as a national serviceman hurtled towards its close, the commanding officer at Mountbatten discovered that I had somehow managed to evade the required number of days for compulsory 'ground combat training.' No one else on camp had so defaulted, so a day was set aside for Senior Aircraftsman Lawrence to complete the arduous training – on his own. A station holiday may not have actually been declared, but I do recall being followed around the station from obstacle and challenge to obstacle and challenge by a very large number of friends and enemies – much as golf professionals are followed onto the eighteenth green by their adoring fans and critical opponents. Alone I climbed poles and netting. I crawled under posts through mud. I ran up hill and down dale with a number 18 wireless set, of almost unbearable weight, strapped to my back, whilst also carrying a rifle and belts of ammunition. I assembled a Bren gun, making certain to align the barrel-locking nut with the retainer plunger and pin, and even worse, I had to shoot at a series of targets with the Bren gun and my .303 rifle.

The last time I had fired a gun had been nearly two years earlier, when I had completely missed not only the target but the entire target area, and so I had, of course, most miserably failed that test. This time, with the raucous noises and the jesting ridicule of my companions ringing in my ears, I determined to do better, to meet the challenge boldly, and to show the baying entourage that I was somebody to be reckoned with in time of war. I planted my elbows squarely and firmly on the ground. I focused my eyes intently on the centre of the target. I breathed in and held my breath. I squeezed, not jerked, the trigger. I scored so many bullseyes that, amid wild cheering, I was awarded the coveted 'marksman' badge. This I deliberately sewed onto the wrong sleeve that night, so that whenever I saluted an officer, he would see that, against all the odds, I had indeed distinguished myself as a military man.

Apart from shooting for the occasional goldfish prize at a fairground, the next time I handled a gun was nearly forty years later, when the Home Affairs Select Committee was considering its report on 'The Possession of Handguns'.

I have many other fond memories of these early years: like the hours I used to spend with my cousin, Alma Cogan, and the family, at their Stafford Court flat in Kensington High Street. Her address was open house to everyone in show business. Around vivacious and glamorous Alma buzzed the young Tommy Steele, Shirley Bassey, the then very slim Diana Dors, and an unknown boy-band called the Beatles. There was Lionel Bart, Lionel Blair and, when in town, Danny Kaye and Cary Grant. They were all enraptured by Alma. Diana's second husband, the comedian Dicky Dawson – a man so naturally funny that Bob Hope sacked him from his job as his warm-up artiste because he was getting more laughs than his boss – used to run me to Paddington Station on

Sunday nights to catch my train back to Plymouth and Mountbatten. Alma would play records on her radio programme which she would dedicate to 'cousin Ivan and all the boys' at whichever RAF station I was currently passing through at the time. It was a heady life for the star-struck.

University

I went up to Oxford in October 1957. To be at Christ Church – known as the House, and the finest college in the university – would have been beyond my dreams, if I had ever had any dreams at school about going to university. Coming from a family with no university history, and a school to which my university potential came as a surprise, I was not at all prepared for the wonder of it all.

The jumped-up son of an Ipswich butcher, Cardinal Wolsey (Henry VIII's 'Secretary of State for all Departments') suppressed the monastery of St Frideswide and, in 1525, built Cardinal College in its place. To match the opulence its founder had achieved, it had to be more magnificent than any other college. When the over-mighty subject fell from power and died, King Henry re-founded the college as Christ Church. Its Great Hall is one of the most splendid in England. On its walls hang portraits of Henry VIII, Elizabeth I, Cardinal Wolsey, and the great men who have been students of the House – prime ministers, prelates, lord chief justices, and men of outstanding and creative fame and distinction like John Locke (the great philosopher), John Wesley (the founder of Methodism), and William Penn (the founder of Pennsylvania). The portrait painters, too, were the most renowned of their day – Romney, Gainsborough, Lawrence, Millais and, in modern times, Sutherland, Gunn, Coldstream and Moynihan. Today's youngsters will recognise the Hall as the setting for Harry Potter's Hogwarts School.

So magnificent and grand is the House that its chapel doubles as Oxford Cathedral. Developed from the twelfth-century church on the site, the cathedral was always intended to combine with the college to be one foundation with two functions. During my time at the college, there was a proposal that an Oxford relief road be built across Christ Church meadow, a matter that required, for some reason, the consent of the government. The proposal never stood a chance, there being in the cabinet at that time, no fewer than five former Housemen. Four of the other cabinet ministers were from Oxford colleges, three from

Cambridge and two from London. The college had also distinguished itself in sport: when I went up in 1957, five of the college first eight rowed for the university boat in the Oxford–Cambridge boat race.

Charles Lutwidge Dodgson, whose portrait hangs in the Hall, had been a tutor (don) at the college 100 years before my arrival. His rooms overlooked the gardens where Dean Liddell's daughter, Alice, used to play: thus, under the name Lewis Carroll, was Dodgson inspired to write the great classics *Alice's Adventures in Wonderland* and *Through the Looking Glass*. In 1960 I helped to organise the Christ Church summer dance, the Black and White Ball, as an Alice in Wonderland function – in her very own garden. To provide the dance music, I gave the fledgling Syd Lawrence and his band its break into the big-time – a fact that, I think, has also never been adequately acknowledged.

At the time, I was one of only a handful of grammar school boys to have made it to this bastion of public school achievement. Rooms could not be found for mere grammarians in the college itself, so for the first year we were roomed out at Park End Street, near Oxford railway station. In my second year I was allowed a room – which is now part of the picture gallery – in Canterbury quadrangle. In my third year I was permitted the not inconsiderable privilege of having my own flat at 3 Beechcroft Road, where I could, and did, entertain as I liked.

In those days girl students attended girls' colleges. Having a girl in your college room, other than for tea, was a disciplinary offence. One undergraduate, seen taking a girl to his room, was stopped by the proctor, the college policeman.

'Its all right,' said the blade, 'she's my sister.'

'No she's not,' retorted the alert official, 'she's a well-known local woman of the streets.'

'I know,' said the young man, 'it is very sad and my mother is most cut up about it.'

Being out of college after 11pm was another offence. Canon Jenkins, one of the great Christ Church personalities, a theologian and an octogenarian with an eye that always seemed to hang outside its socket, in summertime was wont to sleep with his window wide open onto the gardens. Generations of Housemen, finding themselves locked out of college late at night, would climb the walls at their lowest point, which happened to be into his gardens, and then tiptoe past the snoring grandee to the safety of Tom quad.

Although I was given tutorials with one of the brightest scholars of my year, Anthony Browner from Kings School Canterbury (who tragically committed suicide in his second year), and my tutor was outstanding, I was not a particularly successful undergraduate. The astonishment of my parents and my school at my achievement was inadequate motivation for a successful university career, so I was never single-minded or ambitious enough. I worked quite hard but, looking back, I can see that I was not determined enough to hit any particular target and my weapon was only a scatter-gun. I suppose I just enjoyed the social, cultural, intellectual, sporting, and musical atmosphere of the university too much. I did odd things, like becoming social secretary of the Blue Riband Club and founding an organisation called Crime Concern with John Walker-Smith (who became a Conservative candidate and a colleague at the Bar) and Gerald Howarth (who became the MP for Cannock and later for Aldershot). I spoke in good debates at the Union, and earned passing compliments, but it never occurred to me to stand for office or try to become president – which is now one of the very few regrets I have about my life.

Brighton Grammar School did not do rowing, so I had never rowed a racing boat on any river. But one day, fooling around on the college practice boat tethered to the bank in Christ Church meadow, I was spotted by Richard Lander, the House rowing captain and outstanding University Blue, pulling what he described as 'a bloody big puddle'. He invited me to row in bow position in the House second boat in the Summer Torpid races. Sadly, I have to report another of my life's small disasters. Our boat began the season leading all others in the league. But every day, during my membership, we took a beating. Sometimes we were 'bumped' at the finishing post, other times almost at the start of the race. This happened despite huge steaks every night, and following a training programme more punishing than anything I had experienced in the air force. On the final day Robin Whicker, our cox, having shouted himself hoarse during the week, gave a very weak order to 'hold.' Amidst the noise of cheers and boos, I somehow misheard the order as 'pull.' So I pulled. The boat shot hard into the bank where, very sadly, it broke up and sank, depositing all save myself into the river Isis. The lead I had given was not popular. I was chased by my fellow sportsmen along the river bank, seized and tossed without ceremony into the river. There ended my rowing career – for the time being. It revived momentarily almost thirty years later when I was an MP.

In an effort to achieve something at university, I did try to become secretary of the Christ Church Junior Common Room, as a stepping-stone to becoming its president. But I lost by three votes. After the vote I went along to the law library where I announced my latest failure.

'But there are fourteen of us here who would have voted for you if you had only told us there was an election on,' a kind colleague told me.

'That may be,' I replied, 'but I don't believe in canvassing.'

This ridiculous, if gentlemanly, attitude did not of course long survive my entry into politics. The victor was Peter Jay, who went on to become President of the Oxford Union, British Ambassador to the United States during the premiership of James Callaghan his father-in-law, and economic guru at the BBC. He was a much wiser choice.

Christ Church was very generous to me. A bursary was found to enable me to go to Spain in my first long vacation, so that I could learn Spanish and read the original writings of one of the outstanding professors of Roman law, then teaching at Salamanca University. I worked at Spanish for three months, and supplemented my small stipend by teaching English by day and playing the bongos in a club in Barcelona by night. I found this method of learning such fun that I decided to do the same the following year – in Venice. There I learnt Italian at Ca' Foscari (the university), and how to enjoy life even more, with gondoliers who became my friends. When, nine years later, Gloria and I eventually moved to our matrimonial home in Shepperton, our boat, the sixteen-foot cabin-cruiser *Gloria-Sarah*, was brought upriver from its mooring at the Fulham yacht club to our house in great style by Ambrogio and Bruno Palmarin, two of our Venetian gondolier friends. They passed under Walton Bridge, which, in an earlier guise, had been painted by another Venetian – Canaletto.

During other vacations I joined a small group of students selling soap from door to door. We were directed, controlled and provisioned by a dynamic woman in her forties I can only remember as Sue. She drove us to Sussex towns like Worthing and Arundel, and to villages like Bramber and Beeding, in the 1950s version of a Range Rover. The soap, super-fatted and with an inoffensive perfume, was manufactured for a bona fide charity, called 'The General Welfare of the Blind', by blind workers at a special factory. It sold at half a crown for a packet of six tablets, and I received six pence commission for every packet sold. I had to carry a 'pedlar's licence' and wear a badge of authorisation. I was 'teacher's pet' and developed high-pressure doorstep techniques that would have been a criminal offence under modern consumer protection legislation. Most weeks I contrived to be the top earner, at £10 per week. One elderly couple, to whom I had been pitching, slammed the door in my face. Having read the leaflet that I had left on their doorstep, they ran after me calling me back. They wanted to apologise: they thought I had been a Jehovah's Witness. I resolved to speak more slowly and clearly in future. The cause was worthwhile and the 'cold-calling' was enormous fun. It taught me how to be nice to strangers on their doorstep, whilst selling them something they did not really need. After that, canvassing for the Conservative Party was never a problem.

Nostalgia for my university days is even stronger than it is for my school days. One day, after I had 'gone down', I defended a man at Oxford Magistrates Court in the morning, watched Oxford University defeat Yorkshire (with Freddie Truman playing) in the Parks in the afternoon, and in the evening I sat at High Table for dinner (as MAs are entitled and expected to do), discussing politics with the finest academic minds in Britain. Driving home along the M4 with the hood down on my Triumph Spitfire, a sudden deluge soaked me so thoroughly that Gloria would not let me into the house until I had taken all my clothes off – on the village green. That was the sort of day you never forget.

Edward Heath

Eurosceptic though I am, and proud of being branded a 'bastard' by John Major, I confess that another of the most memorable days of my life was when Prime Minister Edward Heath came, in 1971, to speak at a Christ Church dinner (a 'Gaudy'), about his European dream. With him, as guests on High Table, were the world's greatest cellist, Mstislav Rostropovich; the lovely British prima ballerina, Dame Beryl Grey; the Archbishop of Canterbury, Dr Runcie; and assorted Nobel Prize winners. Around Ted sat the Conservative High Command. On his right was Oxford University's Chancellor, Harold Macmillan, and to Mac's right sat the Lord Chancellor, Lord Hailsham. To Ted's left sat the Master of Trinity (the sister college at Cambridge) 'Rab' Butler, and to Rab's left sat former Prime Minister Sir Alec Douglas Home. The beautiful hall was filled with past and present students, and lit only by candles on the tables and the lights on the portraits of the former great men of Christ Church. Ted's speech was intensely moving and the atmosphere, years before Harry Potter, was totally magical.

Afterwards, the Dean asked me to take Ted to the Senior Common Room, to introduce him to the professors and tutors. This proved difficult: he insisted on talking at length to the Organ Scholar about

Mahler's symphonies, and showed no interest at all in those he was supposed to meet and charm.

Unusually for so successful a politician, Ted Heath was often unfriendly to the point of rudeness, to those whom he might have been expected to impress. He must once have been charming enough to win, and to make safe, his marginal Kent seat. He certainly showed more people-management skills than Reggie Maudling when the two, competing for leadership of the Party, addressed a hundred Conservative parliamentary candidates at the 'In and Out' Club in the mid-sixties, at which I was present. But at some stage those political virtues seem to have deserted him.

When Ted was being challenged as leader by Margaret Thatcher in 1975, Nick Scott, the charming MP for Chelsea who served as a social welfare minister for several years and was one of Ted's closest supporters, invited me and five or six other newcomers to his home, to meet and to dine with Ted. The latter was so rude and uninterested in anything any of us had to say, that I advised the generous and kindly Nick that more of such evenings might prove counterproductive. On another occasion, when he was prime minister, I introduced Ted to the Conservative ladies of Burton at a Midlands dinner. They were so put off by his brusqueness and obvious lack of interest in them, that they asked me to vote for Mrs Thatcher.

Strangely, he did not even seem to get on with some of his parliamentary colleagues. Once or twice I saw him sitting alone in the members' dining room, while others came in and sat elsewhere. Ex-ministers complained that he frequently seemed not to know their names. On the evening of the day parliament was first televised, Ted went off to Paris where he stayed the night as the guest of the ambassador. It so happened that the Foreign Affairs Select Committee was also in Paris, and we met Ted after dinner in the lovely British Embassy, a former palace of Napoleon, in the Champs Elysées. Three of us, Peter Temple-Morris, Jim Lester, and myself, stood chatting to him for about twenty minutes, and Ted, wittily for he could be very funny, recounted that day's happenings. The following night I was sitting just behind him in the chamber of the House of Commons when the vote was called. We both stood up at the same time, colliding with each other in the gangway.

'We must stop meeting like this Ted, or people will talk,' I said, rather stupidly trying to be funny, since I was known not to be his greatest supporter.

'Why?' he replied. 'When did we last meet?'

'Only last night,' I said, feeling a bit like a non-person, and thinking that he might be beginning to lose the plot.

Political stirrings

My interest in politics really began when I was at Oxford. It is true that I had been a bit of a trade unionist on the Crawley building site, and as a child I had delivered literature for a family friend standing for Labour on Brighton Council. If I had been over 21, and able to vote at any election, I suppose it would have been Labour. But at Oxford I wanted to learn public speaking, to give me the confidence to speak in court, and the only organisation offering such a service was the Oxford University Conservative Association. So I joined up, and was introduced to the redoubtable Mrs Stella Gatehouse – guide, philosopher and friend to a very long line of future distinguished Conservative MPs. She gave me reading lists so that I might better know what I was talking about – a quite original approach to politics, I thought. I began to find the subject truly fascinating. It soon became obvious to me that free enterprise and privatisation were better than state control and nationalisation; that individual freedom was to be preferred to the centralising power of the state; that Queen, country and patriotism were to be preferred to internationalism (especially to international socialism); and that strong national defence was to be preferred to nuclear disarmament. I realised that I had little in common with the Labour Party, save my working-class background. The first letter that I ever wrote to a newspaper was on the Suez war: it attacked Labour ministers and was published as the lead letter in *The Sunday Times*, the weekend before the 1959 election.

I went on speaking tours of several constituencies, with future Tory parliamentary grandees like Tony Newton, Alan Haselhurst and David Madel. In the 1959 general election campaign, our team warmed up audiences for Neil Martin, the MP for Banbury, and for John Hay, the MP for Henley. Before one speaking engagement we were invited to lunch at the stately home in Wiltshire of a former Speaker of the Commons, Lord Morrison. A tall, distinguished, grey-haired, expensively dressed elderly man, with a commanding figure, was waiting to greet us at the grand entrance. I bounded up the elegant steps, thrust out my hand in greeting, and thanked him effusively for having invited us. He was, he explained, in a voice weary with the patience of the long-suffering, only His Lordship's butler.

Gloria

In my third year at Christ Church I met Gloria – my first and last real love. For me it was both Heaven and the Fall in one. I became totally distracted. It happened in a room in Peckwater quad in Christ Church one Sunday evening in February 1960. I was chairing a meeting, as president of the Oxford University Progressive Jewish Society. The guest speaker, on the topic of the morality of nuclear disarmament, was the Jewish chaplain to the American armed forces stationed in Britain. Sitting in front of me on a sofa was this gorgeous, buxom, long-haired leggy blonde, with the shy look of Doris Day. When she smiled at me I was gone. My reader will, I know, understand how these things can happen.

Gloria was an occupational therapy student at Dorset House in Oxford. Although a Christian, she had come to the meeting out of religious interest, with Gay, a Jewish girl-friend. Gazing admiringly at her, I announced next week's topic: Jewish marriage. Next week she came again. The following week I spotted her with an escort in the Union Cellars. Although I was dressed like a clown, in a bright red shirt with an orange bow tie, I rushed up, insisted that she dance with me, and would not take no for an answer.

After that Gloria would wave to me across the Bodlean library, and bring me sandwiches, which she had made for lunch, in a beautiful little basket, which she had also made at college. We would sit together on the grass in Christ Church meadow at lunchtime, whenever the sun shone. We kissed. She came to my flat and cooked and cleaned. She sold my old battered bike to a friend of hers who was a Fellow of All Souls. I asked her to be my partner at the next Christ Church Commemoration Ball. I doubt whether I could have memorised the quasi-delicts of Roman Law without her. That was it: I was finished! The only university guidance that my dear parents had managed to give me had been: 'Perhaps there you will meet a nice Jewish girl...' and I blew it!

Years later we celebrated our fortieth wedding anniversary with a dinner for a hundred of our closest friends in Christ Church Hall, after attending choral evensong in the cathedral. Gloria came across a photograph of us holding hands by Mercury in Tom quad, a few weeks after we had first met; we had it copied onto the front page of the dinner menu.

If I am an Eastern European Semite at my ethnic root, Gloria must be a Viking. She has imposing Aryan good looks, and a commandingly strong temperament. She had been born and bred in Newcastle, and her family, on her mother's side, were aristocratic Ogles stretching back at least to Norman times. Her family must have lived down any lawless roots, for her grandfather was chief constable of Gateshead. We have incorporated the Ogle family crescent symbol, seen on gravestones in Westminster Abbey, into my knight's coat of arms. Incorporated also is Gloria's name; for the motto is *Gloria Servire Hominum.* I was assured by Bluemantle Pursuivant of the College of Arms, who suggested it, that this means 'How Glorious to Serve Mankind'. I was never brilliant at Latin, but I had a sneaking feeling that the accusative ought to have been *hominem*; and that with *hominum* the motto might mean 'Gloria Services Mankind'. Bluemantle laughed. Gloria said she was not interested in what it might mean. She liked it as it was!

After Oxford, I lived in London where I struggled to get my legal career started. Gloria and I were together a great deal. We used to go dancing to Joe Loss at the Hammersmith Palais. We spent a lot of time with my parents in Brighton and London. Gloria's mother, long divorced from her father, moved down from Newcastle to be with her and Gloria's brother Richard. We were in love, but I did not feel ready for the very considerable commitment of marriage. Understandably, Gloria got fed up. She said that if I wanted to marry her, I would have to go and find her in Venice – whither she was departing forthwith, and indefinitely, with her cousin Christine. This they did. There Christine met, fell in love with and married Paolo, three of whose ancestors were Vendramin Doges who had once ruled Venice. They live to this day in a house on the Grand Canal, which you can just see at the bottom right-hand corner of the famous Canaletto pictures of the Rialto.

After some months I began to miss Gloria a great deal, so I drove to Venice in my Triumph Herald convertible, with my parents – for which, incidentally, Gloria has never really forgiven me. As we swept into the car park at Piazzale Roma, at 2 am, I could see a crowd ahead. This turned out to be a particularly large number of Gloria's Venetian male admirers. Like the male dancers in a Busby Berkeley Hollywood musical, they peeled away as we approached. I proposed. She, to my great joy and relief, accepted. It is what Venice is for. We go back for the annual carnival whenever we can, and dress up in magnificent eighteenth-century costumes. Four years ago we won a prize as 'The most romantic couple in Venice'!

I had been living in the garden flat of a house my father had bought for me in Shepherds Bush. Gloria had been living in Camberwell, which, by coincidence, was to be in my first constituency. She had given up occupational therapy and went to work for De Havilland in their Blue Streak design office in the City, then as a literary agent for DC Benson and Campbell Thomson, one of whose clients was Nicholas Montserrat, the author of *The Cruel Sea*. She helped to give her first break to award-winning romantic novelist Ann Rundle and to Rod Thorp, the author of *Die Hard*. If only she could do that for this memoir!

Later, with Rachel a teenager away at boarding school, Gloria, not one to sit around waiting for her husband to come back from parliament to spend the odd evening or share the odd dinner, decided to reorganise her own life. She became a qualified London Tourist Board 'Blue Badge' guide lecturer. The examination requires the kind of prodigious memory which enables you to answer 200 questions in only 100 minutes, such as: 'What theme is depicted in the fourth section from the bottom of the stained glass window third along in the apse of Salisbury Cathedral?' It is not really surprising that one tour guide, the former London taxi driver Fred Housego, should have become 'Mastermind'. Gloria went into business on her own, and greatly enjoys showing her customers (mainly American), round the stately homes, golf courses, gardens and beauties of the British countryside. Being popular and successful, she has become well known to travelling Americans of a certain income. Most of them are delightful, considerable achievers, and great anglophiles. One of her clients, a very gracious elderly New Yorker, decided to divorce her 85-year-old husband, the head of one of America's greatest international corporations, but to avoid unnecessary unpleasantness settled for only two billion dollars. She has, of course, much to be gracious about.

In this human line of business Gloria has almost as many stories to tell as I have. In 1987, for example, she was taking thirty-three of America's richest by helicopter from Brocket Hall, where they were staying, to the races at Ascot. For the return journey she climbed into the last small helicopter. One of her big business clients, Joe, sat cramped in the back. She put on her headphones. The craft rose 300 feet into the air. She heard the words 'Mayday! Mayday!', wondering for a moment what that could mean. As the helicopter suddenly dropped, spinning groundwards towards a clump of trees, the pilot wrestling to gain control, the penny also dropped for Gloria, and the headline 'MP's wife dies in helicopter crash' flashed before her eyes. They crash-landed heavily on the ground, fortunately staying upright before lurching, shuddering and skidding to a halt. Everyone, thank God, was only shaken and stirred. After a few moments a dazed pilot asked where they were. Long after everyone would have been burnt to a cinder had there been a fire, a little fire engine appeared and began to trundle across the muddy field. Joe said that he was not ready to leave this life just yet and did not want to take any more chances. The survivors completed the journey by limousine, arriving at Brocket Hall to a rapturous heroes' reception.

The owner of the stately home, Lord Brocket, was years later convicted of insurance frauds, arising from his ownership of a fabulous collection of Ferraris. Despite being defended by Desmond De Silva (the distinguished head of the set of chambers I was later to join), he was sentenced to four years imprisonment. Lord 'Call me Charlie' Brocket's reputation was later enhanced by his appearance in 'Big Brother', the stomach-churning reality television programme.

Another Postcript. Eight years later, Gloria was again flying with clients in a helicopter, when she realised that the flight was not only from the same place and to the same place, but it was also on the same day of the same month. Fortunately the Fates were kinder than last time, and nothing happened.

Gloria, like me, is a fighter – but very much braver. She developed osteo-arthritis twenty-five years ago, and has recently had two hip replacements, one knee replacement, one spinal operation to un-trap a nerve, five steroid injections in her spine and four in her shoulders, one shoulder rotator-cuff operation and bone-graft, and has had throat cancer and a breast cancer scare. Yet still she walks her appreciative visitors round the stately homes and gardens of this green and very pleasant land as if she were a spring chicken. Last year she went to see her foot specialist because she could hardly walk, after having seven more operations on her feet.

'How's your general health?' the medical man enquired.

'Fine,' she replied.

'So you are not on any medication?'

'Only ibruprofen.'

'What's that for?'

'My osteo-arthritis.'

'Any other drugs?'

'Only fleccanide.'

'What's that for?'

'My erratic heart-beat.'

'When was that discovered?'

'When I was having a check-up for my throat cancer.'

I am sure that I am a physical coward. I doubt whether any enemy would need to torture me for information. I can only hope that if I ever have to endure pain, I would do so with the nonchalant good humour that my wife and daughter always display when they are suffering.

In ways too many to mention, Gloria has been an inspiration to me. To be able, whatever the stresses of life in the courts or in politics, to go home to a loving wife and the warmth and comfort of a happy home, must surely be, with good health, the greatest of all blessings. There has not been one moment over the past forty-four years that I have been sorry that Gloria married me, nor one day since the day we met that I have not been proud to have known her and thankful for my great good fortune. I have not dared to ask if she feels the same!

Mr. Edw
Sutcliffe
Q.C.

Mr. Ashe
Lincoln
Q.C.

Mr. Ivor Richard

3

Becoming a Barrister and Early Cases

'I see you stand like greyhounds in the slips,
Straining upon the start. The game's afoot:'
(Shakespeare: *Henry V*)

Before trying to enter politics, I needed to become a barrister. Christ
Church students traditionally became members of the Inner Temple, and
I am a follower of tradition.

The Temple, a quiet and historic backwater off London's bustling
Fleet Street, was originally the home of the Knights Templar, a religious
order of fighting monks, founded in 1119 to protect pilgrims on their
way to the Holy Land to fight the Crusades. This holy order was
dissolved in 1312, and the buildings, including the magnificent Norman
church, were given to the Knights of St John of Jerusalem, a rival
institution. Here King John debated a draft of Magna Carta with his
barons before Runnymede. Rumour had it that the holy grail might be
found beneath one of the knightly effigies therein, and it is now besieged
by tourists who have read Dan Brown's *The Da Vinci Code* or seen the
film. The Temple was leased to the lawyers in the fifteenth century, and
has just celebrated 400 years of receiving the Royal Charter – an event
celebrated by a Royal visit and the gift of another Charter by the Queen.
The link between lawyers and the Knights, who had to take a vow of
poverty, is not lost on today's practitioners at the publicly-funded
independent Criminal Bar, who are being forced into poverty by un-
concerned governments.

Tradition and culture sweep and surge like the wind around the
Temple. A beautiful picture, in the central lobby of the House of
Commons, commemorates the quarrel that, according to Shakespeare,
took place in the Temple gardens in 1455, between Richard Plantagenet,
who plucked a red rose, and the Earl of Somerset, who plucked a white
rose. Thus began, so it is said, the Wars of the Roses, which lasted for

39

thirty years. The lovely Middle Temple Hall, lovelier now than the Inner Temple Hall (which had to be completely rebuilt after taking a direct hit during the Second World War), was the setting in 1602 of the Royal Command Performance before Queen Elizabeth I of Shakespeare's *Twelfth Night*. It is said that Will himself performed for his monarch.

The Inns became like university colleges, at which students lived, ate and were taught the law by those who daily practised it, and the title 'barrister' is an academic degree. A barrister must be a member of one of the four Inns of Court, by which he is called to the Bar. As an Inner Temple student I had to eat 24 dinners at the Inn. Wednesday was the usual dining night, which was a pity because on Wednesdays I usually played football for the Christ Church second eleven at home or away. This meant that, even though the trains in those happy far-off days usually ran on time, I could only make the 7pm start for dinner at the Inn in London with the greatest difficulty. So I devised a devilish scheme for getting into the hall after the ceremonial blowing of a horn and the closing of the doors. I would come up through the kitchen, and with Victory, one of the Inn's waiters, walking in step close beside me, I would slide into a seat at the other end of the hall, unnoticed by the Benchers at top table. For a long time this wheeze worked, but one evening I was noticed and rumbled. The knarled finger of a very senior Bencher twisted slowly but surely in my direction, summoning me to his presence. The blood left my face, the hall hushed, and every accusing eye was upon me, as I dragged myself to the Inquisition of the Benchers' table. My Torquemada turned out to be none other than the dreaded Lord Chief Justice of England and Wales himself – Lord Goddard. I suppose that I must have been reprimanded but, that being another wholly unpleasant experience, I have no recollection of it whatsoever. My misbehaviour certainly can have done me little long-term harm, since I was later awarded two scholarships by the Inn, to help me to pay for my early impecunious days at the Bar. The Inner Temple was another institution that has always been good to me and, as far as I know, to every other young aspiring member of the Bar in need of help. I certainly felt very proud when I was elected a Master Bencher of the Inn in 1990.

Having eaten the required dinners, and having also passed the Bar examination, I was called to the Bar on 6 February 1962 by Master Heathcote-Williams. I had no idea what chambers I wanted to join, what branch of the law I wanted to pursue, where to go or what to do. I only knew that I wanted to be a barrister. Like every other barrister to be, I had read and had been excited by the famous murder cases in the Penguin 'Notable British Trials' series. Unlike most of the others, I was also very lucky.

Pupillage

While I was waiting for my Bar examination results, I went to a family wedding where I met and chatted to a man who, it transpired, ran a solicitors' firm dealing mainly with criminal cases. He promised to get me into the finest set of criminal chambers in the Temple. After the wedding I heard no more, so I telephoned him. He told me he had no recollection of having made such a promise, that he must have been drunk at the time, but that if that was what he had said, that was what he would do. Within the week, Manny Fryde, the manager of the firm of solicitors with the largest criminal practice in London (Sampson and Co) had arranged for me to become pupil to the leading junior at the criminal Bar (James Burge), at the most distinguished of all the criminal chambers (Queen Elizabeth Building – known for the sheer volume of its output as 'the Factory'). I was the envy of all my peers.

I got off to an unimpressive start. Robert Goulden, the senior clerk, led me to my pupil-master's room and introduced me. James Burge was 60-ish, tall and rather distinguished looking. Ludovic Kennedy described him well as 'a jovial, sunshiney, Pickwickian sort of man, who always seems to be smiling. Beer and Burgundy seemed to blend with his beaming face...; in short, a very nice man.' I bounded enthusiastically (again) across the room, hand outstretched.

'It is a great honour to meet you, sir, and I am most grateful that you have invited me to be your pupil,' I gushed.

The great man, ignoring my hand, turned away and said, 'I didn't invite you. I don't usually have pupils. You have been forced upon me. And we don't shake hands at the Bar. You will call me Burge, not sir.'

I had to pay my new pupil-master £200, the pupillage charge (since abolished) for the year, which I could just about afford, out of one of my two Inner Temple Scholarships. Over the next few weeks, I went to court almost daily with him to learn my trade. I was allowed to read his briefs, which he was supposed to discuss with me, but he seldom did so. In fact I was given no actual instruction, as is certainly now required. Later, I took some of the cases he was too busy to conduct himself, although I hardly ever received any part of his fee. I had the privilege of sitting in on most of his evening conferences, listening and learning, and after a few months I would write opinions for both his criminal and licensing cases and tentatively hand them to him. He never told me if they were any good, but when he had left chambers to catch his train to Brighton, I would go to his drawer to see how much, if any, of my advice he had adopted to produce his own opinion to the solicitors. Sometimes, I was thrilled to discover, he had shortened mine and signed it as his own.

What I did learn from James Burge, as I sat taking notes of his cross-examination of witnesses, police officers and doctors in drink-driving cases (at which he was magical), was the need for hard work, for orderly argument, and how to get some cases literally laughed out of court. Although primarily a defence lawyer, he was also Prosecuting Counsel for the Post Office at the Old Bailey. I had also to make sure that his papers were in the right order – another vital lesson to be learnt early at the Bar. Even without direct instruction from him, the amount I must have unconsciously imbibed from this eminent man who had such a charismatic presence and command of every witness and court, both in his criminal and his prodigious liquor and then gaming licence practices, must have been very considerable. Only once do I remember him actually giving me advice. We were co-defending in a robbery trial and he passed me a note that read 'Don't try so hard'. That advice I have always ignored.

Unlike today, we did not have to wait six months after our call to the Bar before we could conduct our own cases in court. We could start by taking 'dock briefs'. That meant going down to Quarter Sessions (now the Crown Court) at the start of the session, and sitting self-consciously in a row of barristers desperately anxious for work but trying not to show it. The defendant, who would usually be pleading guilty, would come up into the dock, and the court clerk would invite him to choose any barrister he wished. The chosen one would then go down into the cells, take two pounds four shillings and six pence from his client (two guineas for himself and two shillings and six pence for his clerk), and then discuss what his client wanted him to say to the judge in mitigation of the sentence. That done, the barrister would return to court, and, when his case was called, stand up and deliver his speech.

At London Sessions, where, six weeks after my call, I first perpetrated my advocacy, Nemone Lethbridge was always the prisoner's first choice. This was because she was ravishingly beautiful. I used to sit next to her, if I could, because once she had been chosen, prisoners would come up into the dock and look to the place where she was said to have been sitting, and choose the first alternative barrister they saw – me! Then, as now, little that I said ever seemed to make the slightest difference to the sentence my client would receive in that court. One judge bore the nickname 'Pontoon Jack', because he always gave every prisoner, for whatever offence, and however powerful the mitigation, 21 months. Another, Judge 'Ossie' Maclay, when hearing one of my first pleas for leniency, began nodding in apparent agreement.

'Sit down, he's with you,' horse-whispered an old veteran I thought was a friend, just as I was reaching the purple passage of my speech. I immediately sat down as advised.

'Two years,' said the judge. 'Take him down. Next.' What? Two years for stealing a shirt from a market stall when his children were starving? That was the last time I ever assumed that a smiling and nodding judge was accepting my argument. I feel the same way about juries.

John Streeter, a war hero who had lost both legs when his armoured car was blown up on the way to the battle of Arnhem, was one of the stars of the Factory, and later became the highly regarded Chairman of Kent Quarter Sessions and a senior circuit judge. He told me about a 'dock brief' experience he had once had. His client, a Polish gentleman, did not have the necessary two pounds four shillings and sixpence. 'My wife will pay you this afternoon,' he promised. Streeter was not too hopeful. Later, when he was back in chambers, Robert, the chief clerk, ushered into the room a very buxom blonde lady who claimed to be the client's wife. She was also fulsome in her thanks and praise, and as soon as the clerk withdrew, started to unbutton her blouse.

'What on earth are you doing, Madam?' asked the enormously respectable Streeter.

'My husband told me to pay you,' she began to explain – moments before being shown the door. She left the room, past a line of seated waiting clients, still buttoning her blouse, followed by a red-faced Streeter who, strangers were not to know, was always red-faced and perspiring profusely as the result of his war wounds.

After a dozen 'dock briefs' I was ready. A licence application for a restaurant earned me two pounds; a committal for trial at North London Magistrates Court earned me three pounds; a guilty plea at London Sessions earned me five pounds, as did an inquest at Hastings. My first real trial lasted four days, again at London Sessions, before Judge Henry Elam. It netted me thirty-six pounds, and resulted in my client's acquittal. I was just beginning to experience the single-minded dedication to a cause, the active involvement in the lives of people needing help, the joy of challenging misconceptions, the independence of action within a mysterious and wonderful world of tradition-hewn rules, the power of persuasion and the successes that were to make my life as a barrister so consuming, worthwhile and fulfilling,

My parents were keen to see their only child in action. They came up to London Sessions from Brighton, and sat behind me while I was defending a very red-faced Irishman for driving whilst under the influence of drink. I told him that his case was hopeless, but he pleaded 'not guilty' just the same. It hardly helped that he was unable to stand up in the witness box, because he had ignored my warning not to go to the pub for lunch. I began my final speech, standing in front of the jury. I was not so carried away by my oratory that I could fail to notice that they were all looking not at me, but past me. I turned to see what they were looking at. My proud parents – both fast asleep! Imagine how crestfallen I must have looked. The jury, realising that this was my first case, and seeing my parents so unsupportive and uncaring, must have taken pity on me, for they acquitted my client. He was as astonished as I was, and promptly slipped down the steps of the dock. This taught me an early lesson: a jury's verdict does not necessarily have anything to do with the justice of the case.

I learned another important lesson in my fifth month as a pupil: that you need courage at the criminal Bar. My client was a Jewish philatelist, who had parked his car outside his shop in a street off Trafalgar Square, to unload a delivery of stamps. But the police had suspended all parking, because a member of the Royal Family was to drive by and had already, as I recall, long since done so. It was a trivial case, but there was an important point of law concerning the limitation of police powers and it took many law books and most of the day for me to argue. We were at London Sessions before the gruff, but normally kindly, Judge Frank Cassels. No doubt driven to fury by the time the case was taking, he forgot himself and exploded.

'Your client isn't even British, is he?' he said.

'On the contrary, my Lord, my client is thoroughly and proudly British,' I replied. 'He not only fought for this country as an artillery captain throughout the war, but has won medals for bravery,' which I then proceeded to list.

There was no apology, but I was not interrupted again.

Perhaps I should have known better than to take a point of law, or even one of unfairness, before Judge Cassels. When he had been at the

Bar he had unsuccessfully defended Derek Bentley for murder. A more recent court has observed that both he and his leader, Melford Stevenson QC, failed to point out to the then Court of Appeal how defective in law and fairness the summing-up of Lord Goddard had been; with the result that Bentley was wrongly hanged for murder. He has since been retrospectively pardoned.

Trial changes

Criminal trials in my early days were very different from today. Judges used to be openly biased against defendants, and trials were often rushed through in great haste. Some capital murders only took an hour or two. Malcolm Morris QC, who defended Timothy Evans for famously murdering his wife at 10 Rillington Place, told me that he had had to make his final speech without being given any time to prepare it, at the end of a long and hard day. The judge wanted to send the jury out early next morning in order to start another trial. Fifty years later the hanging of Evans, like that of Bentley, has been held, by the modern Court of Appeal, to have been a deplorable miscarriage of justice.

In those days the police were allowed to give evidence of a kind that would not be allowed today. There was no tape-recording of interviews with suspects, and defences often turned upon discrepancies in the notebooks of the interviewing police officers. There was no closed circuit-television of the scene of crime, no electrostatic document analysis to ensure that notes were correctly kept and honestly recorded, no mobile phone evidence, no facial mapping, and no DNA. Judges were not bound to give directions, as they are now, warning juries against the dangers of identification evidence, or the relevance or otherwise of intoxication, or explain that they should not necessarily hold it against an accused that he had been caught out with a false alibi, or that if he lied to police officers, he might have done so because of panic or to distance himself from a problem which might have nothing to do with his guilt. On the other hand, the prosecution could not bring a defendant's previous convictions to the attention of the jury, unless the defence put those matters in issue, and hearsay evidence was normally inadmissible. There was no requirement for a judge to give reasons for his finding. There was no Human Rights Act and, since there was no European Court of Human Rights, no need to follow its rulings. Before the trial started, any number of jurors could be challenged and removed from the jury box. Juries were not sent home for the night while they were considering their verdict, and in my early days they were hardly ever sent to a hotel. In deciding how late a court would sit, the needs of jurors, ushers, shorthand writers and cleaners, who might have had to collect their children from school, were never considered. Verdicts had to be unanimous. Juries often stayed out until late in the evening, and if they still could not agree they would be discharged, and the trial would have to start again before another jury. In short cases at London Sessions, juries were not even invited to retire: 'Let the front row turn round to the back row and tell me how you find,' said the judges, as they ostentatiously looked at their watches, in an indication to the jury that they were not expected to take too long over their deliberations!

Professional criminals commit different crimes today – although sometimes they do revert to old practices. Some of the old bank robbers have graduated to drug importation or fraud or people trafficking, as safer and more remunerative criminal activities. Certainly there were far fewer drug cases when I came to the Bar, much less serious fraud, and money laundering, as a separate crime, simply did not exist. Even so, the same old families continue to turn up in the dock from time to time: sons of the old villains and even occasionally the old villains themselves. In 1998 I defended for murder the son of an old gangster for whom I had first appeared in 1963.

In many respects, trials are much fairer today. But there are new unfairnesses. Some rules now make acquittal less likely than would have been the case forty years ago. Other changes have stood the time-honoured rules of our criminal law upon their head. When there is a conviction for certain financial offences, the judge is now obliged to assume that the offender has been enjoying a criminal lifestyle for several years, even when there is no evidence to support that assumption, and he may be made to forfeit all his property – even that which is legitimate. Although the traditional 'right to silence' has not actually been abolished, juries are now told that where a defendant has not given evidence and/or has not explained his behaviour to the police when explanation was called for, they can hold that fact against him. The right to make a statement from the dock, thus avoiding cross-examination, has been abolished. Old-style committal proceedings, where the prosecution evidence could be tested before magistrates ahead of a jury trial in order to weed out weak cases, has gone. Juries no longer have to be warned by the judge of the danger of accepting the evidence of accomplices, or women and children in sex cases, without the corroboration of some independent evidence. A female complainant in a sex case cannot any longer, unless there are special circumstances, be questioned about her past, so that a jury may have no idea that she has been free with her favours on other occasions. On the other hand, a jury may now be told about a defendant's previous convictions and propensity to other inappropriate behaviour. Hearsay, or tittle-tattle, is more often allowed against a defendant. Although the prosecution now have to disclose, before the trial, any evidence they have which might undermine their case or assist the defence, this is balanced by a requirement that the defence must disclose their defence and the details of any alibi and defence witnesses, so that the prosecution may be better prepared to challenge it. Under consideration is a restriction upon the defendant's right to call his own expert evidence: even if he does have an expert, and decides not to call him because on balance he may be unhelpful, his report may have to be disclosed to the prosecution so that they can use it against him. The prosecution now have the right to appeal acquittals and to call for sentences to be increased above those imposed by the trial judge. When appeals are allowed, they now more frequently result in re-trials.

Today our laws are proliferating at an alarming rate: over three thousand new criminal offences, set out in thirty new criminal justice acts of parliament in the past decade! The procedures in our courts have become ever more detailed and complicated, and criminal lawyers still have to struggle courageously, as they have always had to do, with judges who assume that a defendant is guilty and who usually try to hold a case together on the side of the prosecution against what are said to be 'clever' (in its offensive meaning) defence lawyers. Life has become much more difficult for a defendant – and for his lawyers.

Outrageously, the fact that this increase in legislation and court rules now means that trials and their preparation take much longer, has been ignored by the last Labour government which cynically attacked lawyers for taking too long over legally-aided work. We have been punished by savage reductions in our fees. No other profession would have put up for so long with its members receiving payment of only forty-six pounds fifty a day before expenses of fifty percent and income tax have to be paid. No other profession would put up for five minutes with the slashing, by no less than fifty per cent, of publicly funded Queens Counsel's fees (and those of their juniors), nor with the increasing amount of work, including more conferences with clients, which is simply not remunerated at all. Furthermore, every change turns out to be a regrettable move towards the fusion of the Bar and the solicitor's professions – a subject I discuss, if my reader will bear with me, much later. But when I began my career at the Bar, nearly half a century ago, the inadequacy of income at the Bar and fusion of the professions were very far from my thoughts.

My career begins

My career really began to take off seven months after I became a barrister. James Burge asked me to make an application for bail in his place, in a watch-smuggling case at Lewes, in which he had been instructed. Customs men, having been tipped off, were waiting to greet a gang of smugglers as they waded ashore from a rowing boat at Dymchurch, on a lonely strip of the Kent coast. Alf Gerard, a well-known villain who had come to collect the gang in his Jaguar, in his hurry to get his boys away, carelessly drove over the foot of an excise man. The gang of five, two of whom including my client were later to be murdered, appeared in the dock in leg-irons and handcuffs.

I addressed the magistrates. I said that I had not been at the Bar very long, but I was appalled to see that men who had not been convicted of any offence could be brought into court shackled like dogs. I asked for them to be unchained before I addressed the court for bail. The kindly chairman of the bench agreed, and as soon as the key could be found, which as I recall took some time, they were unshackled. The defendants were delighted by my audacity. The case received widespread publicity in the national press, for in those days publicity was usually given to preliminary proceedings in the more interesting criminal cases. My client did not get bail, but the solicitor instructing me was also impressed by my brazenness. He was David Napley, the senior partner at Kingsley, Napley and Co, one of the most respected firms in the country. He later became president of the Law Society and was knighted for his services to the law. As a reward for my efforts he gave me the trial of this case as my first really big brief, with Edward Sutcliffe QC, later to become an Old Bailey judge, leading me. I drew a sketch of the principal performers in the trial, which hangs in my chambers today. One of the other junior defence barristers was Ivor Richard, the Labour MP for Barons Court, who also defended in the Great Train Robbery trial, and in due course became British Ambassador to the United Nations, a European Commissioner and then Labour leader in the House of Lords.

Towards the end of 1962 Manny Fryde instructed me to defend Jimmy Fraser (the nephew of Mad Frankie), on my own, in a case that also achieved some national prominence. Detective Sergeant Harold Challenor had decided, rather over-ambitiously, to clear up gang crime on his manor of London's West End Central police station. He arrested men called Pedrini, Oliva, Ford, Cheeseman and Jimmy Fraser, and charged them with conspiracy to demand money with menaces and possessing offensive weapons. The defendants insisted that the weapons had been planted, that their admissions of guilt had been invented, and that they had been beaten up by the police. The jury convicted everyone except my client Jimmy Fraser, although the convictions were later quashed in the Court of Appeal. The Oliva case is an authority on how judges should deal with witnesses who turn hostile to the prosecution. Detective Sergeant Challenor was himself charged with corruption two years later, after he had planted a brick in the pocket of a man demonstrating outside Buckingham Palace, against the state visit of Queen Frederika of Greece. At his trial he was found 'unfit to plead' and was sent to a mental institution. In time, therefore, he became a solicitor's clerk.

Twenty-five years later, when my daughter Rachel was a 19-year-old law student, we were walking together across the foyer of the St Johns Wood Hilton Hotel, on our way to a dinner in honour of the Bulgarian president. There was a deep gravely bellow of recognition from behind us. I turned and saw a large figure advancing towards us.

''Allo,' the man greeted me effusively, 'it's Mr Lawrence. You remember me! I'm Jimmy Fraser. You defended me years ago.' He called over to an older man who was still seated in the foyer. 'Look who's here, Frankie, its our old brief, Mr Lawrence.'

I forced a smile, exchanged an embarrassed word of greeting to Jimmy, and his uncle 'Mad' Frankie Fraser, and hurried off, just in case my old clients happened to be still under police observation. I had defended Frankie when he had tried to break out of Parkhurst prison on the Isle of Wight. Rachel wanted to know who they were and could she meet them. 'Not now,' I said. 'Maybe you will one day!' Michael Howard, when he was Home Secretary, used to say, 'If you can't do the time, don't do the crime.' I am not sure he realised that was also one of 'Mad' Frankie's favourite sayings!

In the middle of the Fraser case Manny Fryde spirited me away to Uxbridge Magistrates Court, to make a bail application for Mickey Ball, who had just been arrested as the get-away driver on a £62,000 London Airport bullion robbery which had taken place on 27 November 1962.

We now know that that robbery had been carried out by members of the notorious south-western gang, led by Bruce Reynolds, to provide funds for the commission of the following year's Great Train Robbery. I failed in my application: the police had more success. They spotted another suspect, Roy 'Weasel' James, one of the train robbers, in the public gallery, and promptly arrested him. Ball, at his later trial was convicted and sentenced to five years imprisonment. He was lucky. If he had not been in prison he would probably have been on the Great Train Robbery, with other members of the London Airport gang who had either not been caught, or who had been acquitted of playing any part in that robbery, and he might have had to serve thirty years.

Stephen Ward

In December 1962 I was having lunch in the London Sessions barristers' mess with John Marriage, a senior prosecuting barrister. He told me that he had just been appearing for the Crown in a bail application in a case that, he forecast, would 'bring down the Macmillan government'. Johnny Edgecombe, the jealous lover of a showgirl called Christine Keeler, had tried to shoot her, and he had been arrested. When his trial took place, three months later, Christine was in Spain. Her story about sleeping with John Profumo, the war minister, and Ivanov, the Soviet naval attaché and therefore almost certainly a spy, had been all over the newspapers, as had the suspicion that Profumo might have been instrumental in helping her to leave the country during Edgecombe's trial. On 22 March 1963, Profumo made his famous statement in the House of Commons denying all impropriety with Christine Keeler, and that he had had anything to do with Christine's absence. These events culminated in his resignation and lifelong disgrace. Then followed the infamous trial of Stephen Ward, charged with living off the immoral earnings of Christine Keeler and Mandy Rice Davies, which was to grip the attention and imagination of the nation. It did indeed bring down the Macmillan government.

James Burge was briefed, by the solicitor J.B. Wheatley, to defend Stephen Ward. I was allowed to sit behind my pupil-master at Marylebone Magistrates Court, and I had to take notes for part of the committal hearings, because Dai Tudor Price (who later became a High Court judge shortly before a sadly premature death), who was to be Burge's junior, was in the middle of another case. I have those notes – and some sketches that I drew – of the girls involved.

Mandy, whose lovely complexion like Dresden china spoke volumes for the skin-beautifying properties of fornication, was told by James Burge in cross-examination that Lord Astor had denied sleeping with her. Her immortal words in response, quoted frequently in conversation, are said to have been: 'He would say that wouldn't he.' Wrong! I have the clear pencil note in my advocate's notebook recording what she actually said. It was: 'Of course it is not untrue that I have had relations with Lord Astor. I'm not going to perjure myself in court.' Still, as a good media story it has run and run – and is still running. I sketched Mandy, Christine and other of the girls in the same notebook, but none of them can compare with the quality of the signed drawing of one of them by Stephen ward himself that hangs opposite my desk in my chambers.

The Great Train Robbery

At 3.03 am on 8 August 1963, the Royal Mail night train from Glasgow to Euston screamed to a halt at Sears Crossing, near Linslade in Buckinghamshire. Armed and masked robbers leapt aboard, coshed driver Mills to the floor, and made off with the then enormous sum of £2,295,150 (£30 million in today's figures). Twelve men eventually received prison sentences amounting to 307 years imprisonment (reduced on appeals to 251 years) for their parts in what has gone down in criminal history as the Great Train Robbery. One of those men was Charlie Wilson. He instructed Manny Fryde to act for him, and I was sent the brief as Junior Counsel. What an amazing coup! Barely out of pupillage, I had landed a brief in the trial of the century.

Unfortunately, it was not to be. Robert Goulden, the senior clerk, decided to overrule the instructing solicitor – as only the grandest of clerks might do – and he took the brief from me and gave it to the Hon. Paddy Pakenham, the son of Lord Longford, the Labour minister who was to champion Myra Hindley. As Robert explained it, since the trial was to take place at Aylesbury Assizes and Paddy, who was senior to me, as a tenant of chambers, was on the Midland circuit, he would not have to pay the daily fee then required of someone appearing off-circuit. So I came to lose a brief in one of the most famous cases of the generation! In the end, Paddy, as junior, represented Wisbey, another train robber, and the Wilson brief went to John Mathew, the famous Senior Treasury Prosecuting Counsel at the Old Bailey. Much later, when

Mathew had taken silk and had become a defender, he represented Kenneth Noye for rceiving the Brinks Mat gold bullion (unsuccessfully), and the alleged murder of a policeman which preceded it (successfully). Charlie Wilson was convicted, and received a thirty-year prison sentence. He did not serve it, for he was sprung from Brixton prison in the most outrageous prison break of modern times.

Another solicitor representing other defendants in the Great Train Robbery trial was Ellis Lincoln. His clever and amusing son Bryan, now a senior solicitor in a prominent City firm, was then a junior solicitor working for his father. He had been a good friend of mine at Oxford, and was sharing my garden flat in Sinclair Gardens, W14. While the trial was in preparation, our flat was burgled. There was nothing of value to take, but Bryan's room was ransacked. At almost the same time, Ellis's offices were burgled. And so were the chambers in the Temple of Ellis's brother, the eminent Queen's Counsel F. Ashe Lincoln, who was representing another train robber, Robert Welch. Were these three break-ins just an extraordinary coincidence, or did someone have a particular interest in knowing, in advance of the trial, the details of the train-robber defence? And if so, who?

Ashe Lincoln, I should add, had had a most distinguished war record as a naval captain. His greatest achievement had been, as a demolition officer, in March 1945, to personally safeguard the famous bridge across the Rhine at Remagen, from booby-trapped destruction by the German army. He was a man of immense courage who thereby enabled the American army to shorten the Second World War. Some years later he was arrested for having a pistol in the pocket of his coat, which he had hung up when dining at the Savoy. As a prominent member of the Jewish community who had reason to fear for his own safety, he carried the gun for protection. Ashe led me several times in trials, but he never spoke to me about the war. When he died, well into his 90s, it was at his memorial service that an Admiral of the Fleet spoke of his conspicuous bravery.

And other cases

My court diary tells me that, in 1963, I spent every weekday (and many Saturdays) in court, sometimes engaged in more than one case in the day. I earned about £10,000 pounds in fees – a fortune in those days, although we were so slowly paid that I often had to wait a year or more for my money and sometimes I never actually received any fee. I started defending other notorious London gangsters, with names like Micky Ishmael, John McVicar, Jimmy Nash, 'Duke' Osborne and later, the Krays. I also began quite a flourishing career defending waiters at Chinese restaurants who, with oriental artistry and amazing dexterity in the use of woks, choppers and boiling oil, were prone to deal with drunks, and other customers who refused to pay for their meals on Thursday nights, by separating them from parts of their body and sometimes from life itself.

In quieter moments I gathered crumbs from the table of my pupil-master's bountiful liquor-licensing practice. I helped to acquire, or renew, drinking licences for public houses, West-End nightclubs like Maxims, and educational institutions like the London Association of Music and Dramatic Art (LAMDA). My stock-in-trade also embraced the securing of gaming licences for the newly respectable licensed betting offices. In the evenings, when neither canvassing nor at my soapbox, I improved my finances, and experience of life, by teaching trainee bookmakers at the London School of Turf Accountancy how to stay on the right side of the law, and law students at the West London College of Commerce how to pass the Commercial Law exam paper. In those days I had to burn the candle at both ends, for it was the only way to make ends meet! I was sometimes so tired that I dozed off, even as I lectured. But I mastered a self-revival technique.

'You in the third row,' I would say, as I felt myself slipping away, 'are you awake and concentrating? What was the last thing I said?'

In January 1964, the publisher and bookseller of the unexpurgated edition of the book *Fanny Hill* went on trial before Sir Robert Blundell, the Chief Stipendiary Magistrate at Bow Street Magistrates Court, charged with publishing pornography. One of the stars in James Burge's chambers, and the advocate I have always most admired, was Robin Simpson. He was briefed for the bookseller, but he could not be in court one day, so I was sent to 'hold' his brief. I had to read the book, of course, and when I had done so I hid it in the piano stool at my flat lest Gloria might see it and corrupt her little mind by reading it. That is how well-brought-up gentlemen used to think and behave, before the 'swinging sixties' took hold of us. But Gloria heard the piano stool lid close, looked to see what I had hidden, found it, and read it anyway. That is how women took control at the dawn of the new iconoclastic age.

At court I was not expected to say anything, but I found myself tempted almost beyond endurance. The distinguished historian, Montgomery Hyde, had given evidence that the book was of very considerable historical interest in its description of seventeenth-century London. Few were aware, apparently, of what he insisted was a most important historical fact: that brothels had existed in Green Street, St James's. Who cared! But I did think that people might be more interested to learn another historical fact: that whenever anyone wanted to get to know Fanny more intimately, all they had to do was to lift her skirt. Women at that period in Britain's proud history, apparently, wore neither brassieres nor knickers. So, when my turn came, I rose from amidst the crowded line of counsel, in the media-packed Bow Street court-room, to cross-examine the witness about this really fascinating piece of social history. Then a blinding thought struck me: the headline in that day's *Evening Standard* might well be: 'No bra or panties for Fanny, says counsel.' I realised, in that moment, that the question I was so sorely tempted to ask would probably bring my fledgling legal career to a premature end. Exercising more discretion than I think I have ever exercised since, I announced: 'No questions,' and resumed my seat.

At about this time I defended a man called Rice at the Old Bailey, for driving while disqualified, and handling stolen weighing scales. A City police constable gave evidence that, while on traffic duty at Aldgate, a car drove past him with the defendant undoubtedly at the wheel. My instructions were that my client, who was known to the police, had never driven that car in his life, and was nowhere near Aldgate at the time. Unfortunately he could not remember exactly where he had been, and so had no alibi witnesses to call. The police officer was absolutely certain this was the man, who was very big and had heavy recognisable Tommy Cooper-like features. With no ammunition with which to show that the police officer had made a mistake, what was I to do? I saw no point in simply suggesting that he was mistaken, and sitting down. So I started to cross-examine him at length about the surrounding circumstances, in case something helpful might turn up. It must have been dreadful to listen to, and the judge did not bother – he lost concentration and then dozed off completely. I went on and on. Then a remarkable thing happened. The witness also lost concentration, and contradicted something he had said earlier and had forgotten. I challenged him on the point. He then made another mistake. I challenged him again. He began to get agitated. Mistakes came fast and furious. Suddenly his face turned grey, and he slumped in the witness box. He was given water and pulled himself together. I asked him why he had collapsed like that, was he unwell?

'No,' he replied to an astonished court. 'I cannot truthfully identify your client as the driver.'

The prosecutor, David West-Russell (later to become a circuit judge and President of Industrial Tribunals for England and Wales), was the first to recover from his astonishment. He asked the judge if he would rise. Judge Block woke up and asked why the application was being made! We went to see him in his room, and explained. He came back into court, stopped the trial and freed my very fortunate and grateful client.

There is a postscript. The police inspector on duty, in Court Five where this remarkable happening had taken place, came up to me as I was gathering up my papers. He thanked me for not making a meal of the unfortunate situation. He explained that the police constable, who had not been long in the force, and was the son of a vicar, had been told by the officer in charge of the case that he had better not show any uncertainty about his identification. I asked what would happen to the constable. He said he thought he might just be disciplined, nothing more. I was foolhardy enough to speak about this incident in what I thought was a private meeting of the Society of Labour Lawyers, in the High Court at the weekend, although why I was attending such a meeting I really have no idea. On the following Monday, a tabloid leader column screamed: 'An unknown lawyer in an unknown case has spoken about an unnamed policeman who, after perjured evidence had been given against an innocent man, told him there would be a cover-up. The lawyer owes it to the rest of society to come forward.'

Next day, a very senior City police officer came to interview me in chambers. I was terrified. Here I was, a comparative beginner at the Bar, and I had caused a real storm by talking publicly out of turn about an extremely serious matter, thereby putting the careers (and pensions) of police officers on the line. I gave my account of the conversation with the police inspector. I was told that he had denied that such a conversation had ever taken place. Did I want to proceed with the complaint? I said that although what I had said was the truth, I had no wish to destroy the police inspector's career, when he was probably just trying to be nice; so I was not making any complaint. Next day the tabloid announced that the lawyer concerned had withdrawn his allegation.

Not too much seems to have happened to the police constable witness either. I saw him often on point duty in Fleet Street. He always saluted me, and held up the traffic so that I could hurry my way from the Temple to the Old Bailey unhindered. Solicitors and barrister colleagues walking with me were most impressed by my surprising youthful influence.

I had to wait forty years before another witness in a case of mine actually confessed, in the witness box, to lying. I was at Leeds Crown Court, defending a paedophile charged with committing two rapes and one indecent assault against a little girl aged eleven years, whom he had befriended. He had an appalling record of some ninety offences in all, several of which were for sexual acts with children, and one of which was for raping a probation officer, for which he had received a six-year prison sentence. This being a second serious offence, under laws introduced by Michael Howard the paedophile was facing a mandatory life sentence. I asked the little girl, who was giving evidence on a television link, and therefore was not actually in the court, whether she ever told lies. She hesitated and then said that she did, sometimes. She agreed that she had told a lie, on another occasion, about her father hitting her, just to annoy her mother. I asked her if she was telling lies about being raped by the defendant. To the amazement of everyone in court, she answered, 'Yes.' The judge could not believe what he had just heard, and thinking that she may have misunderstood the question, tried to put the matter right.

'I think you misheard the barrister's question,' he said. 'You are not saying that the rape did not happen, are you?'

'Yes I am,' said the little girl. 'He didn't rape me.'

A barrister's life is full of surprises! The case against my client was withdrawn from the jury, and 'not guilty' verdicts were entered as far as that little girl was concerned. Later in the week my client was tried again on indecent assault charges before a different jury. It was alleged that he had touched the chests of two other little girls aged nine and ten, and he was sentenced to four years imprisonment with ten years on licence, which meant that he could be brought back to court for further imprisonment 'if' he commits any other offences. I thought 'when' might have been more appropriate.

Gloria-Sarah

In 1963 I bought a sixteen-foot two-berth cabin cruiser, and named it the *Gloria-Sarah*, after both my wife-to-be and my dear mother. I moored it at the Fulham Yacht club, by the railway arches in Ranelagh Gardens. Those were the days of frequent bus and tube strikes and of terrible traffic jams in London, so I decided to take the boat downriver to chambers on any morning when I would not be in court until the afternoon. I would need to anchor at Temple steps, but there was a problem – a great boat called the *Wellington* (still there, but since moved a hundred yards downstream) was already moored there. The owner was the Master Mariners Association, so I asked them for permission to tie up against their boat. They said that they would be delighted to help me, but that first I would need the permission of the Inner Temple authorities, for it was they who must licence access to the Temple steps.

I duly sent my application to Commander Rodney Flynn, the Sub-Treasurer of the Inn, a proud naval man himself, and in due course received a reply. It informed me that the Masters of the Bench of the Honourable Society of the Inner Temple in Parliament assembled were graciously pleased to accord to a member of the Inn the privilege of mooring on the Temple steps, and that a key to the Watergate would be forthcoming. Watergate? What Watergate, I wondered, was there, needing to be opened with a key? There were only some steps down to the water on the other side of the road.

Sitting next to Commander Flynn next day at lunch in the Inn, I asked him what he was talking about. He told me that his Masters, tickled by the unusual application, had asked, appropriately for such eminent lawyers, for a search to be made of the legal precedents. Research had revealed that barristers who used to ply their trade at the court, held upriver at Westminster Hall in the seventeenth, eighteenth and nineteenth centuries, had been permitted by the Inn to moor their boats at the Watergate, and had been issued with a key for access. But of course that had been in the days when the Thames had lapped at the bottom of Middle Temple Lane, and there had indeed been a watergate providing southern access to the Temple. But by the latter part of the nineteenth century the Law Courts had moved to the magnificent new building in the Strand, and barristers no longer had to take to their boats. Furthermore, the Embankment had also been built, and the watergate had disappeared altogether. An amending letter arrived next day advising me to ignore all reference to a watergate and key, and to treat the original letter as permission to moor on the aforementioned Temple steps.

The formalities thus completed, I thereafter made journeys to court by boat: often downstream to Tower Bridge Magistrates Court on Saturday mornings. Harry Stevens, of the solicitors Baldwin and Co. of Tooley Street, used to send me to make submissions of 'no case to answer' for ten guineas a time, on behalf of dockers who had been stopped by the British Transport Police as they left their work-places of a Friday night, carrying hams and other goodies, the legal possession of which they found hard to explain. I used to collect Gloria, motorboat down from Fulham, moor the boat alongside Tower Bridge pier, saunter over Tower Bridge to the court clutching my ten guinea brief, and appear cheerfully before the equally cheerful and charming stipendiary magistrate, Harry Maddocks.

He did not much like prosecutions where the evidence depended entirely on the rule in R v Fuschillo. That case had established a legal precedent during the rationing era of the Second World War. This allowed the prosecution, when charging someone with receiving stolen property, not to have to prove by direct evidence that the goods had been stolen. Mr Maddocks did not like this rule, and insisted that there be direct evidence of theft before he would convict. When that was not forthcoming, he would allow my submission that the prosecution had not properly proved their case, and would award costs to the defence. The weekend, thus satisfactorily begun, would be continued even more satisfactorily as I motored downriver past the dreary undeveloped warehouses or upriver through the leafy green English countryside, aboard the exquisite *Gloria-Sarah*, in the company of my lovely and exquisite future wife.

Many years after his trial in 1940 this same Mr Fuschillo, so it is said, found himself in the dock again, this time before the stern Chairman of London Sessions (another former member of the Factory), W.E. 'Reggie' Seaton.

'Were you not convicted in this court of receiving stolen sugar during the war?' Reggie asked.

'Yes, that was me,' the accused replied.

'Then I shall pass no prison sentence upon you for this offence today,' said the judge, 'as a token of the Bar's gratitude for all the work that your case has provided in the courts over the ensuing years.'

I had many watery adventures with the *Gloria-Sarah*. Fast travel up and down the Thames was, in those days, hazardous for a small lightweight plastic cabin cruiser. Floating debris frequently snapped the pin which, acting as a kind of fuse, held the propeller to the axle, and I would drift at speed on an ebb tide for miles, while hanging over the side of the boat, trying to effect a repair. At other times the plugs would block up and the boat, though consuming petrol at the same rate, would slow down, and I would run out of petrol.

One evening, when I had been invited to dinner with my future mother-in-law at home in Catford, a breakdown occurred on my way back by river from chambers, and I had to go ashore by Lots Road power station at Fulham, in search of a garage. I returned to the boat with a can of petrol to find it high and dry on a sandbank. I panicked, which meant that my efforts to re-start the engine only resulted in my getting the rope twisted around the propeller. It was an hour or more before a kindly passing boat skipper stopped to drag me off the sandbank. By the time I got back to my Putney bridge mooring at about nine o'clock, the tide had turned and I could no longer just float onto it. More half-hours passed. Eventually I was able to wade ashore – to find the boat-yard closed and the exit locked. Exhausted, mud-bespattered, wearing a workman's peaked cap, and carrying my blue barrister's linen bag filled with books and my brief for next day, I grasped and clawed my way to the top of the 15-foot wooden fence onto the road outside, and jumped down – straight into the arms of a sight from the past, a single patrolling policeman.

'Good evening officer,' was all I could think of to say.

'Good evening sir,' was all he could think of to reply. Saluting me, as if it was the most normal thing in the world to come upon a man covered in mud, dressed like a burglar, breaking out of enclosed premises at midnight clutching his loot in a cloth bag, he resumed his plodding way as if nothing had happened. It is impossible not to admire the British Bobby.

One dark, dank, windy Sunday afternoon, when the river and the embankment were deserted and I was alone at the boat's wheel and daydreaming, I heard a loudly revving speedboat breaking the dull silence, and watched as it hurtled dangerously through the arches of Blackfriars Bridge ahead of me. It slammed into something in the water and sank like at stone. The driver obviously could not swim, and was flailing about and sinking in the very choppy water. I barely managed to haul him out. He was very lucky that I just happened to be passing, for there was no one else about. I took him to the nearest river police station up-tide at Putney. He forgot to thank me.

On another occasion, in 1965, I delayed the start of the Oxford–Cambridge boat race. My pin sheered shortly before the flag went up, and the wife of my good friend Ronald Bartle, the Bow Street magistrate (and another star of the Factory), played fumble-fingers with the new pin which she was passing to me from her husband, and dropped it into the river. The boat, out of control, drifted out across the start line. The radio and television commentators were amused, as were their audience, but not, I think, the waiting crews.

Now another of my life's strange coincidences. On New Year's Eve 1976 I appeared at Lambeth Magistrates Court in committal proceedings on behalf of Ronnie Darke, a man with a gangland reputation known as 'Dark Ronnie,' who had given evidence on behalf of the train robbers and was now charged with murder. He, and a companion defended by Kenneth Machin (later to become an Old Bailey judge), were accused of assaulting a man they did not like, and tipping him, unconscious, over a bridge into a stream. The unfortunate victim had drowned. The stipendiary magistrate, after considering my submission that there was 'no case to answer' against my client, eventually, at the late hour of 7pm, agreed with me, and released him.

Darke had been in custody for several weeks, and neither he nor his wife had expected him to be released so soon – if ever. With no mobile phones in those days to give warning, after a celebratory drink or four at a nearby hostelry he made a surprise appearance at his home. He arrived to find that his lady, believing her man to be safely tucked up in prison, had made alternative arrangements for celebrating the New Year, which, he could not help but observe, were even at that early hour well advanced. It was fortunate that there was not another death – and another court case.

Two years later, on 21 November 1978, Darke was hacked to death with a machete, allegedly by TV actor and gangster John Bindon (credits *Up the Junction* and *Poor Cow*). Bindon, who had somehow become a friend of Princess Margaret on the island of Mustique, was later found not guilty of the murder at his trial at the Old Bailey. The scene of the crime? The same Fulham Yacht Club, under the railway bridge near the Hurlingham, at which I had moored my boat and had these exciting experiences in the sixties.

4

Early Politics

'He knows nothing: and he thinks he knows everything.
That points clearly to a political career.'

(George Bernard Shaw, *Major Barbara*)

When I came down from Oxford I decided to take an active part in
politics. I joined the North Hammersmith Conservative Association and
stood twice for Hammersmith Council.

The first time, I had no chance of winning. Three years later I expected
to win, for the Labour majority was small and I had canvassed every
home in Addison Ward once, and some, like the Rockley Court flat of
the beautiful actress and star of *The Forsyte Saga*, Nyree Dawn Porter,
several times. I had not reckoned with boundary changes. Three weeks
before the local elections, Henry Brooke, the Conservative Home Secretary,
altered the ward boundary to include a large part of Baron's Court, the
Labour MP of which happened to be Ivor Richard, my barrister colleague
in the watch-smuggling case. There was no time to canvass the added-
on Labour half of the Shepherds Bush Road and the Goldhawk Road
area and, since it had never seen a Conservative canvasser, I lost by 200
votes. This was my first experience of the unexpectedness, and
disappointment, of politics.

I became Vice-Chairman of North Hammersmith Conservatives, and
on Saturday afternoons and Wednesday evenings I held political 'soap
box' meetings outside Shepherds Bush underground station. These lasted
for about two hours, or until my voice packed up, when I would repair
the vocal damage by sucking Trebor mints. I often had to start collecting
a crowd, I am ashamed to recall, by insulting an innocent passer-by:
'Hallo! Yes, you! The long-haired git!' was one bold approach. If I was
lucky the 'git' would respond so loudly and angrily as to attract the
attention of the uniformed policeman who, in those halcyon days, seemed
always to be on duty at Shepherds Bush Green. Hurrying across to the

scene of an imminent gbh, notebook at the ready, PC Plod's activity would immediately draw a crowd. I would then apologise profusely to the 'git', explain that it was the only way I could attract the policeman's attention and a crowd, and thank him for his contribution to the democratic process. I was never under any real threat of assault, since the sight of an advancing policeman was always enough to make my involuntary assistant disappear speedily into the beyond. Meanwhile a cluster of passers-by would have gathered around my stand, and would linger for a minute or two to hear me begin my oration before marvelling at my impertinence and political opinions, and passing on to re-engage their lives. Wave after wave of homeward bound tube travellers, disgorging endlessly from the depths of the Central Line underground station, would pause to fill the spaces left by those departing.

My weekly text would be taken from the political diatribes of the master soapbox orators whom I regularly watched, drawing daily lunchtime crowds, on the north-east corner of Lincolns Inn Fields. From them I learnt the rudiments of soapbox humour, so necessary if one is to hold a crowd. I also learnt from a pamphlet written by Tony Benn, the distinguished Labour politician, who was later to be my pair in the Commons. To a passer-by breaking wind: 'Excuse me, sir, but are you the *official* spokesman of the Labour Party?' To someone picking up a cabbage from the greengrocers stall next to the underground station, and throwing it at me: 'Look, the leader of the opposition has lost his head!' To the tomato thrower, likewise provisioned and activated: 'Look, my friends, haven't I always told you that the opposition's arguments are thoroughly rotten?' To a Liberal heckler: 'Liberals are like a bunch of bananas. Yellow on the outside, green on the inside; and not a straight one among them.' And to the occasionally well-informed, and therefore particularly irritating, heckler: 'Listen! If everything you know is added to everything I know, I wouldn't know any more than I know already.' It was all terrific fun!

Someone suggested that I should be in parliament. That seemed like a good idea, but how to set about it? First I had to get onto the Conservative Central Office list of candidates. In those days before 'A' lists dictated by the Party leader and 'women only' seats, you had to provide information about your interests, activities, and achievements, and then you would be interviewed by officials and MPs to see how suitable you were. If you got onto the candidates list, your name and history would be passed, together with many others, to any Conservative Association in the country seeking a candidate. They would, in turn, consider your application, and invite applicants in whom they were interested to an interview. On Wednesday evening 10 March 1965 I was interviewed at both the Peckham and Dartford constituencies.

Peckham

Peckham, a south-east London constituency, had been held since the war, with a large majority, by Mrs Freda Corbett, Labour's Chief Whip on London County Council. When she retired in 1970 she was still using, rather charmingly, the sepia election photograph she had had taken in 1945. The seat is now held by Harriet Harman, the New Labour Deputy Leader and former Solicitor-General, who used to brief me in legislative committees in parliament in the days when she worked for the National Council for Civil Liberties. Before the Second World War, and the building of huge council housing estates, Peckham had been a Conservative seat. During my two general election campaigns an elderly man in his seventies, whose name I am ashamed to say I cannot now recall, arrived at the Conservative offices in Queens Road to wish me 'good luck' – having walked all the way from Acton in West London. He told me that he had made this pilgrimage in memory of his mother at every election since she had died, because she had been a maid with Earl Beattie's family, when he had been the Conservative MP for Peckham in the 1930s.

Dartford, by contrast, was a seat so marginally Labour that the Conservatives were expected to win it at the next election. Margaret Thatcher had stood for the seat a few years earlier. Obviously I really hoped that I would be selected there, but my first interview that evening was at Peckham. I did my best before the Peckham selection committee, and they said that they would let me know the result later in the evening. Then I drove on to Dartford and performed. I arrived back at my Shepherds Bush flat just as the Dartford Conservative agent was ringing to invite me to be their candidate. Could I give him an answer there and then? I explained that, as Peckham had interviewed me first, I should wait for their verdict. I sat by the phone hoping that Peckham would not want me. But they did. I thought that the honourable course was to turn down the Dartford offer. Everyone told me I was a fool. 'You are in politics now, and you have to be single-minded: either you want to get into Parliament or you do not.' I obviously was not single-minded enough.

Dartford then chose Peter Trew (the chairman of one of the leading construction companies in Britain) and he was duly elected at the next general election. A modest and self-effacing gentleman, whenever thereafter I ventured anywhere near his Dartford constituents, whether at a party conference or to speak at a constituency dinner, he would insist on telling everyone that I was the one they had really wanted. He served until the seat went back to Labour in 1970. I, of course, failed to be elected for Peckham, at both the 1966 election and at the following election in 1970. My elders and betters told me that I should not have stood twice: again, just not single-minded enough.

My predecessor at Peckham had been Toby Jessel, a member of both Southwark Council and the Greater London Council, who went on to serve as an outstanding MP for Twickenham for 37 years. Opening his campaign in the 1964 election, he handed out blue plastic teaspoons at street corners with the slogan 'Stir it up with Jessel' imprinted on the handles. But there was a problem. Election law required every piece of election publicity to bear upon it the name of the publisher (usually the election agent), together with the name and address of the printer. There being no space for these on the spoon, and sticky labels being useless, Toby was rumbled for a likely election offence. He had to spend much of the second week at the same street corners, trying to retrieve the offending spoons. This incident was well publicised and remembered locally.

One evening, at my first election, I canvassed the Sceaux solid-Labour council housing estate. I knocked on a door.

'Who's there?' bellowed a loud, unfriendly and clearly irritated voice.

'I'm the C-c-conservative c-c-andidate,' I stuttered uncertainly.

'Oh, come in, Mr Jessel,' the voice answered more warmly, and the door opened.

'I'm not actually Mr Jessel,' I began to explain.

'Well fuck off then,' said the man who would have slammed the door in my face had I not got my foot in the opening, and been already half inside. I introduced myself and managed to calm him down. He apologised and offered me a cup of tea.

'Wonderful campaign that Jessel fought at the last election,' he opined, 'what with them plastic spoons – but he didn't win, did he!' He thought a moment then said, 'I'll tell you what. You stand on them street corners handing out french letters with "Stick it up with Lawrence" stamped on them, and we'll all fucking vote for you.' There was, of course, no way that I could have got all the names and addresses on such a small space.

I had wonderful helpers at Peckham. Peter Thorneycroft, not then a peer but later to become chairman of the Conservative Party and who, but for an earlier sensational resignation from the Macmillan government, might well have become the next prime minister, folded raffle tickets at our annual ball. So, in another year, did Henry Brooke, the Home Secretary. Lynda Chalker (later MP for Wallasey, Overseas Aid Minister and a baroness) came to laboriously fold my thirty thousand full-colour newspaper-style election addresses, which were much too thick to go into any envelope. Michael Farrow (a businessman, member of the Greater London Council for Kensington, and now a Common Councilman of the City of London) volunteered to become my chairman for a general election, and stayed on to help for several years. I started the Heath Dining Club, which met at a Cypriot restaurant at Camberwell Green, and managed to persuade a steady stream of Conservative MPs to come and stoke our doctrinal fires. I even had a full-time paid agent. John Dyke was dynamic, friendly, tactful and dedicated. Tragically, when he was driving home one night, two young tearaways in a stolen car overtook a car coming in the other direction on the wrong side of the road, and killed him. He was a very great loss to the party.

When Gloria and I were canvassing the Peabody alms-houses we found Labour's Alderman Mrs Burgess, then over eighty years old, doing likewise. We offered to deliver her Labour leaflets on the upper floors; she took our Conservative leaflets to deliver on the ground floors. Peckham Conservatives always enjoyed a pleasant relationship with the Labour Party, perhaps because we posed so little threat to them. Not, that is, until 1967.

There had been no Conservative councillors on Southwark Council representing Peckham for many years, but our canvas returns that year were so good that I thought we might win both Consort Ward (near the Conservative HQ in Queens Road) and West Ward (around Camberwell Green), where we had managed to get a popular publican, Martin Mulligan, to stand for us. No one else in the Association, not even our dedicated Chairman, Florence Tristram (a local government administrator), or our Treasurer, Jack Rose (a local solicitor), thought we stood any chance. The executive committee chose Mrs Percival, a jolly cleaning lady employed by Southwark Council, to stand for Consort Ward. She won! Unfortunately there was a sensible rule, which we had all failed to notice, that a council employee could not stand for election to the council by which she was employed. She was therefore unable to take her seat, and there had to be an immediate by-election in that ward.

But we had spent all our election money on the abortive campaign and had nothing left for new posters and leaflets.

Florence had the bright idea of asking Mrs Percival's son, Terry, to stand, so that we could use the same 'Vote Percival' posters. We asked him and, trooper that he was, he accepted. Astonishingly, he also won – and went on to serve Peckham as a first-class councillor for several years, until he moved out of the area. Martin Mulligan also won. I never had to pay for drinks at the Golden Lion. Amazingly, six of our other candidates were also victorious, giving us eight out of the fourteen Peckham seats on Southwark Council. The following year there was such a big swing to the Conservatives in London that we even won back control of London County Council. Another political lesson: no seat is ever hopeless when the political pendulum is swinging in your direction.

It may be that the swing had something to do with Enoch Powell's speech, earlier that year, warning that without stronger immigration controls our rivers could 'flow with blood like the Tiber'. I never understood how it was that the man who, as health minister in Harold Macmillan's government had advocated the large-scale recruitment of West Indian women and men to work in our hospitals and to drive London buses, to say nothing of the warm welcome he later gave to all East African Asians, should have set himself up as the scourge of the Heath government for its encouragement of Commonwealth immigration. Enoch was a strange man. I asked for his support as a famous libertarian, for my anti-fluoridation campaign in 1985, on the grounds that mass-medication of the nation's drinking water was an outrageous infringement of the civil liberties he had always fought for. He could not do that, he explained, because he had been the health minister who had tried to introduce the anti-libertarian policy of fluoridation!

As soon as I became Candidate for Peckham, I moved my weekly soapbox from Shepherds Bush Green to Camberwell Green. Although there was no Camberwell tube station, from which a new audience could decant every five minutes, the move worked well for a few months – until London County Council converted the Green into a one-way traffic system. After that, hardly anyone stopped to listen to me, because hardly anyone walked by. So I moved my soapbox round the corner to outside Martin Mulligan's public house. There I found the audience to be much larger and noisier, although, of course, unable to remain standing for long. That pitch soon became a popular meeting point for the local dog population, which would gather on warm Wednesday evenings to find canine companionship – and relief. They found my soapbox to be a particularly useful convenience. A West Indian gentleman stopped one day and asked me if I remembered him. I told him that while his face was familiar, I was very sorry but I could not recall his name.

'It's Andrews, man,' he said. 'You done defend me for brothel keeping.'

I just about remembered him, but not the outcome of the trial. 'Why Mr Andrews,' I said, 'of course I remember you, but what are you doing out so soon?'

'Hey, man,' he replied, 'you done got me off!'

As the official Conservative parliamentary candidate, I was appointed to several local committees. The one I enjoyed most was being a governor of Collingwood Girls School, a position I shared with, among others, Grace Shepherd, the wife of the famous former England cricket captain, David Shepherd, who later became Bishop of Liverpool. I arranged for Judge Jean Graham Hall, who had been a colleague of mine at the Bar, to give the prizes one speech day. At the musical interlude, four little West Indian girls, aged between 9 and 12 years and wearing plaits, stepped up and started playing – a Haydn string quartet. It was one of those particularly moving moments, that happen unexpectedly in life, or sometimes on *Britain's Got Talent*. There cannot have been a dry eye in the place; certainly mine were not. I wondered how many of the white parents present appreciated the statement: look what immigrants in a run-down urban area can achieve if their parents are dedicated enough to make sure that their children get the best education at a really good school.

Harold Wilson called the 1966 general election on 29 March, to strengthen his wafer-thin majority. Unfortunately, that was the very day Gloria and I were planning to get married. 'Instead of wining and dining his family and friends at the London Hilton,' the *South London Press* enthused, 'Mr Lawrence was sweating it out at Peckham Girls School.' I received 8203 votes, and Labour's majority was 12,607. Three days after sweating it out, Gloria and I were joined in matrimony at the majestic West London Synagogue in Upper Berkeley Street, London W1.

Our wedding service was conducted by the brilliant and charismatic Rabbi Hugo Gryn, the senior Reform Jewish rabbi. He had been a child of the Holocaust in Auschwitz, a rabbi in Birmingham Alabama during the race riots, and Principal of the Leo Beck Rabbinical College. He had achieved fame outside the Jewish community as the religious panellist on the BBC Radio Four programme *The Moral Maze*. Gloria had converted to Judaism after a course of instruction lasting several months, under the guidance of the very kind, gentle and talented Rabbi Curtis.

Both great teachers sadly died long before their time. At the wedding we were surrounded by some family and forty or fifty friends. Hugo, who had a considerable influence upon my life, and on the lives of thousands of others, told the audience at our thirtieth wedding anniversary dinner at the House of Commons, which he attended shortly before he died, how he had always used a line from my own short speech of thanks at the Hilton reception.

'People will wonder why so few of our family are here today,' I had apparently said. 'The reason is – we didn't invite them!'

After the festivities, I drove Gloria in my little British racing green Triumph Spitfire to our new home at Shepperton. The journey was eventful. The Conservative slogan at the election, borrowing from the then current Esso tiger advertisement, had been: 'Put a Tory in your tank and your engine won't Labour.' Unfortunately an unhappy Labour voter had taken the invocation too literally, and had stuffed the posters covering my car into the petrol tank. The car did more than labour: it stopped every ten minutes on the 20-mile journey. Arriving eventually at our new home, to spend our first night without central heating in a bedroom with no furniture, I lifted my lovely bride over the threshold. My back has never been quite the same since.

Dunally Cottage

We first learnt about Dunally Cottage, which has been our main home, from an eye-catching advertisement in *The Sunday Times* by the famously honest estate agent Roy Brooks. It read: 'Clapped out clinker-built dinghy for sale with old cottage.' We had been looking for a place on the river, but could not afford anywhere as near to central London as Hammersmith or Chiswick. Docklands was not yet a dream in anyone's eye. Via Richmond, Twickenham, Hampton Court and Sunbury, we came to Shepperton. As with our own first meeting, we fell in love instantly with the house and its setting.

Shepperton, meaning shepherd's habitation, goes back as a settlement 2000 years. Here Cassivelaunus, the leader of the brave Trinobantes, defeated Julius Caesar's Romans in 43 BC. Some writers even think that Caesar crossed from south to north at about here, since it is practically the lowest part of the Thames, and stakes, bones and weapons have been found in the river. After the Romans left, it became part of the Middle Saxon region (hence Middlesex). The first church was built about

AD 650, and it is recorded in the Domesday Book as having seventeen villagers with one virgate (whoever that might be) each, five cottagers, two slaves and a priest. More interestingly, by 1966 it had ten public houses within ten minutes' walk.

Lower Halliford Green, a mile equidistant from both the old village and the new, and upon one corner of which sits our pretty white cottage, is historically a literary haven. In one of the big riverside houses, facing us on Walton Lane, lived the nineteenth-century dramatist Thomas Love Peacock. He loaned his 'cottage' for one summer to his best friend Percy Shelley, the great romantic poet. Opposite us, on the other side of the green is Vine Cottage, in which lived Peacock's daughter and son-in-law George Meredith, another famous poet. Next door to them is Battlecrease Hall, which was something in the Civil War, then variously the home of Lady Hamilton, Nelson's mistress, and of Rider Haggard, author of *King Solomon's Mines*. Dickens in *Oliver Twist* makes his young hero, and the Artful Dodger, hitch a lift in a cart from Sunbury to Chertsey, the next village to Shepperton, through Lower Halliford and therefore past our house. H.G. Wells, in *The War of the Worlds*, has his martians destroying Shepperton church and setting fire to houses at Halliford, while he escapes past our house by boat to Walton Bridge, and then on foot, with the curate, past the back of our house, along the road to Sunbury. In more recent years I would find myself standing in the queue at Budgens behind the late J.G. Ballard, author of the great novel *Empire of the Sun*.

Ours is Shelley's cottage. The roof is Tudor and the house looks as though it was once a wheat barn. We bought it, with its weatherboard exterior, from Digby Turpin, who had filmed television advertisements for Kellogg's corn flakes in the stone-flagged dining room, and for Capstan cigarettes from the capstan-like bollards outside. Although looking like one house, it was in fact semi-detached to Poets Cottage, so named because it had been thought that that was the cottage loaned to Shelley. In 1983, when the then owner of Poets Cottage, Steve Holley (Paul McCartney's drummer with the pop group Wings), sold it to me, I joined the two houses together. We then found that Poets Cottage, whose title deeds date from the mid-nineteenth century, had never been part of Dunally Cottage, whose title deeds as a residence date back to 1720. We were not allowed to remove the timber beams forming the wall dividing the two, because Dunally would have fallen down, so we turned the structure into a living-room feature. As we dismantled the dividing wall of lath and plaster, I found the skeleton of a mouse where two beams joined. It looked as though its nest might have been walled up when the other house was added. It was made up of pieces of faded newspaper. I pieced them together to find that they were fragments of a copy of *The Times*, dated 1833.

If I am right about the walling-up, then two facts would seem to follow. First, that Poets Cottage can never have been Shelley's cottage, since he had died in his little boat *Ariel*, in a squall off the Gulf of Spezia, eleven years earlier in 1822. Second, that Dunally Cottage must all along have been the true Shellean cottage. Here Mary Wollstonecraft Shelley may have begun to write her famous novel *Frankenstein*. Indeed we toyed with the idea of calling the joined-up residence 'Frankenstein's Cottage', but decided that Ivan the Terrible of Frankenstein's Cottage would be too great a temptation for my political opponents.

We now have a stained-glass window where the front door of Poets Cottage used to be. It portrays the face of England's greatest poet. It was ordered by my dear father, who had left school at the age of 14 years and who, while Gloria and I were at work, supervised the reconstruction of the house. When the glazier asked him who he wanted to have portrayed in the window of Poet's Cottage, he could only remember one great English poet. That is why we have Shakespeare in Shelley's window!

POETS COTTAGE, SHEPPERTON   GEORGE PATIENT FEB. 1976

5

New Chambers and the Krays

'*Alea jacta est*' [the die is cast]
(Suetonius, quoting Julius Caesar)

After pupillage, which normally lasts a year, the new barrister, if he is lucky enough to have impressed the existing tenants, may be taken on as a junior tenant in the same chambers. If there is no vacancy he will have to look for other chambers. This is a most demoralising process, and those who cannot find chambers to join may have to give up their ambition to practise at the independent Bar, and work instead for a firm of solicitors, a bank, local government or the Crown Prosecution Service. Often the chambers that has provided pupillage will let the reject stay on for a few months as a 'squatter,' while he or she tries to find a home somewhere else.

I was a squatter for nearly four years at the Factory. I am not quite sure why I was allowed to stay on in that condition for so long. I was certainly in no hurry to leave because I was very busy, and I did not expect to hold onto the solicitors who were instructing me once I left the Factory. They could, of course, have taken me on as a tenant had they wanted to, but it was explained to me that chambers already had one Jewish member! While still a mere squatter, I found myself engaged in a particularly high-profile case.

The Kray blackmail trial

Being neither an East-Ender nor a *Daily Mirror* reader, I had no idea who Ron and Reg Kray were when Manny Fryde instructed me to represent them at Old Street Magistrates Court at the committal proceedings on 15 January 1965, on a charge of blackmail. Nor had I seen the *Daily Mirror* editorial of 13 July 1964 which read:

This gang is so rich, powerful and ruthless that the police are unable to crack down on it. Victims are too terrified to go to the police. Witnesses are too scared to tell their story in court. The police, who know what is happening but cannot pin any evidence on the villains, are powerless.

I only realised how important the Kray twins were when I saw the number of press reporters gathered outside the court, and the media coverage that the case was receiving. The police were certainly out to get them. A team, led by Detective Inspector Leonard 'Nipper' Read, believed that they had evidence of a 'protection racket' being run by the Krays involving a club called the Hideaway in Gerrard Street, in London's West End.

The crime of blackmail is committed when a person, in an attempt to enrich himself, makes an unjustified demand for money accompanied by threats which effectively remove the victim's power to say no to the demand – an 'offer he cannot refuse'. While the bad reputation of the accused may be well known to a jury, the fundamental elements of the crime still have to be proved by the prosecution. If that were not so, anyone with a bad reputation would have to be automatically convicted of any crime alleged against them. In this case the police came nowhere near proving the necessary elements of blackmail against the Kray twins, despite their reputation.

In what used to be the 'committal proceedings', both the prosecution and defence were able to test the strength of the main evidence being relied upon by the prosecution, before a case came before a jury. If the evidence was too weak, there would be no jury trial. For some reason, which I have never understood and to which I objected at the time, parliament effectively abolished this procedure, so that committal proceedings are now more or less a formality with no live evidence being called. An important filter has therefore been removed, and we now have the unnecessary expense of a jury trial in many cases, that have to be stopped by the judge half way through, because there is not, and never was, sufficient evidence to convict the man accused. Not that the filter of committal proceedings was going to be allowed to stop a trial of the notorious Kray twins from going before a jury.

A *Daily Sketch* article reported the bail application I made for the twins on 15 January. 'KRAYS' COUNSEL CLASH IN COURT WITH POLICE' shouted the headline. ' "It is a fundamental principle of law that the defence are entitled to know, and we still do not know, the name of the party upon whom demands are alleged to have been made," said Mr Lawrence ... The magistrate, Mr Neill "Mick" McElligott, told Mr Lawrence that if his clients were committed for trial, he would have the information he needed.' No question in McElligott's court, then, of these particular defendants having a right to be told the name of the person they were accused of blackmailing, so that they could prepare a defence at the committal proceedings! I appealed immediately to the Divisional Court on what used to be called, when it existed, a prerogative Writ of Mandamus to force the disclosure of this vital piece of information. My opponent was the government's top lawyer ('Treasury Devil') Gordon Slynn (later to become Britain's advocate-general in the European Court and then, as Lord Slynn of Hadley, a Law Lord). When eventually we were listed for hearing, it was too late, for we had indisputably to be given this information once the old-style full committal proceedings started; and they had started. For the first, but not the last time, a Lord Chief Justice in the Court of Appeal said to me, 'Hallo, Mr Lawrence. And good-bye!'

The alleged victim turned out to be Sir Hew McCowan, the owner of the Hideaway club and a baronet. But, unhappily for the prosecution, Sir Hew's evidence did not support the alleged crime. He told of a meeting he had had in his flat with Ronald Kray and a man who was the co-owner of the Hideaway. They had discussed a Nigerian investment (the fraudulent brainchild, as it turned out, of another later client of mine, Ernest Shinwell, the wayward son of the Labour ex-cabinet minister Manny Shinwell), and then Ron had expressed some interest in the Hideaway. At a later conversation, in which Reg Kray although also present took no part, Ron had suggested that the basement of the Hideaway might be turned into a casino, and he would see that there would be no trouble at the club by putting in a doorman and receptionist who would be well known to anyone who might be tempted to cause a disturbance. He said that he could fill the place every night with customers. He would want 20% at the start, rising later to 50%. No agreement was ever arrived at about any of this, and the Krays did not even turn up on opening night, although they had booked a table for ten. A drunk called Teddy Smith, who was also in the dock with the Krays, did cause some trouble at the club and Ron told McCowan that that would never have happened if one of his doormen had been on duty.

Some time later there was a further meeting, at which there was talk of McCowan taking an interest in a hotel which the Krays owned, and about getting concessions from the brewers for fruit machines. Then McCowan told Ron that the 50% he was asking for an interest in the Hideaway was too high. Ron asked what he thought would be a fair percentage, and McCowan said he didn't know. At no stage of his evidence did he ever suggest that Ron Kray, who was the only twin with whom he had discussed the matter, had demanded any money from him or had threatened him in any way.

The only other witness to conversations concerning the Hideaway, was Sydney Vaughan, Sir Hew's club manager. He spoke of meeting a man called Johnny Morris, who represented the business interests of the Krays, and who, although the twins were present, did most of the talking. The 20% to 50% was mentioned again, but no one actually said what it was to be a percentage of. The proposition was that the Krays would arrange free publicity, the doorman and receptionist they put in would be paid by the club, and they would introduce customers and visiting film stars, with whom they were friendly, to be entertained there. A proper legal agreement, acceptable to Vaughan, was to be drawn up by solicitors.

Vaughan also told the court that neither Kray had demanded any money, nor made any improper or sinister suggestion or threat or insinuation to him, nor had they frightened him by anything they had said or done. He went further to destroy the prosecution's case when he told the magistrate, 'It was not the Krays but Mr East [a newspaper reporter from *The People*] who put fear into my mind that the Krays could do me harm.'

The prosecution were allowed to treat Vaughan as a 'hostile witness', which meant that they could cross-examine him, although he was their own witness, about a previous statement he had made to the police against the accused. But the actual effect of such evidence is usually counterproductive, because it shows that the witness cannot be believed on his oath, and is therefore too unreliable for the prosecution to rely upon. That was what happened here. Vaughan went further to weaken the prosecution case when he said that he would not have given evidence at all had he not been threatened – by his boss Hew McCowan!

That was it: that was the entire case against the infamous Krays. The prosecution had brought no evidence that could be said to fulfil the requirements of the crime of blackmail. No evidence of money being demanded. No evidence of menaces by the Krays. No evidence of anyone being frightened, except by a story-seeking newspaper reporter who no one suggested was working for the Krays. No evidence of what the percentages spoken about related to. No evidence that the drunken Smith, although known to the Krays, was working for them when he caused the disturbance. No incriminating admissions of guilt made by the Krays to the police or anyone else. If there was to be any agreement, it was to have been properly drawn up by a solicitor; but in fact nothing had been done about it at all in the weeks up to the arrest. I was therefore able to make what I thought was an unanswerable submission: that there was no case of any kind to answer against either Kray. As far as Reg was concerned, he was not present most of the time, and when he was, he took no part in any discussion according to the prosecution's own witnesses.

But, the defendants being infamous gangsters, Mr McGelligott was not one to stop such a case in its tracks for want of something as unimportant as evidence. The public, as members of a jury, would have to decide, he said. In due course they did so – with verdicts of not guilty against both twins.

Before that, however, there had to be a trial. This took place at the Old Bailey, on 8 March 1965. F. Petre Crowder QC, the Conservative MP for Northwood Ruislip, led me on behalf of Ronald Kray, and Paul Wrightson QC led Montague Sherborne (my good friend from the Factory), for Reginald. On the first day, the trial was stopped because a juror had been seen talking to a policeman on the case. There followed a new trial which lasted four days, but the jury disagreed, and were discharged. Another jury sworn in on the 29 March, heard the case for seven days and acquitted both the accused. One of the witnesses who gave evidence on their behalf was a Catholic priest.

As soon as the jury retired to consider their verdicts, my leader went off to the House of Commons to vote – leaving me to hold the fort. I asked the ushers, the clerk and prosecuting counsel to let me know, by telephone to the Bar mess in the usual way, when the jury were coming back. There I sat, in total seclusion, preparing my next case. The hours passed and the daylight faded. Still no word from the court. I ventured downstairs to find the Old Bailey in almost complete darkness. I came across a cleaner.

'What's happened to the Kray case?' I asked. 'Oh they walked hours ago, and a jolly good job too,' she said. No one had bothered to tell me! What Ronald Kray must have thought when neither of his defence barristers was present at his moment of victory, goodness only knows.

About 130 cases after the first Kray trial, I decided that I really needed to be a proper member of a set of chambers, and that I was now strong enough to leave the Factory. I left and, happily, several of the solicitors I had worked for continued to instruct me. I was kept very busy.

One Essex Court

I was invited to join One Essex Court, the chambers of Constantine Gallop QC, a very senior divorce practitioner. He had an excellent criminal team, doing good work for good solicitors. Several members of chambers, Clive Callman, Cedric Joseph, Bill Taylor and John Pullinger, later became Crown court judges. I was warmly welcomed into my new home, where my future now lay in the hands of the clerk, Stan Hicks, a little cockney dynamo, very well connected in the Temple, and well liked by solicitors and their clerks. He always wanted to be clerk to the Attorney-General, and he believed that I would one day hold that office. I am sorry that I turned out to be such a disappointment to him.

Our main rooms were on the first and second floors, and had been, in the seventeenth century, the City of London home of John Evelyn the great diarist. Contemporaneously with Samuel Pepys he had chronicled the Restoration, the Plague, and the Great Fire of London, actually witnessing this last disaster spreading from Pudding Lane right up to his front door.

One day, while admiring the woodwork of craftsmen in the dockyard at Deptford, on the south bank of the Thames, Evelyn took a fancy to a young artisan. He set him up in a workshop of his own at the foot of Ludgate Hill, not ten minutes' walk away, down Fleet Street. Evelyn introduced his young protegé to Sir Christopher Wren, who was then re-building St Paul's Cathedral at the top of Ludgate Hill. He also introduced him to King Charles II. The young man was Grinling Gibbons, and he was to become the greatest wood-carver England has known. His work is to be found at Hampton Court, Windsor Castle and many stately homes and buildings all over the country. To thank his generous patron, Grinling Gibbons presented him, in about 1670, with three lovely fireplaces for his rooms in Essex Court. Although damaged in Victorian times they are still beautiful and their present owners, the Middle Temple, are having them restored to their former glory.

When I moved to my new chambers, most of my big cases came from Manny Fryde. Apart from the Kray gang, I defended Albert Nicholls, who was conducting a private war with the Tibbs gang; the Nash gang, who were conducting a private war with another gang; the Fraser gang; the Richardson gang; the McVicar gang; and almost every notorious gang going at the time. How could I defend members of such gangs? Perhaps my kind reader will wait for my answer until the end of Chapter 6.

In January 1967 John McVicar and his gang were tried at the Old Bailey for the armed robbery of a security van in Mitcham. There had been a tip off, and the waiting police had given chase in their cars. I represented the alleged getaway driver, Billy 'Ginger' Cooper. Shots were fired out of the back of the robber's car as it sped through the busy south London streets at midday. When they found that they had driven up a one-way street into a cul-de-sac, the robbers ran off in all directions. Billy Gentry was cornered in a yard from which there was no escape. Though unarmed, two very brave police officers advanced towards him. He tried to shoot them with his revolver at point blank range. Had there been any bullets left in his gun, the charge would have been murder. The evidence against Cooper was mainly what he was alleged to have said to the police when he was arrested. His defence was that he had been 'verballed': words put into his mouth that he had never said.

There were two very stern-looking middle-aged women on the jury, who could not bring themselves to look at me as I made my final speech. At every good point I made, they shook their heads in obvious and total disagreement. I concentrated all my remarks in their direction. I gave them all I had. It was useless. The jury came back late in the evening. They convicted everyone. Gentry received a 17-year prison sentence. Cooper and McVicar received 15-year sentences. As I walked from the Old Bailey towards a deserted Ludgate Circus at 10.30pm, tired and despondent because of the ineffectiveness of my advocacy, my law books heavy under my arm and my robes and wig in the blue barrister's bag slung over my shoulder, I came upon the two women jurors. They were waiting for me at the bottom of Seacoal Lane, and were in tears.

'We did not want to convict your client,' they told me.

'Then why did you do so?' I asked, not unnaturally I think.

'You have no idea how intimidating it is to be shut up in a room for hours on end with ten men shouting at you,' they told me. Could they do anything to help now? No, they couldn't. The courts, as a matter of public policy, will not go behind a jury's verdict, for that would be to encourage the 'nobbling' of jurors in order to secure an acquittal. We did not then have majority verdicts, but even if we had, two dissenting votes would not have helped my client. I could not help asking a further question.

'You were shaking your heads at everything I said. What made you change your minds?' I asked.

'No, you misunderstood us,' they said. 'We were shaking our heads in total disbelief that the police, badly provoked though they were, could have invented admissions like that.' There was another lesson learnt: jurors who appear to be against you, are not necessarily so!

John McVicar later escaped from Durham prison, earning himself the title 'Public Enemy Number One'. He is now a reformed character, a broadcaster and university lecturer in criminology. A film was made about him 20 years ago starring Roger Daltrey; my local video shop says it is still popular.

In April 1967 I defended a man called Stevens at the Old Bailey, before Judge Maude, on a charge of attempting to burgle a jeweller's shop in Bethnal Green. One of his co-accused was George Evans who, to complicate matters, was usually called Jimmy. The story went that Jimmy, suspecting that his wife was having an affair with George Foreman, the gangster brother of gangster Freddie Foreman, had hidden himself in the boot of a car, and had listened while an episode of the relationship was being there-and-then engaged upon. So upset was he, that he had gone to George Foreman's home carrying a double-barrelled shotgun which he had discharged, less, it was said, with the intention of killing him than of reducing Foreman's capability for engaging with anyone else's wife in the future. This allegation found no favour with a jury when, ten years later, Evans was acquitted of shooting Foreman and of having a loaded shotgun with him. However, the story continues. Brother Freddie, seeking revenge for what had been done to George, got wind of the intended burglary, and went with others of his team to teach Jimmy a lesson. As their car turned the corner, someone inside it called out 'Jimmy', which poor Ginger Marks thought was a call to 'Ginger'. He stepped forward and was most unfortunately shot, by mistake, for Evans. The burglars decided to abort the burglary and make themselves scarce. Someone removed Ginger's body from the scene and, so it is said, he lies entombed to this day in the concrete of the Hammersmith flyover, then under construction. Wherever he rests, no one ever saw

Ginger again. Evans told this story at the trial of Alf Gerard, Freddie Foreman and two others in October 1975 and he was not believed either, as everyone was acquitted. Alf Gerard declared outside the Old Bailey that 'Justice has been done at last.' It really depends, I suppose, on what you mean by justice.

There was also the month-long trial of Charlie Mitchell and others, charged with a dog-doping conspiracy, where the kennel maids had made statements to the police implicating Mitchell. But when they came to give evidence at the Old Bailey, they each said that while they had been witness to the criminal activities of Charlie Mitchell, it had not been *that* Charlie Mitchell sitting in the dock. The police followed them home and took further statements in which they admitted that they had really been got at by *that* Charlie Mitchell. They were recalled to repeat that admission before the jury, and they did so. Charlie Mitchell was found 'not guilty.' Another lesson: never assume that a case is too hopeless!

In one of my early trials I defended a man charged with burgling the Chelsea home of a well-known society woman. His defence was that it had nothing to do with him, and he had an alibi witness to prove it. Unfortunately for him, he could not explain how his fingerprints came to be on both the outside and the inside of the front window. He was duly convicted. Usually such cases are placed in charge of a detective-constable: this one had been placed in charge of a chief-superintendent whom I asked, in the break after he had given evidence, what had brought him to court.

'Hasn't your client told you?'

'Told me what?' I asked. He refused to explain. When I took further instructions from my client for the mitigation speech, he admitted that he had committed the burglary. He said that he had pleaded not guilty because the police had promised him immunity if he returned what he had stolen. He had not been able to do so, but he still felt that the police had betrayed him.

'What on earth did you steal?' I asked.

'Love letters from Princess Margaret to the homeowner – a woman!' he replied. He wanted to tell all. I advised against it. I could not see that telling the judge that he had wasted the court's time with two days of perjured evidence would help to keep his sentence low. I confined my speech in mitigation to my client's attempts to go straight and put his past behind him now that he had a family. He received a two-year prison sentence and appealed. I did not represent him on the appeal, but I heard that he did tell all to the appeal court in his written grounds of appeal. I doubt whether that explanation would have helped to reduce his sentence very much!

Soon after this case, another future barrister joined the Lawrence family.

Rachel

Our daughter Rachel was born on 22 June 1968. She emerged from the womb the victor in a battle she was having with her umbilical cord. She has been at war ever since – fighting her clients' enemies and her own life-threatening illnesses.

You would not think there was anything wrong with her – unless you happen to hear her wracking cough, caused by the thick mucus covering her lungs and stomach, produced by an unremitting lung infection, or notice her occasional court appearances with an arm angled in a splint to carry and hide the intravenous antibiotics, or witness her hasty departures from the dining table when she remembers to inject herself with insulin for the diabetes she contracted when she was 14 years old. She refuses to let her illnesses interfere with a life of seemingly endless partying, social engagements and busy court work at the Bar. She is the true Lawrence role model.

Busy as I was, criminal defence work, being almost exclusively publicly funded, was not particularly well paid, and my income was relatively modest. We decided that Gloria could have a National Health Service birth for the baby and a car, or a private medical delivery and no car. She had opted for the car. I was just finishing a robbery trial in Brighton when Chiswick Maternity Hospital telephoned to tell me to come quickly since mother and child were both in distress. My final speech to the jury was unusually short – though apparently none the worse for that, since my client was acquitted – and I left for London in a great hurry. When I arrived, I found that Gloria was out of danger but in considerable pain. She endured her labour for over 24 hours, barely relieved, she recalls, by my insistence on reading to her, as I sat holding her hand, the latest speeches of Ted Heath, the leader of the opposition.

With the birth imminent a doctor was, of course, nowhere to be found. A midwife sought my help to assist with the delivery. Vainly I argued that it was not right for a husband to witness the birth pangs, and that in any event I was a coward and would pass out when I saw blood. Ignoring my protestations, she tied a gown around me, placed a mask over my face, and ordered me to turn the wheel on the state-of-the-art gas machine. When Rachel finally emerged, shouting and screaming – a trait I could tell was inherited from her paternal grandmother – with everyone struggling to get the cord from her neck, I was struck by how much she looked like me. Then the midwife turned the baby the right way up, and all was well. She had the most beautiful unwrinkled face, and a head full of black hair. I was totally captivated, and slept with her cot by my side of the bed for the next three weeks, with her tiny fingers clasped tightly round my thumb. Rachel demonstrated early common sense. When she woke in the middle of the night for a feed, we gave her warm water, which she must have reasoned was simply not worth waking up for. We had no more disturbed nights.

Despite having a ravenous appetite, Rachel failed to thrive. Our GP did not know what was wrong with her, so we took her to Great Ormond Street Children's Hospital. I reported to Dr Archie Norman, who remained her very caring specialist for many years, that her sweat was extremely salty. The sweat test that was given to her – and which I subsequently lobbied in parliament to become standard for all babies – was positive: she had cystic fibrosis.

This extremely serious, incurable disease occurs when both parents carry the recessive CF gene: there is then a one-in-four chance that they will produce a child with CF. Seven thousand children and young people suffer from the affliction in the United Kingdom. Because, in 1968, life expectancy for this illness was very short, we decided not to risk having any more children with the disease. Today CF is better understood, and with improved diagnosis, dietary management, physiotherapy and improving drug treatments, life expectancy can stretch into middle age and beyond. But when Rachel reached her teens, doctors declared proudly: 'they are living into their teens.' When she reached her twenties, they declared: 'they are living into their twenties'. Now she is 42 and shows signs of continuing indefinitely, God willing.

Aged four she had the Almighty already on her mind. Returning from a shopping trip to Shepperton village with her mother, she announced to all and sundry that she had seen God walking in the village. Sadly, for the Almighty is little known in those parts, it was only our Rabbi,

Tony Bayfield, now the leader of the Reform Synagogue Movement of Great Britain, whom she had spotted. An understandable error!

Rachel was a bright and sporty schoolchild. She won a Latin competition, came first in a chess tournament, and obtained a distinction at Grade 8 for piano playing when she was 16 years old. She holds an LLB in Law at London University, where she used also to appear prominently in their theatre productions, and she was called to the Bar at the Inner Temple by her very proud Bencher father. In due course she joined my chambers and, although no longer together in chambers, we appear together from time to time in the same criminal trial. We did so a few years ago for the international snooker star, Quinten Hann (see Chapter 24). Family links are known to occur elsewhere in the world of crime. Soon after qualifying as a barrister, Rachel returned from court and told me that her client that day had said, 'I'm so pleased that you are defending me, Miss Lawrence, because your Dad used to defend my Dad.' She says she has now been told that several times.

In 1995 Rachel won a Pegasus Scholarship from the Inner Temple and went to Hong Kong for three months, to assist and to observe the work of high court judges Brian Keith and Neil Kaplan. Then, to get some idea of the work of a solicitor's office, she worked as a damages assessor for the leading firm of Simmonds and Simmonds. Perhaps Rachel will become a QC at an early age and, if she has a mind to, go on to become a judge herself. She is certainly a role model for other CF sufferers, and in 1996 was voted CF Achiever of the Year.

In 1999 she delivered what my wife and I considered shocking news. She had applied, and had been chosen from thousands, to appear on *Blind Date* – one of the most popular Saturday night television programmes with Cilla Black as host. I suggested that she go at once for advice to the Bar Council, our governing body, as I had little doubt that taking part in such a programme would be seen as 'conduct unbecoming' a member of the Bar of England and Wales. I was, as usual, quite wrong! Her achievement was greeted as excellent news, and could she get any tickets for the staff? She turned out to be a considerable hit on the programme and, several years later, still gets recognised by taxi drivers, waitresses and court ushers. From her position behind the screen, she rejected a hilariously funny cockney street trader called Darren (who joked that his stuff was so dodgy she had probably defended him already), and a bus conductor (who doubled as a stripper at a night club). She chose the third contestant, a nicely spoken Oxford graduate called Sean. His parents were Sri Lankan. The young couple went off to the Cayman

Islands. There, swimming among the giant stingrays, lazing in the sun and dining romantically by moonlight, there was no romance. They remain just good partying friends.

Rachel used to party continuously. She would ring me in the early hours of the morning, when I was in deep sleep, to ask about some legal problem in her case starting later that day. I would bring to bear all my wisdom and long experience to the matter and advise her.

'Oh, what do you know!' she would say with the wounding ingratitude of children.

I would ask why she bothered to wake me in the early hours of the morning if she thought so little of my advice: and why not ring me at nine o'clock in the evening?

'Don't be so silly,' she would say. 'I couldn't do that. I was at a party!'

Not that Rachel is not serious about her work. We have been in several cases together and she was dedicated, indispensable and skilful. One of her own cases, cited as an authority in the law books, concerns a ticket tout she was prosecuting. He had told a woman police officer that he had no 'sharps' (needles) on him and she searched him and pricked her finger on a hypodermic syringe. On appeal from the Magistrates Court, the Crown Court judge decided that what had happened could not be called an assault by the tout. Rachel persuaded the Divisional Court that the tout had created a danger, since it was foreseeable that the woman police constable might injure herself by searching him, and that was an assault. She had extended the law of assault to protect searching police officers. Academic lawyers were displeased. The Lawrences and the police were not!

I am sympathetic to the pro-life movement, and far from happy about the whole idea of genetic engineering and embryonic stem-cells. Yet how can I justify refusing the chance of a life to suffering CF children? Back in 1968 it was still not possible to detect the disease in the foetus early enough to abort. After brilliant advances in medical science it is now possible. It will always be one of my most dreadful and harrowing thoughts that, if that medical science had been available in 1968, we might well have decided not to have our brilliant, dynamic, beautiful, extremely popular and adored daughter.

That has not been Rachel's only good fortune. On Tuesday 5 October 1999, as Gloria and I were driving up to the Conservative Party Conference in Blackpool, I heard on the radio that there had been a train crash outside Paddington station. A Virgin Inter-City train from Bristol had collided with a local train to Maidenhead shortly after 8.10am. There were deaths and serious injuries. Maidenhead? Wasn't Rachel supposed to be appearing at Maidenhead Magistrates Court that morning? And would she not be getting the train from Paddington at about that time? We were terrified and tried, for 45 minutes, to raise Rachel on her mobile, but failed. I managed to get through to chambers. Yes, my clerk told me, she had been booked to appear at Maidenhead, but she had phoned to say that she was all right: she had missed the train by a whisker! She had been using her new nebuliser, a machine to ease her breathing difficulties, for the first time. It had taken longer than she had expected, and she had arrived by taxi only to see the 8.10 train pulling out of the station. Missing the train did not matter, because the next one would be leaving in 15 minutes, and she would still arrive early at court. She was waiting for it when she heard the loudspeaker announce the disaster.

On the 8.10 train she had just missed was Sun Yoon Hah, a twenty-five-year-old female barrister from Singapore, who was to appear in the same court as Rachel, and whose case was listed to follow Rachel's. Rachel always looks out for other barristers to chat to when she goes to court by train. She would have seen Hah at the front of the train and would certainly have wanted to sit next to her. Tragically, Hah was so badly burnt in the crash that she died four weeks later.

Six months earlier the Nazi nail-bomber, David Copeland, concluding a two-week terror campaign against Blacks in Brixton and Asians in Brick Lane, set off a bomb intended to harm gay people inside the Admiral Duncan public house in Old Compton Street. He killed three and seriously injured seventy-three. Rachel had met an actress friend for a drink in a bar two doors down; they had left minutes before the bomb exploded.

Rachel is surely meant to live.

6

The Kray Murder Trials

'A lawyer has no business with the justice or injustice of the cause which he undertakes, unless his client asks his opinion, and then he is bound to give it honestly. The justice or injustice of the cause is to be decided by the judge.'

(Dr Samuel Johnson, quoted by James Boswell in *Tour of the Hebrides*)

After their acquittal in the blackmail trial, I was asked to represent Ronald Kray as Junior Counsel in May 1968, when he and his brothers Reginald and Charlie were charged (with others) with the murders of George Cornell at the Blind Beggar Public House in Whitechapel, of Jack 'the Hat' McVitie, and, at a later trial, of Frank 'Mad Axeman' Mitchell. These trials set a record for the longest murder trials in British history.

The Blind Beggar and Jack 'the Hat'

Again Manny Fryde had the case, and I made my first acquaintance with the young Ralph Haeems who, some years after he had qualified as a solicitor, inherited the Sampson and Co. criminal law empire from his mentor, and loyally continued to instruct me until his recent tragic death following a heart attack and a triple bypass operation.

The main allegation was that, in March 1966, Ronnie Kray, who had been bad-mouthed by the small-time gangster George Cornell, went up to him in the bar of the public house, shot him in the forehead and walked out. Shortly afterwards, Ronnie told Reggie, 'I've done mine, now you do yours,' and Reggie invited Jack 'the Hat' McVitie, another small-time gangster who had been bad-mouthing the twins, to a small club in Stoke Newington where Reggie stabbed him in the face and body with a knife and killed him.

Enough has been written about the three Kray trials to fill a library, and repetition of the main events and the well-recorded parts of the trials would be tedious. But there are some recollections that might add a little to the folklore, and might correct one or two of the inaccuracies that have crept into the many accounts of others.

The committal proceedings of those two murder trials took place at Bow Street Magistrates Court. They were full of surprises for me. Barristers and solicitors had to run the gauntlet of a daily press barrage, and we had to hold our bowler hats over our faces when arriving and leaving court, lest newspapers print pictures of us 'courting publicity' – which, in those days, the Bar Council considered to be seriously unprofessional. One morning, walking briskly to court from the Temple, a man with an American accent caught up with me, and we chatted merrily as we walked. Later that day, to my astonishment, he gave evidence in the proceedings. When he was asked by prosecuting counsel what his occupation was, he replied that he was a hired assassin! A day or two later, after what must have been a particularly good lunch, the carefree and rumbustious Sir Lionel Thompson, baronet, acting for one of the other defendants, suggested to another witness in cross-examination that he was known by the name 'silly bollocks'. Sir Lionel offered some examples of 'the kind of silly bollocks' the witness was 'well-known for talking': a plot to kill Idi Amin and another to kill the Pope. Society was not so tolerant of vulgarity thirty-six years ago, and 'bollocks', not yet being a reportable word, was indicated in the next day's newspapers by stars. Sir Lionel, a popular character with the villainry, and who had flown bomber sorties in the war, was later to get into trouble with the Bar disciplinary authorities when he chased the driver of a German number-plated Mercedes round the Victoria memorial outside Buckingham Palace, offering him a two-fingered salute.

Another, more disturbing, moment for me occurred when I was accused by the very unpleasant senior prosecutor, Kenneth Jones QC (later to become an unpleasant High Court judge), of examining his confidential trial papers. I had been cross-examining witnesses that morning, relying on detail which, Jones asserted loudly and insultingly during the lunchtime adjournment, I could only have gathered from reading his prosecution papers. He would be reporting me to the Benchers of my Inn for unprofessional and dishonest conduct, and I could expect to be struck off. The old fool had quite forgotten that he had opened the case to the stipendiary magistrate at some length and in minute detail; and he had not the wit to realise that I might have been taking a careful note of what he said. Perhaps he never did so himself, and therefore could not understand anyone else doing it: an indication of the paranoia that was infecting the anti-Kray lawyers. John Leonard, Jones's junior (charming, kindly and, as Senior Treasury Counsel, often an opponent of mine, before he became a distinguished Silk and then a High Court judge), took my arm, told me not worry, and assured me that he would sort his Leader out. He did so, but Kenneth Jones never thought it necessary to apologise for his offensive and absurd mistake, nor did he stop glowering at me whenever our paths crossed. It has always worried me how easily a person's reputation and career prospects might be lost through an innocent misunderstanding with an important person, however stupid.

Another of the allegations with which the Kray twins were charged, was that they had conspired to murder a member of the rival Richardson gang, and were proposing to have their victim executed in the main concourse at the top of the steps of the elegant old Victorian entrance to the Old Bailey, then in use. Two members of the Kray gang actually gave evidence, at Bow Street, that they had been ordered to commit the murder. They said that they had stopped their car outside the entrance, and watched out for their target to arrive at court. The prosecution was even able to produce the weapon that was to have been used: a briefcase with a beautifully constructed trigger mechanism in the handle, attached to a spring-loaded needle. Crafted by a master engineer – none other than 'Split' Waterman, the former British world motorcycle champion – its purpose was to inject potassium cyanide, via the needle, through a tiny hole in the side. The device can be seen today in the police 'Black Museum.' Professor Francis Camps, the leading Home Office forensic pathologist of his day, gave evidence about it. He said that the merest scratch on the leg would have killed a victim in ten seconds. It was not until 1978, over a decade later, that a similar weapon, an umbrella with a spring trigger releasing a ricin pellet, was used, allegedly by a spy called Francesco Giullino, to murder the Bulgarian dissident writer Georgi Markov, at a bus stop on Waterloo Bridge. Fortunately for everyone, the Richardson gang murder was called off, because the two would-be assassins told the court that, as they sat in their car, they saw a man arrive but could not agree that he was the man in the photograph they had been sent to kill. A very lucky gangster!

The two men were not the most reliable witnesses ever to be heard in a criminal court, but the briefcase certainly provided corroboration for their story. Surprisingly, at the end of the Bow Street committal proceedings the stipendiary magistrate, Kenneth Harrington, decided that there was no case to answer. I doubt that Mr McElligott would have come to the same conclusion.

After the magistrates court hearings were over, and Ronald Kray was committed for trial upon several counts, Manny Fryde asked me to choose a Leader. I thought that such a high-profile case should have the best high-profile Silk available – so I went to see Quintin Hogg in his chambers in Paper Buildings.

A lawyer of the highest distinction and fame, and subsequently to become Margaret Thatcher's longest-serving lord chancellor, Hogg had renounced his peerage as Viscount Hailsham when Harold Macmillan retired in 1963, so that he might be free to stand for the leadership of the Conservative Party. Many expected him to become prime minister. The Earl of Home, who had also renounced his peerage to become plain Sir Alec Douglas-Home, was instead chosen to lead the party as the safer pair of hands. When the Conservative government fell to Labour in 1964, Quintin Hogg had returned to his practice at the Bar. In 1968 he was Shadow Home Secretary. He told me that he did not think it right, in his position, to take the case: in other circumstances he would have been delighted to do so. The boundary of the 'cab-rank' principle, by which barristers are not permitted to refuse a 'fare' because they do not like the idea of representing a particular client, becomes a little blurred when politics is involved.

Manny Fryde and Ralph Haeems then asked John Platts-Mills QC to be my Leader in the trial, which started in October – the month that nearly saw the end of the civilised world with the Bay of Pigs crisis. He was the kindest, most charming and delightful of men. He had been Labour MP for Finsbury for six years, losing the seat when it was redistributed, mostly to Shoreditch which already had an entrenched MP. Three years earlier, after the episode of the 'Nenni telegram,' he had been thrown out of the 'Old Labour' party for being too left-wing even for them! In time he became a Bencher of the Inner Temple (about as Establishment as it is possible to be in the legal profession), and in his eighties was elected a Common Councilman of the City of London (also a pretty Establishment organisation). John died in 2001 at the age of 94 years, still practising at the Bar and shortly after making an appearance as auxiliary counsel in the Northern Ireland Bloody Sunday enquiry.

At the reception following his memorial service in Temple Church, many representatives of international Labour organisations, with names like the Bulgarian Workers Music Society and the East German Poetry Appreciation Group, spoke in memory of John's lifetime commitment to their cause. After about one and a half hours of such tributes, I told my ex-parliamentary pair Tony Benn, who had himself delivered a memorable eulogy to John, that I had had about all I could take of so many fellow-travellers.

'I agree,' said Tony. 'Don't you think that we should move that the question be now put?' As Lord Justice Sedley, who had been a member of John's chambers, so aptly said of John, in the course of his fine eulogy in the Temple church: 'He upset apple-carts apparently without trying, cocked a majestic snook at every orthodoxy except his own, and did it all from within the bosom of the very establishment which he had dedicated his life to offending. There's not one of us who isn't the richer for having known John.'

There were some hilarious moments in court. The first arose when the judge, Mr Justice Melford Stevenson, decided that, for ease of identification, the defendants should have a card with a number hanging round their necks. My Leader took immediate objection. They were not cattle. They were at this point innocent men. He had known whole industries walk out on strike for less than that. The judge, thought to be a right-wing Conservative, was unmoved by references to industrial action. When the numbers were hung round their necks, Ronnie Kray stood up, tore his off, and threw it to the ground. The other defendants, as usual, followed his leadership. They were all taken below the court to have the numbers replaced. Ronnie threatened to kill the prison officer if he persisted. He also sent a rude note to the judge. When the sitting resumed, without the numbers but with the atmosphere getting nasty, my Leader sought to lighten the mood. Perhaps one solution, he suggested, might be for the lawyers, who considerably outnumbered the defendants in court, including his Lordship, also to have numbers round their neck for ease of identification by the defendants. When the laughter died down, no one was numbered. John thanked the judge, on behalf of all the defendants, for his wisdom.

Some moments were both hilarious and scary. In the middle of the first trial, my Leader took me off to Churchills the gunsmiths, to demonstrate to us both how the witness Hart's description of the cartridges cascading from Kray's revolver could simply never have happened. Unfortunately for our client, the demonstration showed that the evidence we challenged was indeed very likely to have occurred. John must have dozed off during the demonstration, because to my astonishment he continued to believe in his theory, and insisted in putting it to Hart in cross-examination. When he picked up the revolver to show the jury how impossible the allegation was, blank cartridges cascaded all over the court and everyone fell apart with laughter – even our clients in the dock.

Some moments were just plain scary. Quite early on, Ron Kray told us that he did not want to go into the witness box to give evidence. When the prosecution case was over, John and I went down to see him in the Old Bailey cells, to point out that the evidence against him was so overwhelming, that if the jury did not hear his side of the matter, he stood no chance of acquittal. Ron said he would think about it. The evening before we were due to start the defence case, my Leader told him we needed to go through his account for the next day.

'Not tonight,' Ron said, 'I've got a nice young boy coming to see me. Can we talk about it tomorrow?' We said 'no'. He said 'yes', and of course, he prevailed. Next morning he told us he still did not want to give evidence. John, exasperated, left me to talk sense into our client. But Ron was adamant. I went up from the cells into court, and reported the disappointing news to my Leader.

There is a well-known rule of criminal court practice, long enshrined in judicial precedent, that one cannot make an opening speech to a jury on behalf of a defendant, unless one is calling the defendant to give evidence and at least one other witness, not as to character, but as to the facts of the case. We did not qualify under either heading. Ron Kray's idea of calling as a character witness 'Mad' Frankie Fraser, who had twice been certified insane, and who would have had to be called from his own prison cell, seemed to me unlikely to be helpful. Even so, Ron made clear that he was not going to give evidence. So when my Leader rose to his feet and started to make an opening speech to the jury, I nearly died. I feared that my short career at the Bar was about to end. I could not see myself, at the inevitable inquiry that would be set up to consider whether we had behaved improperly, giving evidence against Platts-Mills. We would both be struck off. Even as I imagined my hair to be turning white, I tugged at John's gown. No response. He was warming to his theme and quite oblivious of me. I tugged and tugged. I was in despair. Mr Justice Melford Stevenson, seeing my distress and guessing at its cause, ostentatiously reached for his Archbold law book, to remind himself of the rules.

Suddenly John stopped in full flow, turned, and asked me why I was interrupting him.

'Ron refuses to give evidence,' I whispered hoarsely.

'So what do you want me to do about it?' asked John.

'Ask for an adjournment,' I suggested in desperation. John turned to Melford.

'My learned junior tells me I must ask for an adjournment,' he said. The judge, trying to make mischief, asked John if he was proposing to call our client to give evidence, and John could not give him an answer. Then a miracle occurred. Ralph Haeems, anticipating an impending disaster, had gone over to Charlie Kray, the third brother on trial in the dock, and told him to tell his brother Ron that everyone was laughing at him for not having the courage to give evidence. It would have been nice to think that Ron Kray, probably the most feared, vicious and uncaring of all who had ever stood in an Old Bailey dock, knowing that his defence team was in real trouble, had decided out of the kindness of his heart to save us. Alas, it was almost certainly his unwillingness to be the object of derision that moved him to speak.

'It's all right, Mr Platts. I'm going into the box,' Ron announced loudly from the dock. Either way, with that one sentence we were free! Perhaps John knew that would happen all along. I only wish he had told me.

My distinguished leader spent long hours with me at weekends in my garden at Shepperton, going through the evidence and compiling his final speech to the jury. The result was always inevitable. At the end of the thirty-nine-day trial, and after a jury retirement of just under seven hours, Ron was found guilty of murdering Cornell and of aiding and abetting Reg in murdering McVitie. The twins were both sentenced to life imprisonment with a minimum of thirty years. I went down to the cells to say farewell to my client.

'Thank you very much for what you and Mr Platts have done for me,' he said without any malice that I could detect. 'We'll keep our fingers crossed for you in Peckham, so that you can become Home Secretary – and let us out early!'

Years later, in 1994, the Burton Conservative Association gave a very grand dinner for Gloria and me and 250 guests, to celebrate my twenty years as MP. It was held in a marquee in the grounds of the stately home of the president of my association, Sir Stanley Clarke. Norman Tebbit (now Lord Tebbit, former cabinet minister and party chairman), had been invited to make a speech in my honour, and Sir Bernard Ingham, Margaret Thatcher's press officer, was to make another. To our total surprise and delight, Baroness Thatcher turned up with her husband

Denis, and sat next to me at the top table. I felt sorry for poor Bernard, who had to do a hasty redraft of his speech which was, of course, intended to be all about the raptures and miseries of working for Mrs T. Norman, in his speech, said jokingly that he did not know why Mrs Thatcher had not made me Home Secretary. When my turn came to reply I explained.

'The reason was quite clear to me, Baroness Thatcher. You will recall that I once told you what Ron Kray had said to me at the end of his trial, about keeping his fingers crossed for me at Peckham so that I could become Home Secretary. So for your Home Secretaries you chose Willie Whitelaw, Douglas Hurd, Leon Brittan, David Waddington and Kenneth Baker. Then you told John Major and he made Ken Clarke and Michael Howard Home Secretary...' Of course that was a joke – I think!

The Kray trials attracted a great deal of media attention and famous people came to court to see what was happening. I turned round one day to find the great Hollywood film actor, Charlton Heston, sitting behind me. I summoned up the courage to ask the star of *Ben Hur*, *The Ten Commandments*, *El Cid* and, later, *The Planet of the Apes*, what had brought him to our court.

'We might make a film about this case,' he replied.

'What part will you play?' I asked.

'Probably you,' he replied.

Of course I did not believe him. He didn't even ask for my autograph!

Mad Axe-man

About six weeks after the Cornell and McVitie trial, Ron Kray was tried again at the Old Bailey, together with Reg and a number of others, for the murder of Frank 'Mad Axeman' Mitchell. Again John Platts-Mills and I appeared for him.

Until recent changes in the law, unless the defence wished it, a jury was not told what previous convictions a defendant had, in case, being human, they became prejudiced against him and did not bother too much about the actual evidence in the trial that they were considering. Prejudice apart, if a jury was going to be told what a villain the defendant was anyway, the police might be tempted not to search for real evidence against a suspect. That being the rule, our first problem was that one would have had to have come from another planet not to have known that the Krays were the biggest gangsters in Britain, had just been convicted of two exceedingly unpleasant gangland murders, and were therefore likely to have murdered other gangsters. What was to be done?

John Platts-Mills and I decided to ask the trial judge, Mr Justice Lawton, if we could question the potential jurors in order to exclude any who had heard of the Krays and their convictions. Although pre-trial cross-examination of potential jurors to discover if they know of the accused, and might therefore be biased against him, takes place in criminal trials in our sister common-law jurisdiction in the United States, where the procedure often takes as long as the trial itself, this was an unheard of procedure in an English court. Yet there was no law actually preventing the process being followed in England, and the judge, very fairly, thought it was worth a try. John asked each potential juror what newspaper they normally read, and if they had ever heard the name Kray mentioned in the newspaper or on radio or television. In those days few people had television, and it seemed, from the answers he received, that few people read even the tabloid newspapers. Those who did, it seemed, only read the sports pages. I thought the procedure might take all day, but within half an hour we had managed to find a jury of twelve men and women who said that they never read or listened to the news and had never even heard the name Kray! If they were telling the truth, their attention spans must have been frighteningly short – which hardly boded well for our trial.

Frank Mitchell, a violent, unsuccessful, and more than usually brainless villain, had been serving a ten-year sentence for violent assault and burglary. He had been involved in the riots at Hull prison in 1962, and in his time had been birched, certified insane, and had latterly been sent to Dartmoor prison. To nearly everyone's surprise in court and outside, it appeared that, despite his record, he had been allowed to live the life of Riley while at Dartmoor. He had become a regular at a local pub, and could go shopping by taxi to nearby Tavistock, more or less whenever he wanted to. He had young girls to keep him happy on lazy afternoons. Prison officers, it seemed, responded to his every whim. This blissful life, sadly for him, came to an end when the Krays decided to engineer his escape and, by so doing, show the world how influential and powerful they still were.

They seem to have had no difficulty getting him out. The 12th of December 1966 was the kind of Dartmoor day when stormy weather made outside work impossible. But that was thought to be no reason why Frank Mitchell's outside work party should not leave the prison for their work-hut on the moors: they did so and played cards, in a hut, for most of the day. At teatime Mitchell left to feed the ponies – and that was the last the prison service saw of him. They found his prison clothes in a lay-by. He was next heard of when he wrote to *The Times* and the *Daily Mirror*, asking Sir David Maxwell Fyfe, the Home Secretary, to give him a release date, in return for which he would give himself up. The Home Secretary was in no mood to bargain: Mitchell must first surrender to the police. Mitchell, not finding that answer much to his liking, carried on living in Whitechapel at the home of Lennie Dunn, a Whitechapel Road bookstall-holder, and minor member of the Kray gang.

Mitchell was content for a while, having been provided with the comforting services of a nightclub hostess called Lisa. In court she described his prowess as a sexual athlete, always warming up for the main encounter with a hundred press-ups. Since this would have weakened the sex-drive of most men, she seems to have been greatly impressed and fell in love with him – and he with her. This made him restless. He wanted more freedom. He demanded action from the Krays, and threatened to go looking for them if they were not more helpful. He became a nuisance. On Christmas Eve he was told that he was being moved to Kent. According to the only witness who gave evidence of this – Alf Donaghue, his principal minder who turned Queen's evidence – he got into a van and was shot by none other than our old friends Freddie Foreman and Alf Gerard. No one in authority ever saw Mitchell again.

The case against Ron Kray was thin. He and Reg might have arranged to have Mitchell sprung from prison, but what evidence was there that they must have arranged, as the prosecution alleged, for him to be killed? Unfortunately Donaghue, as a gangster himself, was hardly a credible witness. There was no other evidence that the Krays had anything to do with the killing. Submissions of 'no case to answer' succeeded before the judge at half-time on the main count, and the jury brought in verdicts of not guilty for all the defendants on the remaining counts.

Alf Gerard, who with Freddie Foreman was also alleged to have disposed of Frank Mitchell's body, could not be found when the police were making arrests, so he was never charged. He died of natural causes thirteen years later in Brighton, in a flat owned by Jeremiah Callaghan, who had been one of the alleged occupants of the car from which Ginger Marks had been shot 17 years earlier.

Appeals

After the Kray trials, we appealed the two murder convictions. We argued that the two different kinds of killing – one shooting by one man, the other a stabbing by another man – should never have been tried together, according to the law as it then was. The Court of Appeal, presided over by the Lord Chief Justice, Lord Widgery, was against us. They said that the rules did not mean what everyone thought they meant; that it was in the interests of justice that the two murders should be tried together by the same jury; and that the press would have found it too difficult to report the trials if they had not been tried together!

John and I argued the appeal on behalf of both Ron and Reg and, after our arguments were rejected, I asked if the court would give me a certificate to allow us to appeal to the House of Lords. My submission was that there was a point of law of public importance, because the interests of the press were surely of less importance than that a man should be tried fairly. The judges were obviously embarrassed by their press reference. Lord Justice James, a charming man, made clear to me that if I insisted on my suggested wording of the grounds of appeal to the House of Lords, the Court of Appeal would not be likely to grant me the certificate. If, however, I felt able to accept the weaker form of words that he was suggesting, particularly as far as the interests of the press were concerned, then they would certify an appeal. On very short reflection, I thought it better to be heard on a weak point than not to be heard at all with a stronger point. This is called judgement!

When I got to the House of Lords I got the immediate feeling that the court had no more sympathy for the legalities, if it meant acquitting the Krays, than the Court of Appeal had had. Lord Diplock asked me why two murders, even if allegedly committed by the same defendant at different times, should not be tried together: an unpromising start, I thought. This was only allowed, under the law as it was at that time, if they were part of a series of similar killings and, the Law Lords agreed with the Court of Appeal, that whatever a 'series' meant in ordinary language, two was enough of a series for legal purposes. As for what was in the public interest, John Platts-Mills, (who was present but not conducting that appeal) records the matter in his autobiography thus:

> Ivan Lawrence ... summed up the argument by saying that what the court must have meant by 'public interest' was 'Everyone knows that the men are guilty and it is in the public interest that they

be found so; and how can that be made more certain than by a joint trial of the two murders.' Lord Donovan answered by gesture and demeanour, although not in words, 'Lawrence, my boy, you've hit the nail right on the head!' Lord Diplock greeted the argument by going off to sleep.

There is a legal saying: 'Hard cases make bad law.' The Kray trials were certainly hard cases.

The Krays also came near to ending my hoped-for political career even before it had started. Sometime later I was invited to the House of Commons to meet the Vice-Chairman of the Conservative Party in charge of candidates. Geoffrey Johnson-Smith (MP for East Grinstead) was, when later I got to know him, far too decent and gentle for the rough and tumble of politics, although he had been both a defence minister and Northern Ireland minister. He had charmed Brigitte Bardot some years before, when as a broadcaster he had famously interviewed her on television. He told me that he was concerned about a rumour that I was a friend of the Krays. He explained that if that were true, it would be rather difficult for me to be recommended as a Conservative candidate. I told him that it was certainly not true. I had merely represented them in court, as had been my duty as a barrister, and I had certainly never met or spoken to them outside the court or prison. He did not tell me where the rumour had come from, but I was not aware that I had any particular enemies, and I guessed that it may have come from the kind of idle, and not necessarily malicious, gossip, you hear round a bar: 'Lawrence? Isn't he the friend of the Krays?' – meaning, isn't he the one that is always defending them? I told Geoffrey that if my integrity were at issue, I would ask all the judges at the Old Bailey to write and vouch for me. He said that it would not be necessary: he was completely happy with my explanation.

Not for the last time I wondered how often fine careers may have been nipped in the bud by gossip and misunderstanding, and for want of an opportunity to explain a situation to someone as fair-minded and careful as Geoffrey. Now that we are entitled to see our files, under the Freedom of Information Act, it probably happens less often, but in those days...

People ask me what I thought of Ronnie Kray. I did not really have the opportunity to make much of an assessment. I spoke to him only during prison conferences when discussing the issues in his case, and, as I have said, he was not very communicative. When I suggested that someone who was well known would have had to have been insane to walk up to Cornell in a public bar full of people and shoot him, he did not tell me that he had indeed once been certified insane! But he had a wry sense of humour. I asked him what he thought of capital punishment. He said he believed in it because it was a deterrent. It was a silly question, really.

For many years Ron and Reg sent me greetings cards at Christmas – just to let me know that I had not been forgotten by them – and after the trials Ron sent me a large framed landscape he had painted in oil, in Broadmoor. It was so awful that for years my clerks would not let me hang it in chambers. Although it does not compare in artistic achievement with the sketch by Stephen Ward of one of his girls, which gazes over my desk, it might, I suppose, have won the Turner Prize. After Ronald Kray died, I asked Sothebys what his painting might be worth. They told me that they had no idea, since they did not deal in the work of criminals. 'What? With all those art forgeries that pass through your hands?' I thought, but did not say.

I also drew my own sketches of some of the characters in the trials. I am not sure how lawful it is to draw in court, but the police printed and distributed copies that have found their way into several books and onto a number of lavatory walls, so it cannot have been too unlawful. I sent a copy of the sketches to Mr Justice Melford Stevenson. He replied: 'Dear Lawrence, Thank you for your assorted sketches. I am pleased to see that for two of us, at least, the Kray trial meant stern application, Yours Melford.'

Defending the guilty

My defence of the Krays nearly always triggers the question every criminal advocate is asked: how can you defend someone you know to be guilty?

Of course you are defending someone who pleads guilty to a crime in court when your task is to persuade the sentencing judge that he is less blameworthy than it may seem. Perhaps the part he played is less serious than alleged, or he may have some reasonable excuse for doing what he did, or he might have some illness which, while not excusing his crime, would justify a lesser sentence. People say to me: how on earth could you defend the serial killer Denis Nilsen? Yes, but he never pretended that he was innocent of the killings: he pleaded guilty to manslaughter but not guilty of murder as he had a right to do if, as we argued, he was deranged.

So the real question is: how can you defend someone who has pleaded not guilty but has told you that he is really guilty? This hardly ever happens, because a British advocate who actively advances a 'not guilty' plea when his client has admitted his guilt – other than where there is a challenge to the prosecution's interpretation of the law – would be committing an offence so grave that he would be 'struck off' and never allowed to practice again! If a defendant insists on proceeding with a 'not guilty' plea, the advocate must refuse to continue with the case, and ask the judge to release him. That is the simple rule: but there is an exception. Since in our system the burden is on the prosecution to prove its case, a defendant, guilty or innocent, always has the right to require the prosecution to prove its case properly by calling its evidence and satisfying the judge that it has the law on its side. But when that happens, and it very seldom does, the advocate is not permitted to make any suggestion in cross-examination of a witness that he knows to be untrue, or suggest that anyone else has committed the crime, nor is he allowed to put the defendant into the witness box to tell the court that he is innocent when he has told his counsel that he is not. Counsel must never knowingly mislead a court: that is the golden rule. What does often happen, is that a defendant who has pleaded 'not guilty' changes his mind during the trial and decides to plead guilty after all: that is, of course, allowed – and welcomed!

So what most people really mean when they ask the 'how can you?' question is: what if your client has told you he is not guilty and pleads not guilty but you know he is really guilty? The answer is simple: you cannot know and be sure that a defendant who assures you that he is innocent is truly guilty until the evidence has been called and tested in a court of law. You were not there! It follows that the advocate is under a duty to represent a defendant according to his plea and he must do so to the very best of his ability however suspicious he may be about the truth. That is why no advocate is allowed to assert his own personal belief to judge or jury in the innocence of his client. As the great Dr Johnson said, in the opening quotation of this chapter, you are his lawyer; you are not his judge. Furthermore, everyone is entitled to a fair trial – whether he is guilty or not. That is what is meant by the 'rule of law'. The verdict is in the hands of the jury or the magistrates not the defence lawyer.

Lest anybody thinks that this is all a bit of a charade or play acting, let me assure them that it most certainly is not. As you will realise, case after case, year after year of my professional life has shown that things are not always as they seem and the unexpected happens quite often. The written statement or deposition taken by a police officer sometimes records what the witness did not actually say and it may actually be repudiated by the witness when he gives evidence. The defendant may be one of 'the usual suspects', and the policeman may have jumped too quickly to the wrong conclusion that the suspect is guilty, and tailored the words he says he heard accordingly. The victim of an assault who was so certain on an identity parade that the defendant was his attacker may not be so certain when he sees the defendant again in the dock. An identifying eye-witness may not in fact, on other evidence available at the trial, have been able to see who the man committing the crime really was from where he was standing or sitting. An expert witness who was so sure of himself when he wrote his report, may change his mind when faced with an alternative opinion voiced in court by another expert. These things happen all the time, and the Court of Appeal, when it reviews the evidence given at a trial, or considers further evidence that was not available at the trial, often comes to the conclusion that a jury's guilty verdict was wrong or at least unsafe.

So the whole procedure of defending a man you may think is guilty before a court has seen and heard the evidence is no charade. You may have been wrong! You may have to change your mind! Anyway it does not matter: you are not the judge and it is presumptuous of you to assume that you are. The thoroughness of our trials these days – much commended by those who have sat as jurors – ensures that as far as humanly possible no one is convicted in a British criminal court of a crime he did not commit. Time and again this thoroughness produces a result that the most convinced by-stander would not have expected. It protects not only the guilty from a false or exaggerated accusation: more importantly it protects the innocent from a wrongful conviction. The difference between the expectation and the result sometimes means thirty years or a life-time of misery remitted from an accused person and his family. To have been able to tease out that difference has been a tremendous and enduring privilege throughout my career.

7

Judges and Villains

'The advocate must acquire the art of being passionate with detachment and persuasive without belief. He must be most convincing when he is unconvinced ... belief, for the advocate, is something best kept in a permanent state of suspension. There is no lawyer so ineffectual as one who is passionately convinced of his client's innocence.'

(John Mortimer: *Clinging To The Wreckage*)

Over the next five years, until I entered parliament, there was hardly a day when I was not in court. I worked in London for nearly a hundred solicitors. The London criminal Bar being smaller than it is today, I often appeared before the same judges – particularly the Recorder of London, the senior judge at the Old Bailey.

Judges

When I began in 1962, the Recorder was Sir Gerald Dodgson, known as 'The Old Wrecker', a pun enhanced by the fact that his directions to a jury would be quite outrageously biased against the defence. He well knew that, as long as he remembered to say the magic words 'any decision about the facts of the case is entirely a matter for you, members of the jury', he would not be criticised by the Court of Appeal. The trouble was that the bias was often conveyed by the tone of his voice: 'The defendant's case is that the slash across the forehead was caused by the flange of the belt buckle' could be made to sound totally ridiculous by the judge's inflexion, and the Court of Appeal would not accept anything they could not see on the transcript. Sir Gerald grew hard of hearing in his seventies. On one occasion, so it is told, a felon on being convicted by the jury was asked, as was then required, if he had anything to say before sentence was passed upon him. The unfortunate replied, 'Fuck all.' Dodgson tapped his clerk on the shoulder and, adjusting his

101

hearing aid, asked what the defendant had said. 'Fuck all,' replied the clerk. 'That's funny,' said Dodgson, 'I could have sworn I saw his lips move.'

He was followed as Recorder by the unfailingly courteous, and fair-minded, Sir Anthony Hawke, who had been a very distinguished senior treasury counsel (Old Bailey prosecutor), and before whom it was always a pleasure for a young man to appear. He used to address a jury as 'Ladies and Gentlemen' – words now, for some reason, considered to be politically incorrect. Before him the defence always felt that a trial had been fair.

Then there was the former England rugby football captain Sir Carl Aarvold, who would give the jury a straight no-nonsense summary of the evidence with an air of laid-back incredulity and humour.

'The defendant told you,' he would say, in a tone that suggested that he might have heard such a tale somewhere or other before, 'that it was a coincidence that he happened to be shopping in that very street and passing that very shop when the real burglar had run out; that it was unfortunate that although out shopping, he had no shopping bag, so his hands were unfortunately empty when the real villain had decided to thrust the television set into them for him to hold; an unhappy coincidence that a police car should have been passing at that very moment; and that he should have chosen to panic and run. A catalogue of coincidences and misfortunes, members of the jury, which the defendant invites you to conclude should not end with the ultimate misfortune that you would find him guilty, though he is completely innocent of this offence.'

But sentencing anyone to prison seemed to be such an unpleasant experience for Sir Carl that he always did so with great dispatch, and with considerable leniency, particularly if he thought that the defendant had been a bit of a sport.

Judge John Maude QC, a tall and striking-looking man with a most beautifully resonant voice, was never Recorder of London, but I must have appeared more often before him than before any other judge. He had once been Conservative MP for Southampton Test, and had also been one of the 'star' Silks in the Factory. He was married to the Marchioness of Dufferin and Ava – upon whom, it was said, Osbert Lancaster's 'Maudie Littlehampton' cartoon in the *Daily Express* newspaper had been loosely modelled – and he was much given to quaint asides to a jury. If you reminded them that a police raid had taken place at 7pm, Judge Maude would turn to the jury of East End market traders and dockers and say, 'About sherry time, members of the jury.'

In one armed robbery case a police officer called Jones, whom I was cross-examining, was giving barely audible evidence. The judge asked him if he was one of the Welsh Joneses. The policeman confirmed that indeed he was.

'Ah!' said Judge Maude, 'then you must have, like all the Welsh Joneses, a strong and beautiful voice. Pray sing after me: do-ray-me-far-so-la-te-do, so that we can see if you are capable of a stronger output.' Police officer Jones did his pitiful best to comply. In an interview for a tabloid newspaper the next day, Judge Maude admitted that he himself 'could not sing for toffee,' and had not indeed done so since he had sung 'Oh for the wings of a dove' as a treble at Eton.

On another occasion, in my presence (so I know it is true), Judge Maude sentenced two homosexuals for an act of gross indecency under Waterloo Bridge and said, 'It is not just the enormity of the crime itself that appals one. It is also the fact that you chose to commit it, under one of London's most beautiful bridges.' Apocryphal reports of that occasion suggest that the judge went on to say, 'Surely the time has now come when you really must pull yourselves together and take yourselves in hand.'

Mr Justice Cassells, a very senior retired judge renowned for his kindness, returned to the Old Bailey in his eighties to preside over a lengthy trial. He invited the prospective jurors to tell him if they had any reason why it might be inconvenient for them to sit for several weeks hearing the case. One man raised his hand and nervously said that his wife was about to conceive.

'I think,' said the very kindly judge, 'that you mean that she is about to be confined. But it matters not whether you or I am right – I do agree that you must certainly be there.'

Many cases have, of course, long since faded from my memory, but others have stuck fast – particularly when I still have the notes. There were bank robberies – so many of them that I was fearful that one day I might be in my bank in Fleet Street on the day of a raid, and recognise former clients, or worse still be recognised by them. There were woundings, firearm offences, murders, manslaughters, gold smuggling, rapes, lorry hijackings, forgeries, larcenies, receivings and frauds: a relentless diet of serious crime. In some I prosecuted, but most frequently I appeared for the defence.

There was the case of O'Connell (I am afraid that I cannot recall his first name) who, with other members of his robbery gang, was accused of attempting to break out of Brixton prison. The others all went to the perimeter wall, where ladders had appeared and a getaway vehicle was waiting. They were caught and either pleaded guilty or a jury convicted them. O'Connell pleaded not guilty. He had climbed onto the flat roof of the island kitchen block situated in the centre of the open square of the prison, burning his hands on the boiling-hot steam pipe. This was nowhere near an escape wall. His defence was that he had not gone to the wall with the others, because he was not trying to escape: he was only taking the opportunity of the confusion to try to demonstrate from the flat roof against the bad prison conditions. Demonstration being no crime, and his explanation being considered reasonable by the jury, he was acquitted. It simply never occurred to anyone in the mid-1960s, before the James Bond films, and it was certainly never suggested by the prosecution, that O'Connell might have been on a flat roof in the centre of the prison, awaiting a lift from a helicopter!

There was 'Captain' Farr, the swashbuckling captain of an English Channel fishing boat, whom I defended at Winchester Assizes for conspiracy to import illegal immigrants into the country. He was caught by the coastguard bringing them ashore at first light, into a little cove along the coast from Portsmouth harbour. His defence was that he had just been out fishing in the English Channel in the middle of the night, minding his own business, when through the darkness he had spied a small rubber dinghy bobbing about on the waves and crammed with poor foreign souls who obviously had been shipwrecked. What else could he do but save them, and bring them to shore where they would find comfort, warmth and safety? Unfortunately, the coastguards, in their zeal, had arrested him before he could report his find at the nearby lighthouse. After the ten-day trial of the captain and his crew, the jury disagreed – a considerable forensic triumph. However, the judge, Mr Justice Park, thought that the case had been too much for me to handle on my own, so he ordered that in the re-trial I should be led by Queen's Counsel. Ian Starforth Hill (later to become the senior circuit judge at Winchester), led me at the retrial, and our client was duly convicted and sentenced to three years in prison.

I had cases where the limits of the rules laid down by parliament or the judges were tested in the Court of Criminal Appeal. Pett and Bird were two scrap metal dealers, whose alibi defence to a charge of conspiring to steal a large quantity of stainless steel so perfectly covered every minute of their movements, and in such detail, that the jury thought it too good to be true, and convicted. The Court of Appeal, however, declaring a new doctrine that could be used whenever they were not happy with a jury's verdict, decided that there was a 'lurking doubt', and acquitted them both. I met my client many years later, when he greeted me enthusiastically as I queued for fish and chips at the Membury service station on the M4. I asked him how he was, and what he was doing: he assured me that whatever he was doing, he was now going straight.

Virtue and Baldessare was an armed robbery trial, in which I was led by John Hazan QC (another barrister friend who later became a High Court judge, before also succumbing to a premature death). The Judges' Rules, which governed police behaviour before 1984, required a suspect, before being questioned, to be cautioned that he need not say anything – like the American 'Miranda' requirement that a suspect must be 'read his rights.' But the Court of Appeal, in our case, managed to interpret the rule to mean that anyone accused of crime could be encouraged to chat away, without having to be cautioned until the prosecution had a case against him – a decision that did much to boost the iniquity of the 'verbal,' of which more anon.

Following another case, in which I was led by the charismatic Sebag Shaw QC (who also later became a High Court judge of great distinction), it was decided that parliament, not the judges, had to change the rules. The waiters at the Caprice, the famous high-class West End restaurant, had not been declaring their tips to the Inland Revenue, and so had not been paying income tax on them. They did not pretend that they had disclosed them, and when charged with tax evasion they were willing to plead guilty. But Sebag's view was that the law was by no means clear on the matter, and could properly be interpreted to mean that the waiters were not required to declare their 'tronc'. He advised them to plead not guilty, argued their case successfully before Judge Maude at the Old Bailey, and our clients were acquitted on the point of law. The Chancellor of the Exchequer made sure that that particular loophole was closed in the next budget. This was the only case I ever had where we barristers actually stopped our clients pleading guilty!

I am sure that some judges found me as difficult as I found them. As the great F.E. Smith is reputed to have said, when a senior judge told him he was being offensive: 'I know I am, my Lord, but so are you. The difference between us is that I am trying hard not to be, and you can't help it!' In one case, I defended a Cypriot called Ptohopoulos, and when the case got to the Court of Appeal, they held that gross discourtesy by a judge to counsel, however unfortunate, is not by itself a ground for quashing a conviction. My client had been charged with living off the immoral earnings of prostitution, and was convicted and sentenced to two years imprisonment and deportation.

The Chairman of Middlesex Quarter Sessions, who tried the case, was the Hon. Ewan Montague QC who was famous for conceiving the remarkable 'Man Who Never Was' diversion, which had so successfully distracted German intelligence away from the proposed Sicily landings in 1944, thereby saving thousands of lives. He was also a very tall man – much taller than Clifton Webb, who played him in the film. Sadly, while it was a proud rule of British law that, in our courts, justice had not only to be done but had to be *seen* to be done, in Montague's court, justice had sometimes to be seen to be believed! To be fair, his summings-up to juries, and the sentences he passed, were usually considered to be reasonable and correct, even by his sternest critics. But he was incapable of controlling himself on the bench during a trial. At the Cypriot's trial, he had ceaselessly interrupted me at every stage, and had made the proceedings look so blatantly unfair that I lodged an appeal and asked Malcolm Morris QC to lead me.

Malcolm was a very senior and respected Silk, and extremely charming, in the old-fashioned style familiar to regular viewers of black-and-white television's *Boyd QC*. He had successfully led for the prosecution in my first big smuggling case. He had been less successful in his defence of Timothy Evans, for the infamous murders at 10 Rillington Place. He told me to find a point of law, because the Court of Appeal would not find against a judge for bad behaviour if they did not have to. I searched and searched and eventually found a point, so weak that neither of us thought it had any merit at all. But Malcolm said it would do, and was quite magical. He demonstrated dramatically, and to the great amusement of the court, the gasps, grunts, groans and guffaws Montague had used to signal judicial impatience with my questions and my speech to the jury. He carried the day. Delivering judgement, Lord Justice Salmon said that, had I put down my brief and walked out of court (as had happened in a case in Liverpool before Mr Justice Hallett, another out-of-control judge), then the defence could have argued, with some justice, that it had been unable to put its case to the jury, and the appeal on that ground would have had to succeed.

'But,' said Lord Justice Salmon, 'Mr Lawrence, with considerable courage and tenacity, and complete courtesy, proceeded to ask every conceivable question, and some that were not even conceivable.' In such circumstances it could not be said that the judge had prevented the defence from putting its case, and the appeal upon that ground would be refused. However, on our ridiculously weak point of law, the court was moved to find more substance.

'On this ground,' said the Lord Justice, 'we find it impossible to uphold the conviction. The appellant may well be a very fortunate man, but this court has no alternative other than to quash the conviction.'

Mine had not been the first complaint against the judge, and Lord Gardiner, the Lord Chancellor, was alerted. The Hon. Ewan Montague QC took the hint and retired early, to give more time to his treasurership of the Middle Temple.

Then there was the bizarre case of a man called Walls, who claimed to be a bishop of 'the Old Roman Catholic Church'. This was a sect, rejected by the true Roman Catholic Church, which, long before child abuse cases became so common in our courts, seemed to have attracted some adherents with very questionable attitudes towards young boys. Walls faced a charge of gross indecency with a young soldier, at the alleged victim's home. He explained to the Canterbury jury, in his defence, that his visit to the boy's house had been a purely pastoral one, in order to warn the father that the boy was having sex with his mother! The jury duly convicted him, and Judge Streeter, no doubt judging the defendant to be effectively mad, if not actually certifiable, sentenced him to a conditional discharge. Walls wanted to appeal. I advised against it. He ignored me. The Registrar of the Court of Criminal Appeal briefed me, because I had been trial counsel, to conduct the appeal, and I had no alternative but to take the case.

I did my feeble best, though it was of course quite hopeless. Lord Justice Winn, who presided over my court, flew into a rage and demanded to know what I was doing arguing an appeal for such a contemptible client on such unanswerable evidence, when the sentence had been so absurdly light. I replied that I was doing no more than my duty on the instructions of the Registrar, but I was upset by the unjustified attack upon me by a senior judge. Later that day, one of the other judges, Mr Justice Donaldson (who was to become Master of the Rolls) sent me a kindly note to reassure me that my brave efforts in difficult circumstances had not gone entirely unappreciated. Shortly afterwards, Lord Justice Winn was found to be suffering from a brain tumour, and died.

I had quite a regular client called John Mangan. He was usually charged with armed robbery but if he was indeed guilty, he was remarkably unsuccessful, and kept being arrested. He so infuriated others in his alleged gang that, on one occasion, a colleague hit him hard with the stock of a shotgun, and left him for dead in the gutter. He recovered, and thereafter had a permanent plate in his head. In one case, it was alleged against him that he had used a milk float as a getaway vehicle. He had the jury in fits of laughter, as he explained in comic detail how little use such a vehicle would have been for escaping from pursuing police cars. He was acquitted.

On another occasion the only evidence against him was an alleged confession to the police, called, in jargon, a 'verbal.' I asked him to turn towards the jury and tell them what a 'verbal' was.

'A verbal, jury,' he bellowed in his throaty cockney voice, 'is when they fucking say you've fucking admitted your fucking guilt, and you ain't fucking said fuck all.' That jury rocked with laughter again.

'With that very clear definition of a verbal,' commented the judge, Commissioner Temple, in his own broad Yorkshire accent, 'I think we'll adjourn for lunch.' Again Mangan was acquitted.

Some time later, when he had been indicted for a robbery set down to be tried at Lewes Crown Court, Mangan managed to persuade a High Court judge that the trial should be moved to the Old Bailey. He had demanded his right to be tried by his 'cockney peers' who would understand his defence better than those 'old country bumpkins at Lewes'.

Speaking of Lewes, there was the case of Mr Saachs who was tried, with two others, at Lewes Crown Court over ten weeks. Shops rejoicing in such names as 'Cheap! Cheap!' had been opened along the south coast. They did not trade from any place for long, because the suppliers only gave four to six weeks credit and, since the bills were never paid, the shop owners found it convenient to move on quickly. This kind of activity was known as a 'long firm fraud'. Mr Saachs owned the company, but its day-to-day running was in the hands of two managers. This was partly because Mr Saachs was an ultra-orthodox Jew who was always about his afternoon prayers in a back room at the very moments when salesmen came to conduct their sales. He was never actually present when anything dishonest took place, so there was no real evidence that he knew of the dishonest transactions. I doubted whether the religious demands upon the time of such an ultra-orthodox zealot would be properly understood by a Sussex country jury, likely to consist, as Mangan had pointed out, of a higher than usual proportion of retired colonels and brigadiers. I could not have been more wrong. While his managers were convicted and sentenced to seven years in prison, Mr Saachs was acquitted of everything except a failure to keep his account books properly. I have found a poem that I wrote while waiting for the jury's verdict – and completed on the train back to London.

The Ballad of Brunswick Street West

A tale of fraudulent, Cash and Carry
Of Gerry, Henry and Bearded Barry
Ran a firm, so it is said,
Ran it right from black to red.

Ran it short on tight liquidity,
Was it crime or just stupidity?
Excess of bad luck? Or false cupidity?
That must be left to the jury's proclivity.

Little Cash and lots of Carry
Menswear's down to Mr Harry,
Businessman from the Elephant precinct,
We can only guess the businesses he's sinked!

Managing director Mr Saachs,
Was he ignorant of all the facts?
Was he deep in hair and perpetual prayer
And never aware of being there?

Their trial a timeless extravaganza
Exhibits, a mass produced bonanza,
Millions of words and waiting on stations,
With William Shakespeare skilled in translations!

Prosecutor Davies stern in stance,
Witnesses withering at his glance,
With Celtic force and Celtic cool,
Brought all within the 'Res Gestae Rule'.

Lawrence, Lloyd-Eley, and Ian Hill
Defended their clients with consummate skill,
But two alas are now savouring bird,
The Almighty came to the aid of the third.

So ends this tale of Cash and Carry
Of Gerry, Henry and Bearded Barry
Running a 'firm' with dreams of clover
At last this bloody trial is over.

About this time I defended a man who had been convicted of murder and sentenced to death in Jamaica. He appealed against his conviction to the Privy Council in London which was, and still is, the ultimate court of appeal from that Commonwealth country, despite the fact that Jamaica had long since been independent. Jamaica either believes that our system of justice is superior to its own, or that it is cheaper to let the UK pay the cost of an ultimate appeal court than to inflict that cost upon the Jamaican taxpayer. I suspect the latter. I had been asked to represent the appellant by the Privy Council '*in causa pauperis*' – that is, for free. I was glad of the experience and of course accepted.

The circumstances of the case were appalling. My client, undoubtedly the leader of a gang of armed robbers, had knocked on the door of a house in Kingston, the capital of Jamaica, shot the owner dead and then burgled the house for trinkets worth nothing. But he had been on 'death row' for two years, and I asked the Clerk to the Privy Council whether, even if I failed in my appeal on his behalf, they would hang him after so long a time.

'Oh yes,' he replied, 'if he has not been hanged already.' Apparently there had been a recent successful appeal against a sentence of flogging – which, it was later discovered, had already been carried out twelve months before the appeal.

A simple, but vital, mistake of law appeared to have been made by the Jamaican judge in his summing-up. Jamaican law was English law, and the judge seemed to have been totally unaware that the English law of murder had been changed. The test of intention to kill, or to cause serious bodily harm, had now to be subjective, not objective. In other words, before a man could be convicted of murder, the jury had to be sure that the evidence proved that he had actually intended to commit the act: it was no longer enough that a reasonable man might assume from the circumstances that there had been such an intention. As such I had what I thought was an unanswerable point.

To my amazement, the Judicial Committee of the Privy Council, consisting of the most senior judges in the land, showed no interest at all in my point of law, and did not even want to hear me argue it. As I walked disconsolately from the Privy Council Chamber in Downing Street, into Whitehall, it dawned on me why the court had shown no interest – the appellant had already been hanged, so any further argument on the law would have been a waste of time. The Privy Council having since developed a 'liberal' approach to appeals against death sentences, some of the Commonwealth countries who wish to keep capital punishment seem now a little keener to have their own final court of appeal.

Other cases attracted the attention of the newspapers. I defended John McVicar's wife who, when the police had come to their flat to arrest her husband, had held them at bay for long enough to let him escape out of the window. I appeared for the top model in the 'She looks better in a shirt' advertisement, accused of receiving a stolen fur coat. I defended a man charged with handling Princess Alexandra's stolen ruby ring. Then there was Miss Priston, the girlfriend of Split Waterman, the world motorcycle champion, who was charged with fraudulently importing gold bullion into Britain.

One particularly interesting case took place at Brighton Quarter Sessions, before the Recorder of Brighton, Sir Charles Doughty QC, who also happened to be MP for neighbouring Hove. My client was charged with receiving a diamond, which the police assumed from the guilty way in which he answered their questions must have been stolen. The problem was that while a respected Brighton valuer of precious stones, giving evidence for the prosecution, insisted that the stone was a diamond worth £25,000, another equally respected valuer, called by the defence, said the stone was only strontium titinate, worth £5. Since the experts could not make up their minds what exactly had been stolen, and the prosecution therefore could not prove that they had correctly charged him with the felony of Theft, instead of the misdemeanour of Obtaining Money by False Pretences, the Court of Appeal acquitted him. Such an argument could never be deployed in the Court of Appeal again, for after my case parliament abolished the distinction between felonies and misdemeanours!

Of course, I was not just appearing in famous and weighty cases at quarter sessions and assizes. I recall one case of little importance, save to my middle-aged client and his accuser, tried at Old Street Magistrates Court before Lewis Sturge – a real gentleman stipendiary magistrate of the old school. My client was charged with 'flashing' at a middle-aged spinster lady in the garden of her house in Islington. She told the court of her deep shock at seeing him, and what he was clearly doing, from the vantage point of her bedroom window. The defendant assured me and the judge that he had done no such thing, and anyway he would have been too far away for her to have seen anything. I persuaded the kindly Mr Sturge that justice could not be done in this case without him going to the house himself to see what could in fact be seen from where the lady said she had been standing. The judge duly adjourned the hearing, and travelled to the scene of the alleged crime. He discovered that nothing at all could have been seen from where the offended lady said she had been standing. When, however he stood on a chair, which had to be placed on top of a table, it would have been quite possible for her to have seen what she had described – as long as she had been looking through a pair of long-range binoculars. I kid my reader not! A miscarriage of justice was avoided by the care and wisdom of a considerate judge – who had not found me too difficult!

Joey Pyle

My next big case turned out to be almost too incredible and not at all amusing. It has to be said that Joey Pyle was well known to the police. He had been acquitted of taking part in the Pen Club murder of famed gangster Jack Spot in 1960 and, although said to be a gang leader himself, seemed to have escaped police attention for ten years. In 1971 Ralph Haeems instructed me to defend him at the Old Bailey for conspiracy to commit armed robbery. The police alleged that, following a tip-off, they had gone to his home, in a leafy and wealthy part of Morden in Surrey, and in the boot of the Mercedes parked in the driveway in front of his house, they had discovered guns and masks for obvious use in an armed robbery. He had been taken with the weapons to Wimbledon police station, where he was charged and held in custody.

On 10 September, I went to Wimbledon Magistrates Court to try to get bail for him. The officer in charge of the case, Detective Sergeant Harold Hannigan, behaved so arrogantly in opposing my application that, most unusually for an armed robbery charge, the magistrates ignored his protestations and granted bail. Pyle then made a complaint to the Metropolitan Police Commissioner, the chief of London's police force, alleging that he had been asked for money by Hannigan not to oppose bail. That complaint was put on hold until the trial was over.

Joey Pyle told a remarkable story. He was a south-west London secondhand car dealer. His business partner, a man called Freddie Sewell, was a well-known villain, wanted by the police in Lancashire for killing Blackpool police superintendent Gerald Richardson earlier that year. By chance, I represented the man charged with harbouring Sewell, the following year at Manchester Crown Court, with Ashe Lincoln QC, as my Leader.

Pyle said that he had been summoned by the police to meet them at a club in Streatham. He went and met a Chief Superintendent of the

Lancashire Police, and a Chief Inspector from the Metropolitan Police. They demanded news of Sewell's whereabouts. Pyle said that he had not seen him for ages and had no idea where he was. The police sounded desperate. The Metropolitan Police were being made a laughing stock by the rest of the country's police forces, for what was seen as their incompetence in failing to find Sewell. Pyle said he was told that, if he did not help them to find Sewell, they would 'fit him up'. That is in fact what they had done, Pyle said, when they came to his house and claimed to have found robbery gear in the boot of his car.

On 2 October 1972 Pyle's jury trial began at the Old Bailey, before a very prickly Judge Gwynne-Morris. Allan Green, later to become Director of Public Prosecutions, was my opponent. The Chief Inspector denied in cross-examination that there had been any such meeting with a chief superintendent from Lancashire in Streatham, or anywhere else. The allegation, he said, was a total fabrication. He gave evidence of an interview with Pyle at the police station from a notebook. I asked if I could look at the notebook. I wanted to satisfy myself that there really was no reference to that meeting at the Streatham club. He refused to hand it to me, claiming that it contained privileged and irrelevant matter. The judge supported him and said that I could not look at the notebook. I argued that I must be entitled to examine the book upon which the police officer was relying to refresh his memory. Judge Gwynne-Morris grudgingly conceded the point – but I could only look at the pages between the paper clips. I said that that would not help me, since I was hardly likely to find what I was looking for in the pages that the police officer himself had marked for inspection.

In a sarcastic tone, intended for the jury – in those days allowed to remain in court when legal argument took place if the parties had no objection – the judge asked me, 'Are you suggesting that this senior officer is lying about the evidence he has just given?' Of course that was Pyle's whole case, so it was a very silly question.

'I am not alleging anything at the moment,' I replied. 'I just want to examine the book which surely I have a right to do.'

'But I have just ruled on the matter,' said the by then irate judge. 'Get on with the case.' I took a deep breath and said, 'I am sorry but I cannot do that. I have my instructions, and if I am not to be allowed to defend my client properly according to those instructions, then I have no alternative but to ask you to release me from the case.'

Now there is nothing judges dislike so much as an abortive trial. If a new barrister has to be appointed, it might take weeks and much expense, inconvenience and disruption to start again. If, on the other hand, the defendant refuses to have new counsel, preferring to represent himself, that often means that the trial will take longer, be more likely to go wrong and in the end result in an acquittal, either by a jury or on appeal.

So Judge Gwynne-Morris, making plain that my behaviour would not be forgotten, reluctantly backed down. I took the paper clips off the book. I turned back the pages. And there, to my astonishment and nearly everyone else's, I found the entry. It showed that a meeting with the Chief Superintendent from Lancashire at a club in Streatham on the date suggested had indeed taken place.

It was a great moment for the defence. The officer had lied on oath or, as he explained it, with so much on his mind, he had 'completely forgotten' about the meeting. This did not mean, of course, that the police had planted the weapons on Pyle, but it was a very serious blow to their credibility. Again, I learnt the lesson that it is sometimes necessary to stand up to awkward judges at the Bar, and the young advocate must have the courage to do so if necessary, as long as he is polite.

But that was only the first of the misfortunes that befell the prosecution at this trial. The arresting officers gave evidence that, having found the guns and robbery equipment in the boot of Pyle's Mercedes, they took them immediately to Wimbledon police station, carrying them inside to be registered at the station sergeant's desk, through a door leading directly from the car park. Not true, Pyle told me: the guns, which were certainly not his, had been brought to the station sergeant's desk through another internal door leading from somewhere inside the police station.

'So what?' I asked him. 'What does it matter what door they came through?'

'They are lying about it,' he replied, 'they brought them from inside the police station.'

Of course, if the weapons and masks had been 'planted' by the police they would have been more likely to have put it all together inside the police station, where they would have some privacy, than in the car park where anyone might have seen what they were up to. It still seemed a bit far-fetched to me, for the police to be lying about which door they had come through.

But Pyle was adamant. He said that if I could catch the police officers out on that matter, it would be another lie with which to nail the main false allegation. He was so certain that the uniformed station sergeant – who had nothing to do with the Flying Squad detectives from New

Scotland Yard – would, if he were honest, bear him out, that I told Allan Green I wanted the sergeant called as a witness. I did not ask my solicitor to take a statement from the officer, because I did not want to alert the police about the importance of the door. There was always a risk that the detectives might tell him what their evidence had been, and how his evidence might harm them. But it was a dangerous course for the defence to take. The general rule is never to call a witness unless you know in advance what he is going to say: he might, in the witness box, forget what he was supposed to say, misremember the truth, or simply not be prepared to help.

But Ralph Haeems and Pyle convinced me that the risk was worth taking. We had already caught the detectives out in one monumental lie, so they were obviously not being too careful in covering their tracks. It also occurred to me that, if DS Hannigan had behaved as arrogantly at the police station as he had behaved at the bail application, there might be no love lost between the uniformed sergeant and detectives from the Flying Squad, who had just barged into the station and proceeded to take over the place.

The station sergeant went into the witness box. The risk turned out to have been well worth taking.

'Can you remember which door the detectives came through with the guns?' I asked him.

'Yes, they came in through the inside door,' he replied.

'You sound sure about it. Are you?' I asked.

'Yes. I am quite sure,' he responded.

'Why are you so sure?' I asked.

'Because I thought it was rather odd at the time. If they had just brought the guns to the police station in a car, why were they not bringing them in through the car park door?' was his reply.

What joy – in those days – to find evidence being given by a completely honest police officer! This was a much heavier blow to the prosecution's case, because there could be no other explanation than that the guns had indeed been planted on Pyle.

But it got even worse for the prosecution. When Detective Sergeant Hannigan gave evidence, although his years of experience made him sound very professional, he came apart when he told the jury that he carried one of the guns into the police station in his pocket.

'Were you wearing the same suit that you are wearing today?' I asked him. He thought it was, or one very like it.

'Show us how you carried the gun in your pocket,' I requested. He tried getting it into the pocket, but it kept falling out. The jury was not greatly amused. Game and set! But not yet match. That came after two further witnesses crumbled the prosecution's case.

The first was Pyle's next door neighbour. He told the jury that he had been standing and shaving, by the front window overlooking the driveway at the front of Pyle's house. A car had screeched up and had disgorged what seemed to him to be 'a car-load of thugs'. He has seen them rush up to Pyle's front door, and he was about to telephone the police when a police car had arrived with lights flashing, and uniformed policemen got out. They had started talking to the other men, and the neighbour realised that he might have mistaken police officers for thugs, and that everything was under control. Minutes later, he left home to get his train to work in the City. He had to pass Pyle's Mercedes parked in the drive sideways on. The boot was open. It was empty. He was sure of that because he was inquisitive about what had been going on, and if it had been crammed full with guns and other articles he could not have failed to notice, for he had passed the car no more than two or three yards away. But the police had already given evidence that they did not remove any of the guns and robbery gear from the boot of the car at Pyle's house, and that they had driven the car to the police station with the contents exactly as they had found them.

Try as he could, Allan Green could not shake the neighbour in cross-examination. This was hardly surprising. He happened to be a respectable and mature City solicitor of good character, who had no reason to dislike the police or perjure himself for a villain, even if he was his next door neighbour. We had caught the police lying again about their main allegation.

There was yet another crippling episode for the prosecution's case, which was pure courtroom melodrama. I had called Pyle's wife to give evidence about the way the police had behaved when, on the day before the arrest, they had come to the house with a warrant to search for stolen jewellery. They had left empty-handed. She had the appearance of a very respectable middle-aged woman, soberly dressed and modest in manner; a typical decent housewife from that particularly affluent part of Surrey. It had not really been necessary for the prosecution to cross-examine her at all, since the evidence she had given was peripheral to the issue and she was, after all, the defendant's wife, who might be expected to give a favourable gloss on events for her husband.

But DS Hannigan was driving Allan Green mad, as he sat behind him mumbling throughout the trial, watching his case fall apart. He insisted that Mrs Pyle be attacked and discredited. And, as so often happens in court as in life, the attack had completely the opposite effect from that intended.

'Have you ever been in trouble with the police?' she was asked.

'What are you talking about?' she replied, visibly shaken. Green, embarrassed, put to her that she had been convicted of importuning as a prostitute in the 1940s and early 1950s – nearly thirty years earlier. There was a long pause and silence. Mrs Pyle started to sob quietly. Then she lifted her head, looked towards her husband in the dock and said, so softly that she was barely audible, 'He never knew. He never knew.'

There was a gasp from the crowded court. It looked as though that question might destroy a marriage. Then her husband, from the dock, called out in an anguished voice, 'I never knew. I never knew,' and repeated it several times, each time more dramatically. There was silence in the court. Not a dry eye anywhere. Looking back on the moment, it ought to have been melodrama at its most unconvincing, but at the time it was just incredibly moving.

At the end of the trial, Joey Pyle was speedily acquitted. Judge Gwynne-Morris, crusty, unreasonable and unpleasant though he had been, announced that he was going to do something that he had never done before. So seriously did he take the police misbehaviour in this case, that he had decided costs should be awarded to the defendant, not 'out of public funds', as was usual, but directly against the Metropolitan Police. I assume, but was never told, that some kind of enquiry must have followed.

A postscript. Three years later Detective Sergeant Hannigan was charged with corruption: he had demanded a bribe from a defendant in another case, in return for not opposing bail. He pleaded guilty and was astonishingly sentenced by Mr Justice Melford Stevenson to a conditional discharge, with a recommendation that he see a psychiatrist.

'You have suffered enough,' the *Brighton Evening Argus* reported the judge as saying.

So angry was Joey Pyle about being framed that, shortly after the 1972 trial, he was said – although he has denied it in his autobiography – to have given information to a newspaper about a friendship between the Soho pornographer James Humphries, and Commander Ken Drury, the head of the Flying Squad. Thus began to unravel a whole cesspit of police corruption in London. Drury received an eight-year prison sentence. Commander Wally Virgo, the head of the Obscene Publications

Squad received a twelve-year sentence, subsequently quashed, together with the conviction, on appeal.

The Police Commissioner Sir Robert Mark was reported as saying, 'A good police force is one which catches more criminals than it employs' and that the CID 'must be the most corrupt organisation in London.' Certainly 'Operation Countryman', the investigation later set up to get to the bottom of police corruption in the region, received practically no cooperation from the Metropolitan police force. But over this period a succession of chief superintendents, chief inspectors, and a large number of smaller fry, found themselves in prison, in the dock, or taking early retirement from the force. A total of 74 police officers were investigated, 13 were jailed, 8 were dismissed and 12 resigned. It was a truly dreadful time for criminal justice in Britain.

Joey Pyle stayed out of serious trouble until 1992, when he was sentenced to 14 years imprisonment for distributing heroin. His wife divorced him.

The Old Bailey bomb

On 8 March 1973, about 60 cases after Joey Pyle's, I was in one of the new Old Bailey courts on the second floor, and half-way through a three-week armed robbery case, when just before 3pm the judge, Mervyn Griffiths-Jones, the Common Serjeant, received a message that there was a bomb outside the building. We were enjoined to leave the courtroom speedily – through the public entrance in the front of the court, outside which was the bomb! No one thought of telling us to leave by the back of the court where the bomb was not! I was last out, staying to tie up my brief and tidy my papers. This done, and with my arms full, I was about to push through the swing doors leading out into the hallway when the bomb exploded. Glass rained down on the other side of the door. Those who had hurried out ahead of me were not so lucky. When the dust settled and the noise abated, I went over to the window at the front of the court building and looked out. The sight was as desolate as a nuclear winter. Thousands of windows had been shattered in the tower blocks opposite. Cars had been hurled into the air. The buildings and a public house opposite were badly damaged. People lay on the ground in shock, or were picking themselves up out of the debris. Billy Rees-Davies QC, the one-armed Conservative MP who had been defending in another trial, was standing at the top of Seacoal Lane, in the middle of the debris, black cape blowing out in the wind, looking for all the world like the Avenging Spirit. Jeremy Hutchinson QC, a left-wing campaigner against capital punishment, brilliant defender from the Factory, and now a Social Democrat peer, stood beside me.

'What would you do to them now Jeremy?' I asked him.

'Hang them,' he replied.

The IRA Price sisters Dolores and Marian and Gerry Kelly, after months of careful preparation, had organised the placing of car bombs outside four public buildings in London that day. One bomb was defused, the other three exploded. Mercifully, only one person died, although 180 were injured – mostly by broken glass. It surprised me that the IRA had been able to place their bomb right outside the Old Bailey, for ordinarily a permanent parking ban made it impossible to park outside the front of the building. But on the day planned for the Old Bailey bombing the Transport and General Workers Union just happened to have arranged a one-day strike in London, and parking restrictions had been lifted. Only then did it become possible for the bombers, provided they got there early enough, to park the car where they did. To think that, after all that careful planning, the bombers might have been unable to get their car-bomb any where near the building but for the strike decision taken just one day earlier.

Gerry Kelly, who received two life sentences in relation to that day's bombing, escaped from the Maze prison in 1983, was caught again in possession of a cache of arms in Amsterdam in 1986, and was released from prison in 1989. He was rewarded with the post of minister in the new coalition government at Stormont.

Judge Aarvold

Mr. Jeremy
Hutchinson
Q.C.

Hon. Ewen Montagu QC

Salmon J

Mr. Malcolm Morris QC

Michael Corkery QC

Judge John Maude QC.

8

A Seat in Parliament

'Say, for what were hop-yards meant:
Or why was Burton built on Trent?
Oh many a peer of England brews
Livelier liquor than the Muse,
And malt does more than Milton can
To justify God's ways to man.
Ale, man, ale's the stuff to drink
For fellows whom it hurts to think:
Look into the pewter pot
To see the world as the world's not.
And faith, 'tis pleasant till 'tis past:
The mischief is that 'twill not last.'

(A.E. Housman: *A Shropshire Lad LXII*)

In 1970 I fought Peckham again in the general election, which the Conservatives won with Edward Heath and which all the main public opinion polls said would not happen! This time I received 8232 votes, 29 more than last time but still not enough. It was obvious that if I was ever to get into parliament I would have to leave Peckham, and try to get adopted for a seat I had some chance of winning.

I asked for my name to be put onto the Conservative Central Office candidates list, and I applied to over 30 constituencies. Despite being selected to open the key debate on industrial relations at the Party Conference in Blackpool in October and doing it according to subsequent speakers 'splendidly', 'excellently', even 'brilliantly' – although opposed by the Liverpool Edgehill candidate, Michael Howard – not one of them even invited me to an interview. Billy Rees-Davies had once told me that, very shortly after the war, he just happened to bump into the chairman of the Conservative Party in the street, and had been invited there and then to be MP for Thanet. Obviously things had changed since those days!

121

Finding a seat

On the wise advice of Bill Henderson, the chief Central Office agent, I rewrote my long and boring biographical details and produced a much shorter version. In it I revealed, provocatively, that I was both a member of the Monday Club (right wing) and the Bow Group (left wing). I was invited for interview at the next eleven seats for which I applied: they all wanted to know how I could be a member of both groups. I explained that while the Monday Club (which did not have quite the connotation of extremism it has since enjoyed) was a ginger group attempting to ensure that the Tory Party did not lose sight of its fundamental principles, the Bow Group provided the party with an opportunity for young thinkers to put forward constructive ideas for future policy while their minds were still fresh. There was a place for me in both. Seven constituencies thought that there was a place for me in their finals.

Chertsey and Walton was one. It was a new constituency which promised to yield a good Conservative majority, and as it was situated just over Walton Bridge, only a few minutes away from Dunally Cottage, it would have been perfect for the Lawrence family. There were five stages of selection, one of which was a visit to our house by the committee, to see how we lived! Gloria was asked, in those days before political correctness, if she was Jewish. I seemed to have done well through four of the rounds, and found myself, the favourite according to the constituency agent, in the final with Norman Fowler, John Wakeham and Geoffrey Pattie. The final selection took place on a swelteringly hot Saturday afternoon, with everyone in shirtsleeves, and all the windows of Addlestone Village Hall wide open.

I was last to be interviewed, three steaming hours into the process. We all had to wait our turn outside in the car park. When my time came, I hurried inside feeling confident. But hardly any of the seventy faithful gathered to select their candidate even bothered to look up. No welcoming applause. No smiles. No friendly glances. Nothing. Totally dead! After I had been introduced, I made a feeble attempt to establish some kind of rapport with those I was so anxious to lead to electoral victory.

'Relax,' I said. 'You are looking nervous.' No response. 'Don't try to be funny,' Gloria had told me. She was obviously right. I tried another tack:

'Important things first. This will cheer you up. England have just bowled Australia out for 136 runs at Headingly.' Still no response, even to news that exciting. My heart sank. Not for the first time (and certainly not for the last) an audience seemed totally uninterested in anything I had to say. One of the other candidates must have already swept them off their feet, and they had already decided that they had no need of me. I was right. Geoffrey Pattie was duly selected, and won at the next election with a majority of 11,963.

I let a day or two pass, and then dropped in to see the Conservative agent to ask what I had done wrong. He said I had missed only by a whisker, and that I had had the most enormous bad luck. I had failed with my test score opening because Geoffrey Pattie, himself a member of the MCC, had earlier started with the same cricket gambit, and had received a rapturous response. One of the selectors thought that I must have overheard that gambit through the open windows to the car park, and had marked me down for misjudged opportunism. To make me feel a little better, the agent also told me that the fact that I was Jewish had no more than the most marginal effect upon the result. Since I had apparently only lost marginally, I was enormously reassured.

I next found myself in the final at Thanet East, another new constituency which was to yield a Conservative majority of 6597 at the next election. With me were Michael Howard and Jonathan Aitken. After my speech and interview, the chairman came out and said there was one matter to which the selection committee needed to know the answer: would I come and live in the constituency? I was told that my reply would make a difference. I said that of course, when I was elected, I would buy a house in the constituency and come to live there. But it would be unfair on Rachel, who was happily at school where we were living, to move until then. I would of course want to spend every weekend nursing the constituency. Jonathan, who was single, and a very attractive candidate, did not have the same problem: he promised to move to Thanet immediately. He was selected.

Then I was in the final at Chester, which had enjoyed a Conservative majority of 7005 in 1970. I was against Peter Brooke and Peter Morrison. To make us welcome, there was a drinks reception on the lawn of the Duke of Westminster's stately home, at which the finalists circulated to demonstrate their social and conversational skills. Everyone was very friendly and encouraging, and I took to the Chester Conservatives immediately. Sadly they did not take to me, and Peter Morrison won. I drove back from Chester via Burton, a constituency that had just started its selection process.

Introduction to Burton

I arrived early in Burton-upon-Trent, the heart of the Burton constituency, and drove around the streets. At the last election John Jennings, the retiring Conservative MP, had had a majority of 4365 in a straight fight with Labour, but as I drove through the streets I could see that he must have been a miracle-man to have won the seat at all. What I saw, not having had time to venture out into the lovely country villages, was street after street of drab Victorian workers' terraced houses and quite a bit of urban decay. 'No,' I thought, 'not another five years fighting an essentially Labour seat I cannot win!' I considered dropping into the constituency office and telling them that I had decided to withdraw my name. Since that would have given me a black mark and blighted any other attempts, I suppressed that feeling and dutifully presented myself at the appointed hour.

Not being over-anxious to win, I must have sounded rather laid back. That might not have been a bad thing, for the line between laid back and quietly confident is narrow.

'Why did you choose to apply for Burton?'

'Because you were kind enough to invite me.'

'But what is your connection with Burton?'

'None.'

'Surely you have family connection or close friends here?'

'No.'

'Well, I expect you drink the beer we produce in Burton?'

'No, I am afraid I am not a drinker.'

'What do you know about farming?'

'Nothing.'

Comment from the chairman: 'I think Mr Lawrence has won his way into the next round: he's the first really honest candidate we've interviewed!'

In the final I beat Nick Budgen, who went on to win Wolverhampton South West, and Michael Latham, who was the victor at Melton Mowbray. Both, of course, very honest men who became much admired MPs, though from different wings of the party. Years later, when I was browsing through the old constituency records, I discovered that eighty members had voted for me, and three each for the runners-up.

One of the three, who had not much liked the look of me at the time, was Councillor Gordon Wyatt, a retired bank manager, who became Chairman of the East Staffordshire District Council on several occasions. He also became one of my staunchest supporters. Tragically, when he developed incurable cancer, he ran a rubber tube from the exhaust pipe to the inside of his car, sat in the car with his lovely and devoted wife Joan, and, sipping their favourite gin and tonic and holding hands, they departed this life together.

Before my selection, the Burton officers had taken an unusual decision. They had decided that they were all too old and should make way for a younger team. John Jennings would be 72 years old at the next election but was not too happy to be asked to retire. He had been a schoolteacher and had represented Burton with distinction in parliament for nineteen years, holding onto the seat by only 236 votes in 1966. He had also been the senior chairman of the House of Commons committees dealing with Bills – a position that sometimes led to a seat in the House of Lords. I tried to get him a knighthood when I was elected, but Ted Heath and Humphrey Atkins, the chief whip, would not hear of it. John had been strongly against Britain joining the Common Market, and had refused to support the Heath government in the lobbies, so had to be punished – '*pour encourager les autres*'. It was a great pity.

The constituency chairman, 80-year-old Sir Clifford Gothard OBE, was to become the president. He had been knighted for his lifetime of service to the Conservative Party, and was the sort of person who had no difficulty in combining the additional roles of Chairman of Marston's Brewery (the makers of 'Pedigree' beer), Editor in Chief of the *Burton Mail* (the main local newspaper), senior accountant of the oldest accountancy firm in the town and a local magistrate. A younger man, 63-year-old Danny Wallace, became chairman. A dour Scotsman, who had been a lieutenant-colonel in the Sherwood Foresters and had fought at El Alamein and Anzio, he was both the chief magistrate on the Burton bench and the head brewer at Allied Breweries, where he had invented the famous 'Double Diamond' beer. Mrs Alma Thompson, an ex-school teacher well into her eighties, handed over as chairman of the Conservative women's branch to Councillor Elsie Layden, who was in her fifties. A new agent, David Simpson, and myself as the new candidate, both in our thirties, completed the team.

At a meeting of the Association soon after my selection, a former Mayor of Burton, Alderman Michael Fidler, asked if it was true that I was a Jew. There was a shocked hush. Before I could answer, Councillor Dini Hunter, a powerful-looking, obviously strong-willed woman with an Austrian accent, leapt to her feet and declared, 'Zat is a disgraceful qvestion.' I was not quite sure why. Then Councillor Ann Ball, another woman of presence, also leapt to her feet, and this time in a strong Greek accent declared that she was ashamed to be in the same room as Alderman Fidler. When calm was restored, I said that I was proud to have been chosen for such a happy cosmopolitan constituency, and that I would, of course, be delighted to take part in church services, as indeed I had done in my last constituency. I was grateful that both women, and their delightful husbands, always remained among my staunchest supporters.

A tall, good-looking and impressive-sounding man in his forties, asked me at the same meeting for my views on housing planning and development.

'You must be the local builder,' I said, 'so I had better be careful how I answer.'

Everyone laughed, because he was. This was Stan Clarke, whose mother had been in service in his village of Barton-under-Needwood, and who had driven himself from plumber's mate to becoming the largest property developer in Staffordshire. He later became the owner of Uttoxeter racecourse in the constituency, and of several other racecourses throughout England, a member of the Jockey Club, was knighted for his services to horseracing and charities, and in his last years was both High Sheriff and Deputy Lieutenant of Staffordshire.

In preparation for such high offices, Stan became president of Burton Conservatives. At my adoption meeting in 1997, for which he and his lovely wife Hilda had especially flown back in a helicopter from Aintree, he said that there were two certainties he could forecast for the coming week. One was that I would be re-elected as Member of Parliament for Burton: the second was that his horse, Lord Gyllene, would win the Grand National. Sadly, he was only right about the second – upon which Gloria won £400. She knew better than to bet on the first.

The Conservative headquarters, at 9 St Paul's Square in Burton upon Trent, to which thousands of people were to come to my Saturday morning advice sessions ('surgeries') over the next quarter of a century, had been the lovely old vicarage of St Paul's Church – built, as had most of the few fine examples of Victorian architecture in Burton, by the brewers. Sir Clifford Gothard, who owned the property, offered us the top floor of the building to be our constituency residence. We knew that a flat 'above the shop' would be asking for trouble, so politely declined. Sir Clifford offered us another of his properties, a farmhouse on a 400-acre estate, five minutes outside the constituency in South Derbyshire, whose MP was then George Brown and later would be Edwina Currie. Being brought up as town dwellers, we loved the idea of living in a country house – especially that country house – and accepted.

Grove Farm, with a fifth of a mile of chestnut trees leading up to the house and a fifth of a mile of lime trees leading away from it, was to be our splendid constituency home for the next 19 years. It had originally been in the grounds of Drakelow Hall, the home of Sir Nigel Gresley, who had built the London, Midland and Scottish Railway to its greatness. The post-war Labour government had commandeered and demolished the Hall, and upon the site, had built the largest electricity generating power station in Europe. Luckily, you could not see the cooling tours from Grove Farm – unless you peered between the trees and looked up! The dining room of the Hall was reassembled in the Victoria and Albert Museum in London, to become an example of Victorian stately-home design at its best.

During the power strikes and the three-day week that drove Prime Minister Heath to call the general election in February 1974, Drakelow power station was heavily picketed round the clock. I had to drive almost into it, and past it every day of the election. Either because my impact on the area as candidate had been so feeble that nobody knew who I was, or because nobody cared, I was neither picketed nor stopped on my way into or from Burton while the strike and the election campaign lasted.

Far more famous political figures than me went unrecognised at that time. Just before the election campaign started, several hundred miners, engaging in the industrial action that the government was attempting to stop by court injunction, marched in protest up Fleet Street in London to the Law Courts in the Strand. I happened to be appearing in the High Court in an appeal and, after lunch at the Inner Temple Hall, three minutes from the court, I walked back with Sir Peter Rawlinson, the Attorney-General. He was seeking on behalf of the government, in another court in the building, the very injunction against which the miners were marching, and so was much in the news and being publicly reviled in the left-wing media. Crossing Fleet Street together, we had to pass through the demonstrating ranks of men and women bearing placards declaring 'Down with Rawlinson' and much else. They most politely made way for us. Had they but realised that they were making way for the very person against whom they were so bitterly demonstrating, they might not have been so polite!

Honey-trap

Two weeks before the election was called, Gloria and I decided to go to Moscow for the weekend. Thompsons, the travel agents, were offering a package tour for only £40, and it was too good an opportunity to miss. Gloria wanted to be 'Lara for a day', and be driven in a troika through the snow-covered woods around Moscow. Our hotel was the Intourist on Gorky Street. This turned out to be premises of the KGB.

Other passengers on the flight worked for the British Steel Corporation, which happened to be developing a novel technique for vulcanisation – the bonding of rubber to steel. This held out considerable potential for the British construction industry, and was obviously a target for Soviet industrial espionage. The Russians made a big play for everyone on the plane, and each of us was approached on some pretext or other. Whether we were touring the city, or just standing around in the hotel lobby, Russians came up and asked us to sell them our jeans, our cameras, our watches and practically anything else. A doctor on our flight was approached in the hotel lobby by a Russian who said how surprised he was, being a doctor himself, to have bumped into a kindred soul – and would his new friend like to change some currency? That would certainly have been a criminal offence. Two young Portsmouth Technical College students were followed across Moscow by someone who kept hiding behind trees, and who finally emerged, one hour later, from behind some books in the Moscow University library.

Another of our group lost his wallet. The hotel staff claimed to have found it, and he was taken to an interrogation suite minutes before we were to leave for our flight back to London. His interrogator alleged that someone had obviously been cut from a family photograph found in the wallet and that, since his purpose in coming to Moscow must have been to visit that person, it was necessary to know that person's name. If he refused to give it, they would have no alternative but to hold him for questioning, and he would miss the flight home. To miss a pre-paid package-tour flight would be very expensive. It was even possible that someone might be frightened enough to be prevailed upon to post a letter on his return to England, as the price for his release, and then find himself caught in a spy trap.

Despite the 'cold war', no one had alerted us to the danger of such approaches. Worrying incidents had certainly been occurring. A few months earlier, a tourist was reported to have 'accidentally' fallen out of a window on the twenty-first floor of the same Intourist Hotel. This was surprising, since all the hotel windows were permanently sealed against the cold, and could not be opened. Then there had been the unfortunate episode with Commander Anthony Courtney (the Conservative MP for Harrow East and a former Head of Naval Intelligence), who had been caught, a year or two earlier, in a 'honey trap' in a Moscow hotel. The Russians had circulated compromising photographs to his Association officers, who promptly de-selected him as their candidate at the next general election. These episodes were very much in my mind when I met Olga.

Gloria and I were sitting in the hotel nightclub, attempting to eat a barely edible meal. Across the room, an exceptionally pretty blonde, with short hair and an even shorter mini-skirt, kept smiling at me. Being British, and naturally friendly to natives abroad, I smiled back. Gloria did not smile, and asked me what on earth I thought I was doing. I said that I thought I was about to be picked up by someone working for the KGB, which presumably had the whole hotel staked out. Gloria said I was paranoid. I suggested that if she went off to the ladies room, we might be able to find out which of us was right. Gloria, sport that she was, agreed – and exited stage right.

The blonde immediately stood up, and leaving her companion sitting alone at the table, cat-walked enticingly towards me. My heart missed several beats. She said nothing, but floated passed me, brushing her bare thigh accidentally against my hand – which happened to be gripping the table edge in sheer panic. I thought that this might possibly be a signal, so I got up and followed her out of the dining room. She waited for me to catch her up, and took my hand. By then I had broken into a sweat. We sat down together in the hallway. I made sure that my back was against the wall. We conversed thus:

'Why did you follow me out?' she asked.

'Why did you smile like that at me?' I countered.

'Because you looked so nice. What is your name?'

'Ivan. What is yours?'

'I am Olga. So you are Russian, Ivan?'

'No, I am not Russian, but you obviously are.'

'No, I am Italian.'

She was lying. Apart from her very Russian looks, I had heard her speaking what sounded like fluent Russian to the waitress. What I thought was a little sinister was that my passport, which had been taken from me on arrival at the hotel earlier that day, happened to have nothing but Italian entry and exit stamps in it, from the several Italian holidays I had taken with Gloria. I wondered whether Olga's masters also knew that I was likely to be elected to parliament shortly. She wanted to speak English and told me some far-fetched story about how she came to be in Moscow on an errand for her Italian husband. She did not explain why she was sitting in the Intourist nightclub with another man who looked very much like a Russian.

'Do you like me?' she asked, disarmingly. Not, of course, wishing to give offence, I assured her that I did. She seemed delighted, put her arm in mine, and suggested that we could perhaps go somewhere upstairs together. That's it, I thought! She wanted to take me to a room where a photographer would be hiding in a wardrobe, ready to take photographs as soon as we had our clothes off, and they would be filed away by the KGB until I became prime minister.

'Forgive me,' I forced myself to say, 'it was lovely meeting you, but I think that I had better get back to my wife.' I stood, bowed, made my excuses and left while sweating profusely and shaking like a jelly. I returned to my table. Olga not impressed by the faint-heartedness of Englishmen, returned to hers.

'Hallo, Romeo,' Gloria greeted me cheerfully, 'and how was it for you?'

I told her exactly how it had been. She said that Olga's table companion, a handsome young man, had come across and started to engage her in conversation. She had not had the same difficulty that I obviously had, in telling him to get lost.

A few days later the election was called, and after my election, one evening in the Commons members' lobby, I mentioned the collective experiences of our package-tour flight to a senior Conservative MP. He agreed that tourists to the Soviet Union ought to be warned about the dangers awaiting them, and advised me to report my experiences to a Foreign Office minister. So I went to see the Junior Minister, Roy Hattersley, in his room, and de-briefed with him and an official. Roy showed no interest whatsoever. Another MP friend suggested that I should talk to a lobby correspondent and, naively, I did so. It resulted in a half-page story in the *Daily Mail* under the large heading 'Ivan and Olga', a photograph of me and a silhouette for Olga.

Geoffrey Howe, even then a man of considerable importance in the party, said that he was sorry that I had got such bad publicity. Oh dear! Black book again! However, later that summer I opened a church fete in the village of Kingstone in my constituency, where the vicar, Reverend Gledhill, brought me comfort. He introduced me, announcing to the crowd of celebrants how delighted and privileged the parish felt at being represented in parliament by someone with such high moral principles that he could resist the predatory advances of a beautiful Soviet spy sent to entrap him. I received an extremely warm reception from the crowd when, on welcoming them to the fete, I confessed that I could not remember who had said, 'Politics is the second oldest profession – and greatly resembles the first!'

General election, February 1974

We returned from the excitement of Moscow to the thrill of a three-week election campaign. I spoke in thirty-three unheated village halls, sometimes three in an evening. My speech, updated daily according to the national election situation, was a standard diatribe against 'reds under the bed'. A man called Bert Ramelson (or was it Bertram Elson?), featured prominently in it. He had been unwise enough to say that the Communist Party only had to mention something in the spring for it to become Labour Party policy by the autumn. So the question posed by the Conservatives at the election was: whom did the electorate want to be ruled by – the communist-influenced trade unions, or a democratically elected non-communist government? The electorate chose, wrongly of course. Had this been the European Union we could have ordered a re-run, or several re-runs, until the voters came up with the right answer! But that would be for later. The country ended up with the misery of a 'hung parliament'.

My canvassing team was small. Leading it was Cedric Insley, an immensely enthusiastic paint salesman who later became chairman, and then president, of the Burton Conservative Association. He also became chairman of the West Midlands Conservatives, earning for the dedication he and his wife Fay had shown to the cause over forty years a well-deserved CBE. He is now a popular district councillor and he has been Mayor of East Staffordshire. Good friends from London, Robert Johnson (later to become a High Court judge), his regal wife Linda, and my 'pupil' at the Bar, Bryan Niblett (later to become Professor of Computer Science at the University of Wales and a well-known arbitrator) came up to help me. At every election we were generously loaned an all-weather Range Rover for our 'battle-bus' by Jim Leavesley, a local industrialist and brother-in-law of Stan Clarke, but even so we could only canvass a small number of streets in the three weeks of the campaign. I resolved in future to always have a large team of canvassers, and nearly always thereafter achieved that aim.

I cannot move on without paying tribute to the many voluntary party workers in Burton, without whose dedicated efforts, over the next almost quarter of a century, neither I nor my party would have enjoyed much success. There were my dedicated chairmen, men and women like Joe Harvey (an ex-chief constable), Rob Robertson (the managing director of the Blithfield Reservoir), Keith Hornby-Priestnall (a heroic wartime submariner), Joan Cullen (the first woman army officer to enter Belsen, and who could never thereafter speak of the horror), Dan Harrison (the dynamic health club entrepreneur and former brewery drayman), Danny Wallace, of course, and others like Alex Fox (who became Conservative Leader of East Staffordshire Borough Council), Phillip Atkins (who became Conservative Leader of Staffordshire County Council), John Hicklin (the retiring ex-manager from Lloyds steel foundry) and the many councillors and activists, alas too many to mention, who gave up so much of their time and energy for the Conservative cause. Then there was the brilliantly effective line of Conservative agents: the paid party organisers, who were always able to cajole, coax and charm the volunteers to ever greater effort.

One or two of the Conservative party's heaviest national hitters visited Burton during my first campaign. Michael Heseltine came round the town with me in a loudspeaker van. I drove; he spoke.

'Good afternoon ladies and gentlemen,' he said quietly and with boundless courtesy, 'this is Mr Michael Heseltine, the Aerospace Minister, speaking to support your Conservative parliamentary candidate Mr, er, er, er, ah, yes, Ivan Lawrence.'

It was a complete waste of time. No one paid the slightest attention. In fact no one had time to look up from their daily labours, or could even hear a word he said, before we had driven past. I asked Michael if he would mind taking the wheel while I took the microphone, to show him how we did loudspeakering in Burton. I turned the power up to full, and bellowed as we passed the Bass brewery: 'Keep 'em out! Keep 'em out! Keep 'em out! Don't let Benn nationalise our beer and ruin our breweries. Keep Burton Conservative. Vote Lawrence for Burton.'

We could tell that this message was reaching home, from the number of two-fingered acknowledgements we received everywhere we went. The more economical one-fingered salutation, doubtless indicating that I should stand and win at least one more time, did not replace that gesture until the 1980s. For months afterwards, Michael would come up to me in the tearoom and corridors of the Commons, grab my arm and intone: 'Keep 'em out! Keep 'em out!'

He came many times to Burton during elections, and his visits were always great fun. At another election I strode out ahead of him into the Burton shopping precinct, loudspeaker in hand, proclaiming excitedly: 'He's here! He's here! Yes, he's here! Who's here? Tarzan is here and wants to meet *you*. Him Tarzan. Me Ivan. Come and say hallo to Tarzan the great Tory beast in the Conservative forest.'

There was always a good-natured reception, and our supporters were able to hand out hundreds of Tory leaflets to the happy shoppers.

In my first election campaign, in the village of Leigh at the Uttoxeter end of the constituency, as rural an area as it was possible to see, Gloria decided that she had had quite enough of my wimpish witterings, and spoke out boldly.

'I don't agree with my husband about social security and student grants. Nobody should be entitled to state handouts, which we all have to work so hard for, unless they really need and deserve them.'

As a man (or woman), the audience of thirty plus rose to their feet and applauded. It was soon all round the public houses. The new Tory candidate called Ivan Lawrence was really a woman.

It took me time to win the confidence of my constituents. That I may have done so by at least the 1983 general election became clear when Gloria canvassed a house in Yoxall, on the southern borders of East Staffordshire. A little boy answered her ring at the doorbell.

'Is your Mummy in?' asked Gloria sweetly. 'Will you tell her I'm calling on behalf of Ivan Lawrence.'

The little boy ran off excitedly to tell Mummy the glad tidings, and returned to tell Gloria that Mummy said would she come upstairs and see her. Gloria ventured up, and arrived at the bathroom, where the lady of the house was sitting in the bath – stark naked.

'I'm so sorry,' said Gloria.

'No, it's me who should say sorry,' said the lady. 'I thought it was your husband.'

The constituency of Burton had been represented by Liberal MPs until the Second World War, when John (later Lord) Gretton, crossed the floor to join the Conservatives. John Jennings warned me that my refusal to hold out the hand of political friendship to the Liberals, as he had done all his years as MP, would cause a Liberal to stand at the election, and would cost me my seat. He was wrong. A Liberal did stand, but I hung onto the seat in the February 1974 election with a majority of 3303, and only slipped back to a 2098 majority in the election that

Harold Wilson called in October 1974, to strengthen his slender hold on power.

I had some good luck in my first election. My original Labour opponent had been charged with rape and so had to withdraw. He was replaced by David Hill, a Labour party researcher who, having failed to defeat me, became head of the Labour Party's publicity machine until the mid-1990s, and then followed Alastair Campbell as Labour's spin-doctor in chief. I won the first election with 23,496 votes to Labour's 21,398, with the Liberal, Keith Stevens, a friendly farmer, coming in third with 7969 votes.

And so, on 28 February 1974, I became the very proud MP for the brewing centre of England. Three hundred square miles, half rural, half urban, containing in population and activities as generous a mixture of all that is best in Britain as it was possible to find. Burton was known not only for its beer, its markets and its Uttoxeter racecourse, but also as the home of Marmite, Bovril, Branston pickle, Tutbury glass, Pirelli tyres, JCB earthmovers, BTR industrial plastics, Lloyds steel foundry, British Gypsum, Marley Tiles, Robirches pork pies, and fruit machines.

The next twenty-three years of my life were swept up in a perpetual maelstrom of causes, personal, local, national and international, the sheer volume of which astonishes me as I sit down to ponder where exactly those exciting years went.

I always spent the day following my six successful elections touring the streets and villages of the constituency in the Leavesley Range-Rover, loudspeakering my thanks to all who had put their confidence in me, and promising that I would continue to work hard for everyone regardless of their politics. On my first such outing I found Dave Stacey, the Labour-supporting *Derby Evening Telegraph* reporter, sitting tired and emotional by a lamp-post, and I invited him to travel with me on the tour. He told me how impressed he was by the large number of people who came across to wish me luck, or who waved from their windows and the entrances to their shops as we passed. He promised always to report me fairly – which he did.

I had an odd relationship with the local media. There were no fewer than twenty-seven editions of local newspapers covering the constituency each week, and I needed to feed as many as I could with news and opinion. The task was becoming impossible even before the advent of the faxes, e-mails and text messaging that must now make the life of an MP all but unbearable. The *Burton Mail* was my main newspaper. When I first arrived in Burton it was a really dreadful rag. Sir Clifford's policy, as editor-in-chief, had been to exclude all attacks on John Jennings, and to publish in full anything he said in parliament, on any subject. This, of course, killed local political interest stone dead.

At the first opportunity, I went to see the editor. I pleaded with him *not* to report my speeches in full, to feel free to publish genuine attacks upon me but to give me a right of reply; that way there would be some chance of getting people's interest. This worked at first, but after a while they forgot about giving me any right of reply, and undue coverage was given to some correspondents who were clearly mad. They were the kind of correspondents, to whom, when they wrote to me directly, I would respond, as Disraeli had done: 'Dear Mr Bloggins, I think you should be told that some offensive idiot is writing letters using your name. You might want to have him stopped. Yours sincerely etc.'

I was libelled from time to time: it was par for the course. Occasionally I would threaten action and get an apology. This would be published in print so small that no one could see, on a page which no one would ever read, and so long after the libel that no one would realise what it related to. The truth is that an MP needs the media more than the media needs the MP, so I never actually sued the newspaper. There were also such marvellous headlines as 'Refuse dump chaos: MP steps in'; 'Silent vigil: MP speaks out', and my favourite, 'Porno film row: MP acts'. In time the *Burton Mail* became known, after a prominent left-wing trade union leader of the time, as 'The Lawrence Daily'. I could not have been more pleased. I felt I had earned that accolade.

9

My Early Years as an MP

'Every tradition grows ever more venerable ... The reverence due to it increases from generation to generation. The tradition finally becomes holy and inspires awe.'

(Nietzsche: *Human, All Too Human*)

I doubt whether anyone who has not been a member of parliament can really appreciate the feeling of awe that comes upon the new MP when he or she first walks into parliament, sits in the chamber, and becomes part of the historic democratic process, with all its splendid pageant and tradition.

For nearly 600 years the Palace of Westminster has been at the very centre of the nation's life – and now this wonderful place was to become for me, a nobody in particular, my workplace and the centre of my life. Throughout my 23 years in parliament, I often went into the chamber to sit through a debate in which I could make no contribution, or even in which I had little particular interest, just to remind my soul where I was, and how important and almost sacred it all was to me.

And when my political soul had been touched enough – which I am afraid happened quite frequently when, in the 1970s and 80s, debates dragged on through the night – the soul of the lawyer in me led me to sit on my own, in the dimly lit vastness of Westminster Hall. Here, for hundreds of years, had sat the Royal Courts of Justice – the courts of Chancery, of Common Pleas, of Kings Bench and of the Exchequer. In this very hall, in February 1649, King Charles the First was tried by a court of some 57 commissioners who, he insisted, had no power to try him, and who then found him guilty of treason. Here, too, were held the trials of the Earl of Strafford (Oliver Cromwell's general in Ireland), of Warren Hastings (Governor-General of India), and every state trial until the late nineteenth century. At the far end of the hall one can still see the entrance to what was the court of Star Chamber. And outside the Hall, in New Palace Yard, William Wallace, the great

Scottish hero, was hung, drawn and quartered; and the head of Guido 'Guy' Fawkes was skewered onto a pole, as was the disinterred head of Oliver Cromwell – dreadful reminders to the many ordinary people of London who in their daily lives used Westminster Hall as a market place or social centre, of the high price of treachery.

In my first days, I went into the chamber to listen, and to get the measure of the place – and of my colleagues. One Friday afternoon, as I sat on the opposition benches minding my own business, a short, dark squat man whom I had never seen before, came up to me and barked out an order: 'Object when the next Bill is announced,' before turning and hurrying away. I later learnt that it was usual Friday afternoon procedure for the Speaker to announce a string of Private Member's Bills, which, if not objected to, would automatically pass through to the next stage without any debate. The main political parties did not much like these backbench Bills, and they often objected to them. The Bill would then be put back to a date when it could be debated properly, and opposed. But neither the government nor the opposition wanted to be seen objecting to Bills – for example, providing a free mechanised wheelchair for every disabled person – which the media might have popularised but which would have cost a fortune, lest a national frenzy were triggered in the weekend tabloids. In such circumstances the government would get an unsuspecting backbencher to object to it. Unless the press gallery had been tipped off in advance about the objection, they might not be able to see who was actually objecting. As Sir Michael Caine might say, not a lot of people know that – and certainly I did not. Perhaps there ought to be a training programme for new MPs.

Anyway, I did not object. In fact nobody objected. The barker rushed over to me in a rage and asked, I thought a trifle unreasonably, why the bloody hell I had not objected as he had instructed me. I told him that I was not in the habit of being ordered to do things, by someone who I did not know, and who had not bothered either to introduce himself or to explain why I should object. I asked him who he was. He told me he was a Conservative Whip called Nigel Lawson. I had not been in the place five minutes, had not yet made my maiden speech, and I was in the 'black book' again, for being unreliable and too stupid to recognise, respect and obey a future outstanding Chancellor of the Exchequer.

I just missed something even more momentous, on one of those very early days. Never being sure that I would be able to leave the Commons before the last train to Walton-on-Thames at midnight, and parliament having a good free car park, I mostly drove into London from Shepperton. The journey took me just over an hour. Usually my route home began round Parliament Square, right turn along Horseguards Parade, left into the Mall, and up Constitution Hill past Buckingham Palace, to Hyde Park Corner. On Wednesday 20 March I decided to try out another route: along Birdcage Walk to Buckingham Palace, then turning up Constitution Hill and missing out the Mall. This was a fortuitous change for me.

Three friends of mine, Kevin Winstain (a senior barrister in my chambers), Brendan Quirke (a solicitor, loyal to me and to chambers), and Brian McConnell (a *Daily Mirror* crime reporter, whom I had got to know when he covered the Kray trials), had invited me to join them for a drink at El Vino's wine bar in Fleet Street. I had to refuse, because I needed to be in the House for that evening's votes. I was fortunate to have such an excuse, for these were three really thirsty Irishmen and I would have been way out of my league. After an hour or three, they departed that famous hostelry for the Irish club in Eaton Square. This happened to be at about the very time that I was leaving the House. Had I taken my usual route up the Mall, I could well have been just behind or even just in front of them.

Halfway along the Mall their taxi came upon a limousine and another car slewed at an angle across the road. A man with a revolver was shooting into one of the cars. Kevin and Brendan, in no condition to get involved in violent intervention, took evasive action – onto the taxi floor. Brian, exercising the fearlessness for which the British press is renowned, decided that he was fit enough to get stuck in. He got out of the taxi and advanced towards the gunman.

'Give me that gun immediately,' he ordered the astonished attacker. He was rewarded with a bullet in the chest. He did not find out until he awoke later in hospital that he had in fact intervened in an attempt to kidnap Her Royal Highness The Princess Anne. Her chauffeur and two policemen were also shot and wounded – the revolver of her bodyguard having dramatically and most unfortunately jammed at the crucial moment. Others coming onto the scene wrestled the gunman to the ground. Ian Ball, the attacker, was quite mad, and in due course went to Broadmoor where he remains to this day.

For his act of bravery, Brian McConnell received the Queen's Medal for Gallantry, and probably never had to pay for a drink again. Had I been on the scene, whether in drink or not, I have little doubt that I would have shown the same exemplary bravery – as Kevin and Brendan.

Fortunately. Her Royal Highness was unharmed, though, of course, well and truly shaken.

A Tunisian holiday

The summer parliamentary vacation being the only time I could accept criminal trials lasting more than a day or two, we began the habit of going away over Christmas. In 1974 Gloria, Rachel and myself took another very cheap package-tour holiday for a week to Tunisia, where we greatly enjoyed ourselves. We flew with Laker Airways.

As we were taxiing for take-off at Tunis airport for the return flight, the pilot announced that he did not like the sound of one of the engines, and was returning us to the airport lounge so that it could be inspected. The hours began to tick by, with no information, and the many children with us growing hungry and restless. The passengers due back at work in England next day, and the parents of the smaller children, began to wonder aloud what was happening. Through the airport lounge window onto the runway we could see our plane, and one or two men, who did not seem to be in too great a hurry, gesticulating with what looked like pocket torches and screwdrivers in their hands.

I searched for a flight attendant (in those days called an air-hostess), to find out how long we were expecting to be there, but there was no one in sight. An hour later, and four hours into our waiting time, I managed to find an attendant who told me that no one had told her what was happening either. I asked if we could have food and drinks. She said there was nothing available at the airport. I asked whether we could make telephone calls to those waiting for us to arrive at Heathrow. She did not know about that: there were no mobile phones in those days and long-distance calls would have cost a fortune, even if a public telephone could be found at the airport.

Rumblings of discontent grew ever louder. Then one of the passengers stood up, called for order, announced that he was a trade union shop steward, and proposed that we organise ourselves immediately for action. A group of us would march on the airport operations tower, and make known our demands. I gulped in astonishment. Did this idiot not realise that, only a few months earlier, there had been an attempted hijacking at this very airport? Hostages had been taken, and the Tunisian authorities had blown the plane up on the runway!

I felt obliged to say something. I did not divulge that I was a Tory MP, of course, lest it provoke the militants to even more immediate action. I did, however, say that I thought we should wait a little longer before doing anything that might upset our sensitive hosts. There was a murmur of support, and a new urgency was given to my search for someone who could tell me where the captain of the plane could be found. I eventually came upon a flight attendant who reluctantly divulged the captain's whereabouts: he was sleeping at the Hilton Hotel. What? While we were all hanging around dog-tired, broke, with nothing to eat or drink, children becoming fractious and all held in ignorance of what was happening, the captain and his merry crew were relaxing in five-star luxury?

Armed with the captain's name and hotel room number, I rang him. He was not best pleased to be disturbed. I let him have it. I was a lawyer, and I would be suing the airline. I was an MP, and I would be raising this matter on the floor of the House. There was about to be a riot from a lot of angry blast-furnace workers and shop stewards. An international incident of terrifying proportions was about to be unleashed, as armed security guards, recently experienced in anti-terrorist action, mowed down innocent passengers with their machine guns. Moreover I would be speaking to Freddie Laker personally, about the cruel and callous way his airline treated the women and children who had entrusted themselves to his care. The world would hear of this – if, as increasingly became unlikely, we survived this terrible ordeal.

The captain suddenly sounded concerned. He told me that there was mechanical trouble with the plane, but that engineers were fixing it.

'What, with pocket torches and screwdrivers?' I asked.

'There is nothing more I can do,' he said.

'Oh yes there is,' I responded, raising my voice over the telephone. 'First, you could get out of bed and come to the airport. Second, you could find out exactly what is happening with the plane and when we can expect to be airborne. Third, you could brief the stewardesses to update us or, better still, do it yourself. Fourth, you could make sure the women and children, particularly, had some food and drink. Fifth, you could arrange for us to telephone our homes to reassure worried families without us having to pay. Finally, you could please do all this immediately, and meet me at the lobby entrance in fifteen minutes.'

The captain, although he cannot have been too happy with my tone of imperious command, and certainly ignorant of the fact that I had long ago been but a senior aircraftsman, conceded the need for action. Another lesson learned: MPs frighten the life out of officialdom and therefore wield considerable influence. I returned to the concourse, gathered the heads of the families about me, explained what had happened, and won general approval for my action. We were, though, all worried about flying at all in a plane that the screwdriver and pocket-torch gang might just be pretending to have mended.

The captain arrived, and set in train everything I had asked for. He confessed to me that he also had his doubts that the repairs were being effected by mechanics who knew what they were about. According to Laker Airways, no other plane was immediately available, but they were trying to re-route a jumbo jet that had been flying Arabs to Mecca. This was bound to take some time. I said that he could hardly expect everyone to hang around the airport terminal, and asked why he could not arrange for us all to be put up at the Hilton Hotel until the new plane arrived. My air of authority as quite obviously a leader of men continued working: he agreed, and arranged it. Next morning a bus collected us from our luxurious hotel, and we flew back – only 26 hours late. Laker Airways collapsed soon afterwards. I hope that the cost of this adventure was not the reason.

Unknown to me, one of the passengers on our flight happened to be the editor of the *London Evening News*, then still in existence, widely read and influential. It seems that I had not just impressed myself. Unlike the doubtful publicity I had received over Olga, an article in the evening edition on the day we returned did me no political harm whatsoever. Parliamentary colleagues patted me on the back. Ministers congratulated me. Secretaries smiled encouragingly. My political future was assured. My only disappointment was that this time, I had no church fete to open.

The House of Commons

1974 was not a good year for the British people. After the general election, which Labour had only won by 301 seats to the Tories' 297, and there was soon a hung parliament, Harold Wilson gave the miners a 35% pay rise, some nurses received 50%, teachers 32%, top civil servants 28% and local government officers 13%. Inevitably the economy was in chaos and inflation shot up – from 16% to 20%. We were only permitted to take £50 with us when we went abroad, and proud Britons were humiliated when European friends felt so sorry for us they would insist on paying for everything. In Cyprus, for which we had part responsibility as a guarantor power, a civil war broke out and there was slaughter. From Northern Ireland, conflict spread to the mainland, with bombs exploding on a coach on the M62, in Pall Mall, at Marble Arch, at the Tower of London, in a public house in Woolwich, at two public houses in Guildford and Birmingham and even in the MPs' offices, off Westminster Abbey . There were many deaths, and much maiming, mayhem and misery. As if the year was not bad enough, we also failed to beat Germany in the World Cup. So to cheer Britain up, and to strengthen his weak majority, Harold Wilson decided to call another election in October. But the nation refused to be cheered, and gave Labour no more than a three-seat majority over all the other parties.

On 1 May 1974 I delivered my maiden speech in defence of the grammar schools that Labour was hell-bent on destroying. It gave me an opportunity to pay tribute to my predecessor John Jennings, who had been a local teacher and headmaster. We were not supposed to be party political in our maiden speeches, but we were allowed to speak of the needs of our constituencies. So I spoke about the two excellent Burton grammar schools which were being forced to become comprehensive, despite the fact that they provided high-quality education, gave parents some choice in the education of their children, and yet were to receive no more money to fund the changes. This was educational vandalism in the name of social engineering, yet the truth was that it would be the children of the working-class families who were mostly enjoying the privileges of Burton's grammar school education, who would be the real losers. Labour either could not see it, or did not care.

The speech went down very well in the constituency. Some activists in the local 'Save our Schools' campaign, from Labour and Liberal backgrounds, decided to join the Burton Conservatives and to work for us. Later, the 'kangaroo courts' being run from Birmingham by the Transport and General Workers Union, together with the widespread anger at their leader's abuse of power, were also to bring trade unionists and former Labour supporters into the Conservative camp to work for my re-election. Reg Prentice, the education secretary, who put the Labour government's case against me in my debate, dramatically resigned from the government and his party five years later, and crossed the floor to join the Conservatives. The issue that moved him so greatly was the destruction of the grammar schools! So I invited him to Burton to boost our campaign. He came, and his visit, very popular on our side, unnerved Labour activists in the constituency. Shortly after this visit, Reg became a Conservative minister.

* * *

After the 1974 defeats, the Tory party had to decide whom it wanted to lead it: Ted Heath, the two-time loser, or someone else. The officers of the 1922 Committee (the body consisting of all backbench Conservative MPs), at a famous meeting at the Carlton Club, decided that Ted must go. Margaret Thatcher – a woman! – decided to throw her hat into the ring.

We organised meetings in Burton and in Uttoxeter, to see how our party workers felt about her. To my surprise, since most of our activists were traditionalists, these gave her overwhelming support. I said that I would, of course, take their views into account in making my own decision, but I was unhappy about sacking our leader just because he had lost two elections in one year. So I supported Ted on the first ballot, and he lost. Although I very much wanted Mrs Thatcher to succeed him, I did not vote for her on the second ballot either. She was so obviously going to win, and win handsomely, that I cast my vote for Geoffrey Howe, a friend whom I did not want to see humiliated. I was one of only 19 MPs who voted for him. The vote being by secret ballot, I never told him or anyone but Gloria. I admire Geoffrey for his very considerable achievements as Solicitor-General, Chancellor of the Exchequer and Foreign Secretary – but now I am afraid, although still a friend, I find it difficult to forgive him for his betrayal of Margaret Thatcher and his role in bringing her down.

There being national astonishment that the Conservative party should have chosen a woman leader, Margaret Thatcher arranged meetings with groups of her backbenchers, and sought advice about making herself and the party more acceptable to the electorate. I suggested that she would do that by visiting as many large factories as possible, to let the doubters and the workers see her and realise just how right the party had been. She took the advice. I also suggested that every Tory candidate and their spouses should have a photograph taken with her, to display in constituency offices, something that had apparently never been done before. My picture still hangs proudly in the Burton office – and we have a copy at home. Unfortunately, I must confess to my reader that these two suggestions were, I think, about my only contributions to the future greatness of Thatcherism.

Roy Jenkins wrote that Margaret Thatcher despised people. He was quite wrong. She was charming and friendly not only to backbenchers but to most other people who met her, precisely because she did like people. Never too busy to stop for a chat, she always took time to help her parliamentary colleagues by signing birthday cards for our very old or sick constituents. She used to join us for lunch or dinner in the Commons dining room, and she had a disconcerting tendency not to leave, out of the politeness of her upbringing, until we had also finished. On one occasion, when my daughter Rachel was six years old and Mrs Thatcher happened to be sitting at dinner on the next table, Rachel nagged me to be introduced to her. I did so. They talked on and on about Easter bunnies and little girl's things, while matters of state waited. On another occasion, Gloria and I had invited the widow of Dr Alan Freeman, our local Conservative county councillor, to dinner in the House. We introduced her to Margaret Thatcher, by then prime minister, who resisted all efforts by her stalwart aide, Michael Alison, to drag her away for more urgent business, so that she could stay to chat and commiserate on the loss of the husband whom she had never met. We are all human, and we do not forget such kindness.

But things did not really improve for the Conservatives after Margaret Thatcher's election as leader. Whenever party fortunes sink, we are inclined to believe that it has never been like that before. It often has. In fact, things were so bad at that time that Rear-Admiral Morgan Giles, war hero and MP for Winchester, tried to steady the ship and bring us to our senses. At a meeting of the 1922 Committee he rose to his feet, and in loud and commanding stentorian tones exhorted us all with the words, 'Pro bono publico: no bloody panico!'

Things only really began to improve for the party, after Harold Wilson stepped down as prime minister. He had said that he did not intend to stay long after the 1974 election, but it was still a surprise to nearly everyone when he resigned on 16 March 1976, just after his sixtieth birthday. His successor, James Callaghan, only knew five days before – at about the same time as I did.

During a debate on government spending, I was sitting at a table in the 'aye' lobby, signing letters to my constituents. Labour was about to suffer a major defeat by 28 votes, because 37 of its left-wingers refused to support the government. While the debate was in progress, and the noise level in the chamber was beginning to rise, the door from the chamber burst open, and a very red-faced Wilson rushed out. He had to say something to someone, and I was the only one there.

'Well if that's how they fucking want it, they can fucking have it,' he expleted to me, then turned and rushed off. Moments later, while I was still savouring the moment at which a British prime minister sought to

145

share a historic moment of party grief with me, the same door burst open again, and Labour's Chief Whip Bob Mellish descended the same stairs. He too felt the need to say something to someone, and I was still there.

'At least your ex-fucking leader could make up his mind. That's more than our fucking leader can do,' he too expleted to me, and he also turned and rushed off. It was quite fun being there at such a small but vital moment in our national cavalcade – and noting the elegance of the language used by great persons.

My early attempts to speak in the chamber were not very successful. I was, it is true, called to speak several times by Speaker Selwyn Lloyd, but only to fill in the minute or two before the front-bench speakers were timed to wind up the debates, as they usually did thirty years ago. After several months of such treatment, I complained to him. Had I not been in the House long enough to be allowed to make a speech lasting ten minutes with some content? If I went on failing to catch his eye for a proper speech, there was not a great deal of point in my being in parliament. Selwyn was grumpy and not particularly friendly to new boys, quite unlike his more popular and encouraging successors, George Thomas and Jack Wetherill. But after my complaint he did become less grumpy towards me, and started calling me to make proper speeches now and then. So I spent hours in the chamber, trying to be active at question time and in debate. I also endeavoured to make myself useful to the party by producing briefing papers, on such political-legal issues as Labour's disgraceful handling of the Shrewsbury picket affair and then of the Clay Cross miners.

In May 1976 I was in the chamber when the Labour government, on the parliamentary ropes because one of its ministers had died, thereby cutting its effective majority to one, was about to lose its flagship bill to nationalise the aircraft and shipbuilding industries. The clever Tory MP for Tiverton, Robin Maxwell-Hyslop, had persuaded Speaker George Thomas (and his team of advisers), that the Bill, because it was 'hybrid' (a mixture of private and public elements) had first to be dealt with, according to the rules, by a Select Committee. Since this would delay the Bill for months, the government decided to table a motion to nullify the Speaker's ruling. As if that was not bad enough, when it became clear that the government was going to lose the vote, it decided to cheat. It did this by counting Tom Pendry, a government Whip as a voter, when he had agreed to 'pair' with a Tory colleague not to vote. 'Pairing' is a traditional and widely used informal arrangement, founded on mutual trust, whereby two MPs on either side of the House agree not to vote on an issue so that neither side can score an advantage. To cheat on this was about as disgraceful an offence to hallowed constitutional and parliamentary procedure as it was possible to commit.

Possibly ignorant that abuse had occurred, and triumphant (or inebriated) at their surprising victory, Labour MPs broke with tradition and jumped onto the benches singing the Red Flag. In sheer exasperation, Michael Heseltine, the Conservative frontbench spokesman on the Bill, picked up the mace, the symbol of the Queen's authority, and made mock offer of it to Labour. More outrage and noise. The Speaker suspended the sitting for 'grave disorder.' The editors of the tabloids, the cartoonists and television (before parliament was televised) chose to leave as the enduring image of the day the picture of Tarzan in a loincloth furiously brandishing a club, rather than the far more significant and infamous behaviour of a Labour government cheating to secure its policy of nationalisation by any means.

A cross-party issue

If there is any theme about my political recollections, it is how being a politician interlinked with my being a lawyer. One example of this occurred very soon after I entered parliament, when the legal powers of arrest by the Transport Police, the subject of many of my Tower Bridge criminal cases, became a political issue.

It was then a central principle of our criminal law – not yet qualified by legislation – that a person accused of crime had a right to remain silent, and did not have to explain himself: the burden of proving guilt lay entirely with the prosecution. To require the accused to prove his innocence when crime was alleged against him was generally accepted as placing excessive power in the hands of the police. If it were otherwise, the police might not always choose to remember, when giving evidence in court, that a defendant they believed to be guilty had in fact given an innocent explanation. There was also the danger that someone, incapable of explaining himself, might be wrongly convicted. But for some reason, the Transport Police had been given the power, not vested in any other police force in the land, to arrest, and charge, when there was no other evidence, those found leaving British Transport property in possession of articles which they would not or could not explain.

My friend Ian Percival QC (the MP for Southport and later Solicitor-General in Mrs Thatcher's government), told me that this power had

147

reappeared in the latest British Transport Private Bill, and was expected to go through 'on the nod,' unless someone objected to it at the next Friday afternoon sitting. I duly went into the chamber and shouted 'object', in the approved way, so that the Bill had to go over to another date to be more fully considered. British Transport, of course, found this most irritating and inconvenient. Their lawyers descended upon me. Did I know what I was doing? I thought I did. Did I realise that by objecting to the Bill as a whole I was putting in jeopardy the future of British Transport? Possibly, but then needs must. What did I want? The deletion of the one offending clause that went contrary to the whole spirit of British justice. Certainly not! They seemed confident that either political forces would be brought to bear upon me from on high to withdraw my objection, or that the demands of my barrister's practice would make it impossible for me to be present to shout 'object' next time the Bill came up in the chamber. They misjudged both me and my party. I kept being present on Friday afternoons to shout 'object'. They kept coming to see me. I kept repeating my objection. They continued to do nothing to remove the clause. I decided to enlist powerful support.

If one looks upon political ideology as 'circular,' rather than 'linear,' one can see how the libertarian 'right' might sometimes go full circle and link up with the libertarian 'left.' This happened during my political career with a number of issues affecting the liberty of the subject. Some of my strongest supporters against the mass-medication of the water supply by fluoridation were left-wingers like Tony Benn. So it was with the civil liberty issue of the burden of proof. I asked John Mendleson, the extremely left-wing Labour MP for Penistone, to help to persuade his government of the danger of allowing the Transport Police to continue to have this power. My barrister colleague, Alex Lyon (who was MP for York and Minister of State at the Home Office, and who later married his private secretary at the department, Claire Short), was not much interested in the point when I raised it. But such was the knife-edge upon which Harold Wilson's first government was balanced that he showed much more interest when Mendleson raised it with him. The clause was eventually withdrawn and I withdrew my objection to the Bill. The future of British Transport was, after all, safe in my hands.

Capital Punishment

My first really big parliamentary moment came on 11 December 1975 when, having been lucky in a ballot for backbench motions, I moved

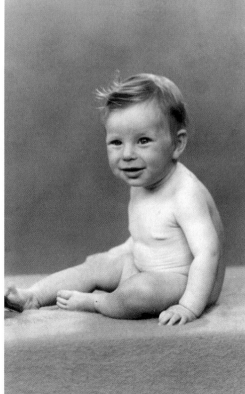

Left: My parents' wedding.

Below left: With my mother and father, aged seven.

Below right: Me, aged six months.

Left: My cousin, 1950s pop singing star Alma Cogan.

Below: BGS cricket team.

Above: Our wedding: 3rd April 1966 at West London Synagogue, Upper Berkeley Street.

Left: At my call to the Bar – before my cases and causes took their toll!

Below: Rowing on the Thames in the 'Legal Eight' boat with Greville Janner (losing his wig), Ken Hind CBE (MP for West Lancashire) and Sir Nicholas Lyall QC (MP for Mid-Bedfordshire and Solicitor-General).

Above: With Margaret Thatcher and Gloria, 1976.

Below: A visit to Burton by Aerospace Minister Michael Heseltine, February 1974, with Gloria, Cedric Insley and Danny Wallace (Chairman).

Campaigning in Burton: *Above,* a walkabout in Burton market, *Below,* with farmer constituents.

Left: Presenting my National Lottery Bill to Speaker Wetherill.

Below: *Times* cartoon following Home Affairs Comittee meeting with MI5.

Bottom: As a Home Affairs spokesman with Robert Maclennan (Liberal Democrat) and Tony Blair (Labour).

Some Kray trial
personalities, sketched by the author.

Babes in Wood court uproar

UPROAR broke out in a court today when unemployed labourer Russell Bishop was cleared of murdering "Babes in the Wood" Karen Hadaway and Nicola Fellows.

Fighting erupted at Lewes Crown Court when the not-guilty verdict was announced. Bishop's brother Alex screamed with delight and leapt from his place in the public gallery into the dock.

He was immediately grabbed around the arms and throat by prison officers and policemen.

Bishop's mother Sylvia who

had been shaking with emotion shouted: "Let me get at the boy."

As she and her husband Roy leapt to their feet they were surrounded by more policemen and scuffles broke out.

Mrs Bishop shouted and swore at a policewoman as punches started to be aimed in all directions.

In the middle of the mayhem Bishop himself shouted at his family: "That's enough, let's have some respect—pack it in."

● "I'll sue over agony."—Page Five.

Russel Bishop: "Let's have some respect."

Above L–R: The Kray twins; Denis Nilsen – serial killer; Daniel Morrell – 14-year-old victim of the bin bag beasts murder.

Left: Russell Bishop – acquitted of Brighton *Babes in the Wood* murders.

Below: 27th July 1963 – Mandy Rice-Davies (left), who rose to fame for her part in the 'Profumo Affair', sits in a car with Christine Keeler after the first day's hearing at the Old Bailey in the trial of Stephen Ward.

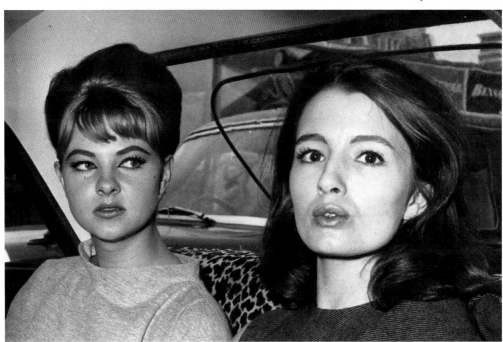

Left: Portrait by Stephen Ward of one of his ladies.

Below: There being no photograph as wireless-operator on a storm-tossed speeding target-towing launch on a NATO exercise in the Atlantic in 1956: this as captain and crew aboard the Gloria-Sarah becalmed on the Thames at Putney 1973.

Above: With Refusenik leader Professor Lerner and former Labour Defence Secretary Roy Mason in Moscow.
Below: With Israeli Prime Minister Yitzhak Shamir in Tel Aviv.

Above: With President Pinochet and Jim Lester MP in Santiago, 1984.
Below: With Israeli Prime Minister Binyamin Netanyahu and MPs David Sumberg and Greville Janner in London.

Left: With Inkatha Freedom Party President Chief Mangosutha Buthelezi in Kwa Zulu Natal.

Below: Burton Conservatives 1977. L–R David Simpson (agent); John Starkie (Conservative Central Office agent); the MP, me; Sir Clifford Gothard (president); the MP's wife; Lady Gothard; Councillor Elsie Layden (Women's Chairman); and Joe Harvey (Association Chairman and a former Chief Constable).

Left: With Pakistan Prime Minister Benazir Bhutto.

Below: With Indian Deputy Prime Minister Jagjivan Ram.

Welcoming Her Majesty The Queen at Burton railway station, 1983.

'That this House demands Capital Punishment for Terrorist Offences causing Death.'

I had caught the moment. The bombing campaign of 1974 had continued into 1975. As well as the terrorism in Northern Ireland, there had been horrifying atrocities in London, when brave soldiers and innocent citizens had been blown to pieces in the streets. A public opinion poll indicated that 88% of the public supported my motion. It was more likely than it had ever been, since the abolition of the death penalty a decade before, that parliament would respond to such very strong public opinion, and might vote for the death sentence to be restored, at least for killing by terrorists. Unusually, I was given a full day debate, and the House was crowded. The Prime Minister attended, and the Leader of the opposition never moved from her seat.

My opening speech lasted, with interruptions, for almost half an hour. I gave three reasons for a favourable vote: the failure of life imprisonment to deter such killings; the likelihood that more innocent lives would be saved; and my belief that we could not continue flouting the wishes of the overwhelming majority of the people we represented in parliament.

I listed the bombing atrocities which had occurred for the second year running: at the Naval and Military Club in Piccadilly, at two telephone exchanges in London, at Selfridges, at Harrods, at a shopping centre in Bristol, at a waterworks at Walthamstowe, at John Lewis's in Manchester, at a jeweller's shop in Kensington and at a boutique in Victoria. Then, after a short lull in which bombs stuffed with iron screws and ballbearings deliberately to cause the maximum horrific injury, had been defused by brave soldiers in Hampstead, bombs went off again in Putney and Bond Street. Ross McWhirter, a prominent Conservative candidate, was assassinated, and an attempt was made on the life of Ted Heath. Bombs tore people apart at a public house in Caterham, in the foyer of the Park Lane Hilton, at the Portman Hotel, at Green Park underground station, at Lockets restaurant in Westminster, at a trattoria in Mount Street, in Connaught Square, in Scott's restaurant, Walton's restaurant and in a public house in Maidstone.

'In all,' I said, 'since this House last voted that life imprisonment was the best we could do by way of a deterrent, there have been 30 bombs, 243 people injured and, by divine providence, only 10 people killed in England. The violence has got worse. The bombs now come without warning and have been planted more indiscriminately. They have been made more bestial in their nature and we have had the first doorstep assassination ... There is a widespread belief that when we are forced to withdraw our troops from Northern Ireland there will be an amnesty for political terrorists.'

Was capital punishment a deterrent? I insisted that ordinary voters believed it to be, and that they were as likely to know what deterred ordinary people as any academic or senior police officer. The IRA clearly believed it was: they not only used capital punishment themselves as a deterrent, but on the last occasion that parliament had debated the subject, their leader had been worried enough about the harm that it would do to the terrorist cause to threaten to take the life of two British soldiers for every terrorist sentenced to death.

I attempted to answer each of the objections raised against capital punishment: martyrdom, reprisals, hostages, jury acquittals, use of juveniles, the uncivilised nature of vengeance and the rest. Despite a challenge from Brian Walden (the Labour MP for Birmingham Ladywood, later to become a television personality) and Labour cries of 'scaremongering,' I ended with the forecast that, if we did not take public concern seriously, a likely consequence would be that the public would take the law into their own hands – as had already happened in Northern Ireland, when Protestant loyalists, despairing of government action, had turned to terrorism.

The debate contained some really excellent and powerful speeches. Most speakers conceded that capital punishment might well be a deterrent, but argued against restoration both as a matter of principle and on the ground of impracticality. Labour's John Mackintosh, the former Conservative Home Secretary Robert Carr, the future Conservative Foreign Office Minister Ian Gilmour, and the Liberal Emlyn Hooson QC, all thought that it would stimulate not diminish terrorism, and that it would be too difficult in practical terms to restore it. On the other hand, Sir Hugh Fraser (my senior political neighbour as MP for Stafford) said that the death penalty would be a statement of the community's total abhorrence of an outrageous crime; Eldon Griffiths (speaking for the Police Federation), said that rank and file policemen were overwhelmingly in favour of restoration; and Mark Carlisle (a former Conservative home office minister and future Secretary of State for Education), said that he had changed his mind from being an abolitionist to becoming a restorationist, both because in his view it would deter, and because he was persuaded by the strength of public opinion.

The Home Secretary, Roy Jenkins, wound up the debate against my motion. He said that we owed our constituents our judgement even against their strong views. The Commissioner of Police for London had told him that to bring back capital punishment would weaken the police, and that was also the opinion of the great majority of those who had responsibility for dealing with terrorism. I said, in the very brief reply I was allowed, that three groups of people would think we were out of our minds if we said no to the motion: the police, the public and the terrorists themselves, who were certainly not deterred by life imprisonment with its probability of amnesty.

The House voted 232 for my motion and 361 against. Parliament had once again defied the wishes of the people upon whose votes we depended. Roy Jenkins, not wishing to court further unpopularity, refused to go on any television programme to discuss the matter with me.

A few weeks later, after we had been playing soccer together for the House of Commons (Westminster Wanderers) against the press, I drove the Reverend Robert Bradford, the Ulster Unionist MP for Belfast, to Heathrow. In the debate, he had made a very powerful speech, supported strongly by the Reverend Ian Paisley, in which he warned that the terrorists would win if we compromised our attitude to the punishment we inflicted. He went from the airport to his constituency office to hold his weekly surgery. There, an IRA gunman walked into his office – and shot him dead.

I was given an armed guard in the constituency, and my constituency offices had to be altered to provide better protection for the constituency agent, first David Simpson and then Shirley Stotter, the staff and volunteers. Two armed policemen would sit outside the room in which I held my weekly surgeries, and would follow me everywhere for the next two years.

On Friday 30 March 1979 at 3.30pm, I finished dictating to Felicity, my secretary, and rushed out to collect my car from the House of Commons car park. I was trying to miss the worst of the Friday afternoon traffic to Burton, but I had first to collect a brief from chambers to read over the weekend. I drove quickly to the Temple about a mile away. There was a phone calling for me as I hurried up the stairs. It was Felicity.

'Thank God you are all right,' she said, 'A bomb has gone off in the car park, and someone was leaving in a car. I thought it had to be you.' Since it must have taken a few minutes for news of the bomb to reach her, and I had taken only five minutes to get to chambers, I must have missed the bomb by seconds.

It seems that two members of the Irish National Liberation Army, pretending to be workmen, had managed to get into the Commons underground car park to place a mercury tilt-switch and explosive under the car of war hero Airey Neave. As he drove up the slope on his way out, it blew him to pieces. He was Margaret Thatcher's campaign manager and had been destined to become her Secretary of State for Northern Ireland. I had given him a lift back to his flat in my car, only a day or two before.

Ronnie Bunting, the INLA chief-of-staff, was shot dead at his home the following year by – his widow always insisted – the SAS.

10

Politics Takes Over

'Politics are almost as exciting as war, and quite as dangerous. In war you can only be killed once, but in politics many times.'

(Sir Winston Churchill)

Politics, like any other trade, has to be learnt and requires total commitment. More than that, you can only really enjoy politics if you get fully involved. I spent the next few years doing just that. My criminal practice took a back seat.

What I found so appealing about being an MP was the range of interesting activities that came with serving the three masters in the public arena – my country, my political party and my constituents. You also have to like and get on with people, because that is what politics is all about. If most people bore you or get on your nerves, then politics is not for you. It helps if you believe that your party's policies will improve the human condition, for then you will want to spread them by word and influence. What happens when you have to choose between these three masters? Fortunately, it does not happen very often, but when it does I believe that nearly all MPs would put country first, constituents second, and their own political party third.

Country must be pre-eminent, for would not most people be prepared to go to war and, if necessary, die for it? If your party leaders decided to surrender the sovereignty of Britain to a European super-state and you believed that Britain should remain a sovereign nation ruled by a British parliament with a monarch at its head, would you be able to support your party?

But, of course, to become an MP and remain in parliament, you have to be elected: so your constituents are next in importance. They have got to like or at least respect you, and feel that you are doing a good job both in looking after their personal interests and representing them and the constituency at Westminster. There develops an almost mystical link between you. They may come to look upon you as their champion – even if they did not vote for you or share your politics. And you go back to the constituency at weekends, as much to charge your political batteries and to draw strength from your political life force, as for any other reason. You owe it to your constituents to work for their causes, and to help them and their families in their hour of need. Having the magic letters MP after your name gives you, as I have already said, the influence which helps to get many things done: a letter of complaint from an MP causes a stir and often results in action not only from ministers, civil servants and local government officers, but also from chairmen and managers of industry. I always wrote to the secretary of state in person, whom I could corner in a lobby or a corridor in parliament: I never wrote to the government official I was advised to contact. If my activity did not involve the government, I wrote directly to the chairman or chief executive of the company concerned: I never wrote to the 'human resources director' or sub-managers. By going directly to the top man or woman you nearly always achieve better results, because chiefs are the people who have the power to remove the incompetent, or, as the Americans say, 'to kick butt'!

Surgeries

Now that the 'expenses' scandal has so sadly lowered MPs in the public estimation, it is timely to recall how hard we all used to – and I do not doubt still do – work. I held 'surgeries' in Burton every Saturday morning. Constituents in need of help or advice would book an appointment with my office, but I never turned anyone away who came without a booking. If they could wait, I saw them at the end of my list. For 23 years my surgeries were full, and I never once had to advertise them in the local papers – so I lost that opportunity for free publicity. The surgery over, I would lunch at a nearby fish and chip shop, where my constituency agent, neighbouring MPs, councillors, town hall or other officials, and a variety of strange people got into the habit of joining me. Lunch over, I would visit disabled constituents who wished to see me, in their homes, attend meetings of organisations in the constituency, attend fetes and bazaars and, if I had no more pressing engagement, go along to cheer Burton Albion, the local football team, in whichever of the non-professional leagues they were currently appearing. On summer afternoons, when the sun was shining and people were in their gardens, I really enjoyed my canvassing. I recorded their problems on the spot, with my pocket tape recorder, which my secretary would convert into correspondence on the Monday. My constituents were always delighted (and impressed) to see immediate action being taken. For most of my years, I was writing about 200 letters a week on behalf of my constituents. I spent the parliamentary breaks, regarded by the media as our lengthy holidays, in the constituency, visiting factories, farms, industries, businesses, hospitals, schools, offices, old people's homes, local government departments, the police, the Crown Prosecution Service and a variety of social and charitable organisations. Even when I had to travel abroad with select committees in the vacation, I always made sure that I spent enough vacation time in the constituency. No one could – or ever did, as far as I know – accuse me of being a lazy MP!

Inadequate housing and social relationships were the most frequent problems. Overcrowding, council housing dilapidation and damp, problems with electricity, gas, the water supply, telephones, unpopular housing developments, defective roads, inadequate trains or bus services – the aggravations to daily life seemed relentless. There was also domestic violence, truancy and poor social service provision. There were also the neighbours from hell.

Then there were the difficulties facing local industry and businesses. The brewing industry, although one of the nation's successes, had labour problems, pollution problems, take-over problems, taxation and public house monopoly problems. Unhappily, because it was partly as a result of ill-thought-through policies of the Thatcher government, the beer-making part of the brewing industry is now much depleted in Burton. Other local industries faced planning, competition, transport, utilities and government red-tape problems. Farmers always had problems – of bovine tuberculosis, BSE, foot and mouth disease, agricultural subsidies, export bans, pollution restrictions, or low returns leading to the shortage of farm workers – with many farmers going out of business.

I lobbied at Westminster for a seemingly endless number of local causes: a second road bridge over the River Trent; flyovers across the A38; safer main roads in the constituency; bypasses for Uttoxeter and Tutbury; a new Burton hospital; an intensive-care baby unit; closed circuit television in public car parks and shopping areas; more policemen on the beat; a new magistrates court and police station; higher local government and police grants; and for job-producing subventions from central government. A member of parliament's constituency concerns and activities are continuous, diverse, and, if his endeavours are successful as many of them are, extremely satisfying. I do not think that the ordinary voter has any idea how much a busy MP has to do in his constituents' interest – I certainly did not before I decided that I wanted to become an MP.

Mostly I was being a social worker: sometimes I was even a psychologist. On one occasion an irate local GP, having waited in the queue to see me for much of the Saturday morning, demanded that I do something about a very minor road problem in a village. I let the doctor, who was upset and angry, go on and on. The loss of what must have been a precious morning of free time, and the degree of anger, seemed to be a high price to pay for such a small problem that I could have dealt with by post. I asked what the real problem was, and I was accused of not listening, 'like all MPs'. Then, bit by bit, the real reason for the visit emerged. The doctor just had to confide in someone about an acute personal and family problem. I listened and I was concerned. But at the end I had to say that I was no psychologist and, with the best will in the world, I felt that I could not be of much help. I said that some stressful professions, like the church and medicine, appointed one of their number locally to be a 'stress councillor', and since I was sure that there must be a local doctor who fulfilled that function, I would immediately try to find out who that was.

'Don't be so silly,' the doctor said, 'I *am* the "stress" councillor!' We both dissolved into gusts of laughter, and I was thanked for helping to lift the burden. Could any expensively trained psychologist have done more?

Burton's Muslim community

Muslims from District Mirpur in Pakistan formed the largest immigrant community in Burton. Soon after I became MP I was invited to join them to celebrate an important day, and to make a speech. They forgot to tell me what they were celebrating, and not wishing to show my ignorance, I did not ask. But I did telephone the ethnic minority desk at Conservative Central Office, and they told me that it must be the anniversary of the birth of the Prophet Mohammed. So I read up about the great man, and prepared a fine speech. Unfortunately, the celebration turned out to be in honour of Pakistan's Day of Independence, which I had not read up. As so often with my speeches, it did not matter very much. I began by saying that Pakistan would never have been founded if it had not been for the Prophet Mohammed – and went on to deliver my speech about his great works. My hosts were impressed by my deep interest in them, and my wide knowledge of their history, and there began a mutually respectful friendship that continued for nearly a quarter of a century.

In the 1983 general election, one street in the centre of Burton, whose residents were largely from the Pakistani community, put on a terrific display of support for me. Conservative banners, with my name writ large, stretched across the road, large portrait posters of me appeared in most of the windows, and as I canvassed door-to-door, men, women and children greeted me with their babes in arms, as though this would be a campaign to remember. I was almost embarrassed! When I eventually lost my seat, my closest Muslim Conservative workers were the ones with tears running down their cheeks.

Over the years the Muslim community in Burton grew in number as family members from Pakistan joined their settled families, and new families were started. I helped to get planning permission for one mosque, followed a few years later by another. I mediated conflicts between the groups within the community. I attended meetings and gave encouragement to the Community Relations Council. Practically every week families came to my surgery because the Home Office had turned down their young daughter's application to marry a man of their own religious faith and culture in Pakistan, and their wish to bring him to Britain to settle as fiancé or husband. I found out why that had happened, explained the reasons to the family, advised on the chances of a successful renewal of the application – and commiserated. Occasionally the girl would contact me later to say that she did not want to marry the man intended for her, but that if her father found out that she had approached me, he would be very upset and angry.

One delightful gentleman wrote enthusiastically to me as follows:

'Dear Sir, I would ardently present dinkum supplication to your goodself, for your kind perusal regarding the application made and lodged by my wife, to the British Embassy in Islamabad... Despite the fact that both my cases are pregnant with irrefutable authenticity and free from animadversion, I totally fail to understand the cornucopia of their lop-sided determination and impending procrastination despite bombardment of the correspondences sent by my solicitor.' He went on to ask me to write to everybody without unnecessary delay, and ended: 'I'm optimistic that a prompt electrification of magnanimity and your meticulous bathing with an aromatic soap of your highest globally-traversed consideration and approach could only give me a sigh of relief and solace from this mushrooming agonising and writhing suffering and despondency. I'm looking forward to seeing your good-self soon!'

He had obviously swallowed a dictionary! How could I have failed to pull out all the stops? I think I was successful – his wife was, after all a legitimate dependent.

I did not have as much success with male fiancés, who would often just arrive at Heathrow airport without any 'entry clearance' certificates. For some years, the sponsoring family member was able to ask his local MP to call up the immigration officer at an airport and stop the immediate deportation of the unqualified arrival, until his application had been more fully considered. Since long-haul flights from Pakistan or India tended to arrive in the middle of the night, MPs had to be woken up to provide this service. It was not popular at Westminster and, as the numbers and frequency of the demands for this service grew, it was eventually stopped.

It became clear to me that the process of granting and refusing these applications was thoroughly unsatisfactory and caused a great deal of emotional suffering. The sheer volume of applications, and the often doubtful qualifications of the civil servants burdened with the decisions, drove me to the conclusion that the fairest way to deal with the problem would be to introduce a cap on numbers. No one at the Conservative top table agreed with me. It has taken the massive growth in the number of immigrants under New Labour to move us in that direction.

In 1974, the size of Burton's immigrant community was small, and the elders of the family were able to keep their youngsters out of trouble. The whole family would be employed in the family business or in industries such as the biscuit factory in Ashby, which had come to rely upon labour from the Pakistani community. In time, as the community expanded, control became more and more difficult. As the elders lost influence, conflicts within the community grew, some youngsters began to be troublesome and problems proliferated. I had to try to be all things to all people. Not that the Burton immigrant community was particularly difficult. Mostly they were delightful and fitted well into the town, providing a wide range of public services, employment, professional support and sporting achievement. It was just that working for social harmony in a multi-racial society demanded a considerable proportion of the working life of an urban MP in the Midlands. I was fortunate that, being a member of an ethnic and religious minority myself, there was mutual respect and understanding between us for all of my years as Burton's MP.

The Burton Breweries Charitable Trust

For most of those years, I was also chairman of the Burton Breweries Charitable Trust. This had developed from a company, created in 1899, by the no fewer than forty Burton breweries then in existence. Its original purpose had been to preserve and to protect Burton's natural hard water which, filtering through the gypsum and gravel layers, gave Burton beer its world-renowned taste and quality. It had a secondary purpose: to look after the welfare of the skilled artisans who sank and maintained the wells, tapped the water and brewed the beer. When I became chairman, the company was called the Artisans Dwelling Company, and it owned many houses built to let to brewery workers for very low rents. My fellow directors were the managing directors of the four breweries still remaining in the 1980s and 90s – Allied, Bass, Marstons and, at first, Everards. We decided that since there now existed a welfare state, there was no longer a need for that particular kind of philanthropy. So we sold the houses to the local council (and to some of the tenants), and converted the money into a managed fund, from the interest of which we made grants on a regular basis to help organisations looking after young people in the Burton constituency. We had quarterly meetings at each of the breweries in turn, examined the investments for our fund with a professional adviser from one of the major finance houses in London, and allocated the gifts on the advice of the Staffordshire County Council Youth Officer.

Over 15 years, scouts, guides, Duke of Edinburgh award candidates, ethnic minority youth clubs, and individuals needing sponsorship for musical instruments or sailing ship training, received over £100,000. When I was no longer the MP, the breweries presented me with several hundred bottles of best Burton Ale with my picture on the label and a summary of these achievements, to give to my friends. Unfortunately there was a 'sell-by date' on the bottles – and I had passed mine!

Royal visit

In 1983 the Queen was coming to Burton. As Duke of Lancaster she owns the ruins of Tutbury Castle, which had housed the captive Mary

Queen of Scots for most of 1569 (while she was suspected of being complicit in Lord Darnley's murder), and for most of 1585 (when she was implicated in the Babington plot to murder Queen Elizabeth I). Then, from Chartley Castle on the border of my Burton constituency, Mary had been taken to Fotheringay to be tried and beheaded. Queen Elizabeth II also owns much of the surrounding farmland. The monarch, in a truncated version of the ancient 'royal progress' around England, visits her properties and, of course, the cities, towns and villages of the kingdom. Burton was very excited at the prospect of a royal visit – especially the children who could look forward to a day off school.

But shortly before the great event, the visit was cancelled. The Staffordshire police, at a time of widespread terrorism, said that they could not guarantee Her Majesty's safety when she arrived, as was proposed, by air at a small private leisure-flying airport, three miles outside Burton-upon-Trent. This seemed to me a poor reason for causing so much disappointment to so many people. The Queen would have been in no greater danger in Staffordshire than anywhere else she bravely went to be with her loyal subjects in the realm. I fired off letters and telephone calls, making myself a thorough nuisance to palace officials, the police hierarchy and local government officers alike.

Under the onslaught, officialdom relented, and at 10am on Friday 23 July, the royal train pulled slowly into a Burton railway station festooned with beautiful displays of flowers in hanging baskets. The Queen, her courtiers, ministers and other dignitaries alighted – to meet yet more dignitaries, the Lord Lieutenant, the chairman of the council, his chief executive, the aldermen and myself, together with our wives ranged along the platform.

Lest she disappoint the people of Burton, and perhaps to placate their angry MP, Her Majesty had decided to spend the night in the train at a railway siding up-line from Burton. It was a typically thoughtful and generous gesture. It may be that the warm and genuine greeting that she received in the constituency helped to remove any reservations the palace might have had about her next visit in 1986, when she came again, to name Burton's newly reconstructed district hospital, the 'Queens Hospital'.

Workload

Looking back over my 23 years as an MP, the sheer volume of my constituency activities staggers me. I had conducted 1100 weekly surgeries totalling 4000 hours of personal interviews; I had visited over 1500 local organisations; attended nearly 2000 engagements in the constituency (most of which were not party political); taken up over 33,000 personal problems for my constituents and written over 100,000 letters on their behalf. At my last election in 1997, I felt proudly able to boast that most families in the Burton constituency had been directly helped by me at some time. Sadly, for such is politics, this did not stop me losing my seat!

But apart from my work in the constituency, in the months after my first election, the pattern of my life away from the constituency also changed. When I was not in court, I would spend at least two to three hours a day going through the post and dictating letters to my secretary. The rest of the day I would spend reading newspaper articles, preparing speeches and articles of my own, broadcasting on national and local television and radio, meeting constituents and experts to discuss problems of national and local politics, and attending the daily party meetings on topics occupying parliament, held every hour on the hour in the evenings. I went into the chamber whenever there was a debate that particularly interested me. There is, of course, not enough time in the day to be knowledgeable and active on every political issue, so I concentrated on law and order and foreign affairs, with less frequent forays into social welfare, education and treasury matters. An MP has to trust the advice of those in his party who have made themselves experts in the subjects in which he has had no time to take a close interest. He has to rely as well on the whips, who guide him into whichever is the appropriate lobby, to vote in the party's best interests. Parliamentary activity is so hectic and complex that it is impossible for an MP to conduct his life in any other way.

I used to be on the go from early morning to late at night. My father had to phone my secretary to make appointments to see me when he was in London! Apart from lunch and dinner times, I never relaxed for longer than to snatch a quick cup of tea in the tearoom. After 23 years in the House I could not tell you what any of the barmen in the Commons bars or the smoking-room looked like, because I hardly ever went into them. Some evenings I would find myself shifting from foot to foot, and then realise that I had done nothing to make myself comfortable all day.

I once rushed out of the members library across the narrow public corridor to the members men's lavatory, unconsciously unzipping my trousers en route. Inside, I found myself standing next to Maurice

Macmillan, the MP for Farnham and son of Harold Macmillan. I told him how fortunate I thought I had been not to have bumped into any female colleague or secretary in my semi-undressed state. He told me that he had seen Winston Churchill in the same place in the same situation and had upbraided him thus: 'Winston, your fly is undone.'

To which the great man had replied, in his famously gutteral lisp, 'Maurice, that is not a matter which need cause you any particular concern, for it is a fact well-known, that a dead bird *never* falls out of its nest.'

It is strange that the contempt in which MPs today are held as a class is hardly ever directed at the individual MP who is admired and respected in his own constituency. This is obviously due to the work demanded of and done by the modern MP, and the respect that he or she must now show to constituents. Things have moved on from the days when, back in 1774, Anthony Henley, the MP for Shrewsbury, could show his contempt for his constituents who had asked him to oppose the Excise Bill:

Gentlemen,
I received yours and am surprised at your insolence in troubling me about the Excise. You know, what I very well know, that I bought you, and by God I am determined to sell you. And I know, what perhaps you think I do not know, that you are now selling yourselves to somebody else. And I know, what you do not know, that I am buying another borough. May God's curse light on you all. May your houses be as open and common to all Excise officers as your wives and daughters were to me, when I stood for your rascally Corporation,
    Yours,
        Anthony Henley

In my early days, I was one of the 'Friday MPs.' We were a band of half a dozen or so brothers who did the party's 'dirty work' on a Friday. Barely acknowledged, like the operatives of MI5 or MI6, we made sure that there were always Conservatives present for any Private Member's debates that were contrary to Conservative policy, and we were ready to take an active part in them, and to talk them out so that they made no progress. Our labours made it possible for our party leaders in particular to be in their constituencies or about the country on political business, instead of at Westminster hanging around in case there was a vote. This usually meant that Gloria had to collect Rachel after lunch, from her excellent Westward School in Walton-on-Thames, and travel in heavy Friday North Circular traffic to meet me at the Hendon home of our very kind friends, Josephine and Montague Sherborne (my talented colleague in the Kray trials and much else), as near to 4pm as possible. Then the three of us would begin the long haul together up the M1, M6 and A38.

In rain or snow, in the days before the M40 was built to take some of the strain from Friday night traffic heading north, the journey was seldom pleasant and was often horrendous. If we were lucky, we would arrive at Grove Farm by 8pm, get Rachel off to the babysitter, change clothes and arrive at the evening function – late. In my early days people would look at their watches and mutter to each other. They seemed to think that all we had had to do was to roll out of bed at the farm, throw on some clothes and hop along to the evening engagement. David Simpson, my agent, had to train everyone to start evening functions an hour later than they had been used to, and not to expect the MP and his wife until an hour after that. It was only as the economy flourished, and Burton became less provincial and parochial, with more of its businessmen working in London and the other major cities, that there was more understanding of the time constraints of an MP who, of necessity, had to be based in London.

Demanding as the MP's work was, I never wanted to give up being a practising barrister. Sir Edward Gardiner (the prominent QC and Conservative MP for Fylde), advised me early in my parliamentary life that I had to choose between my two professions or I would not achieve my potential in either. But had I been ambitious to become a High Court or any other judge I would not have stood for parliament: and had I been ambitious to become a government minister I would never have continued with my career at the Bar. The truth was that, harbouring neither of those ambitions, I happily continued with both my careers.

I would have no regrets whatsoever, though the hours were long and the path was not always easy, were it not for having a family. I very much regret that I was not as good a husband or father as I ought to have been. Looking back now, I can see that my life as a QC MP was, in truth, rather selfish. It certainly required a very understanding and independent-minded wife. I was exceedingly fortunate: I could not have found a more loving, or long-suffering partner if I had searched the whole world.

In those days one could, just about, carry on working as both an

MP and as a practising barrister. The House did not meet until 2.30pm and, because of the time taken by ministerial questions and statements, ten-minute rule bills and other lesser business, there was no obligatory voting, in the normal way, until 7pm or 10pm. Main debates would not start before 4.30pm, which would normally allow a barrister to get back from a London court, although Petre Crowder QC had not been able to make it in the first Kray trial. It even allowed one famous Labour ex-minister to get back from his own trial at the Old Bailey, in order to vote.

John Stonehouse, who had been the Labour candidate for Burton in 1955, became Labour MP for Wednesbury in 1957, and then, when that constituency was abolished, he became MP for Walsall North. Attractive, as well in personality as in presentation and appearance, he rose rapidly in the Labour Party, becoming successively Junior Minister for the Colonies, Minister for Aviation, Postmaster General and then Minister for Posts and Telecommunications, before the Wilson government fell in 1970. While in opposition he embarked upon a commercial career, failed with several companies, and found himself the subject of a Department of Trade Investigation for financial irregularities when £700,000 was found to be missing from London Capital Securities, a company he had established, ostensibly for the purpose of assisting refugees from Bangladesh. With suspicion against him growing, he absconded to the United States in November 1974, leaving behind his wife and three children. Then a pile of his clothes was found on a beach in Miami. He appeared to have committed suicide. In fact he had done no such thing. He had faked his suicide and had fled to Melbourne, Australia, where, assuming the identity of a dead constituent, he began what he hoped was a new life, together with his pretty young Commons secretary, Sheila Buckley.

Unfortunately for them the alert Australian police, investigating irregularities in his immigration application, and thinking that he might be the fugitive English peer Lord Lucan, then being sought worldwide for the murder of his child's nanny, arrested Stonehouse. He was deported back to Britain, where he was charged with eighteen counts of conspiracy, theft, forgery and insurance frauds. He was tried at the Old Bailey in 1976, convicted and sentenced to seven years imprisonment. He was released after three years, because he had suffered three heart attacks and had to have major surgery. He married Sheila in 1981, had a son, and died at the age of 62 in 1988. Few in parliament knew that Stonehouse, who resigned as Privy Councillor and MP on his conviction, had been for a decade or more a Czech spy. His codename, appropriately, had been Twister.

While he was on trial at the Old Bailey, I was also engaged in the building, so we used to travel back to parliament together at the end of the court day, on the underground. We did not speak about his trial, but his conversation about political events always sounded a bit odd. He spoke of himself in the third person – Stonehouse did this or that – as if trying to make me think that he wasn't all there. Despite an enormous amount of pictorial newspaper coverage of his trial each day, no one on the tube, or passing us as we walked, seemed to recognise him. I remember two city gentlemen loudly discussing the case in the tube – blissfully unaware that the subject of their discussions was actually strap-hanging next to them as they talked!

Over my 23 years in parliament, it became more and more impossible to carry on two full-time careers. The select committee system developed. This outstanding democratic parliamentary improvement, producing far greater control of the executive than I think parliament had ever had, meant that those who served on these committees had their mornings taken up with committee sittings. Committee stages of Bills also began to take place more frequently both in the mornings and afternoons. As I became more senior, and more actively involved with foreign affairs or law and order issues, I found that even free mornings had to be given over to meetings with ministers, broadcasts, speech-writing, preparing articles, and committees, in addition to dictation time with my secretary. So the amount of legal work I was able to do fell to about a quarter of my original practice, with long weeks and even months when I could not do any court work at all. Since I was practising less, becoming a Crown Court Recorder was all the more valuable in keeping me informed about the real world of the courts, and I was able to form a more realistic view about what was going wrong with the legal system and government proposals to reform it. I was also able to sit for a week or two whenever I wished.

Today the situation is even worse for anyone thinking of holding a job outside parliament. The House actually meets for its main business on three mornings a week. The media, being more demanding and important, requires considerably more commitment. The sheer volume of material that the MP now has to process through fax machine, e-mail, and mobile phone must make it all but impossible for the criminal practitioner to survive in parliament. You can, of course, write opinions and articles, give advice and have conferences, for this work can be done before parliament sits or after it has risen; but I doubt whether it is any longer possible for the criminal lawyer MP to make regular daily appearances in court. He may certainly be in trouble with his constituents if he has to disclose an outside income for 'moonlighting' on a second job!

As a result, the days of the old-style QC MP, and with him, the old-style Solicitor-General and Attorney-General, not to mention the old-style Lord Chancellor, who used to preside over the House of Lords sitting as the highest appeal court in the land, seem now to have gone for ever. As for the Recorder, the Human Rights legislation may have made it impossible any longer to be both an MP and a judge, and thus to carry out both legislative and judicial functions. I can only feel proud to have been one of the last of the tradition of practising barrister QC MPs.

Working under such workload, the one thing I had to have was an efficient, capable and devoted secretary. Ah, dear Felicity!

Secretaries

As a newly elected MP I was expected to take on my predecessor's secretary, and so, at first, I did. Pat Smith, though suffering with a seriously crippled leg in a metal brace, was marvellously crisp, sensible and brave. Unfortunately she was so efficient that she did not think that I could keep her fully occupied, so she was also the secretary to Eldon Griffiths, the energetic Conservative MP for Bury St Edmunds, ex-minister and spokesman in parliament for the Police Federation. Pat thought it would be better if he did not know that she was also working for me. So when, in the middle of dictation, we would hear Eldon bounding up the stairs, I would have to sneak away like a guilty lover, and hide in a cupboard until he had gone! Although he was usually quickly in and out, so to speak, I got fed up with this arrangement. Hiding in cupboards, for whatever reason, was hardly my style – even at that young age. So Pat introduced me to Felicity.

Felicity had been Jack D'Avigdor Goldsmid's secretary, when he was MP for Lichfield. She was a very 'nice', almost 'genteel' lady, in the old-fashioned meaning of the words, of uncertain age and a spinster, living with a much-loved cat. Her father had been somebody in the old Empire, and she was well liked by the other secretaries and knew the ropes. But she would, I think, have found the new regime of computers, faxes, e-mail and the internet thoroughly uncongenial. Mobile phones would certainly have been impossible, for unhappily, as her 18 years in my service dragged on, she became increasingly deaf through diabetes. This made her irritable, and she would, in her later years, sink into an understandable depression. This meant that my research assistant, Samantha (Sam) Walker's first job on arrival in the morning would be to sift through the wastepaper basket, and rescue any important-looking letters – and even the occasional cheques from solicitors – which had found their way there unopened. I worked outside Felicity's room in the corridor, where I could keep an eye on her, and make sure that important telephone calls reached me. I also had to make sure that I read and signed every letter before it went out, as occasionally, irritation and boredom led dear Felicity's mind, and fingers to wander aimlessly over her typewriter.

I found that I had accepted an invitation to 'speqaqk' to a Round Table; raised a problem with the Principal of Stoke-on-Trent College about a 'gobbledey gokop training scheme'; and generously offered to 'amd wprle' with a lady parish councillor, whom I also said I would be pleased to 'belp' whenever she asked. One lady I addressed, rather impolitely, as 'Mrs Babel Jones', and to another I tendered my congratulations on a successful 'him replacement'. To yet another I expressed my pleasure that, having had an operation, she had 'not recovered'. In 1991, I wrote saying that, speaking for myself, I would not want to see sanctions lifted until 'Sadam Hussain was removed and all fear about his treatment of Kuwaitis, Kurds and Iraqui Shits' (a misprint for Shi'ites) was also removed! I suppose I was lucky that she had not mis-spelt 'Kurds' as well!

When Felicity reached retirement age, I was able to take on the redoubtable Sue Dennis, who having been secretary to Peter Lillie, the prominent Conservative cabinet minister, was the embodiment of secretarial near perfection. Together with Sam Walker, Rachel's very bright and lively school-friend, as my research assistant, my office reached a level of output, efficiency, and political 'nouse' that I had only dreamt of having for the past 18 years.

When my 23 years in parliament came to their inevitable end, I returned to full-time practice as a barrister. But I found that nearly all my old solicitor clients had died or retired, and that their firms had long since reorganised, amalgamated or just ceased trading. To those who think that politicians are just in it for the money, I should point out that my MP's income was very much less than I would have been earning at the Bar – even with the expenses, which were much more modest in my time.

But the truth is that I loved every minute of my years in parliament, and if I had my time again, I would not think twice about making the financial sacrifice. I am not sure that my family would agree!

11

More Causes

'So long as a man rides his hobby-horse peaceably and quietly along the king's highway, and neither compels you or me to get up behind him – pray, sir, what have either you or I to do with it?'

(Laurence Sterne, *Tristram Shandy*)

What the office of MP gave, above all else, was access. Access to information, access to ministers, access to other decision-makers and to those with their hands on the levers of power. This access was invaluable not only in the service of our constituents, but also in support of any wider political and social causes we cared to pursue.

After my debate on capital punishment, I did not follow that cause much further. Other MPs, like George Gardiner (the courageous and single-minded MP for Reigate), initiated Commons debates calling for restoration, and I naturally supported him and took some part. I still believe that this country would be a safer place if we had the death penalty. International human rights commitments apart, there might even be, in some quarters, less objection now than there used to be to capital punishment: for on the one hand, the level of murder from knives and guns has soared, and on the other hand, we are better able to protect those mistakenly accused with a string of previously unavailable resources, such as DNA, the abolition of the false 'verbal' (by tape-recorded interviews with suspects), the requirement of stronger warnings by judges to juries on the dangers of identification evidence, electrostatic document analysis, mobile phone records, closed circuit television and the Criminal Cases Review Commission. But an issue that stands little chance of parliamentary success is a waste of limited 'cause time.' And there were other more promising causes for me to espouse.

Referendum campaign

One cause was the referendum campaign in May and June 1975, to ratify Britain's entry into the Common Market. I supported this cause with enthusiasm, spending a great deal of time campaigning throughout the constituency on the back of a lorry, mid-week as well as at weekends, together with Keith Simpson, the Liberal candidate for Burton. A united Europe would be a bastion of peace, and never again would European nations go to war against each other. But this was to be a Common Market only, or so we were promised. That is what it was called. We were assured by both Prime Minister Harold Wilson, and former Prime Minister Edward Heath, that it was a lie put about by the anti-common marketeers that our courts would be governed by foreign courts (except in the limited field of trade), or that we would lose any of our sovereignty as a proud nation state. On the contrary, we would be gaining sovereignty as our mutual security powers were pooled with the other five nations. When the words 'slippery slope' came to mind, they were always brushed aside by our great leaders.

This referendum cause was a success, because by its means the country voted overwhelmingly in favour of Britain staying in the Common Market. Later, when the reassurances we were given turned out to be false, and the question became whether and to what extent we were being required to surrender even vaster chunks of our sovereignty so that we could take the road towards a federated super-state, I fought the referendum cause again for the opposite reason – see later!

Compulsory seat-belts

The driving instructors of Burton persuaded me to take over the mantle of President of the National Association of Approved Driving Instructors (NAADI), from Gerald Nabarro MP. An exceedingly popular public performer, he was renowned for speaking his mind, through a handlebar moustache, with gusto and good humour. But he was retiring from parliament. This position gave me a platform from which to campaign for road safety. It also gave me some status, as I threw myself into the libertarian campaign to stop the wearing of seat-belts from being made compulsory – a battle which went on for years, and for which I always had full NAADI support.

It seems strange, now that we take the compulsory wearing of seat-belts for granted, to recall just how bitterly fought was the campaign for and against this safety measure in the 1970s and 80s. I was never against the wearing of seat-belts, and I always wore one myself. What I was against was everyone being *forced* to wear them. So I joined a small team, led by Ronald Bell QC (MP for Beaconsfield) and Anthony Fell (MP for Yarmouth), opposed to this serious restriction of our liberty. Over several years, whenever the subject came up for debate in Private Member's time on Fridays, we would keep talking until it was too late to advance the business. Although we were the campaigners, many MPs, peers and ordinary people were unhappy at being forced to wear seat-belts, and strongly supported our stand.

It seemed that everyone knew someone who would have died had they been seat-belted into a crashing car, because they could not have been thrown clear or would have been unable to escape when the car caught fire. Even the ultra-respectable RAC argued that it would be wrong to pass a law that forced people to do something that might kill them: seat-belt wearing should be encouraged, they said, but not made compulsory. Others opponents argued that the law would be impossible to enforce, and an impossible law would only bring the law generally into disrepute.

The only British academic to have carried out a thorough and systematic survey of the countries which had introduced compulsion, Dr (now Professor) John Adams, of University College, London, demonstrated that generally held perceptions of seat-belt safety were completely mistaken. If seat-belt wearing saved lives, he asked, why was there no evidence in any country, where seat-belt wearing was compulsory, of a reduction in road accident deaths for that reason? In fact, he demonstrated, the decline in road accident fatalities and serious injuries, then taking place in every first-world country as modern cars became safer, was actually greater in Britain without compulsion than in the other countries where there was compulsion. Statistically, therefore, compulsory seat-belts could be shown to cost more lives than they saved, and that we were actually safer in Britain without seat-belt compulsion, than we would be with it. He thought that the reason for this might be what he called 'risk compensation': that unbelted drivers, like rock-climbers, were more careful than those who drove with the over-confidence of the seat-belt wearer. The figures certainly showed that not wearing seat-belts compulsorily had been safer for pedestrians and cyclists. Once again libertarianism and evidence seemed to be against the do-good impulses of government. Once again also, there was no limit to the determination of civil servants, the medical authorities and the government to conform with other countries in Europe that had introduced compulsion. In 1983 the Thatcher government, of all governments, introduced this further advance of the 'nanny' state, when Norman Fowler (Secretary of State for Transport and MP for Sutton Coldfield), tacked compulsory seat-belts onto a denationalising Transport Bill. By ensuring that a vote against compulsory seat-belts would have meant that all the other sensible proposals in the Bill would have failed to become law, even doubting libertarians duly allowed the measure to pass.

To this day I have never seen a serious refutation of the Adams analysis. We opponents were just considered to be mad; and being beaten, I went on to fight for other causes that still stood to be won.

Israel

I joined the Conservative Friends of Israel (CFI) to support an interest group with which, of course, I had a very close cultural and religious affinity. Furthermore, my efforts for Israel always had the support of my constituency officers: very necessary if you are using up time you would otherwise be spending on your constituency.

Before I was sent to the Suez war zone in 1956, I had been asked to declare for the record whether, as a Jew, I would be prepared to fight against Israel if that should become necessary. Israel had been stopped by Britain and France, almost at the gates of Cairo, from completing its own military action against Egypt's nationalisation of the internationally owned and operated Suez Canal, in order that we might be able to claim the glory of the invasion. There was, therefore, an outside chance that we might have had to put our troops into battle against the Israelis. I replied that since I was British, not Israeli, if it were necessary in Britain's interest for me to fight against Israel, I would consider it to be my duty to do so. I was, of course, mightily relieved that it did not happen.

As a CFI member (and later as Vice-Chairman and, briefly, Chairman) and also as a member of the Board of Deputies of British Jews, I have visited the Holy Land many times. Jews and non-Jews who joined me on these visits, and who, in Britain, harboured doubts about Israel's militarism, settlement building, and aggressive behaviour towards the Palestinians, usually changed their minds when they saw the nature of the constant threat that Israel bravely faced. Apart from the tremendous thrill, of which it is impossible ever to tire, of being in the Promised Land, visiting its historic sites and meeting its people, I have had so many stimulating and heart-warming experiences with Israel and Israelis over the years.

I was in Tiberius in 1980, at a grand reception for the leading Jewish figures from the Soviet Union who had been allowed by Gorbachev to leave for the first time: a cause I describe in Chapter 15. In 1981 I was one of five hundred delegates, from sixty countries, at the World Jewish Congress in Jerusalem, at which I spoke on behalf of British Jewry, a very considerable honour.

In January 1985 I had the incredibly moving experience of being at Tel Aviv's Ben Gurion airport to welcome planeloads of fatigued, bemused and bedraggled black Ethiopian Jews to Israel. These were the second wave to have been secretly airlifted out of that country, in what was called 'Operation Moses'. Said either to be descendants of the tribe of Dan (one of the twelve tribes of Israel), or of Jews who had left the Egypt of the Pharaohs to establish their own Jewish kingdom in Africa, or, most romantically, to be the descendants of Menelik, the child of the union of King Solomon and the Queen of Sheba, 30,000 of these tent- and forest-dwelling adherents of the pre-Hebrew teachings of the Old Testament went on to settle in Israel. To see the joy and wonderment on the faces of the little children, as they learnt to ride bicycles in only five minutes, and to adapt to such household marvels of Western civilisation as the low-flush toilet, was quite something. Since then I have had the privilege of talking to some of these first black Jews to become Israeli diplomats.

But I think the most moving Jewish experience of all came towards the end of my MP years. I was in Warsaw, attending an international conference on the growing world drug problem. On the evening that the meeting ended, and not being due to fly back to London till the next afternoon, I went with some of the other participants to the hotel's casino – and won £100 at roulette. I decided to spend my winnings on a taxi next morning, to take me to see the death camp at Auschwitz. The girl on the hotel booking desk told me that it was too far away and I would miss my flight back. She suggested that I go instead to Majdanek, which being just outside Lublin was much nearer. So after an early breakfast, I set out alone with my taxi driver.

Although it was a freezing cold, bleak, morning, I was still very surprised to find no other visitors at all to the camp. The driver managed to find a caretaker who told me, incredibly, that few people ever came to Majdanek, and none on the Sabbath. There was certainly no Visitors Centre. This may have been because, unlike Auschwitz where one and a half million Jews had died, and there are always queues of visitors, only 300,000 Jews had been slaughtered and then cremated or buried at Majdanek.

The caretaker escorted the two of us round the camp, which is much smaller than Auschwitz-Birkenau, with all its huts and buildings still standing. Had it been the height of summer, I would still have felt chilled to the marrow of my bones. There were moments when I found that I could hardly draw breath. I was shown where, in one day alone, 18,000 men, women, and children had been unloaded from lorries, shot as they stepped to the ground, and fell or were kicked into a massive trench. In one of the huts, empty Zyklon B gas canisters, the contents of which had been piped into the shower heads fifty years earlier, still lay where they had been thrown. Nearly everything was where it had been when the Allies liberated the camp, although the area was kept clean and tidy by the caretaker's small staff. There were the spine-tingling heaps of gold tooth fillings, extracted from prisoners to help finance the Nazi war effort; the human hair shorn for some other dreadful purposes; and the stomach-churning piles of children's shoes.

We were all in tears. Prince Charles came years later and was in tears. Everyone should go to see Majdanek, and cry. We must never forget what man is capable of doing to his fellow man: how the decent inhabitants of a town like Lublin could pretend that they did not know what was happening, as they wiped the thick ash from the cemetery chimneys off their window ledges. Nor forget why it was so necessary for the State of Israel to have been created. I became a trustee of the Holocaust Educational Trust to help to keep that memory alive.

Had I any ambition to become a minister in Margaret Thatcher's government, it is unlikely that I would have advanced my chances by arguing with her, as I did from time to time, over Israel. Although always a supporter of that nation, she had to take advice from a Foreign Office which, because it was full of ex-ambassadors who had served in the twenty-three Arab and other Islamic states, was overwhelmingly Arabist. Under such pressure, she was sometimes persuaded to speak and to act against Israel. She allowed Israel's enemies to have offices in London. She had almost been persuaded to welcome talks in London with PLO officials on the future of Israel, before they had fulfilled a promise to forswear terrorism. On that occasion the CFI, then led by the redoubtable Michael Fidler (the Conservative MP for Bury), managed to persuade her against such action at the very last minute. I had another argument with her over Israel, which I describe later.

She appointed one British ambassador to Israel who had little time for the country or its people. He could be deliberately undiplomatic. In the front room of his official residence, frequented by Israeli politicians, he had hanging over his fireplace one of the series of paintings by the great Victorian artist David Roberts, depicting imaginary scenes of brightly turbaned Arabs seated at the Pool at Shilo, or wherever. The trouble with these undoubtedly beautiful pictures was that they had become icons for ex-patriot Palestinians, and were therefore offensive to the Israelis. In the end the ambassador had to be removed, because an ambassador who is undiplomatic and distrusted by the host government is of little use to either country. One of the first actions of his more tactful successor, Patrick Moberly, was to replace the Roberts painting with one by a modern Israeli artist, which made Israeli visitors feel much more welcome. Even so, our consul-general in East Jerusalem had the right to bypass the ambassador, and to report directly to the British Foreign Office about Arab issues: a somewhat unusual deviation from the diplomatic norm, which must have been insulting to an ambassador for its offensive implication that he could not fully be trusted.

I used to speak out for Israel in parliament, even when, or perhaps I should say especially when, it was unpopular. The Holocaust and the necessity for a Jewish homeland apart, the achievements of that little democracy, in creating a garden in a desert and becoming a world leader in scientific research, though encircled by dictatorships hating both its religion and its people, and subjecting it to constant terrorism and war, are truly phenomenal. Under that kind of seemingly endless attack since the foundation of the state in 1948, the arrogance, and sometimes the aggressiveness that has so often characterised Israel's approach to even its friends in the outside world, are understandable. That aggression is often tempered with humorous fatalism: as Golda Meir used to say of Moses, 'He led us all over the desert for forty years and then left us in the only part of the region that has no oil!' And as others have said of the same great leader: 'If, when he left Egypt, he had only turned right instead of left...'

In the early 1980s, when CFI MPs were in Mettula, discussing Israel's relations with its northern neighbour Lebanon with Israel's surrogate Christian militia leader, General Lahad, there was a terrifying bang outside the building in which our meeting was being held.

'It's only a fighter plane going through the sound barrier. It happens all the time,' Lahad explained.

'If that is the explanation,' I asked him, 'why has everyone in the street outside thrown themselves to the ground?'

Lahad was trying to hide from us the fact that this was, of course, just the latest shell attack from Lebanon, which used to occur almost daily. It was yet another attempt by the PLO to terrorise the town's population, despite the fact that by day it was full of Arab workers. Even now, people in Britain do not seem to realise, for television does not often report these events, that Israel has been subjected to shelling, suicide-bombing, shooting or other violent and murderous attacks, practically every week of every year since the 1970s.

That is why Israel, having kept its side of the UN bargain by withdrawing all its troops from Lebanon in 1990, by July 2006 had had enough of Hezbollah, the terrorist organisation, which, far from honouring the UN resolution calling for its withdrawal, had stepped up its attacks on Israel. Tragically, Israel discovered that it was unable to finish off the terrorists, as the United States and British government had both allowed and expected them to do. Unknown to our intelligence (and presumably to Israel's), Iran and Syria had been secretly building up that organisation's strength and military capability to the point where the once fearsome Israeli army found itself unable to stop the bombardment of Israeli towns and cities in the one month it was given by the international community to complete the task.

Even more recently, having honourably and at enormous risk abided by the international call to hand back Gaza to the Palestinians, the Israelis have had to live with rockets being fired daily by a Hamas-ruled Gaza. When they dare to respond by taking out rocket positions, often deliberately sited in heavily populated areas, or by closing down Palestinian crossings into Israel, they are reviled by swathes of the international community. For me, that cause continues, though there is little I can do to help.

The Canadian constitution

Another political argument I had with Mrs Thatcher concerned Canada. In 1979 Premier Trudeau asked Britain to release ('repatriate') our ultimate control of the Canadian Constitution to Canada, while they would remain part of the Commonwealth. Since the 1936 Statute of Westminster,

Britain had made clear its readiness to give up any constitutional power it enjoyed as head of the Empire, to any requesting country. Canada, having become in all other senses a self-governing country, could have its own final say over its own affairs whenever it wished. But the Canadians themselves had refused to make the request over the next four decades, mainly because the provincial Canadian leaders had found it impossible to agree among themselves, and therefore had thought it better to leave things as they were for the time being. Many thousands of Canadians laid down their lives for the Empire in the two world wars, a fact brought home to me recently when I went to the battlefields of Flanders, and visited the beautifully kept graves of the fallen.

But in 1979 a lively and colourful campaign was launched in Britain *against* repatriation. Verbal battle was joined in the central lobby and committee rooms of the House of Commons at Westminster, first by some of the Canadian provincial premiers, reluctant to concede this further power to Premier Trudeau, and then, when Trudeau had bought off the premiers, by Native American chiefs who did not trust Trudeau to accord them what they considered to be their land rights.

Regaled in magnificent headgear and colourful national dress, the chiefs lobbied us. They could not believe that we were preparing to let them down. They came with documents proving that 'the Great White Queen' (Victoria) had, 100 years earlier, pledged to the Indians, now called the First Nation, the very rights that Trudeau was denying. Sad as any act of betrayal must be, nearly everyone in the British parliament of all parties, now thought that enough water having flowed under enough bridges, and the world having so greatly changed since the time of Queen Victoria, we had no real alternative but to respond positively to the request from the head of a democratically elected Commonwealth government. But there was an 'awkward squad,' and I was a member. It was otherwise rather eminent.

The squad – Sir Derek Walker-Smith QC, Sir Charles Fletcher-Cooke QC, Sir Bernard Braine, Jonathan Aitken and myself – was concerned not about the principle of total self-government, which we all accepted without demur, but about the timing. For the Canadian Supreme Court was at that very moment considering the position of Quebec and First Nation land rights, and that body, being the highest authority under the Canadian Constitution, it seemed to us prudent to await their verdict, only a few weeks away, in case it ran contrary to that being advanced by Her Majesty's Government. We wanted to avoid any possible embarrassment to the Queen.

What happened to our merry band was bizarre. Instead of ignoring us – for what did it matter if a mere handful of the House of Commons voted against the motion on such a principled ground – we were subjected to sustained and intense pressure to change our minds, first by the Chief Whip, then by the Solicitor-General, followed by the Attorney-General, the Lord Chancellor and then, finally, by the Prime Minister herself. When Charles Fletcher-Cooke and I were summoned to her presence, she seemed to be almost in tears. She pleaded with us not to vote against the government, and having no wish to cause her or the government, distress, we all agreed to abstain. The Bill went through with no votes against.

No one has ever explained to me why the Prime Minister was so upset about such a small group of objectors, or why it was so important that there should be no dissenting vote in the House of Commons. I guessed that maybe Trudeau had threatened something as serious as the withdrawal of NATO over-flying rights in Canada, but no one would, or did, ever tell me.

Football and other sport

Hardly, it is true, a parliamentary cause, but in the breaks from such campaigns and parliamentary duties, I played football for the House of Commons Westminster Wanderers soccer team, against the press, other parliaments and 'all-stars'. I was at my best playing in a position, little known to football tacticians, which might be described as 'all over the field', and so was, quite obviously, totally useless. Our captain, for a time, was Malcolm Allison, the famous England player and First Division manager. He had a plan: and we were thoroughly briefed. Our secret weapon was to play an 'off-side' game. The weapon was as useless as I was, because there was never anyone left to protect our gallant goalkeeper, the Walsall Labour MP Bruce George, when Malcolm's ruse failed. So we lost all our matches – by scores like 13 nil. When we summoned up the courage to dispense with Allison's generous services, we did not actually start winning – but we certainly started losing by much smaller margins.

Once, against Reading United, I found myself marking a man with a particularly well-developed stomach, whom I thought I recognised. I asked his name. It was Roy Bentley, my idol, the great Chelsea and England centre-forward who had become the Reading manager. On another occasion, fed up and humiliated by being given the circular run around every few minutes by a man half my size, I pulled him back by his shirt, on the blind side of the referee, and asked his name. It was Jimmy Greaves, the great England inside-left and star of Chelsea and Tottenham Hotspur. What I would not have given to have met these great players 30 years earlier when, as a football mad schoolboy, I used to write away for their autographs!

We had our own stars, of course. There was Ken Clarke (the Nottingham MP, future Home Secretary, Chancellor of the Exchequer and Lord Chancellor), playing it always seemed in his 'hush puppies'; Peter Bottomley (MP for Woolwich and now MP for Worthing West), who was much faster as a swimmer, but whose loyal wife Virginia (later to become Secretary of State for Social Services and for the National Lottery) was always vocally active in support on the touchline; Bryan (now Lord) Davies (who had once played for Ipswich); and the lanky and surprisingly skilful Earl of Craigavon. At Crystal Palace one Sunday afternoon, the well-known TV host and broadcaster, David Hamilton, found himself so carried away by our astounding football skills against his team, the All-Stars, that he dropped his trousers to 'moon,' I think the word is, before a huge crowd.

This part of my sporting career came to an untimely end when, in an inter-parliamentary soccer match, I attempted a foolhardy tackle upon a ten-foot defender from the Dail (the Irish parliament), and ruptured myself. And so, in my forty-fifth year, I was obliged to hang up my boots. The rest of the team will have breathed a big sigh of relief!

Lest anybody thinks that we were not elected to parliament to sport ourselves at the taxpayer's expense, I should perhaps make clear that, as well as having a lot of fun and exercising our unfit bodies ('*mens sana in corpore sano*'), we did raise worthwhile sums of money for the Moorgate Tube Disaster Fund, and a number of children's charities.

One fine day in 1985 I even resumed my short and unsuccessful rowing career and joined in a parliamentary regatta to raise funds for St Margaret's Church by Westminster Abbey. All hands were called to an array of boats manned (and womanned) by ministers, back-benchers, journalists, clerks and even Olympians. One boat, crewed by Old Etonians, disappeared downriver in a furious race with the 'Avon Ladies', crewed by ministers' wives. Another called 'No Turning Back', and crewed by the driest of the dry, was launched, of course, by the Prime Minister, and straightway rammed a number of other boats, thereby making little progress. One of her predecessors, James Callaghan, did the splits attempting to board his boat, and was nearly lost in swirling waters far murkier than anything to be found on the dry land of politics. I was privileged to be a member of a boat named 'Legal Eight', which was otherwise crewed by bewigged past, present and future solicitors and attorneys-general, and which was coxed by Greville Janner, wearing a black cap once worn by judges passing sentences of death. We rowed up against the tide to the start at Lambeth Bridge. After thirty or forty exhausting strokes we turned, and going immediately out of control, hurtled down-tide to collide with Westminster Bridge in only three strokes, narrowly missing an enormous refuse barge by Waterloo Bridge. We had to be towed back – from Wapping!

Not naturally given to foolhardiness, I feel that I must confess to my reader, since I want my memoir to be frank and honest, a further occasion when I engaged in reckless sporting behaviour. It happened in October 1988, after I had delivered a speech against the abuse of press freedom to a conference of newspaper editors at Victoria Falls in Zimbabwe – an occasion opened with a welcoming speech from President Mugabe (in those days a respected and popular figure), and attended by the press barons Tiny Rowland and Rupert Murdoch. I cannot think what made me do it, unless it was to win back favour with the media that I had forfeited with my speech against the press. Anyway, physical coward as I have admitted to being, I went whitewater-rafting down the Zambezi! The editors were short of one person to fill a raft at 6am, the morning after my speech, and I was easily persuaded to help them out. We were assured, as the dangers of the several rapids were explained to us, that if we tipped over, a following raft of native Zambezians would speedily fish us out of the raging surf. In the event we did not tip over, but unfortunately the Zambezians did. Since we were well ahead of them, I do not know whether they had anyone to fish them out.

I was not told before setting off that, if I fell into the water, there was a nasty little bug that burrowed into one's veins and eventually stopped one's heart. Nor was I told that crocodile eggs would from time to time survive the perilous drop over 'the smoke that thunders', the Victoria Falls, and survivors had grown into a colony of adult beasts only too hungry for a juicy breakfast of press-men and their associates.

I hope that I do not need to persuade my kind reader that duty calls a member of parliament far more often than reckless pleasure. And so it was that at 7am one Saturday morning in December 1990, Gloria and I drove down the M6 from Burton, on the way to an all-day judicial seminar in London, at which I hoped to improve my efficiency as a judge. It began to snow heavily. When we reached the hill at Corley, we happened upon articulated lorries scattered and stalled all over the road. Unable to get past, we could do nothing but sit and wait – for eighteen hours! The entire Midlands froze, and thousands of vehicles slithered to a halt as the temperature tumbled. I was among the very lucky. I had my adorable wife, a full petrol tank with the engine running to keep us warm throughout the ordeal, a radio, music tapes, a pocket TV set, crisps, nuts, biscuits and several bottles of Burton beer, which I always kept in the car for when I had to thank someone for rendering me a small kindness. What we did not have, of course, in those far-off primitive days, were mobile phones. Eventually, around midnight, and after a day with no traffic movement whatsoever, someone in the Midlands police force hit upon the brilliant idea of removing a small part of the central reservation, so that we could turn back along the unaffected motorway lanes. No one in authority had thought of doing that all day! They also set up a most welcome, but long overdue, hot drinks stand in the lay-by. We drove back a little way along the M6 and spent the night at the Holiday Inn in Birmingham.

The following Tuesday, several MPs who had been caught up in the misery raised in the Commons the deplorable police failure to react, for eighteen hours, to the horror of mass breakdown on one of the nation's main arterial highways. The sketch-writers had a fun day. Andrew Rawnsley, of the *Guardian* wrote:

> The House of Commons was plunged into chaos yesterday as a dense blanket of MPs descended on Westminster to complain about the snow. The bitter conditions – with some backbenchers gusting up to gale force – were some of the worst in living memory. Kenneth Baker, who had braved the weather to answer their questions, was trapped on the government frontbench for several hours. Or so it seemed. On and on they went about the snow, burying the Home Secretary alive. No MP fell on him more thickly or heavily than Ivan Lawrence, the bombastic Conservative MP for Burton.
>
> 'The whole thing was quite disgraceful,' blustered Mr Lawrence. 'I was stationary on the M6 for eighteen hours – in the company of my wife.' Mercifully, Mrs Gloria Lawrence is understood to have survived that dreadful ordeal and is now expected to make a full recovery.

My former next-door constituency neighbour, Matthew Parris wrote in *The Times*: 'A hundred hearts went out to Mrs Lawrence.' And Quentin Letts, in the *Daily Telegraph* wrote:

181

As nightmare scenarios go, there can be few things to match being cooped up in a metal box for 18 hours with a politician. That terrible fate actually befell Mrs Gloria Lawrence at the weekend... Mr Lawrence, disclosing that his only comfort throughout the ordeal (apart from his wife) had been a supply of Burton ale, complained that he had not seen a policeman... Given that he was tilting back sharpeners on the public highway, this was probably just as well.

One unsympathetic constituent went further. Writing to the *Burton Mail*, he accused me of being a disgraceful hypocrite on law and order, since I was quite prepared to fulminate against drinking and driving, yet had imbibed, on my own confession, three bottles of Marston's Pedigree, Ind Coope Burton Ale and Bass White Shield while in a car on the M6. He had totally missed the point: I had not been driving anywhere for 18 hours!

All too often, the dedication of members of parliament in the service of the public is easily ridiculed: but it is worse when we are ignored.

12

1981: Queen's Counsel

'If a man love the labour of his own trade apart from any question of success
or fame, the gods have called him.'

(Robert Louis Stevenson)

Everything seemed to be happening politically in 1981. The election of
Michael Foot, a brilliant parliamentary orator, but whom someone
unkindly called 'a leg-end in his own life-time', to Labour leader, and
his Party's reversion to hard-line socialism, provoked the 'Gang of Four'
(Roy Jenkins, Shirley Williams, David Owen and Bill Rogers), to break
away from the Labour Party. This led to the formation of the Social
Democrat Party – and eventually to the creation, under Tony Blair, of
New Labour. Labour tore itself apart over Europe, with most trade
unions and political leaders wanting to pull out. There was more IRA
terrorism in England when Sir Stuart Pringle, the Commandant-General
of the Royal Marines, had his legs blown off in south London; a gallant
bomb disposal officer was killed defusing a bomb in Piccadilly; the home
of Sir Michael Havers, the Attorney-General, was bombed; and the
Reverend Robert Bradford MP was murdered (as I have already related),
in his Belfast surgery. Bobby Sands, elected to Westminster for Fermanagh
and South Tyrone as a member of the IRA, died after a ten-week hunger-
strike, as did nine other members of the IRA. Violence flared up and
exploded in the streets of Brixton, Bristol, Birmingham, Wolverhampton,
Preston, and Toxteth on the outskirts of Liverpool. In San Francisco,
the newly elected American President Ronald Reagan survived an
assassination attempt, as did Pope John Paul II in Rome. President Anwar
Sadat, the Egyptian peacemaker with Israel, was not so fortunate. In
this atmosphere of pandemonium and madness, Sir Keith Joseph, the
Conservative right-wing idol and Secretary for Trade and Industry,
announced to an astounded back-bench committee of Tory MPs that
he was going to bail out British Leyland and the car industry, by taxpayer

funded subsidies – about as un-Conservative an action by the government's super-Conservative as could be imagined.

Two of the only bright spots that year were the wedding, obviously made in heaven, of Prince Charles and Lady Diana Spencer at St Paul's Cathedral; and for me, the achievement of one of my few real ambitions.

Queen's Counsel

On 16 April 1981, I became a QC – a position described by toastmasters as 'One of Her Majesty's Counsel Learned In The Law'. To achieve this august rank, and the right to have these letters after one's name and to wear a silk gown in court, is not merely a high honour, it is recognition by some of the most senior and successful barristers and judges that one has achieved a level of excellence in an area of legal practice. It is that most cherished of all attainments in professional life – a mark of the approval of one's peers. It is also an indicator, to those needing the services of a senior barrister, that the work is likely to be of a high standard. While it might be expected that the award of such a badge of honour will herald higher earnings, competition being keen it could also lead to less work: some, therefore, prefer not to seek the honour. Indeed many barristers, who have risen to the rank of circuit or High Court judge, have never become Queen's Counsel. Useful as it may be as an indicator of seniority and skill, it is nowadays considered by some to be elitist, and as such, out of place in this world of political correctness. This despite the fact that appointments to the rank of Queen's Counsel (or King's Counsel, if the monarch should be a male) can only be achieved today after a lengthy (and costly) process of open and independent selection by committee, without regard to colour, gender, sexual inclination or disability and, in future, it is even going to be subject to peer evaluation. But so much of the work is publicly funded, and the fees that the government are prepared to pay have been so savagely slashed, that inevitably the days of such a rank and honour will be numbered. When that happens, it will be the end of yet another proud British tradition that has always served a useful and important purpose, domestically and in the world of international business beyond.

Earlier in the twentieth century, MPs who were practising barristers automatically received the title of Queen's Counsel, and they were known as 'parliamentary silks'. By the time I was elected that route had long been abolished, although the title was still awarded to ministers of state who had given up their legal practice and so had been prevented from gaining silk. So, not being a minister, I could only become a silk by the normal route. Yet although my seventeen years seniority, and the size of my practice at the Bar, might have entitled me to the honour had I not been an MP, my applications kept being turned down. I suspected that I might have found my way into the 'black book' for some reason, and I asked Sir Ian Percival, the Solicitor-General, if that was so. He thought it unlikely but promised to ask the Attorney-General, the leader of the Bar.

'No, you are not in any black book,' Sir Ian reported reassuringly to me, 'but the problem is that we have a parliamentary tradition not to give silk to Conservative MPs, unless we can match him or her with a Labour applicant (and vice versa), and there is no one eligible to become a Silk in the Labour Party. You will have to wait until a Labour candidate presents himself.' Totally ridiculous as this obviously was, I am immensely grateful to Labour's Lord Gifford, himself a distinguished lawyer, for applying the following year.

The advantage of being 'in silk' is that you usually, though no longer always, work with junior counsel who, together with your instructing solicitors, make up your team. Good juniors, who are prepared to help a leader by grinding through the boring and detailed bits, and who bring experience, flair and wisdom to a case, are a joy. Over twenty-five years I have been privileged to lead men and women of real quality who have put my own limited abilities to shame and have taught me much more than I could teach them. Men like Robert Flach, Cedric Joseph and Ali Mohammad Azhar, whose wise guidance consistently turned my cases from disaster to success. Charles Conway, whose cross-examination in the magistrates court laid the foundation for the acquittal of an alleged murderer; David Martin Sperry, whose sharp-eyed discovery of a stain on a piece of wall-paper, missed by the forensic scientists, spared another from a murder conviction; and David Haeems, whose alert observation of a sex instruction video saved yet another innocent man from many years of imprisonment for rape. There were women, too, like Kali Kaul, whose diligence in a fraud trial helped to save a surveyor from the total destruction of his life; and Lauren Soertz, whose astute knowledge and grasp of legal precedents led to the acquittal at half-time of a man wrongly accused of a contract killing. Some of my juniors have become leaders and judges themselves. All of them, working as a team, helped me to success in trials that our clients might have hoped for but could never have expected.

Although I have little difficulty remembering my juniors through the years, I have more difficulty remembering all my leaders. Perhaps this is because my juniors were always very helpful, while I was of much less use to my leaders and I have thought it better to forget them. Of course, I do remember the best: James Burge, Victor Durand, Jeremy Hutchinson, and Bernard Gillis stand out – and others I have mentioned in this memoir. But Peter Taylor once asked me if I remembered such and such a case. I said I did not. He described an event in that case. I still had no recollection. The result was amazing, he told me. I still had no recollection. 'But I led you in that case,' he said. And I had no recollection of having been led by the future Lord Chief Justice of England and Wales!

Nuclear Iraq

In the third week of June 1981 I was lunching alone in the members' dining-room when the Prime Minister joined me. Mrs T was, as usual, sweetness and light, and chatted about some of the matters then occupying her attention. Boldly, I took the opportunity to ask her why, at prime minister's question time a day or two earlier, she had attacked the Israeli bombing of the Iraqi nuclear reactor at Osirak, and why she was so certain that Saddam Hussein was not building up a nuclear military power potential.

'Because I have been into the matter with a tooth-comb and there is no jot or tittle of evidence to back the claim,' she said.

'But haven't the Foreign Office shown you the Mossad file, which, my Israeli friends assure me, clearly proves Iraq to be importing weapon-enriched uranium, delivering it to secretly hidden weapons factories in mysteriously disguised vehicles, and masking the camera lens trained on the radioactive core of the plant, in breach of their international obligations?' I asked. Mrs Thatcher repeated the bit about the tooth-comb, and left the table in what seemed to me to be some considerable irritation at my obtuseness.

Within a few days something unusual happened. She appointed Sir Percy Craddock, one of our most senior ambassadors, to advise her personally on foreign affairs matters. The media wondered what was going on. Was the Prime Minister unhappy with her briefings from the Foreign Office? Why had she set a gamekeeper to become a poacher? I cannot say that she took that step as a result of what I had said to her, but her surprising action certainly followed very soon after our conversation. It seemed that, whatever the reason, she was not too happy with the Foreign Office. Unfortunately, the man she chose was so distinguished and dedicated a gamekeeper that he may have been incapable of becoming a poacher, and the arrangement appeared neither to have worked nor lasted.

From what we now know about the Iraqi nuclear development, and Saddam Hussein's refusal to allow the weapons investigators to do their work, together with the use of poison gas to destroy 8000 Iraqi Kurds at Hallabja in 1988, and 30,000 Iraqi Shi'as in northern Iraq in 1991, we must surely conclude that Margaret Thatcher and the Foreign Office may have been wrong about the insignificance of the Iraqi nuclear reactor. We can only be very thankful that the Israelis made sure, in 1991, that Saddam did not have a nuclear capability when he invaded Kuwait, and during the Gulf War that followed.

Did he have this capability by 2003? The 'dodgy dossier' aside, it seems incredible that Saddam should have refused permission to the weapons inspectors to complete their search if he did not have weapons of mass destruction, for that course was certain to result in a destructive onslaught upon Iraq, by the Americans and their British and other allies, and an end to his regime – which is, of course, exactly what happened. It is true that no weapons were found, but then neither, for months after the invasion, was Saddam Hussein – although everyone was looking for him. I wrote a letter to *The Times* in April 2003: 'Since the coalition, with all their resources, have been unable to find Saddam Hussain, can we be sure he exists?' They felt unable to publish it; it was probably too long!

Even now, can we be so certain that the weapons of mass destruction never existed? That they were not moved out of Iraq into neighbouring countries?

Closed shop

A few weeks after my argument with the prime minister, in July 1981, I staged a small demonstration in the Commons, with a ten-minute rule Bill, to remind the government of the strength of feeling in the country against the tyranny of the closed shop: trade unions refusing to allow anyone to work for a company unless they were members of the union. This had of late stopped too many people working, like the famous

Walsall tea ladies who had refused to join a trade union. It had also threatened thousands of small businesses, whose production could be brought to a standstill by secondary action. It was called the Trade Union, (Freedom of Association) Bill, and Andrew Alexander, in the *Daily Mail*, described it as 'one of the more interesting ten minute rule Bills (parliament) has seen for a while'.

In my speech introducing the Bill, I said that the object of the exercise was to remind the government that 186 Tory backbenchers had signed a similar 'early day motion', and that a poll of trade unionists had shown 80% to be against the bully-boy tactics and kangaroo courts of the trade unions themselves. I did not seek to abolish the closed shop, only to help employees to obtain and keep their jobs irrespective of trade union membership, by making a trade union agreement void in law, and therefore unenforceable in the courts. My Bill was, I argued, 'a moderate and reasonable measure', consistent with our obligations to international human rights, and similar to measures that had already been introduced in other countries. 'We are right and close behind you,' I told Jim Prior, the Employment Secretary. Cyril Smith, the Liberal spokesman, tried to speak against the Bill – so much for liberalism – but the attempt at demolition of my Bill came from Labour's Kevin McNamara (MP for Kingston-upon-Hull Central), who turned in what the papers described as a 'poor' performance.

We lost, of course, by 136 to 114 – what the *Daily Telegraph* called a 'temporary reverse' – with under half the Tories voting for it. Jim Prior was not willing to be pressured into any change just yet, and Ted Heath was against any change at all, so the payroll vote was not as enthusiastic as it might or ought to have been. But the point was made and taken.

Before long the blot of the closed shop was removed from the statute book, and Tories found much support in the country when Mrs Thatcher removed that abuse of trade union power, thereby reversing one of the ratchets of socialism.

The man who murdered a judge

In November of 1981 I defended John Smith at Leeds Crown Court, charged with murdering the highly respected Judge William Openshaw, who sat at Preston Crown Court. Smith had stabbed the judge twelve times, to death, and was insane. Eventually he was arrested as he stood at the top of Blackpool Tower, preparing to throw himself off. In anticipation of the spectacle, a large crowd had gathered.

The first issue to be considered at his trial, at Manchester Assizes, was whether he was fit to be tried, or to enter a plea. The jury found that he was fit. At the announcement of this verdict Smith created a disturbance in court, so the judge, Mr Justice Lawson, let him lie down on the floor of the dock. Columns of cigarette smoke rose from the dock throughout the trial.

Smith had gone to Judge Openshaw's house in Preston to kill him because, as he explained to the police, he had sent him to borstal many years before. Horrifyingly, Mrs Openshaw had surprised him as he was stabbing her husband in the garage of their house. Smith ran off, flagged down a passing car, and, holding the driver at knife-point, made him drive to Scotland. At the end of the day Smith abandoned the car and driver and ran off. There were therefore two positive identifications: by Mrs Openshaw, and by the car driver. In addition, the driver saw Smith throw the knife out of the car window, and noted where it had fallen. It was retrieved by the police and became an exhibit: it was covered with Smith's fingerprints and the judge's blood. When Smith was arrested he made a statement to the police in which he said that he had once gone to London with a knife to stab the Lord Chancellor, Lord Hailsham. He had found out where the Lord Chancellor lived, and had taken a bus to his home in Barnes. He told the police that, as he was walking towards the house, the thought had come to him that Lord Hailsham had never done anything to hurt him, so he had turned round and had gone back to where he was staying.

Smith refused to give instructions to my solicitors or to me, and half-way through the prosecution's evidence he decided that he did not want me or his solicitor to represent him any more. He had wanted me to read out a statement that he had prepared. I said that it was for him to read it out, for in those days the accused could make a statement himself from the dock instead of giving evidence. He insisted that I do it for him. I told him that was against the rules. He said that he had briefed me to break the rules. I said that if he thought that, he was very much mistaken. He told me that he did not want any more to do with me, so I informed the judge of the situation and left the trial. Mr Justice Lawson asked my female junior to remain and to assist the court by keeping an eye on Smith's case, and this she nobly did. He was convicted of the murder – but by a majority verdict of eleven to one. One member of the jury seems to have thought that the case had not been proved against him. How scary!

Judge Openshaw's son, Peter, has honoured his father's memory by becoming successively Honorary Recorder of Preston, a member of the circuit Bench, and is now a most distinguished High Court judge.

The Mountnessing silver bullion robbery

In December 1981, I flew to Tampa Florida for a weekend speaking tour for the Association of Trial Lawyers of America, a prestigious American legal group that I had addressed two years before at their Mid-Winter Convention in Monte Carlo. Repeat invitations followed, and I spoke at the Orange County Bar Association Annual Dinner, a Florida Bar Association lunch and met, over the years, a large number of delightful and exciting American trial lawyers, many of whom come often, with their wives or husbands, to London.

One of their annual conferences took place in London in 1981, and the Criminal Bar section wanted to see a criminal trial at the Old Bailey. It so happened that one of my cases, described by the prosecution as 'the most valuable robbery ever in Britain' was starting in Court Five, a very small court which could not accommodate the hundred American trial lawyers who wanted to attend. A roster was therefore arranged, and over the next week a steady stream of them trooped in and out of the court. Among the spectators, they joined senior police officers investigating police corruption.

On 24 March 1980, a lorry carrying 321 ingots of silver bullion, worth £3.5 million (about £23 million by today's value), travelled from its depot in east London's Tooley Street, along the A13 Commercial Road on its way to Tilbury Dock. At about 11.10am the driver came upon what he thought was a traffic census road-block near Mountnessing, and was waved into the side of the road by a policeman, and several official-looking men who appeared to be from the Ministry of Transport. The officials approached him, and as he leant out of his cab to speak to them, one of them drew a gun and ordered him out of the cab. The robbers then got in – and drove straight off with the load.

Today, when security systems and security guards are everywhere, it is astonishing to realise how little security consciousness we once had. There had been the one usual security attendant, driving his usual white Alpine security car behind the lorry. No problem, in the heavy traffic, for the gang to separate him from his charge. There was no two-way radio in the cab of the lorry, and mobile phones had yet to be invented;

the driver had not been warned not to stop; and the route, about which no one had bothered to inform the police, was the one invariably used for such journeys. The insurance company insuring the load was registered in East Germany, and seemed to be little concerned about its security.

The case against my client, Bob Deanus, was that, although he was not present at the robbery, he had been the vital supplier of the transport information and the facilitator of the conspiracy. The evidence upon which the prosecution relied came from one Mickey Gervaise, and an alleged admission to the police by Deanus of his guilty participation in the plot. Gervaise was what was known as a 'supergrass' – a species of villain who had been promised immunity if they gave evidence for the prosecution in big cases.

The practice was seemingly rife at the time, of London's detectives having regular informants who, besides receiving much reduced sentences for 'grassing' on their mates, would benefit by receiving some of the reward money and sometimes by their police contacts looking the other way when they committed other crimes. Some of the policemen in the case were shown to be lying, and one of the senior police officers was probably a villain himself. Certainly there can have been no doubt that their star witness, Gervaise, was one of the worst criminals ever to have come before the courts. Although he had only been convicted on three occasions, his crimes numbered over 34, and were valued at over £3 million. He was also the gang leader and brains behind this heist.

Deanus's defence was that Gervaise, by pleading guilty to the robbery and promising to give evidence against the others, knew that he would receive a greatly reduced sentence. But he had falsely pointed the finger at Deanus as one of the conspirators because he held a grudge against him: he believed that Deanus had cheated him out of £12,000 from the sale, some time earlier, of emeralds in Amsterdam. When Deanus had explained to Gervaise that the emeralds had been stolen from him at Heathrow, when he had taken his eye off the duty-free bag into which he had put them, Gervaise had not believed him. Deanus also alleged that the police had invented his so-called admission of involvement in the robbery.

Deanus read a statement from the dock at his trial instead of going into the witness box and giving evidence. While this meant that the value of his account was worth less, since he had not been tested by cross-examination, it did mean that any previous convictions or compromising behaviour would not be revealed. Statements from the dock have long since been disallowed, and now the law has changed so that bad character evidence can be given even if the defendant does not give evidence. But the prosecution in Deanus's case were furious that he had made allegations against the police and their star witness, and had refused to go into the witness box. They felt particularly frustrated because they were unable to put to him in cross-examination that he had, through his solicitor, actually written to the court indicating that he was intending to plead guilty!

Surprisingly, for the law provided no basis for it, prosecuting counsel applied to the judge for permission to reopen their case, after Deanus had made his statement, in order to put that letter in evidence. Even more surprisingly, the judge allowed it, and the evidence was duly given. To complete the list of surprises, despite this information, which the defence could not deny, the jury acquitted him!

Perhaps the jury had believed neither Gervaise nor the police. For in the course of the case it had emerged that twelve bars of the silver bullion, valued at £100,000, had inexplicably gone missing while it was in police custody. Furthermore, £300,000 of reward money was paid out for information from a police informant leading to the recovery of the silver, and there was some suspicion that some of the money had found its way into police pockets.

One or two of my guests from the Association of Trial Lawyers of America told me that it was just like being back home!

13

The Falklands War

'Even now that it is all over, it is hard to grasp the enormity of what has happened: in the last quarter of the twentieth century, Great Britain has been to war and has fought on a scale and in a manner not seen by this country since the second World War. A naval task force of 100 ships has sailed 8,000 miles to the South Atlantic to engage an enemy invasion force off the last outpost of a forgotten empire.'

(*Sunday Times* Insight Team)

My reader will not be surprised to hear that I make no claim to have actually done anything to win the Falklands war, which broke out in April 1982. I did, however, make a six-minute speech in the House, seven weeks into the war. I suggested that a united House would be helpful encouragement for our troops, and that a decision for or against action should be made before our land forces, being made to wait on their ships and unaccustomed to bobbing about in the storms of the South Atlantic seas for long periods, became incapable of performing any task at all. It is heartbreaking to have to recall that the greatest single disaster that befell our troops was the bomb which hit the troop carrier *Sir Galahad* off Bluff Cove when the Rapier anti-missile tracker defence system failed, eight days before the Argentine surrender. It killed 55 Welsh Guards – who had been waiting too long to disembark.

Shlomo Argov

When the Falklands war started, Sir Michael Havers QC (Attorney-General, MP for Wimbledon and later to become Lord Chancellor) told me that Israel was thought to be exporting arms to Argentina, and asked me if I could do anything to help. I went to see Shlomo Argov, the Israeli Ambassador, at the embassy, and told him that Her Majesty's Government would be most grateful if the exports could be stopped.

He was a brilliant man of immense, though sometimes aggressive, charm. He was certainly fond of Britain, having studied at the London School of Economics, but there was always a touch of bitterness there. When I asked him about it, he told me that he had been betrayed by the British army on one occasion. At the end of the Mandate in 1947, when he was only 18 years old, he had been in command of a crack Palmach unit of the Israeli army. It had been assigned to take over an important observation post from the British army in the north of the country, on the border with Lebanon. A time had been agreed for the hand-over, and his unit had arrived at the appointed time, only to discover that the British had left some time earlier, allowing the post to be taken over by an Arab unit. As a result, the Israelis had had to fight to gain control of the post, and unnecessary loss of life resulted. In particular, he had lost a close friend and, I believe, he had been wounded himself. 'Do you wonder that I am bitter?' he asked me. I did not.

When I went to see him about arms to Argentina, he began to lecture me.

'Haven't the British drummed into us over the years that the most important imperative in international commercial life is that contracts, properly entered into at arm's length, have to be honoured? Now you are asking me to break a contract?'

'But in time of war against your friends, surely the breaking of such a contract would be justified,' I replied.

'Friends?' he countered. 'Is it the action of friends to help our enemies? Why do you allow the PLO, who terrorise your Israeli friends, to have offices in London where they plan our destruction?'

Touché – I had myself been campaigning to stop the PLO being allowed to operate in Britain.

Shlomo walked across the room to his secure telephone, lifted the receiver, and asked to be put through to Menachem Begin, the Israeli Prime Minister, in Tel Aviv. After a few moments the telephone rang back, and he had an animated conversation in Hebrew, which I could not understand. He said we must wait, and over lemon tea and cinnamon biscuits, we chatted. About fifteen minutes later Shlomo was called back to the phone. More animated conversation in Hebrew. He came over to me with a stern look on his face.

'You must understand,' he said, 'that the order for these weapons was placed long before the conflict arose, and this is a private contract over which the State of Israel has no control. But,' he said, allowing himself the hint of a smile, 'the transport logistics are another matter, and the Prime Minister has assured me that plans will be made to route their delivery via the North Pole! As long as you are quick with the war your government need give the matter no more thought.'

I passed on the encouraging news to Havers. He assured me that the government would be very pleased with my efforts – and relieved. They may have been, but no one ever bothered to tell me the actual outcome – although I think I might have been told if any Israeli arms had ever been delivered.

A few weeks later, on the evening of 3 June 1982, as Shlomo Argov was leaving the Dorchester Hotel under police guard following a diplomatic dinner, he was shot in an assassination attempt, and was left totally paralysed by a bullet which lodged in his brain. One member of the assassination team from the Abu Nidel faction of the PLO, the Palestinian terror organisation, was shot dead on the spot by Shlomo's alert Metropolitan Protection Officer. The other two were arrested within the hour, their getaway car index number having been noted. They were later tried for attempted murder at the Old Bailey, pleaded not guilty, and were convicted and sentenced to 30–35 years' imprisonment.

As for Shlomo, the finest surgeons were flown in from all over the world to save his life. They succeeded. Most of his friends thought it would have been better if they had failed. I went to visit him in the Hadassah Hospital, near the Mount of Olives in Jerusalem. It was dreadful. His mind was sharp enough to remember my name and he launched into a tirade against the British. His body was full of pain which his doctors assured me was only in the mind. He lived a life of what must have been utter misery for a further 21 years until, in February 2003, peace came to him at last.

Within a week of the assassination attempt, the Israelis retaliated. They bombed, and then invaded, Lebanon, where the terrorists had been harboured. They stayed in occupation of the south of that country for 18 years. Goodness knows how many thousands more died as a result of the attack on Shlomo Argov. It is said that he had been against the invasion. I doubt very much that he would have been against Israel's response to the continuous bombing by Hezbollah, surrogates of Iran and Iraq, that has tragically taken place since, in 2006. He was a fighter, a patriot, and a very brave man.

The sinking of the *Belgrano*

After the Falklands war I was involved, as a member of the Foreign Affairs Select Committee, with the parliamentary enquiry into the sinking of the Argentine battleship, the *Generalissimo Belgrano*, which had taken place just before 8pm on Sunday 2 May 1982.

Some in the Labour Party, led by Tam Dalyell, Labour MP for Linlithgow, and spurred on by journalists, had accused Margaret Thatcher of unnecessarily sinking the *Belgrano*, with the loss of 321 (originally thought to have been 368) of the crew of 1138. This accusation came to a head in the middle of the 1983 general election campaign later in the year, when Mrs Thatcher was answering questions on a television phone-in programme. A housewife put the allegation to her, and the Prime Minister was so upset that anyone should seriously think that she or her cabinet were capable of such a horror, even in time of war, that, unusually for her, she gave a less than convincing reply. The allegation was always absurd. Apart from anything else, operational decisions of this kind are only taken after advice from the military High Command. To clear the air, and to remove all doubt, the All-Party Foreign Affairs Select Committee decided on an enquiry.

The argument against Mrs Thatcher, put by Dalyell, was that 'she coldly and deliberately gave the orders to sink the *Belgrano*, in the knowledge that an honourable peace was on offer'. Furthermore, the *Belgrano*, when it was sunk, was actually steaming away from the combat zone on its way home: 'Why, if it was going back to port,' Dalyell asked, 'was it necessary to sink it?'

The committee addressed these and related questions. We interviewed cabinet ministers, their military advisers, and ambassadors. We inspected documents and records – and particularly the 'top secret' military intelligence known as the 'Crown Jewels,' which were the records of the submarine *Conqueror* which had actually sunk the cruiser.

The first question was, did the retreating *Belgrano* still pose a threat to our forces? Could the ship have turned round? Or could it have played some other part in an attack? Our admirals certainly thought so. The ship had 15 guns with a range of 13 miles, and it also had Seacat anti-aircraft missiles. Its escorting destroyers were thought to have Exocet anti-ship missiles, with a range of more than 20 miles. Their view was later confirmed by the Argentine Naval Commander himself, Rear-Admiral Lombardo, who told the BBC *Panorama* television programme, that the ship and its escorts were going to form part of a pincer movement coming back against the Task Force. The committee concluded that it would have been unreasonable for the British naval authorities to have reached any other conclusion than that the *Belgrano* still posed a threat when it was sunk, that its sinking was therefore militarily justified, and that to have authorised any other course would have been a dereliction of duty by the government.

What of the Peruvian peace proposals? Did the cabinet know of them when the order was given to sink the *Belgrano*? In any event, had they been acceptable to both the British and the Argentine governments? Since the British were not involved in negotiating the proposals, nor were they consulted, it is academic whether they would have been acceptable or not, had they known about them. In fact they turned out to be little different from the proposals that had been put forward by the US Secretary of State, General Al Haig, a few days before, and which had been roundly rejected by the Argentine Junta. General Haig himself told the committee that he did not think that we were on the verge of any settlement when the *Belgrano* went down.

Nevertheless, the allegation was that Mrs Thatcher knew about the Peruvian peace proposals when she gave the order to sink the ship. Unfortunately that hare had been set running either by Haig's misunderstanding of the situation, or by his loose use of language. He told the *Panorama* programme, and subsequently wrote in his 'memoirs,' that he had got the impression that Francis Pym, the British Foreign Secretary, had accepted the proposals in principle by Sunday lunchtime. Pym vehemently denied that. He told our committee that no positive proposals, to agree or disagree, were brought to his attention until the day after the sinking. His explanation was confirmed to us by both the British Ambassador to the US, and the British Ambassador to Peru, both of whom had been closely involved. We put this discrepancy to General Haig. He told us that he had no reason to contradict what Francis Pym had said to us. In other words, the allegation was a load of nonsense! We concluded that the British War Cabinet was not aware of the Peruvian peace proposals when the order was given to sink the *Belgrano*.

After the *Belgrano* had been sunk, the Argentine fleet returned to port and never left it during the remainder of hostilities. The *Belgrano* incident distracted attention from the fact that the war was not of our making, and that the Falkland islanders had the right to decide who they wished to have ruling them. As far as I know, no apology was ever made to Margaret Thatcher by her parliamentary accusers who, by their persistence, in the end succeeded only in making themselves look foolish.

There is no doubt that the United States, although not openly coming out in support of Britain in the Falklands war, did much behind the scenes to help our victory – particularly with the provision of the latest technology and of intelligence, and, in one famous incident, by attempting to rescue a fallen helicopter and its crew. That 'special relationship' between the two countries may well have been one of the forces later driving the Blair government, despite considerable opposition from the media and the Labour Party, to side with President Bush over the invasion of Iraq in 2003. It certainly had a lot to do with what was known as the Westland Affair in 1988, when Michael Heseltine, the defence Secretary in favour of a European helicopter, walked out of the Thatcher government over the Prime Minister's support of the Sikorsky helicopter, which was unwanted by the generals, but backed by the Americans: for General Haig wrote in his memoirs, 'I called in my marker.'

Dreadful as the Falklands war was, with its loss of 255 British lives and three or even four times that number of Argentinians, there were positive far-reaching consequences for good. In Argentina Galtieri and his military dictatorship were toppled and replaced by a democratic government. For Britain, our reputation in the world rose considerably, and the electoral victories of the Thatcher government that followed ensured that the ratchet of Thatcherism had time to become well nigh irreversible. For the Falkland islanders, the subsequent regulation of fishery licensing and the peaceful farming of their sheep with its internationally acclaimed wool, has given them considerable prosperity. Whether the revival of Argentine ambitions which have sprung from the recent discovery of oil beneath the island's waters will provoke further conflict, we will have to wait to see.

14

1983: Denis Nilsen

'Variety's the very spice of life,
That gives it all its flavour'
(William Cowper, *The Timepiece*)

Another year full of variety for me was 1983. I visited Hong Kong, Taiwan, Israel, Chile and Spain; fought a successful general election; became a Crown Court Recorder; and defended in of some of my most high-profile cases.

Taiwan and Hong Kong

I met Vincent Siew, the Taiwanese Director of the Board of Foreign Trade, when we both attended a foreign leadership course at the School of Foreign Service at Washington's Georgetown University the previous summer. He invited me, as an active Conservative MP, to Taiwan as the guest of the government of the People's Republic of China. He wanted me to learn more about his country, its relations with Communist China, its approach to commercial piracy, and to meet some of its important politicians, military men, judges and industrialists. I said I would be delighted to accept, if Cathay Pacific would let me exchange the first-class ticket he was offering me for two economy tickets, so that I could take Gloria. I also wanted us to stop over in Hong Kong. Although Taiwan said no to the arrangement at first, they relented when Cathay agreed to it.

So on 4 January Gloria and I flew to Taiwan, stopping for three days en route in Hong Kong. There we had meetings with Sir Edward Youde (the Governor), the British political advisor Robin McLaren (later to become Ambassador to China), John Griffiths QC (the Attorney-General), and interior, security, education and trade officials. Gloria met the Tourist

Board and was invited to return soon to train the colony's new tour guides. Her work commitments prevented her from taking up the generous offer, and she was not too keen to leave Rachel (or me) for several weeks.

Hong Kong, an amazingly vibrant and outstandingly successful British colony, was in 1983 in a state of considerable apprehension and nervousness. The 99-year lease, which Britain held from China, was coming to an end. Our government was deep in negotiations with the People's Republic, in an effort to ensure that the political and legal institutions, which had given the colony its political stability, rule of law and phenomenal trading position in the world, would not be destroyed when it returned to the ownership of what was then a comparatively repressive and economically backward communist superpower. Yet we held hardly any bargaining chips. I later made four more fact-finding and goodwill visits to Hong Kong with the Commons Foreign Affairs and Home Affairs Committees over this worrying time. We held public meetings, met important individuals and produced reports to parliament, hopefully demonstrating both to the people of Hong Kong and to the People's Republic, the British parliament's deep concern for the colony's future.

I tried several times to speak in the House of Commons in support of Hong Kong, but debates on the colony's future were short, held at a late hour, and preference had usually to be given to the real Hong Kong experts. Geoffrey Howe, then Foreign Secretary, won an undertaking that there would be no substantial change for fifty years, but the fact that final decisions on political and legal issues were to pass to Beijing left us with more hope than confidence. After 1989, the horrific repression of Tienanmen Square had remained in everyone's memory. From time to time there have been signs that China might renege on their Hong Kong agreement, although by and large it seems, thankfully, to be holding.

Ten years later, I was offered a very well-paid case in Hong Kong, but it was expected to last up to a year, and I could not have remained a member of parliament. Rachel played her part, winning an Inner Temple Pegasus Scholarship to Hong Kong for three months, where she marshalled for two High Court judges, Neil Kaplin and Brian Keith, and worked in the personal injury department for Simmonds and Simmonds, the leading City of London solicitors. She goes back when she can afford it, for the rugby sevens. Hong Kong is such a thrilling place, and the three of us loved our visits there.

Three days after our Hong Kong stopover, Gloria and I flew to Taipei and received VIP treatment. We were driven everywhere in limousines with flags flying and motorcycle outriders. We were also flown in a windy and noisy military aircraft to the frontline town and port of Quemoy, five miles from Red China, accompanied by twelve Italian members of parliament. After a few glasses of rice wine I had to make a thank-you speech on everyone's behalf – in less than perfect Italian. Our host, the general with responsibility for defending Taiwan from invasion, was even more affected by the rice wine than I was. A Taiwanese tradition requires a guest to toast the host by lifting a glass in his direction, to which he is expected to stand and respond with 'gumbay', his replying toast of welcome. After fifteen such toasts, the poor man could only stand with difficulty, and could not remain standing at all. He joked, 'I am now a very red Chinese!'

There would probably have been no better time for the Red Chinese army to have invaded Taiwan!

A few weeks later, the military plane in which we had flown to Quemoy crashed, killing everyone on board.

I returned to domestic political activities in England. With the experience of two very sad constituency cases, I helped to persuade the government of the need to introduce a crime of child abduction, to help mothers whose children had been kidnapped by their foreign fathers and taken abroad. I successfully lobbied ministers for money to build the long-overdue Tutbury bypass in my constituency. I managed to secure a promise of improved train services from Burton to Birmingham and Derby. In a Commons speech I supported the call for the privatisation of the water industry. At a conference of the Guild of British Newspaper Editors, I defended the Contempt of Court Act against an attack by journalists and the Law Society. In a speech to Uttoxeter Conservatives, I attacked the Campaign for Nuclear Disarmament saying:

Because Europe would not rearm, Hitler invaded Poland. Because Czechoslovakia, Hungary and Afghanistan were weak, Russia invaded them. Now the Russian leader, Yuri Andropov is saying: 'let no one expect unilateral disarmament from us – we are not that naïve!' If we want our children to live in a safe world, then there is no alternative to protecting them properly with the nuclear deterrent that had kept peace in Western Europe for 37 years.

In the midst of these great issues of world and national politics, I had also to attend to my legal practice. Because I had no political job in government, I was able to do so.

John Goodwin

Whenever Stan Hicks, my stalwart clerk, thought that I was in danger of taking politics too seriously, or that I was getting forgotten at the Bar, he would get me into court. This also helped to relieve my ever-flagging financial condition. And so, in March 1983, Jeffery Gordon briefed me to lead David Ashby, at the Old Bailey, in defence of John Goodwin, charged with the crime of nobbling a jury.

Goodwin was alleged to have masterminded a plot to bribe jurors at his trial on charges of burglary, involving jewellery, gold and silver worth £1.25 million. The plot was foiled by the courage of a waitress who refused the cash offered to her on several occasions, and reported the matter to the police. The conspirators had been obtaining information about jurors from milkmen, publicans, postmen and delivery boys, and the jurors had each been offered £1000.

The police evidence against Goodwin, however, turned out to be rather unsatisfactory. One police officer gave evidence that, by chance, he had just happened to overhear Goodwin say something highly incriminating as he sat at the next table to him in a café near the Old Bailey during the trial. He assured the jury that he had not been involved in any way in the Goodwin case, and had never seen Goodwin before. It was just a coincidence that he happened to be stationed at the same police station as officers who were engaged in the trial. When I asked him, in cross-examination, how he knew that what was being said on another table might be important enough for him to listen closely and then to write down every word he heard Goodwin say, he suddenly remembered that he had, after all, once seen Goodwin; that was when Goodwin had been on trial in another Old Bailey court. He had on that occasion, he explained, caught sight of him through the glass in the door. The problem with that explanation was that it was untrue: the glass on that door at that time had, according to other evidence, been covered up for security reasons – especially so that no one could see inside the court.

Two other police officers in the case were not much better witnesses. They said that they had been standing together, and had closely observed Goodwin's car pull away from a building. Unfortunately, one officer remembered clearly that it had gone to the right, while the other's clear recollection was that it had gone to the left. Other police witnesses gave evidence that contradicted the computerised record of what they had reported at the time. The jury cannot have found the police evidence too convincing.

However, the main evidence of the conspiracy was to come from two women who had told the police they were actually present at a meeting at which Goodwin had arranged to nobble the jury. One came into court, took one look at Goodwin in the dock, burst into tears, and refused to give evidence. The judge ordered her to be taken down to the cells. The other woman came into court, looked at Goodwin and promptly announced that she was not going to be a 'grass.' The same judicial fate awaited her. Although neither witness actually identified Goodwin, the jury naturally drew its own conclusions. He was convicted and sentenced to seven years' imprisonment. His eight co-defendants, seven of whom had pleaded guilty, received sentences of between two and four years. Old Bailey records, the judge was told, revealed that over nine months there had been attempts to interfere or intimidate jurors in no fewer than fourteen trials.

'Uncorrupt justice is part of our freedom,' said Mr Justice Talbot, when he passed sentence, 'and when you attack that you attack us all.'

My application for leave to appeal against the conviction was turned down by the single appeal judge, whose task is to filter out weak applications. We took the case to the full Court of Appeal, arguing that the identification evidence, in a case in which the police evidence was so badly flawed, needed to be more than merely the tears of the women and their refusal to speak.

I opened my case at 10.30am, and battle raged all day between myself and the prosecutor, the Senior Treasury Counsel and my friend and mentor from The Factory, Kenneth Richardson. At times the court seemed to be with me; at other times they were obviously not. At 4.30pm, when we were soon to rise after a really hard day and I was tired, I committed an unforgivable forensic sin – I lost self-control.

'If I went back to the Temple and told my colleagues that the Court of Appeal of England and Wales had considered that identification evidence like this was wholly satisfactory, I would be laughed at!' I was astonished to hear myself saying.

'We'll see about that!' muttered Lord Justice Lawton, rising angrily with his brother judges, and storming out of court. I turned to Jeffery Gordon sitting behind me and apologised abjectly for my dreadful behaviour that was bound to have lost me the sympathy of the court, and with it our client's case.

'Not at all,' comforted the kindly Jeffery, whom many years of marathon running had made sympathetic to the weakness and failings of others. 'That was exactly the political-type jolt they needed to get them thinking sensibly.' I had the miserable feeling that I had let down my client and the entire Bar. I prepared to make a grovelling apology to the court next morning.

The court reassembled at 10.30am. Fred Lawton swept in, and before I could say anything he said that it had been a dreadful case with no apparent merit whatsoever. However, if asked whether the court could put their hands on their hearts and say that the identification was completely safe, the three judges agreed that they could not do so.

'However suspicious we are, we have to look at the quality of the evidence and the quality was lacking.' They felt obliged to allow the appeal and to quash the conviction.

I was flabbergasted! Jeffery tugged at my gown and told me to ask for costs.

'We can't,' I said in a loud whisper. 'You heard what Lawton said about the merits of the case. They will come down on us like a ton of bricks for being ridiculous and ungrateful.' Jeffery persisted, and since barristers have to act on instructions, and Jeffery's instructions were unmistakably clear and firm, I had little course open to me but to obey.

'May I ask for costs, my Lords,' I mumbled.

'Costs?' exploded Lord Justice Lawton. 'On what conceivable grounds?'

'Your lordship's decision came as such a surprise,' I weakly replied, 'that I am afraid that I have not prepared myself with the answer.' I reached for Archbold, the criminal lawyer's bible, to remind myself of the costs regulations.

'A surprise?' thundered this most distinguished judge, 'Surprise? Why, you told us yesterday what would happen to us all in the Temple if we came to any other conclusion!' Before I could get my astonished self together, he added, 'I suppose you would argue that if the single judge had given you leave to appeal, we would have had to grant you your costs, because they would have to follow the acquittal. Since we have found that the single judge was wrong to refuse you leave, then you must have your costs, mustn't you?'

'Of course, my Lord,' I answered fawningly. My instructing solicitor was grateful on behalf of his client. I was enormously relieved that I had not made such an ass of myself as I had thought.

While John Goodwin had been in prison, his wife Shirley had been kidnapped by a gang with sawn-off shotguns, and had been kept chained up at a deserted holiday camp on the Isle of Sheppey. A ransom of £50,000 had been demanded. From his prison cell Goodwin, working with the police, trapped the gang. Mrs Goodwin was released and the gang leaders were caught, arrested, charged, convicted and, in June 1984, sentenced – the leader Charles Pitt to 18 years imprisonment, and his son-in-law Sean McDonald to 8 years.

John Goodwin had certainly led a charmed life. In 1981 he had been charged with being a member of a gang attempting to break into Barclay's Bank in Whitechapel, with thermic lances. At the first trial the jury had disagreed. At the re-trial he pretended that he was having a heart attack, and that trial was abandoned. At the third trial the case was stopped when he produced a tape-recording of a detective constable and a detective inspector, in the process of taking a bribe from him. No evidence was offered against him. The policemen were charged and tried at the Old Bailey, but presumably since Goodwin, the principal witness against them for the Crown was such a villain, they too were acquitted. A third police officer, who had been convicted after a jury trial, even had his conviction quashed in the Court of Appeal.

The following year the supergrass Micky Gervaise, a jeweller serving a six-year sentence for crimes involving £6 million, and who had been the prime mover in the Mountnessing silver bullion robbery for which my client Deanus had been charged, made a statement implicating Goodwin, and his friend Brian Reader, in a series of burglaries amounting to over £1.25 million. But at that trial, he said that he had been ordered by the police to give false evidence against them. That trial, too, had to be stopped. At the re-trial both defendants were acquitted. The judge told Goodwin that he left the court 'without any stain' on his character.

I have lost track of my client John Goodwin since then. He has certainly not asked me to defend him again. I was fortunate in not losing track of my junior at the Goodwin trials, David Ashby. At an early stage of the proceedings he had asked me if he could be absent for a short time to be interviewed for the Conservative parliamentary candidacy for Ashby in Leicestershire. 'Ashby for Ashby' being the perfect electoral slogan, I told him that he had to go. David was selected, elected and served that town and north-west Leicestershire with loyalty and dedication for fourteen years. He later became an active member of my Home Affairs Select Committee. Sadly his political, though not his legal, career came to an end when he unsuccessfully sued the *Guardian* for libelling him as a homosexual. As more and more prominent homosexuals seem to be 'outing' themselves, and the attitude of society has changed so much towards them that the law protects them against any form of discrimination, that may well be the last time anyone will be able to claim that being called a homosexual has diminished their reputation among right-thinking members of society – the test for defamation.

The evil of jury nobbling has more recently led to a change in the law permitting trial without a jury in exceptional cases – one of which has now taken place. The concern of all those who believe in jury trial must be that this will be the slippery slope leading to more and more trials before a judge alone.

Back to politics

As 1983 progressed, I seemed to get even busier. I spoke in parliament on the Marriage Bill, supporting proposals for extending the places at which marriage could be solemnised: I hoped that more people might want to get married. I lobbied Peter Walker, then Secretary of State for Agriculture, with the suggestion that the problems facing pig farmers might be reduced if the government helped the industry to improve its poor marketing. I attacked the Labour controlled Staffordshire County Council for proposing to close three Burton primary schools without being able to explain to parents why such disruption of their children's education was necessary. And I urged upon the local health authority the need for a special care baby unit for Burton General Hospital, which was thereafter soon provided.

I also helped with one campaign of particular importance for sufferers of cystic fibrosis, Rachel's illness. Tadworth Court Children's Hospital, in the Reigate constituency of my friend George Gardiner MP, was a subsidiary of Great Ormond Street Children's Hospital, set in tens of acres of parkland round a Queen Anne mansion. It provided hospice and respite care to children suffering advanced forms of degenerative cystic fibrosis, and their families. It was threatened with closure because it had become too expensive to maintain. George and I campaigned on the hospital's behalf. I managed to secure an adjournment debate, at the end of 1982, to draw attention to the threat and said:

The uniqueness of this hospital is that it is what some hospitals claim to be, but few really are – a home. It is a place of happiness, providing care and hope for children who are terribly sick, and for some who have little hope of life. To those children, Tadworth is a second home, to which they are happy to return time and again. It is a home where the parents can go to live for short periods with their sick children and be sustained themselves, where they can gain some respite from the despair of coping at home with the most handicapped of children. It is a place where parents who are cracking up under the strain can receive friendship, advice and help.

In March, after a visit to Tadworth by Health Minister Kenneth Clarke two months earlier, the brilliant campaign, conducted by George Gardiner and the nurses and administrators round the offices of the *Sun* and other national newspapers in Fleet Street and in parliament, bore fruit: the hospital would remain open and receive support from both government and private charitable funds.

Immediately after the Goodwin trial, I went to Madrid to attend a meeting at which diplomats from many countries were preparing for the Helsinki follow-up later in the year. It was a joy to see with what swashbuckling panache our representatives performed, and how warmly enthusiastic the Eastern European countries were towards the new Thatcher government. 'The British are back,' they kept declaring. Two days after that, I went to Israel to attend a conference of international parliamentarians, held over three days in the Knesset. I took the opportunity to visit Shlomo Argov in the Hadasseh hospital. I flew back on the Friday for the Burton Conservative AGM, and on Saturday chaired a public meeting in Burton Town Hall I had organised to see how we might improve employment prospects in the constituency.

My judicial career began in March when I was appointed an assistant recorder of the Crown Courts. There followed a week of instruction, sitting with Judge James Mendl as he tried cases at Knightsbridge Crown Court. After Easter I had a week of constituency engagements in Burton, took part in three debates in the Commons on housing, finance and young people, and made a speech on law and order at the annual conference of Senior Probation Officers in Porthcawl. Then, at the end of May, a general election was called.

General election 1983

My campaign began, as it always did, with the ritual destruction of my urban poster sites by Labour supporting youths, followed by a press attack by me upon the vandals for traducing the rights of others as members of the Labour Party, and then the Labour candidate's denial of any Labour involvement in the desecration. As the campaign got under way, helped by the efficient organisation of my agent, Hugh O'Brien, and the magnificent support of Burton Conservative officers and workers like John and Norah Hicklin, Cedric and Fay Insley, Keith Priestnall, Joan Cullen and the families of Stan Clarke and Jim Leavesley, I found the reception on the doorstep and at public meetings to be particularly warm and encouraging. It was not just the Falklands factor. It began to seem that the Thatcher government had not only managed to reverse the 'ratchet of socialism', but there were actual signs of improvement in the economy. The poll tax had yet to be introduced, and the sun shone literally as well as politically. Michael Foot was swept away, and Margaret Thatcher's Tories surged back to power again on 9 June with a majority of 144 over all other parties and a majority of 188 over Labour. My own majority rose by 1846 to the unheard of heights, for a marginal seat, of 11,647.

As I was driven round the constituency next day, thanking voters for renewing their faith in me and the Conservative party, someone threw an egg at me which just missed Cedric Insley. I caught it and threw it back more accurately. I suppose that, as an assistant recorder, I should not have done that. I certainly enjoyed it more than I had enjoyed an earlier incident in the campaign, when my loudspeaker had awakened a night-worker. Driven to a violent frenzy, he had run after me in the street brandishing a knife. He was brought to the ground with a rugby tackle – by his wife! That taught me two important lessons: one, that in a democracy you cannot please all of the people all of the time; the other, that the women in Burton were not to be crossed, especially by their husbands!

Stan got to work again, and I was in court through most of the summer vacation. Then, as we approached party conference time, I found myself engaged in another high profile case.

David Martin

At mid-day on 14 January 1983, Detective-Sergeant Peter Finch of the Metropolitan Police drew his revolver on a man sitting in a yellow Mini that had stopped in traffic in London's Earls Court Road, and shot him five times in the head and body. He then pulled the man out of the car, and started hitting him about the head with the gun. The man was so badly wounded that he nearly died.

The officer was not only behaving as no police officer should ever behave, but he had been terribly mistaken in his identification. He thought he was shooting a man called David Martin, who had been arrested some months earlier for armed robbery and the attempted murder of a police officer, and had then escaped from Marylebone Magistrates Court on Christmas Eve. The man Finch actually shot was an innocent passenger in the car, a 26-year-old film technician named Stephen Waldorf. The Metropolitan Police had to pay the equivalent of half a million pounds in compensation for this attack by Finch and a Detective Constable Jardine, and both stood trial for attempted murder and attempted wounding nine months later at the Old Bailey. They were cleared of all charges. That Finch had been allowed to have the gun with which he had shot Waldorf was quite disgraceful – as I shall explain a little later.

Martin remained at large for only two more weeks after the Earls Court blunder. He was arrested on 28 January when, following a movie-like chase along the Northern Line underground tunnel between Belsize Park and Hampstead, he found his exit blocked by police advancing in the other direction. When ordered to put his hands up, he refused and carried on walking towards his captors: he was lucky not to have been shot.

David Martin was an intelligent and colourful character. He had strikingly handsome, if feminine, features, and long flowing fair hair. His trial was reported in full each day by tabloid, broadsheet, TV and radio, and both Ralph Haeems and I received daily letters to pass on to Martin from his adoring female fans. But he was also a suicidal, gun-crazy and violent criminal. He was said to be 'an arrogant pervert' by some who knew him. He bore the nicknames of 'Houdini in drag' (having escaped arrest several times dressed as a woman), and 'King of the twirlers' (because of his skill as a lock-picker). One former inmate at Gartree prison told a reporter from the *Daily Express*: 'Martin used to break out of his cell at dead of night, open security door after security door until he reached the governor's office, where he delighted in stealing the cigars.'

On 21 September 1983 he stood trial at the Old Bailey facing an indictment alleging fifteen offences. I was leading John Caudle for the defence; Kenneth Richardson led John Nutting for the prosecution. The alleged offences ranged from car thefts, burglaries of business premises, theft of guns and ammunition, possession of firearms to resist arrest, armed robbery of £25,000 from Brinks-Mat on a delivery to Lloyds Bank, grievous bodily harm to the security guard, to attempted murder of a police officer. Martin had a bad prison record, having been to borstal for possessing a firearm to resist arrest, and having already served a nine-year prison sentence for conspiracies to steal and to obtain property by a forged instrument, and also for prison riot. When he was arrested he told the police, 'I could have killed the lot of you.' At his trial he said that he had been determined to resist arrest or kill himself, because he could not face another prison sentence.

Seldom can a defendant have been given so many benefits of the doubt. Of the fifteen counts in the indictment, Martin admitted taking part in the theft of the money, but the jury acquitted him of armed robbery and causing grievous bodily harm to a security guard. He admitted burglary of the offices of the magazine *Gun Review*, but the jury acquitted him of two other burglaries – of a Covent Garden gunsmith, and a West End security equipment office. They also acquitted him of car thefts and related offences, and, more seriously, of having guns with intent to endanger life. They did, however, convict him of the lesser offence of having with him a gun with intent to resist arrest.

He admitted his guilt to the offences where there was positive and reliable evidence. Where there was no such evidence, the jury seem to have accepted Martin's explanation of events, and appeared not to want to convict him in any case where they did not have to do so on the evidence. They accepted that he may have thought that the bank money was going to be snatched (theft), but that he did not have any idea guns were going to be taken or used, which would have made his crime one of armed robbery. They were also prepared to accept that he had not been the man who had shot at the security guard, and that he did not know the man who had been responsible for the shooting had with him a gun which he was prepared to use. They accepted that he was just borrowing a Mercedes from his friend, who might not have told him it was stolen. His same explanation for being in a stolen Volkswagen Golf was also accepted. He admitted being in possession of security and electronic equipment that had been stolen in a burglary, but he denied being the burglar: when he burgled premises, it was always professionally done, he explained to the jury, with a specially made key. Not for him the vulgar method employed in that case by the burglar, who had sawn his way in.

Even with his good looks and a kind of pop-idol status, it may seem surprising that the jury can have been as sympathetic as they were to this prolific offender. There were certainly two areas of the trial where the prosecution case was strongly disputed.

Just before midnight on 5 August 1982, Martin was caught inside a film-processing laboratory off Portman Square in London, pretending to be a security guard. He had nearly succeeded in bluffing his way past a real security guard, when two police officers, passing the building and alerted by the burglar alarm, had arrived and challenged him. He later explained to the jury that he had been to the premises several times before, for his purpose had been the crime of video piracy, there being on the premises machinery for copying 20 video films at a time. He had tried to run away, but was brought down on the stairs with a rugby tackle by one of the officers. Both officers seized him and one put him into a headlock. Martin said the other officer had his arm and was twisting it so hard that the pain was excruciating – a fact which, that officer fairly conceded at the trial. Martin managed to work a hand free and took a gun, which he just happened to have with him, from his pocket. Unfortunately it was loaded, and in the struggle, with a hair-pressure trigger, the gun went off accidentally, and shot Police Constable Nicholas Carr in the top of his thigh. Martin said in evidence that he had no intention of shooting anyone, but was panicking because of the pain, and was desperate to get the police off him.

But what was he doing with a loaded gun in his pocket? He explained to the jury that the major criminals who were behind the multi-million pound video piracy had not been happy when he had told them that this was going to be the last run he would make for them. Fearing that they might come to the premises and attack him, he had taken the gun – for self-defence only. Unfortunately for his account, the silver revolver, which the police said had been used, did not have a hair-pressure trigger: it required quite a pull to set off a shot. Martin's explanation was that the gun produced by the police was not the gun he had used. He had used another larger gun. Another had indeed been found on him, and that did have a hair-pressure trigger, but since the cartridge that had been fired had somehow been lost, it could not be proved conclusively which gun had in fact been used. Furthermore, Dr Clarke, the firearms expert called by the prosecution, said that it was difficult to see how the gun he was alleged to have used could have been so carefully positioned so as to cause that particular wound.

I submitted to the judge, Mr Justice Kilner-Brown, that there was no case to answer on attempted murder: if Martin had wanted to kill the police officer, he had earlier opportunities to do so, and had shown no such intention. I was successful. As Martin had admitted to possessing the gun, and to drawing it against an arresting police officer, the jury had little choice but to convict him of causing grievous bodily harm to PC Carr with intent to resist his arrest – which they did by a majority of eleven to one.

The second, and far more worrying, aspect of the trial concerned what happened when the police had arrested Martin on the second occasion outside his flat. After his original arrest at the video-copying premises, he was charged, and remanded in custody. But on one of his appearances at Marylebone Magistrates Court Houdini had escaped. On 13 September 1982 he bought a gun in a gun-shop, and the shop owner, suspicious because he was unsure whether the purchaser was a man or a woman, had called the police. They knew exactly who the purchaser was. Ten of them lay in wait for him as Martin came up to his flat in Crawford Street in the lift.

The account the police gave in court was that DS Finch, of the Waldorf incident, not realising that the person who looked like a woman and who was swinging a handbag was Martin, went up to him as he put the key in the door and said, 'Excuse me, love.'

Martin had turned round with a gun in each hand and said, 'I will have you. I will blow you away.'

A struggle had taken place, and Martin had pointed a gun at Finch. Another armed officer, further up the corridor towards the lift, thinking that Finch was about to be shot, shot Martin first.

Martin's account was wholly different, and as it turned out appeared to be more consistent with the evidence and common sense. The police had given him no opportunity to draw a gun; they just shot him as he got out of the lift on the way to his flat.

The police version was full of holes. They could not explain why, believing Martin to have been someone who had shot a policeman, they could have been so laid-back about arresting him. Were they really so incompetent, this crack unit from the Flying Squad, that they had surrendered the element of surprise in their favour, and had let Martin walk out of the lift and along the corridor before they had approached him? Did DS Finch really believe that this was an innocent woman walking along the corridor? They must have known full well that this was the escapee and police shooter for whom they had been lying in wait! They knew that David Martin often dressed as a woman, the shopkeeper had described the gun buyer as a man dressed as a woman, they knew what car he was using, they had staked out the public house opposite the block of flats where Martin lived, and they had their personal radios at the ready. Yet, on their accounts to the jury, they had all managed to miss him driving up in his car, getting out, walking in through the front door of the block of flats and coming up in the lift. Theirs was the unlikely story.

As if that did not throw enough doubt on the police version of events, they had difficulty explaining why, if he had been shot at his front door as they alleged, the pool of blood was several yards back at the lift – where Martin said he was in fact shot. Nor could they satisfactorily explain why, if their account of what happened was true, the handbag and keys Martin had been carrying had been recovered by the lift, not by his front door. Nor why, if the revolver and door-keys had, on the police account, been dropped before he had been shot, his blood was on them. Nor could they explain how, if Martin had turned to face the police officers with the guns in his hands, he had been shot in the back of the neck! On practically every other important detail, such as which of the two guns he had actually threatened the police with, where he was standing when he was shot, whether he continued to stagger after the shot, on which shoulder he was carrying the handbag, different officers gave different accounts.

Worst of all, the seven officers present at the shooting all denied on oath that after Martin had been shot in the head and fallen to the floor, Finch had sat upon him, and pistol-whipped his face. They had not, of course, been warned that the prosecution would be producing evidence from other police officers that the pistol-whipping had indeed taken place, that a police doctor would be confirming that the wounds on Martin were consistent with pistol-whipping, and that Finch, who was not allowed to give evidence, had actually made a statement admitting to doing it!

In those circumstances, it was hardly surprising that the jury disbelieved the police. On 11 October, David Martin was acquitted of all the charges save those that he had admitted to committing when he gave evidence. Of the fifteen original charges, he was convicted of only four.

Two matters were certainly more surprising than the jury's verdict. It was astonishing, after Finch's behaviour on Martin's arrest, that he was ever permitted to carry a gun again. If he had been banned, Steven Waldorf would not have been shot.

Also surprising, in all the circumstances, was the sentence that the normally moderate Mr Justice Kilner-Brown passed upon Martin: 40 years imprisonment, which translated to an effective 25 years. That was the kind of sentence Martin might well have received had he been convicted on all the counts alleged against him. As it was, such a sentence was savage, and seemed to me to be about 15 years too much.

I went down to the cells to see him. He was in shock. I told him that I was reasonably confident that we would get the sentence down on appeal. He told me that he could not serve any prison sentence of even ten years, and he was going to top himself. I reported this immediately to the senior prison officer at the court. 'Really!' he said, in a tone of voice that I took to mean that he was not unduly bothered by the prospect. I left the Old Bailey and drove to Blackpool for the Conservative party conference.

One month later Martin was found dead in his cell at Parkhurst prison. He had hanged himself with a piece of flex from a washing machine. No one could explain how he had got hold of it or, it seemed, how the prison officers could have missed seeing it when they had earlier carried out a thorough search of his cell.

While Martin had been on remand at Brixton prison, Denis Nilsen had apparently fallen in love with him. That was why Ralph Haeems and myself, with the formidable Robert Flach as my Junior, came to represent Nilsen at his trial at the Old Bailey two weeks later.

Denis Nilsen

On Tuesday 8 February 1983, Dyno-Rod, the drain-clearing company, was called out to remove a blockage at 23 Cranley Gardens in Cricklewood, north-west London. The refuse engineer who answered the call at first thought that the problem was rotting chicken meat. Closer examination indicated that it was something very different. The finding led to the arrest the next day of Denis Nilsen, one of the tenants of the house – for murder.

He was a 38-year-old civil servant, working as an interviewer at a local Job Centre. Just before his arrest Nilsen had told a colleague at work: 'If I'm not in tomorrow, I'll either be ill, dead or in jail,' and they had both laughed. At the house, evidence of three killings was discovered. At 195 Melrose Avenue, another house at which Nilsen had been living earlier, and to which he took the police, were found the remains of twelve more bodies.

The truly gruesome serial killing spree had started in late 1978. We know the details of the victims, how they were killed, why they were killed and where parts of their bodies could be found, because Nilsen spoke frankly to the police for 30 hours and wrote 50 notebooks about his exploits, with positional sketches of the bodies. Three other near victims, who had either managed to escape or were set free by Nilsen, gave evidence at his trial. Four others, who were likewise entertained by Nilsen at his home, were not called to give evidence. The author Brian Masters has turned Nilsen's ramblings into a definitive and classic account of the workings of the mind of a serial killer. In *Killing for Company*, Masters writes: 'Nilsen is the first murderer to present an exhaustive archive measuring his introspection. His prison journals are therefore a unique document in the history of criminal homicide.'

There were exceptions, but mostly Nilsen either targeted young homosexuals who were job hunting at his office in the Job Centre, or his victims were young men he had met in a public house during the evening. Before he took them home to spend the night with him, he established that his prospective victims were unlikely to be missed by their families, who, unhappily, had completely lost interest in their own sons. Nilsen apparently craved company so much that, when his victims wanted to leave, he strangled them, making sure that they were dead by drowning them in the bath. He would then wash the bodies, lay them on his bed, sexually fantasise about them, and go to sleep besides them. Later he would put the bodies under the floorboards, for future retrieval and sexual abuse. When the odour became too unpleasant he would cut up the bodies, using his training as an army cook. After boiling heads, hands and feet in a pot on the stove, he either destroyed the body parts by burning them in the garden, or he would wash pieces of the body down the sink or lavatory. Sometimes, if there was too much, he dumped bags of the human remains in public open spaces. One witness, happening upon a plastic bag hanging up in a Cricklewood bus shelter, found it to contain some body parts.

Nilsen explained to psychiatrists that his mental troubles had started when, at the age of six years, he had seen his grandfather's corpse. He complained at Brixton prison, 'No one wants to believe ever that I am just an ordinary man.'

On 24 October 1983, Nilsen stepped up into the dock in Court One at the Old Bailey. He was charged with only six of the murders, and two attempted murders. He pleaded not guilty to murder, but guilty to manslaughter by reason of 'diminished responsibility'. He also pleaded guilty to the attempted murders, for which there could be no defence of 'diminished responsibility'.

The only issue for the jury to try, as far as the murders were concerned, was whether Denis Nilsen was more or less normal and had the intention to kill (or its alternative, an intention to cause really serious bodily harm), in which case he was guilty of murder; or whether his responsibility for the killings was so diminished by mental impairment ('diminished responsibility') that he was guilty only of manslaughter. This was both a legal and medical issue. At the end of the day it did not really matter, as far as the length of his actual sentence was concerned, of what crime he was convicted. Now that we no longer have capital punishment in the United Kingdom, the sentence for both multiple murder and multiple manslaughter would have to be life imprisonment, and either way Nilsen would need constant medical care and treatment, and he could never be released so long as he remained a danger to the public. However the jury decided, Nilsen had killed many times and was not – cannot have been – mentally normal. Although that must have been painfully clear, the jury had to go through the artificial process of making a judgement between murder and manslaughter as if it really did matter.

At the end of the trial, they convicted him of murder. Did they really think he was normal? Unlikely! My guess is that they convicted him of murder, not because they thought he was all there, but because they had little confidence either in the medical evidence that they had heard, or in the complicated law that we lawyers had tried to explain to them. It certainly could not have been easy for them to follow what any of the psychiatrists were talking about. Was it not Sam Goldwyn who said, 'Anyone who goes to a psychiatrist needs his head examined'?

The jury must have thought that the one way they could stop Nilsen ever walking the streets again to commit more killings was to find him guilty of murder: for then they could be sure he would remain in prison for life or as long as the system allowed. And that is the rub: psychiatrists and lawyers have not yet worked out a formula for mental impairment that really makes sense to a jury. This may be because in most cases where defendants are convicted of manslaughter by virtue of 'diminished responsibility', the matter does not even go to a jury: the prosecution and defence psychiatrists agree about the defendant's mental state before trial.

We could not plead that Nilsen was insane because there was no evidence that he was suffering from a mental disorder like schizophrenia. Had there been such evidence the jury could have understood that, particularly if the psychiatrists had been agreed upon the matter. What we did have were statements from psychiatrists that he was so mentally disturbed, albeit to a degree less than insanity, as to make him not always responsible for his actions. But the prosecution did not accept those statements – that is why we had to argue the case before a jury.

As it turned out in court, the psychiatrists, on both sides, were a disaster. They had difficulty explaining themselves. They contradicted each other. Sometimes they even contradicted themselves.

We first called Dr James MacKeith, a most distinguished psychiatrist (whose work on false confessions helped to free the Guildford Four, the Birmingham Six and Judith Ward from convictions for IRA bombings), to say that Nilsen was suffering from a personality disorder that had led him to separate his mental and behavioural activities to such a degree that it indeed qualified as 'diminished responsibility'. This is defined in the Homicide Act of 1957 as:

Such abnormality of the mind (whether arising from a condition of arrested or retarded development of mind or any inherent causes or induced by disease or injury) as substantially impaired his mental responsibility for his acts and omissions in doing or being a party to the killing.

But, after somewhat lengthy (and sometimes quite aggressive) cross-examination by prosecuting counsel Allan Green, when MacKeith was asked again, 'Do you yourself think that he was suffering from diminished responsibility?' he gave the astonishing reply, 'That is for the court to answer.' He refused to confirm that Nilsen was suffering from 'diminished responsibility' because, he explained, 'diminished responsibility' was a legal not a medical term! I wish he had made that clear before we had decided to rely on his opinion.

After that somewhat unhelpful start for the defence, we called Dr Patrick Gallwey, also to say that Nilsen was suffering from 'diminished responsibility'. He told the jury that he had made a special study of the kind of mental condition suffered by Nilsen: it was called, amazingly, the 'Borderline-False-Self-As-If-Pseudo-Normal-Narcissistic-Personality Disorder'. Everyone in court laughed. It was only with the utmost difficulty that I managed to pry the expert away from that form of words to a shortened form that we agreed would be called a 'False-Self' syndrome. This condition manifested itself with the sufferer sometimes being normal and sometimes being paranoid or schizoid. The strain of keeping the abnormal at bay, the psychiatrist explained, led to sudden breakdowns that were violent and psycho-sexual, and they showed in an absence of feeling, so that people were treated as objects. I was not sure that such behaviour was too dissimilar from that of some of my colleagues in parliament, but I said nothing. Nilsen's behaviour certainly followed this pattern and was therefore a serious personality disorder. But did it amount to 'diminished responsibility'?

Again, despite what we had been led to expect, Dr Gallwey could not quite bring himself in the witness box to agree that it was something called 'diminished responsibility.' He would only go so far as to say that he could not see how a man could be guilty of malice aforethought (the necessary criminal intent) if he was without feeling, because feeling was an integral part of a person's intent and motivation. The defence were now desperate, and I was beginning to feel rather foolish. Neither of our psychiatrists had 'come up to proof' and said what they had assured us, before they gave evidence, they were going to say. The trial began to look like a complete waste of time.

But all was not lost, for we had not yet heard from the prosecution's psychiatrist, Dr Paul Bowden. Another psychiatrist of the highest distinction, he had been called to rebut what was expected to have been our evidence of 'diminished responsibility'. But his evidence was no more helpful to the prosecution than our experts had been to the defence. He told the jury that he 'felt strong sympathy for the defendant' and believed that he understood Nilsen imperfectly. Although he did say that he saw nothing particularly symptomatic of mental aberration amounting to 'diminished responsibility' about Nilsen's behaviour or explanations, his credibility as a witness became rather suspect when he told the jury that, in his opinion, masturbating over the corpses was not a sexual act. Nor was powdering the corpses: that was done only to mask the smell. Nilsen had walked out of one interview with Dr Bowden, not because he could not cope with the memory, but because he was feeling remorseful. The 'False-Self' syndrome of Dr Gallwey was just a theory impossible to refute. He admitted in cross-examination that although he had said in a report, of 20 September, that he was unable to show that Nilsen had an abnormality of mind, he had later filed a report that had said precisely the opposite – that he *did* consider that Nilsen was suffering from an abnormality of the mind.

'How was that?' I asked, 'and which was it?'

Dr Bowden explained that he had originally thought that abnormality of mind and mental disorder were the same thing, but now he had to admit that he was wrong. You would have thought that an expert would have sorted that one out before he had become an expert! I put to him the various ways in which Nilsen had behaved, and suggested that common sense might seem to indicate that they were examples of abnormal behaviour. Dr Bowden did not think that there was very much strange about Nilsen's behaviour at all. It was true, he said, that most remand prisoners committing, or attempting to commit, suicide were suffering from mental disorder, but when Nilsen attempted it, that must have been an exception – despite the fact that he had originally thought otherwise.

How convincing could all this conflicting medical evidence have been for the jury? No wonder they were confused. In my final speech, which was uncharacteristically short, I tried to cut through the confusing psychiatric mish-mash of evidence:

> We have an old Latin phrase in the law: it is '*res ipsa loquitur*' and it means that the facts speak for themselves. If you think that this man, who killed fifteen young men, none of whom had harmed him in any way, and that what he did to the bodies afterwards was perfectly normal, then you will convict him of murder. But if you think that at the time he did it, he must have been almost as mad as a hatter, then the only rational verdict you can come to is manslaughter by virtue of diminished responsibility.

The jury was out a long time considering that single issue. On 4 November 1983, after consideration for a day and a half, they came to a majority verdict of ten to two, that Nilsen was guilty of murder. I suspect that they took the safe way out, for it occurred to me that they might have thought it was just too dangerous to find him guilty of manslaughter: for that would be to let psychiatrists, like those they had seen and heard, decide when it might be safe to let him back into society!

Nilsen took the verdict very philosophically. 'I have now a guilt and punishment complex. I am convinced that I deserve everything that a court can throw at me,' he told Brian Masters.

I thought that the Nilsen verdict, and indeed the trial itself, were profoundly unsatisfactory. Not because Nilsen has been removed from circulation in society for the rest of his days – for on his own admission he had killed fifteen young men without the slightest justification. Rather it was because, despite all the advances we have made in medical science, and in rationalising the criminal trial process, we still seem to be incapable of apportioning degrees of criminal responsibility for crimes committed by people with some mental abnormality. The Nilsen trial highlighted, in the words of Anthony Storr in his postcript to Brian Masters' remarkable book, 'the gulf which still exists between legal and psychiatric ways of thinking'.

There is always a reason why criminals commit crime. It may be greed or lust. It may be because they are drunk or on drugs. They may be unable to control their anger when provoked, or their sex drive when tempted. They may be suffering from mental illness or serious personality disorder. Aside from those cases, where the question is whether the police have got the right person, guilt or innocence is usually a relatively simple matter for ordinary people on a jury to decide. With all the facts before them, they can make a judgement about whether it was the defendant and whether, if it was, he behaved reasonably in all the circumstances or not.

But where mental disorder is the reason for the killing, it must be difficult enough for juries to come to the right decision on the conflicting evidence of psychiatrists about symptoms and what their significance is. The task becomes impossible if the experts themselves are not clear in their own minds what the law actually requires of them.

The courts have been trying these issues for over 100 years, and yet we still have not resolved this confusion between psychiatry and the law. Surely, as Anthony Storr has said, 'Both lawyers and psychiatrists need to find a common language in order to understand each other and become able rationally to communicate.' Twenty-seven years after the Nilsen trial, there remains a more fundamental need: we still do not have recognised and accepted standards by which criminal responsibility can be fairly judged for those who are not mentally normal. Perhaps the reason why no serious attempt to resolve the problem seems to have been thought to be worthwhile, is that whatever the jury's verdict, the sentence to be served will be the same.

Confusion cannot lead to just verdicts. We need a reclassification of mental disorder in the light of modern psychiatric knowledge, and with it a restatement of the legal rules that should govern criminal responsibility in the light of that reclassification. The Nilsen trial judge, Mr Justice Croom-Johnson, was working upon just such a re-classification: tragically, he died before he could produce it. The Coroners and Justice Act 2009 makes an attempt to clarify the meaning of 'diminished responsibility', but I am not convinced that it goes far enough to remove all obscurity.

Chile

A few days after the Nilsen trial, Alan Rusbridger, the editor of the *Guardian* wrote:

Mr Ivan Lawrence QC, the Conservative MP for Burton, has, in his capacity as top silk, spent much of the past couple of months in the company of Messrs. David Martin and Dennis Nilsen. Time for a change of company. He is off to Santiago to meet General Pinochet.

And so, after speaking to the Gedling Constituency Conservative supper club, to a Burton Conservative Women's cheese and wine party on the last day of Nilsen's trial, and holding a surgery for most of the next day, I returned to Shepperton to pack my bags for a visit to the country of the reviled dictator.

The Bow Group, of which I have been a member for 50 years, had organised the two-week visit, at the invitation of the University of Chile, and I went with Jim Lester MP, Gloria Hooper (MEP for Liverpool and later, as Baroness Hooper, to become a health minister and Leader of the House of Lords), Michael Stephen (later to become MP for Shoreham), Nirj Deva (later to become an MP and then MEP for south-east England), Keith Best MP, Mark Robinson MP, Michael Lingens and Patricia Comrie.

I can only say that Chile turned out to be nothing like I had expected. We were given, and we took, every opportunity to meet and question not just President Augusto Pinochet and members of his right-wing regime, but anyone in non-terrorist political life opposed to his regime. We spoke with members of the main political opposition, trade union leaders, left-wing intellectuals, the editorial staffs of left-wing journals, human rights activists and even displaced and jobless people in their temporary camps, who had been from time to time the target of police repression. I could not help wondering in what Communist dictatorship such freedom would be allowed.

We knew, of course, of the bloodshed, torture, police repression and censorship that had followed the coup ten years earlier, and in which thousands had died. But dreadful as this was, the worst estimate of the numbers involved scarcely registered on the Richter scale besides the millions slaughtered under Stalin, Mao Tse-Tung and other regimes in Cambodia, Vietnam, Korea, Afghanistan, Ethiopia, or since in Yugoslavia, Rwanda, Iraq and Sierra Leone. It was not as if Pinochet's coup had replaced a period of peace and harmony. On the contrary, it had occurred at the demand of democratic political parties of both left and right, because the Chilean people were outraged at the state violence, and the fact that their Marxist President Allende had found it necessary to protect his palace with Cuban mercenaries.

By 1983, although we found press freedom restricted, we were surprised to be told by the editor of one opposition journal, *Analisis* (who was himself on bail awaiting trial for inciting protest) that his revolutionary writings could still be freely bought and read at any newspaper kiosk in Santiago. So could the speeches of political leaders opposed to Pinochet. Torture, deplorably, was still continuing in Chile – and was probably endemic in South America. But its existence, we were told, had more to do with the civil courts having no control over the military – the mark of every dictatorship – than with political ideology. When we met the leader of the copper workers union, he showed us scars from burns on his back, and explained that this had happened when he had been demonstrating in a street and the police had picked him up and placed him on a pile of the demonstrators' burning tyres. This was how police in totalitarian regimes could be expected to behave he said; he did not suggest that he had been subjected to brutality on the orders of the president. Archbishop Fresno of Santiago, and human rights agencies which he supported, told us of the 50 or 60 cases currently causing them anxiety, but that was nothing like the number we had expected to hear about when we had arrived. He also told us that there had been few if any disappearances since 1977, and that Pinochet had allowed 2000 exiles to return home. Regular demonstrations against the regime did take place, and 40 people had died in recent years, but a demonstration of 250,000 shortly before our arrival had passed off without military or police repression or any serious disturbance.

Lawyers told us that a judge in Valparaiso had just ruled against illegal detentions, that the judiciary were now becoming more independent, and that they were now being allowed to speak out against human rights abuses. Businessmen told us that the orderly free enterprise economy was beginning to make them and Chile prosperous. Women told us they felt safe walking alone in the streets. Jewish leaders in Santiago (where there were six synagogues) said that they were unaware of any anti-semitism or racism in the government (whose foreign minister was a Jew), and non-Jewish members attended synagogue services as a sign of respect on the High Holy Days. Shortly before our arrival, Chile's large middle class had given 67% backing in a referendum to a proposed constitution – promising democracy by 1989.

All but the most apoplectic knee-jerkers would have to concede that the widely held belief that Chile was still being ground under the jackboot of a mass-murdering bloodthirsty dictator owed little to reality, and that some effort was certainly being made to correct the wrongs of the past and to bring Chile into the arena of accepted nations. The country was reaching out, particularly to Britain, because historically we had been a friend, having given them the founder of their nation, Bernardo O'Higgins, a navy created by Lord Cochrane, and generals even now with surnames like Gordon and Sinclair. Our Chilean guide was called Luz(y) O'Shea. To us it seemed that the real problem now was that democracy was unlikely to be achieved as long as Chile had no fewer than 62 political groupings. With such political divisions, the military would continue to have public support if only for the sake of stability. Nevertheless, having enjoyed democracy for the 175 years before Pinochet, our group felt sure that it would soon return to it. It did so in 1990, following a plebiscite which removed Pinochet from power in 1988.

He continued to serve as commander-in-chief of the Chilean army until 1998, when he retired and became senator for life. He came to London for medical treatment and was arrested at the request of a Spanish judge for crimes for which he had immunity in Chile as an ex-President. The British government refused to surrender him and he was kept under house arrest – at the famous Wentworth golf course in Surrey – until March 2000, when he was released back to Chile on medical grounds. On his arrival he rose from his wheelchair to greet the hundreds of his supporters who had come to welcome his return. He died nearly seven years later at the age of 91.

Sir Anthony Kershaw

Norm St John Stevas

Peter Thomas

Ian McKenzie

15

Campaign for the Release of Soviet Jewry

'Of course the walls have ears, but if you speak up they will hear that you have not forgotten us: that's why we can live in hope.'

(Dr Victor Brailovsky, on my visit to his Moscow home in 1982)

It was Greville Janner who persuaded me to take up the cause of Soviet Jewry. Greville (now Lord) Janner QC, the Labour MP who followed his father Barnett (later also Lord) Janner, to become MP for Leicester North West, is a living dynamo. His dedication to Jewish causes, and his success in winning support for them, has been phenomenal. Among his many other activities, he set up and developed the All-Party Committee for the Release of Soviet Jewry in the British parliament, the European Inter-parliamentary Committee for Soviet Jewry, and the British and Inter-parliamentary Committees against Anti-Semitism. He was the driving force behind the War Crimes Act 1991, which enabled Nazi war criminals to be prosecuted, and ensured that the Holocaust would be remembered by future generations. He has continued to devote his strength and influence to that cause as chairman of the Holocaust Educational Trust, and to securing the return of art treasures and money looted by the Nazis, to the families of their former rightful owners. He has also been an outstanding president of the Board of Deputies of British Jews (the Jewish parliament), and vice-president of the World Jewish Congress. His achievements, and courage have been the greater because his single-mindedness has inevitably made him enemies in parliament. Through Greville I also became a member of the Board of Deputies, and Vice-Chairman of the European Inter-parliamentary Committee for Soviet Jewry.

At least since the pogroms under the tsars, Jews have suffered for their race and faith in Russia. As a separate ethnic group, they were subjected to discrimination. As adherents to a religion, they were reviled by the atheistic Soviet state. As Zionists, disposed to leave Russia and live in Israel, their loyalty was suspect. It followed that access to higher education for young Jews was restricted, good jobs were therefore difficult for them to obtain or to hold, and there was a determination by the Soviet state to wipe out both the religion and the culture. Soviet Jews were physically attacked, and their attackers were not brought to justice. Many were forced to live in relative poverty. Without jobs, they were prosecuted for their 'parasitism' in living off others. Scientists were denied their intellectual life-blood of access to libraries and to their colleagues for the interchange of ideas. Trumped-up criminal charges were brought against them, their trials were unfairly conducted, and sentences were draconian. Religious teachers, called 'prisoners of conscience', were particularly harshly treated, and insuperable obstacles were put in the way of those who wanted to leave the Soviet Union. In twenty years, although a quarter of a million Jews had been allowed to leave, 400,000 had been prevented from doing so. In 1979, 51,000 exit visas had been granted: by 1985 the number had fallen to 1000. Those who had applied to leave and been refused were known as 'refuseniks'.

After the Second World War, the doctrine spread and took hold throughout the civilised world that everyone has certain basic human rights and, because some countries embrace neither democracy nor the rule of law, the enjoyment of those rights should no longer be a matter for individual countries and their governments alone. Henceforth, they were to be everyone's business. This utopian doctrine was accepted by the overwhelming majority of the members of the United Nations in the General Assembly's Universal Declaration of Human Rights in 1948. In 1975 the Soviet Union, desperate to become a more acceptable part of the Western world's flourishing economic scene, and despite having refused at first to sign the Declaration, changed its mind and signed up to it. It went further: it also signed up to what was called the Helsinki Final Act. This was a treaty, agreed at a conference of the United States and Canada together with all 33 European states (except Albania), held in Finland's capital city in that year. It was not a binding treaty, but a statement of political intent and commitment to the renunciation of force and respect for the security of those countries. It also called for the development of trade and cooperation between the nations, and the liberalising of contacts and human rights. There was a commitment to follow through every few years, with a review of what action had been taken following the agreement at Helsinki.

The first review was to be held in Belgrade in 1977. At the preliminary meeting, to agree an agenda, the Soviets made clear that they were not going to allow human rights (and the plight of Soviet Jews), to be discussed at all. They threatened to withdraw from the Helsinki process altogether if the subject were included. But if the Western countries walked out of the process because of this veto, who would suffer the most? The Soviets! Having been the strongest protagonists of the Helsinki process, and having the most to gain from forging stronger links with the West, they had the most to lose if the process failed. So we members of the Inter-parliamentary Committee went to Belgrade and lobbied each country's ambassador, in an attempt persuade them to call what was obviously a Soviet bluff.

Our lobby was successful. The bluff was called, and the Soviets backed down. As a result, in Belgrade later that year, at Madrid in 1980, at Vienna in 1986 and at other conferences in Ottawa, Helsinki, Berne, London, Paris, Copenhagen and Moscow in the years up until 1991, the appalling record on human rights in the Soviet and eastern bloc came under continuous international exposure and attack.

1984

In 1984 the Commons Foreign Affairs Select Committee (to which I had been appointed just before the 1983 general election), decided to inquire into UK–Soviet relations. We invited our opposite numbers on the Foreign Affairs Commission of the Council of the Supreme Soviet to come to Britain and give evidence to us. That invitation was accepted, and on Tuesday 18 December 1984, in a joint meeting with the Inter-parliamentary Union, we met in the Grand Committee Room off Westminster Hall, and questioned them on a wide range of subjects. Their chairman was Mikhail Gorbachev, then no more senior or important than any member of the Politburo or Secretary of the Central Committee of the Soviet Communist Party. But by then he had been marked out for future greatness, and was known to have been chosen to be President Chernenko's successor as President of the Soviet Union. He was, moreover, a man with whom, Margaret Thatcher announced while he was in London, she 'could do business'.

But at the parliamentary public meeting, both Norman St. John Stevas (then MP for Chelmsford and now a Lord) and myself asked him how he explained the gap that existed between the Soviet constitution, which guaranteed freedom of religious expression, assembly, equality of races and forbade unjustified arrest, and the treatment actually being meted out to Soviet Jews. He waved aside the question, refused to respond, and moved on quickly to speak about other matters.

At the crowded reception following the meeting, in the adjoining Inter-parliamentary Union room, I cornered the unfortunate Mr Gorbachev.

'We are sorry that you brushed aside our concerns about human rights,' I said, perhaps rather adventurously. 'We happen to think they are extremely important, not only as a matter of principle, but also because your failure to honour the commitments you signed up to at Helsinki on human rights makes us wonder how much reliance we can place upon your signature on any future arms reduction treaty.'

The man shortly to wield supreme power as the president of all the Soviet republics and who would be signing such a treaty, glared at me, I thought a trifle menacingly. I was thankful to be on home ground. Then, through an interpreter, he spoke.

'Don't lecture me about human rights,' he fumed. 'Look how you British betray human rights by having three million people unemployed, by shooting people in Ireland who only want their freedom from your colonialism, and by hammering workers, who only want to earn a living, into the ground at Wapping.'

Whether it was his briefing or his understanding which was at fault, I do not know, but I had certainly made him angry. He passed quickly along to receive more questioning on the subject, doubtless more tactfully addressed, from Greville Janner.

Several years later, after he had been deposed, Mikhail Gorbachev came back to parliament to attend another social gathering. I met him again and reminded him of our last meeting.

'Ah,' he said disarmingly, and without an interpreter, 'everything always looks so different later.'

1985

After our first working session at Westminster, the Praesidium of the USSR Supreme Soviet invited us for a return visit, and in July 1985 the Foreign Affairs Committee invaded Moscow for ten days. Gorbachev having indeed moved on to higher things, their new chairman was academician Boris Ponamariev, a candidate member of the Politburo who, as head of the KGB, had provoked angry human rights demonstrations when he had last visited London. To us, he was gentleness itself. His vice-chairman, Leonid Zamyatin, was the far more intolerant of the two, and was therefore later appointed Soviet Ambassador to Britain. Our discussions with the Praesidium were, however, friendly and courteous. We talked about every East–West topic we could think of, from Afghanistan and the Middle East to international terrorism, nuclear and conventional arms reduction and the world economy – *plus ça change!*

Although the Kremlin itself was richly and beautifully decorated, and its furnishings magnificent, the rest of Moscow was totally drab and depressing. Its economy felt like that of post-war Britain thirty years earlier. We were staying at the National Hotel overlooking Red Square, which had once been Lenin's Moscow residence, and was meant to be one of the best Moscow hotels; but there were no plugs for the washbasins and the staff suggested that I take down one of the heavy curtains to use as a blanket to keep me warm in bed. With hindsight we can now see how inevitable major change in the Soviet Union would be. The hotels are reputedly much better today.

While in Russia our committee visited a collective farm, met local government officials and talked with representatives of the Russian church. We met the one Rabbi of the one remaining synagogue in Moscow who, because he only enjoyed 'puppet' status, obviously felt unable to speak freely. Nigel Spearing, the Labour MP who was our resident transport expert, took us to marvel at the artistic splendour of the Moscow underground stations, with their magnificent stained-glass windows – and the memory of the hundreds of lives given to their construction in Kruschev's time. We attended a ballet at the Bolshoi, which, either because of its overt anti-semitism, or its manifest artistic imperfections, provoked our in-house cultural guru, Norman St. John Stevas (who after his ennoblement became Chairman of the British Arts Council), to walk out in the middle of the performance.

A BBC investigating team happened to be in Moscow at the same time as we were, and they wanted to film us talking to ordinary Russians in a park during the lunch hour. Unhappily, they could not find anyone who wanted to talk to us, and the filming session looked as though it was not going to take place. So, with Jim Lester (the Conservative MP for Broxstowe and a stout internationalist), I waded into a long stationary queue for blinzes and lemon tea and, in a loud voice I declared that of course no Russians wanted to speak to us, because they had never even heard of William Shakespeare. That really got them going!

'What you mean we don't know William Shakespeare,' said one, 'I read *Macbeth, Hamlet* and *Henry Fifth.*'

'And I read *Romeo and Juliet* and *Othello*,' joined in another.

'We all learn Shakespeare at school,' explained yet another. Everyone began talking to us at once.

'Bloody marvellous how you did that,' said the BBC reporter, his cameraman filming feverishly.

At a meeting with the Procurator-General (the Chief Prosecutor), we were assured that it was quite impossible, in the regime over which he presided, for Jews to be being prosecuted on trumped-up charges. He invited me to be his 'personal guest' in the Soviet Union for a month, when he would show me the workings of the Soviet legal system, and how happy all the Jews really were. On my return to London I wrote to accept his very kind offer, and said how much I was looking forward to his hospitality. That was, of course, the last I ever heard of it. I cannot say that anyone was surprised.

On a previous visit to Moscow, three years earlier, in the depths of winter and with the temperature at 30 degrees below zero, several of us MPs (including Roy Mason, Labour's former Secretary of State for Northern Ireland) and our wives had visited the leading 'refuseniks' Victor and Yelena Brailowski, Vladimir Slepak, and the Lerner circle of academics in their homes. They had been orchestrating the drive for exit permits. Now, on the assurance that we could meet and talk to whoever we wanted while in the Soviet Union, we invited Professor Alexander Lerner to meet members of the Foreign Affairs Committee for breakfast at the National Hotel. He told us that he was not allowed into the hotel, and had been stopped from meeting foreigners. Sir Anthony Kershaw (MP for Stroud), our redoubtable and be-monocled chairman, therefore arranged a press conference at the other end of the hotel, so that when all the 'minders' were facing the wrong way, we were able to spirit Lerner into the hotel and into what we had been assured was our totally private room. There he told us what was really going on in the way of human rights abuses to Jews and other dissidents in Moscow.

Some time later, at a Soviet Embassy reception back in London, I was taken to one side by one of their diplomats. He told me that they had taken a dim view of our little ruse and an even dimmer view of the lies being told to us in our discussion. I asked him how he knew what we had been talking about in our room, since his people had promised us it would be completely private. He told me, with an attempt at a Humphrey Bogart smile, that in the Soviet Union, nothing was private.

While in Moscow we also had discussions with a number of Soviet organisations. One, the Institute of World Economy and International Relations (IMEMO), was chaired by Yevgeny Primakov, later to become Soviet prime minister under President Boris Yeltsin. A little fellow, Professor Sasha something or other, kept interrupting our exchanges to make observations which we had difficulty in following. When the meeting ended, we collected ourselves together to go off for the weekend to Suzdal, a town east of Moscow, for some Russian trade union style relaxation, to which we were, of course, very much looking forward. Primakov said that he would very much like to meet us again, and whispered to me that that would, of course, be without Sasha! As for the weekend, Sasha informed us, undeterred by our obvious dismay and absence of enthusiasm, that he would be coming with us. He turned out to be our KGB 'minder'.

That Saturday night our team dined alone on unappetising food and undrinkable wine in the drabbest of Stalinesque municipal buildings. The evening might have been uneventful – had it not been for Sasha. Ian Mikardo and Peter Shaw, Labour MP grandees both, recounted witty and enthralling yarns, after dinner, of the halcyon days of British Socialism. Peter Thomas and Norman St. John Stevas, Conservative MP grandees both, told no less witty and enthralling tales of Thatcher behind the scenes and modern Conservatism. Then Sasha, sitting forlorn and ignored at the end of the table, banged his spoon loudly on his plate.

'I want tell Russian joke,' he said.

'Oh, no, not that,' we all said. A Russian joke was bound to be no laughing matter. But we could not stop him; he was after all our host. In fact he told such a funny joke that I have borrowed it unashamedly for nearly all my after-dinner speeches. It goes like this, though my reader must imagine the changes of accent.

An Englishman, a Frenchman and a Russian are each extolling the virtues of their wives.

'When I go to work in the morning,' said the Englishman, 'I wave goodbye to my wife who I see, through the kitchen window, sitting astride her horse – and her feet touch the ground. This is not because in England our horses are stunted of growth. Oh, no, it is because in England our women have beautiful long legs.'

'And when I go to work in the morning,' said the Frenchman, 'I say goodbye to my wife – and my hands encircle her waist. This is not because we Frenchmen have very big hands. Oh, no, it is because in France our women have beautiful slim waists.'

'And when I go to work in the morning,' said the Russian, 'I slap my wife on her behind. And if, when I get back from work, it is still wobbling, this is not because our Russian women have very big behinds. Oh, no, it is because in Russia, we have the shortest working day!'

I will remember Sasha long after I have forgotten all the important Russians I met – except, possibly, Mikhail Gorbachev.

Our committee ended our extraordinary Moscow week with a final session with our hosts at the Kremlin. As we rose to leave, I asked Chairman Ponamariev what they would want to say to Margaret Thatcher if they had thirty seconds to express a point of view. He thought for a moment and said, 'We would ask her to use her influence with Reagan to stop the Americans developing Star Wars.'

There it was! Proof that the Soviets really did believe, as indeed their own research at Krasnoyarsk behind the Urals was telling them, that the laser-directed Strategic Defence Initiative was quite capable of taking out their defences against nuclear attack. And they were indeed very worried about it, contrary to what many Western experts insisted on telling us. It was also evidence that the Soviet Union realised it did not have the financial resources to match the threat. At this time, the Soviet people, now having access to Western television programmes, were beginning to make clear to their masters that the massive military defence expenditure was depriving them of the benefits of a Western-style consumer revolution and could not be allowed to continue.

Over the next twelve months, with Gorbachev now president, the old guard led by Andrei Gromyko were sidelined, and the pace of arms reduction negotiations gathered speed. Over the next decade, the Soviet empire began to crumble. To have been there in the Kremlin at such an epoch-turning time was a truly memorable experience – for someone who was only a backbench MP and a knock-about Old Bailey lawyer!

Gorbachev, the radical reformer, introduced glasnost (openness) and perestroika (reconstruction), and the floodgates of momentous European change were opened. Although he believed that it was only through the structure and bureaucracy of Communism that his reforms could be made to work, the other nations making up the Warsaw Pact did not agree and demonstrated their disagreement in no uncertain manner.

1989

The year in which it all happened was 1989. While the horrific slaughter of Tiananmen Square, within days of a Gorbachev visit, strengthened the grip of Communism in China, in Europe Soviet Communist power was collapsing. The Chinese government had no intention of letting that happen to them. In February the Soviet Union exposed its vulnerability by pulling out from Afghanistan, where it had lost 16,000 men and women, with another 35,000 wounded. In March demonstrations in Hungary led to the fall of Kardar, and withdrawal from the Warsaw Pact in May. In June Solidarity was elected to power in Poland, and withdrew from the Warsaw Pact on the election of Lech Wallensa, as a non-communist president. In September Austria opened its border with Hungary, and in October Hungary declared its independence from the Soviet Union. In that month also, Honneker was removed from office in East Germany and on 9 November the Berlin Wall came down and there was dancing in the streets. In December the Czechs removed themselves from the Soviet Union and the Romanians got rid, horribly, of the Ceaucescus.

With the Soviet Union and its hold on power disintegrating, it is surprising that the superpower was at all concerned about the small minority of Jews who wanted to leave.

1990

In January 1990 the Soviet Foreign Minister invited Professor Rosalyn Higgins (then a lecturer at the London School of Economics and legal adviser to the Foreign Affairs Committee) and myself to go to Moscow to help the Russians to draft a law, which would be International Convention on Human Rights compliant, and which could allow the tens of thousands of 'refuseniks' and dissidents to leave the Soviet Union. The *Daily Express* was ecstatic. 'Britons fly to Russia's rescue', shouted their headline. 'Two top British lawyers ... a life-line to the Soviet Union ... a further example of the high regard Mr Gorbachev has for British democracy – and the Prime Minister.'

We flew out on 12 February and, over two days, had drafting meetings with Soviet Foreign Office ministers and lawyers. They were open to most of our recommendations and agreed to recommend their adoption – Rosalyn was after all Britain's true 'top expert', and went on to become the very distinguished President of the International Court of Justice at the Hague. Walking together back to our hotel late one night in the deepening snow, across Red Square, past Lenin's tomb, we chatted over our astonishment at how rapidly the world seemed to be changing, and we wondered how long Lenin would be allowed to remain where he lay, looking like a waxen doll. He is still there.

There were issues still remaining, and I was promised by our Foreign Office that they would arrange another opportunity to meet the Russian 'exit' lawyers at the approaching Helsinki follow-up meeting. So, in continuing hot pursuit of the cause, I attended that meeting, on 26 June, in Copenhagen. Unfortunately, it was the day that Rachel was to receive her London University degree of Bachelor of Laws at the Royal Albert Hall from the Princess Royal – and I was not going to be there. Once again my career, and other obligations, had come before my family.

I met Yuri Reshetov, the head of the Soviet Human Rights Directorate, and he talked to me about the progress of our draft proposals. He said that President Gorbachev was under pressure not to concede too much in the proposed Exit Law, or five million Jews, most of them highly qualified, would want to leave the country. Nevertheless we did discuss the outstanding problems – whether the Law should apply retrospectively, the need for an effective appeals procedure, passports, and some of the particular cases that were causing concern in the West. The situation under Gorbachev was definitely improving, and the number of Jews leaving the Soviet Union was beginning to rise.

In July I accompanied parliamentary colleagues John Gilbert and Clive Soley (Labour) and Roger Gale (Conservative), to Ulan Bator, the capital of Genghis Khan's Outer Mongolia. We were to monitor that country's first-ever democratic election, which was widely expected to herald the end of the hated Communist totalitarianism that had held the nation in thrall for decades. No one spoke English, but the Mongolians were exceptionally warm with their hospitality, and they sat us in exotic tents to eat enormous hunks of lamb on knifepoint, washed down with fermented horse's milk – sometimes, it seemed, with bits of horse still in it! We inspected ballot boxes at voting centres, as members of a theatre audience are invited to inspect a conjuror's box of tricks, and we satisfied ourselves that every potential voter had easy access to a secret and private vote with a legible ballot paper. On the election day voters flocked to the polling stations, many proudly wearing national dress, and hundreds having journeyed impossible distances across the Mongolian steppes on horseback. Who won the election? The only organised party: the Communists!

While we were there, preparations were being made for the arrival of United States Secretary of State, James Baker. Ulan Bator was flooded with CIA agents and staffers, and every hotel was taken. Vehicles and supplies were flown in. You would think that Genghis Khan himself was returning to the seat of his power. Then the great man made an unfortunate blunder. He told an American television audience that one of the purposes of his visit was to shoot wild geese in the Gobi desert! The animal lobby in the US went mad. The visit was hastily cancelled. The cost must have been enormous enough to pay for many Mongolian democratic elections.

On the way back to the UK I was asked to stop off for two hours in Moscow to meet Chairman Fyodor Burlatsky, of the Human Rights Committee of the Supreme Soviet, then working on the final stages of the Exit Law. Burlatsky said he was pleased to be able to tell me that there was no longer much for us to argue about. The only major issue remaining was the need to get rid of the excuse of 'state security' for refusing to issue exit visas (because it was too wide), and to replace it with 'knowledge of state secrets' (which was much narrower). I asked what had happened to the fear that five million Jews would leave. He said that Gorbachev's view was now that even if that number did leave, most would want to return to the new Soviet Union. It was a satisfying visit, spoiled only by the baggage handlers at Moscow's Scheremetyevo airport. Taking advantage of my short stopover they had a field day with my luggage, breaking it open and removing the lovely cashmere sweaters I had bought for Gloria and Rachel in Mongolia, the home of cashmere. I did not complain too loudly: our own leading international airport had itself just acquired the nickname 'thief-row', after one widely publicised criminal trial in which I do not remember being invited to play any part.

I hurried back from Moscow, to sit as a Recorder at Middlesex Crown Court, where all my attention had now to be concentrated on a case involving a young woman charged with shoplifting £4-worth of cosmetics from a store in Oxford Street. Such was the switchback life of a QC MP!

Soon after that Moscow meeting the Exit Law was finally introduced and over a million Jews left the Soviet Union. Few have returned, despite the de-communisation of the countries that made up the giant confederation that has since been dissolved. Russia, the largest of the countries, was for a decade welcomed into the bosom of the West and, highly questionable responses to the breakaway movement in Chechnya apart, found itself less and less attacked internationally for contempt for human rights.

But more recently, demonstrating an authoritarianism we might perhaps have expected from a former head of the KGB, President (now Prime

Minister) Vladimir Putin started flexing his international political muscles. With missiles threateningly pointed in the direction of the West, the cutting-off of gas and oil resources to uncooperative dependent former parts of the Soviet Union, the arrest of political dissidents, the introduction of restrictions to the new democracy, the assassination of journalists critical of his regime in Russia and abroad, the hanging on to power when his time as president was over, and generally demonstrating nostalgia for the old Soviet Union, it began to look as though Russia might be up to its old and traditional tricks. The invasion of Georgia confirmed international fears.

There may now be even less reason for Russia's Jews to want to return.

16

1984–5: PACE and the Brighton Bomb

'The man who is tenacious of purpose in a rightful cause is not shaken from his firm resolve by the frenzy of his fellow citizens clamouring for what is wrong, or by the tyrant's threatening countenance.'

(Horace, *Odes: Book 3*)

In 1984 parliament passed one of the most important pieces of crime legislation of all the years in which I was a member of parliament: PACE, the Police and Criminal Evidence Act. What it was intended to achieve, and what to a very large extent it has achieved, has been a substantial reduction in miscarriages of justice. This laudable aim has not, and can never be, totally achieved by any act of parliament, however momentous. Indeed, several of this country's most infamous miscarriages have occurred since the passing of the 1984 Act. Nor has such success as has been brought about in recent years resulted from this legislation alone: there have been other statutes like those that created the Crown Prosecution Service and the Criminal Cases Review Commission. But by throwing light into the dark corners of our criminal procedure, by codifying, clarifying, and modernising many of the activities of the police as they stop, search, seize property, question suspects, arrest, detain and charge them, the whole business of our criminal justice system was transformed and massively improved in this year. And of all the measures introduced by this act of parliament, the most effective and far-reaching has surely been the introduction of tape-recorded interviews of suspects.

Tape-recording police interviews

Since my working life was split between making laws and seeing them implemented in our courts, it was inevitable that one of my continuing parliamentary 'causes' would be the reform of the unsatisfactory parts of

237

the criminal justice system. Sometimes this meant supporting government legislation; sometimes it meant resisting government attempts to change the system, when by operation of the law of unintended consequences, the changes seemed likely to make the situation worse.

When I had been in full-time practice, before I became an MP, most of my cases seemed to be taken up not with direct evidence that my clients had committed a crime, but with challenging police evidence that my clients had admitted their guilt on arrest, or had otherwise incriminated themselves. Where such evidence was truthful, my clients often accepted that they had indeed admitted their guilt, and they would go on to plead guilty at court. Of course there must have been cases when a defendant, having immediately owned up to his guilt, might have been persuaded by others accused with him to change his mind and pretend that the police had invented it. But in too many cases of serious crime, false allegations were made that the defendant had confessed his guilt when he had done no such thing.

The device of the falsely alleged admission of guilt was popularly known as the 'verbal', effectively so described by my client, John Mangan, in an earlier chapter. That the police ever invented confessions or admissions of some guilty act was, of course, vehemently denied, for the consequences, if it were ever proved to have happened, would be prosecution for perjury, imprisonment and the ruin of a life and that of a family. But it certainly did happen and, incredible as it may seem, it used to happen often. I was told, by someone who was there, that when Nipper Read gathered his team around him shortly before the arrest of the Krays, he gave the order that under no circumstances would 'verbals' be tolerated. The fact that 'verballing' took place was, in my experience, largely ignored by the judges, who thereby encouraged its use, and judicial and academic references to the term 'verbal' only started to surface in the 1980s.

The prosecution frequently invited juries to believe that admissions of guilt had been made in circumstances that were either highly unlikely or totally ridiculous. In case after case, where the plea at trial was 'not guilty', it would be seriously suggested that professional armed robbers, with long years in prison behind them, and facing many more years in jail, immediately after being reminded that they did not have to say anything and that if they did, what they said would be written down and given in evidence (against them) at their trial, were alleged to have meekly admitted their guilt. This would happen before they were allowed to have their solicitor present, and when the only other witnesses were police officers. Often these alleged confessions would be made when there was no other evidence of any kind against the accused. Time and again juries, left with the question of whether they believed the police evidence or not, simply disbelieved them. As a result, guilty men, against whom there may well have been other strong evidence had it been looked for, and even in some cases where it had actually been adduced at trial, would walk free.

Dishonest police evidence usually concerned the police officer's notebook, to which he was allowed to refer to remind him of the words actually said to have been used by the accused. He could do this provided the note had been made at the time that the event had occurred, or very soon afterwards, while the events were fresh in his memory. So, the police witness always swore on oath that the note had been made 'contemporaneously'. Sometimes, under cross-examination, they could be driven to admit that the note was not so 'contemporaneous' after all, and that their memory was nowhere near as good as they were pretending it to be. Sometimes, they could be caught out lying about what appeared in their notebooks – as Joey Pyle's case demonstrated. Sometimes one police officer would contradict another. Sometimes the circumstances in which the note was said to have been written turned out to be too incredible for words: a jury might be assured that a notebook had been miraculously written up, in the clearest neatest handwriting, by a police officer travelling in a police car at 60 miles an hour along a bumpy road. Sometimes, the numbered pages in the book were out of sequence, so that events taking place at a later date just happened to find their way into the pages of a notebook dealing with an earlier date. Sometimes, it could even be shown that the original pages had been taken out and that pages had been added, because the staples had been put back into the book the wrong way round. Sometimes, a different type of paper had been put into the notebook, and you could see this by holding it up to the light. Sometimes, by sprinkling the page underneath the one with the alleged admission with a chemical, experts could expose an imprint that did not match the page above it. All of the above happened at some time or other in cases of mine – and I was not the only barrister practising at the criminal Bar.

So widespread was the practice that it may even have happened that honest officers, truthfully denying that they had 'verballed' a suspect, would be disbelieved by a jury simply because the false 'verbal' was so well known in certain communities. It is both astonishing and disgraceful that, faced with so many acquittals, the judges took so long to say or do anything about it.

Of course there had always been a simple answer to the problem: tape-record every interview by police of a suspect at the police station, and give a copy of the tape to the defence, to guard against any tampering with it by the police after the interview. Any interview away from a tape-recorder might even be made inadmissible. At a stroke, nearly every allegation of police 'verballing' would disappear, defendants would have to plead guilty at their trial if they were guilty and had said as much to the police in interview, and the result of cases where they pleaded not guilty would depend not on what they were alleged to have said verbally to the police in unlikely circumstances, but on whether the police had found enough real evidence against a defendant to justify a conviction. A lot of the nastiness would go out of criminal trials, and young police officers would feel that they had embarked upon an honourable career, because they were not being attacked in court all the time for alleged dishonesty.

Sensible as tape-recording would have been, the police were always against it. They would not agree to it under any circumstances. Perish the thought that it was because they wanted to continue their freedom to 'verbal' suspected villains, but they were always unable to give me a sound reason for their opposition. I wrote articles in national newspapers, suggesting that the matter was so important that, if the police continued to object, and the government persisted in supporting the police objection, it might even be worthwhile, as a *quid pro quo*, to offer some surrender of a defendant's automatic right to silence.

I argued the cause of tape-recorded interviews in speeches in parliament and outside, challenged police officers in private and on radio and television, and I lobbied a succession of home secretaries. I was not, of course, alone in doing this, but even the Phillips Royal Commission on Criminal Procedure, which reported in 1981, only tiptoed round the possibility. Eventually, after many years, the good sense argument won. In 1983, Leon Brittan, the most determined and effective of Home Secretaries, introduced the Police and Criminal Evidence Bill, which, with many other sensible provisions, ensured that never again would the police have to rely on dodgy notebooks to establish a case against a villain.

There were many other campaigns – some successful some not so. I argued for a simpler definition of the crime of theft that juries could more easily understand: not successful. A simpler format for the new 'caution', when the right to silence was later qualified by statute: successful. A statutory increase of sentence where an offence had been aggravated by race hatred: successful only after New Labour came into office. A Criminal Cases Review Commission, with a wider remit than the Court of Appeal had for considering appeals, in possible cases of miscarriage of justice: successful. A national crime force to deal with certain crimes: partially successful. But I do not believe that any of them were as important as the Police and Criminal Evidence Act of 1984, because that Act tackled the opportunity for police malpractice at its root.

The Brighton bomb

The achievement of better law, order and justice were, unhappily, not the only such occurrences of that year. The 1984 Conservative Party Conference was held in Brighton in October, and half-a-dozen of us from Burton attended. After the conference ball on Thursday night, we all decided to go on to the Grand Hotel, a couple of hundred yards from the Conference Centre, to mix with the famous. I walked to the hotel along the seafront with the others, but did not join them for a drink in the lobby. I had been staying during the conference week at my family home in Montpelier Road, half a mile up into town, and knowing that my mother and father would be waiting up for a chat, I walked home – and missed the bomb.

At 3 am the IRA blew up the Grand Hotel in a dramatic and horrifying attempt to wipe out the prime minister and her government. They succeeded in killing five people and injuring thirty-four others. One of the dead was Sir Anthony Berry, the MP for Southgate, with whom I had walked along the seafront that very afternoon, talking about the conference, the state of the country and his support for Israel. The bombers, almost by a miracle, missed Margaret Thatcher. She had come out of the bathroom of her hotel suite at room 629 only moments before the bomb totally destroyed it. Norman Tebbit was seriously injured, and his wife Margaret was crippled and paralysed for life. The Burton team were buried in the falling rubble but, thank God, were otherwise unhurt. Barbara Makin and George Lawson were shocked but resilient, though Hugh O'Brien, our constituency agent, kept coughing up black stuff for months.

As soon as I heard about the bomb on the early morning news, I rushed down to the Grand Hotel to see if I could be of any help. By the time I arrived I was, of course, surplus to requirements: so I just stood on the seafront outside the hotel with Julian Amory, the Brighton Pavilion MP, talking over the horrifying events and their likely consequences. One, of course, was to make us redouble all our efforts to destroy the IRA.

In due course, Patrick Magee, the lead bomber, was caught, tried and convicted for his part in the atrocity in 1986. He was jailed for thirty-five years: but, sickeningly, was released with 400 other paramilitaries in 1999, as part of the Good Friday agreement. Since leaving prison he has insisted that he was neither sorry nor ashamed of what he had done, and that his action had made a contribution to the peace process!

1985

1985 began for me with four days in the constituency. I visited a rehabilitation centre for juveniles in action in Derby, and a youth training programme in Burton. I toured wards in Burton hospital, and sat in on a Barton-under-Needwood parish council meeting. I received a delegation lobbying for the retention of a village traffic scheme, chaired a quarterly Burton Artisans Dwelling Committee meeting with the brewery managers, conducted my usual full Saturday morning surgery, and travelled to Derby football ground to see Burton Albion outplayed by Leicester City – hardly surprising, really, since Derby were three leagues above Burton. At the weekend, I flew to Israel with the Conservative Friends of Israel.

There meetings had been arranged with President Chaim Hertzog, Prime Minister (now President) Shimon Perez, the next Prime Minister Yitshak Shamir, other ministers and political leaders, and members of the Israeli parliament (Knesset). We also met generals in the 'war zones' at the Golan Heights and the Lebanese border. We discussed the peace process with the Jewish Mayor of Jerusalem and the Arab Mayor of Bethlehem, with academics, industrial leaders, charitable organisations and members of several settlements and kibbutzim – over thirty meetings, to which should be added sightseeing in Jerusalem, Jericho and Massada, and a swim (or more accurately a float), in the Dead Sea.

Thus spiritually and educationally refreshed, I was back on the Monday to face my parliamentary activities. A morning seminar at Chatham House with the Foreign Affairs Committee; a meeting with the prime minister on a matter which I have long forgotten (but it is in my diary!); lunch with Peter Stoddart, the editor of *The Times*; an interview on a BBC 2 television programme, and an appearance on the radio on the Jimmy Young programme; a speech in the Commons on Hong Kong;

and the first of my parliamentary speeches on one of my very particular causes – the campaign against water fluoridation.

Water Fluoridation

I was just about the most unlikely person ever to involve himself in a campaign accusing the 'authorities' of abusing science and medicine to control the lives of ordinary people. It was 'nutter' territory, like belief in alien attacks, letters written in capitals and underlined in green ink, the sort of thing conservative (with a small 'c') MPs fear most to see in their morning post. Besides I was trying to build a reputation as a sensible and well-balanced lawyer on whom the government could depend as 'a safe pair of hands', just in case I should ever start to harbour ministerial pretensions. I had never heard of water fluoridation nor, frankly, when I first learnt about it, could I have cared less about it. Then the Sub-Committee on Social Services and Employment of the Commons Select Committee on Expenditure, chaired by Renée Short MP (the Labour MP for Wolverhampton affectionately known as 'Red Renée'), of which I had been made a member, began an enquiry into 'preventive medicine' in November 1975.

Parliament was concerned then, as it still is today, with the high and ever-increasing cost of the National Health Service. So the committee set out to discover whether taxpayers' money was being spent in the most efficient way for the benefit of the nation's health. 'Prevention is better than cure' is great wisdom: but 'preventive medicine' is a vast subject. Sometimes it involves ethical questions, like whether people should be forced by law to wear seat-belts and crash-helmets. Its range is wide too, covering environmental pollution, inadequate housing, education – activities which usually only involve the Department of Health when people become victims. The committee decided to concentrate its attention on those areas of the DHSS empire where a relatively small diversion of resources might have a significant effect: so we studied alcoholic drink, cigarette smoking, family planning and abortion, diet, counselling, exercise, screening – and dental health.

The medical and dental industries were determined to add fluoride to the drinking water because, they claimed, it would reduce the incidence of caries in children's teeth – as commendable an aim as could be wished. Reluctantly, at first, I began to take an interest. For reasons which I shall explain, my modest contribution assisted our highly regarded parliamentary committee (on which, incidentally, the future Labour Foreign Secretary Robin Cook also served) in coming to the conclusion, despite the efforts of almost the entire dental profession, that: 'We are unable to make any recommendations on the use of fluoride in the general water supply.' The committee had simply failed to be convinced by what it had heard from the so-called experts.

In fact, the reasons for keeping fluoride out of the public water supply are very strong. Fluoridation, being mass-medication, is both ethically and morally unacceptable. Before prescribing a medicine, the doctor has to know the patient, what is wrong with him, and how he may be helped by certain treatment, but with mass medication this cannot happen: whoever orders such medicine knows nothing about the patient. In some parts of the British Isles, a high proportion of the population does not even have any teeth: why should they be forced to subject themselves to a treatment that cannot benefit them? Most people, if asked in public polling, want nothing to do with any form of mass-medication. Councillors voting against the people's wishes are as undemocratic as the dentists are unethical. In the early 1980s, fluoridation of the public drinking water also happened to be illegal.

For any medical substance to be added, there has to be a law permitting it, as there was for chlorine, the addition of which can prevent typhoid. But there was no law that permitted the addition of a dental medicine called fluoride to the water. A woman with no teeth, with the support of anti-fluoridationists, sued the Scottish water authorities in the High Court of Scotland, for illegally adding fluoride to Scottish water. After the longest civil trial in Scottish legal history, she won her case, and the government did not waste its money in an appeal. Fluoridation was declared to be, as we had argued that it was, illegal: if parliament wanted to continue with it, it had now to introduce a law to make it legal. This, to my party's shame, it proceeded to do.

It was not just the infringement of civil liberties, the illegality or the undemocratic nature of fluoridation – serious as these matters undoubtedly were – that drove me to fight against it. It was also the realisation of how much ignorance about the health and safety of the matter there was amongst the so-called 'experts' who came before our committee to recommend it. They were vague as to its benefits, and either had not read, or did not care to consider, reputable reports that questioned both the efficacy and safety of fluoride. Witness after witness strongly advocated the fluoridation of the public water supplies because, they said, there was no evidence of it causing any harm. Yet there were studies, from universities (and Nobel Prize winners) all over the world, concluding that fluoridation caused a great deal of harm. As I looked further into the subject, I got angrier and angrier.

When the Water Fluoridation Bill (introduced by the government – appropriately enough, in 1984 – to make legal what the Scottish court had ruled was illegal) was at its Report stage on 5 March 1985, I entered the Guinness Book of Records for making the longest speech in Parliament that century! Accompanying a photograph of me 'in full spate' on the front page of *The Times*, a columnist reported that, 'The perpetrator of the longest speech inflicted on the House of Commons this century, denied yesterday, in a voice undimmed by 4 hours and 23 minutes of stultifying oration, that it had been his primary intention to bore the government into submission.'

Kinder observers suggested that it might have been a filibuster, but that had certainly not been my intention. The purpose of a filibuster is to stop legislation happening. I knew that I could not stop the passage of the Bill by a speech, however prolonged. No, my purpose was simply to get onto the record some of the conclusions of these research institutions worldwide, that water fluoridation was relatively unbeneficial and posed positive threats to the health of the nation, threats which the experts stubbornly refused to even contemplate.

It will perhaps surprise many people that fluoride is one of the most potent poisons known to man. Those who wish it to be added to our drinking water do not deny its potency as a poison, but they insist that, at one part per million, its toxic effects are non-existent. They continue to do this in the face of a growing number of scientific reports that, at little more than this level, it causes cancer, heart disease, bone malformation, muscle weakening, affects brain function and discolours the teeth. One reason for this may be that half of the fluoride ingested never passes out of the body: it accumulates in the system in quantities that far exceed the acceptable proportions laid down by the World Health Organisation. Furthermore, fluoride is already ingested from tea, beer, and foods processed with fluoridated water. It can be found in the very air we breathe, in those parts of the country where aluminium is smelted, bricks are manufactured and chemical fertilisers are produced. Fluoride is also added to most toothpaste, so goodness knows how much of it is swallowed by small children every day. In the areas where it is permitted to be added to the public drinking water, the proportion of parts per million consumed must be many times greater than the amount considered to be safe. That is why it becomes so cumulatively dangerous.

I had much to speak about without any need to filibuster. My research assistant Dani Okarmus had mined the material assiduously. I have been told that an MP colleague had gone into the Central Lobby to greet constituents. He told them that I was speaking interminably in the Chamber and they asked what I was speaking about.

'About four and half hours,' the MP replied.

'No,' said one constituent, 'I mean what is his subject?'

'Oh, I don't know,' my friend replied, 'he hasn't said!'

Some months later I decided that I must do something about the reputation for being a parliamentary windbag. My speech has even featured in the game of Trivial Pursuit. The opportunity presented itself at a dinner of the Burton Leander Rowing Club when I was called upon to speak – seventh – at 12.45am, and after much alcohol had passed the lips of the guests. The toastmaster introduced me:

'My Lords, Ladies and Gentlemen, pray silence for your member of parliament who will give his address.'

'My Lords, Ladies and Gentlemen,' I said, when the applause had died down, 'my address is Grove Farm, Drakelow, Burton-upon-Trent, to which I am returning immediately. Good-night, and thank you all!'

That speech went down almost as well as its rather longer predecessor. A columnist from *The Times* telephoned me next day to ask whether it was true that, having made the longest continuous speech in parliament for a century, I had now made one lasting under ten seconds, which had to be one of the shortest. I told him that while true, my short speech had not been original: Lord Birkenhead, the Lord Chancellor, had performed the same feat more famously in the 1930s. The newspaper report next day failed to carry that qualification: it spoilt a good story, I was told.

To be fair to myself (for who else will be?), much of my speech time in the House of Commons was taken up by helpful (and unhelpful) interventions from my parliamentary colleagues. My friend, the late David Renton (Lord Renton of Huntingdon QC), told me that for a long time he had kept a copy of the debate by his bedside, because he thought some passages were so funny that he could be hastened into sleep with a smile on his face. When, for example, I had reached the point where I was discussing the evidence that fluoridation at very low levels poisoned the food chain, and that trout eggs did not hatch, the Scottish members became particularly activated. Nicholas Fairbairn (anti-fluoride) said that he called his secretary Trout and would not want to see any experiment of any kind performed on her. John Golding (anti-fluoride) said he wanted the Minister of Health to answer that point, and Ken Clarke (pro-fluoride) intervened to say that, although his advisers knew about bees, cattle, and people, they were stuck when it came to fish. He then went across the Chamber and sat on the Labour Front Bench, which upset Labour's Gwillam Jones (anti-flouride) who said that this confirmed the totalitarian socialist nature of the Bill, while someone else explained that the move had only been for Ken Clarke to give his 'hush puppies' an airing. At about 6am, Toby Jessel (pro-fluoride) intervened to remind me that I had offered him a lift home. The wittily outrageous Nicholas Fairbairn then took exception to Edwina Currie (pro-fluoride) coming into the Chamber wearing a very tight t-shirt advertising the Trent and Mersey Water Authority, and carrying out a running commentary, from a seated position, so that he was not able to hear all my speech. She, observing that the honourable member appeared to be well 'watered', offered to pour water down his throat when he became spreadeagled on the Chamber floor. Fairbairn retorted that if he ever found the honourable lady spreadeagled on any floor he would not be tempted to do more than step over her.

At one stage, my good friend, the Right Honourable Sir Bernard Braine (MP for Canvey Island and very pro-fluoride), felt provoked to interrupt me on a point of order, to complain to the Speaker that I had surely been abusing my position in parliament. He reminded the House that he had held the previous record for a three-hour speech, but he said that he had at least been speaking on behalf of thirty-six thousand of his constituents. I pointed out that I had been speaking on behalf of fifty-six million of mine. At 8.20am, Speaker Wetherill had to call for order and warn that if I was continually interrupted and fed with further distracting thoughts, I would be likely to lose altogether the thread of the excellent speech he considered that I had been making.

Unfortunately, with all the mostly well-meant interruptions through the night, I had not, after over four hours, been able to get my parliamentary speech much past the introductory remarks. At 9.45am, I said that having 'only dealt with one of the five amendments to which I was asked to speak, perhaps I could now move on to–'

'The Old Bailey?' suggested my room-mate Michael Colvin (anti-fluoride). Oh dear! I had almost forgotten. I had to leave for the Old Bailey at once, for when the court had risen the day before, I had been in the middle of cross-examining a police officer and I needed to finish. I was in course of defending Billy Hickson, halfway into a three-and-a-half month trial. He had been charged, with two of the infamous Knight brothers and four others, with participation in the largest cash robbery, of Security Express, in British legal history. On my hurried way to the Old Bailey, I found myself being pursued by paparazzi desperately anxious to take my picture. At least that is what I thought – until they rushed past me to take pictures outside the court of blonde bombshell film star Barbara Windsor (Mrs Ronnie Knight), who was about to give evidence on behalf of one of her brothers-in-law.

Ladies from the Burton Conservative Association, spearheaded by our no-nonsense agent Shirley Stotter, a few days later enlivened proceedings by coming down to London to observe their MP at work. Unfortunately, they missed my parliamentary performance, and decided instead to attend at the public gallery of the Old Bailey, to hear my final speech in the trial. Its end, an hour or two later, must have come as a great relief to them, for they broke into applause. The judge, unused to such a disturbance, took a dim view of this loyal display of support, and ordered my highly respectable admirers to leave the court immediately, or they would be taken down to the cells to cool off!

My parliamentary speaking record cannot now be broken. Shortly after the fluoride marathon the government changed the rules, so that MPs proposing amendments to Bills could be cut short in House of Commons debates. Another blow to protect government from parliamentary interference with its work! Some unkind judges may wish that such a rule could be introduced to shorten my jury speeches. Sometimes you have to take a little time with a jury and judges always want speeches to be short. But they are not always right. One very experienced High Court judge, presiding over one of my early armed robbery trials at the Old Bailey, was kind enough to pass me down a note complimenting me on my final speech, but hoping that he might be forgiven for saying that it was too long for a completely hopeless case. It was not hopeless at all: the jury acquitted my client in less than fifteen minutes.

The Water Fluoridation Bill passed into law in the autumn of 1985, after I had made another, much shorter, speech, beginning: 'As I was saying when I so rudely interrupted myself...', and mass medication, by the addition of this rat poison to the water supply, became lawful. It is frightening that the benefit of any doubt about fluoridation's safety is not given by our political masters to the people they are supposed to be protecting. But whether or not it was to be put into the drinking water in any particular part of the United Kingdom was to depend on whether the local health committee recommended that action to the local water authority. The water authorities have not been too keen about it. Before they comply with any request, they want assurances from the government that they will be compensated if they are ever successfully sued for harm done to anyone's health in the course of the preparation, delivery or use of the dangerous material. Since governments have always refused to underwrite such costs, the proportion of the public drinking water being fluoridated nationwide today is only marginally more than it was in 1985, and is less than 10%.

New Labour proposed to introduce a measure which would allow for any failures to be underwritten, and to give the health authorities the right to demand fluoridation by the water authorities, provided that they are satisfied that the public in that area wished to have it. Since the health authorities are driving this illiberal and undemocratic change in the law, they are unlikely to be impartial in assessing public opinion. The pro-fluoridation lobby has declared that a recent public opinion poll demonstrates public support. It depends, of course, what question is asked. If you stop people in the street and ask them: 'Would you support the addition of fluoride to the drinking water if it will relieve children's toothache?' there can be little surprise that two-thirds of the public answer 'yes'. Reliance upon such a question surely casts doubt upon the integrity of those who seek to impose their medical or dental will on the rest of us, however honourable their intentions may be.

Although the World Health Authority recommends fluoridation, it will also come as a surprise to many that the United Kingdom and the Republic of Ireland are the only countries in Europe that permit its use. All other European countries have either never allowed it or, having been persuaded of its undesirability, have actually banned it. As the number of reputable detractors grows, and the evidence of harm proliferates, it can only be a matter of time before this procedure, objectionable in both principle and practice, will be banned in Britain. It is a pity that so much harm will be done to so many by so few health dictators before that happy day arrives.

Cyprus

In April 1985 I went to the lovely island of Cyprus, and that too became one of my parliamentary causes. The division of that country is surely one of the great political tragedies of modern times. Because the UK has responsibilities for the island, both as a member of the Commonwealth and as one of the international 'guarantor powers' under a treaty of

1970, the Foreign Affairs Committee, in 1985, carried out an enquiry into the possibility of reunification. Our report was little liked by the British government, the Greek government, the Turkish government, the Greek Cypriots or the Turkish Cypriots. It was, therefore, widely considered by commentators to be a very good report.

The island of Cyprus, 140 miles long by 60 miles at its widest point, is only a stone's throw from Turkey. It has had many overlords throughout history. Mycenaeans, Assyrians, Persians, Romans, Byzantines. King Richard took it for England in the Third Crusade of 1191. Turkey took it in 1571, and held it until the Ottoman Empire began to collapse in 1878, when it was leased to Great Britain. We annexed it in 1914, and it became a Crown Colony in 1925. In the 1940s and 1950s, British servicemen died in continual fighting against EOKA, a terrorist group seeking *enosis* (union) with Greece, which was also engaged in fighting with a Turkish resistance group called Volkan. To rid ourselves of the problem we gave Cyprus independence in 1960, with Archbishop Makarios as president. As a 'guarantor power' we retained two sovereign military bases on the island at Dekalia and Akrotiri, which also had strategic importance for Britain in the Mediterranean. There was more fighting in 1963–4, and President Makarios was imprisoned. He was only released in 1970, when he agreed to a Treaty dividing power in the island, in rough proportion to the sizes of the Greek and Turkish populations. The Greeks, with about two-thirds of the Cypriot people, would have the presidency, and a majority of the members of parliament, and the civil service would be split between the religious communities. This treaty was never implemented.

Meanwhile, on the Greek mainland, Papadopoulos led the Colonels in a coup in 1967, and took control of Cyprus. In 1973, power was seized from the Colonels by Ioannides, and Makarios was overthrown. In 1974, Turkey invaded Cyprus and remained, later declaring the north of the island to be a self-governing republic – The Turkish Republic of Northern Cyprus – holding that position, in the face of United Nations sanctions, right up to the present time.

Britain and the West have been staunchly pro-Greek in the past two decades, which is why until very recently, all aid and assistance has gone to the Greek south. The Greek south thereby enjoys a standard of living three times higher than the Turkish north. Such a disparity cannot be just.

Few who attack the Turks for their 'illegal' occupation of half the island realise why this happened. Nicos Sampson, a fascist gangster bent on *enosis*, seized the presidency of Cyprus by force in July 1974, and sent troops into the Turkish communities of the north of Cyprus, burning villages, raping the women and slaughtering the children. Thirty-eight Turkish villages had to be abandoned by 14,000 villagers, and 10,000 Turks in Famagusta faced starvation. Entire villages and their populations were being wiped out. The prime minister of Turkey, Bulent Ecevit, begged Harold Wilson, the British Prime Minister, to use British troops from the sovereign bases, in exercise of our 'guarantor powers', to stop the ravaging of northern villages and towns. Wilson refused. He said that enough British troops had died in Cyprus. Ecevit said that if Britain would not act, the Turkish army would have no alternative but to invade the island in order to protect the Turkish-Cypriot enclave.

And that is what happened, five days after the Sampson rampage began. The Turkish army moved in, and drove the Greek army back south to the 'green line' at Nicosia, sacking Greek villages as it went and taking possession of Salamis. They have refused to withdraw. Since then, Turkish settlers have crossed from Turkey to settle and build up the Turkish population. The Turkish government said that they would only withdraw their army when the Greek Cypriots agreed a constitution fair to Turkish Cypriots, and enforced by a power that could ensure that no more people would die. Since the Turkish invasion, hardly anyone has died in Cyprus from the conflict: and that is what matters most to the Turkish Cypriots. They have a strong argument.

The political problem now is that so much time has passed since the invasion that the settlers have taken root, and the old leaders, the Turkish-Cypriot Denktash and the Greek-Cypriot Clerides, who had shared a common past when they were part of the old united Cyprus, and who it was always hoped would come together to work out a peaceful solution, are no longer in power. The momentum for uniting the island, with the two religious communities living side by side and governing jointly, has faded, particularly since the south remains so much better off under the current stalemate. This situation seems not to have changed, as many thought it might, although Cyprus has become a member of the European Union.

I had joined the Parliamentary Friends of Northern Cyprus, not because I was anti-Greek, but to support the politically weaker side until such time as their argument was heard and understood. I made friends in the north and took part in debates in the House, and discussions outside, in the hope that progress might be made to resolve the conflict, and bring peace and unity to this lovely part of the world and its delightful people.

At the farewell dinner after one of our parliamentary visits, I proposed the following toast to our hosts:

> Visits abroad by British MPs,
> Have been known to cause natives to take to the trees,
> To board up their homes,
> Lock their women in towers,
> And send for assistance from neighbouring powers.
>
> To North Cyprus we came, not as foe but as friends,
> To learn for ourselves what the future portends,
> To do what we could,
> To bring peace in the sun,
> To an island divided by dogma and gun.
>
> Now our visit is over and our task all but done,
> We thank you for what has been really great fun.
> We have walked and we've talked
> And we've wined and we've dined,
> And our hosts have been welcoming, generous and kind.
>
> So to President Denktash and Kenan, our hosts,
> Your guests rise to give you the sincerest of toasts:
> To a Cyprus united in justice and peace,
> Where Turk walks with Greek, and hostilities cease;
> To a beautiful land which will prosper and mend,
> And visitors flock to admire (and to spend),
> Where its people are happy and so much at ease
> That they will always welcome – more British MPs.

I will never be Poet Laureate, but it was a little unkind, I thought, for the Greek Cypriots to oppose my becoming chairman of the UK Branch of the Commonwealth Parliamentary Association because of my wish for a united Cyprus. Or perhaps it was because my poetry was so bad!

When Greek Cyprus hosted the CPA annual conference in 1992 in Nicosia, a notice was pushed under the doors in the hotel of the British delegation, telling us that it would not be well thought of by the host country if we visited Northern Cyprus. I ignored this, and went the next day to Kyrenia to see David Daine, the British high commissioner, and President Denktash and his ministers and advisers. Our Foreign Office Minister, Lynda Chalker, came north with us. The Turkish Republic of Northern Cyprus may not have been internationally recognised, but the island was still part of the Commonwealth, and I certainly felt an obligation, while we were in the country, to visit such an important part of it. Nevertheless, we tried to keep the visit quiet, not because it was wrong, but because we had no wish to rub Greek Cypriots' noses in it. Next morning, some Greek Cypriot MPs invited me for breakfast, and there I was verbally attacked for going to the north.

'Do you want to resolve the problem through dialogue with the north?' I asked.

'Yes of course we do,' they answered.

'Well that was what we were trying to do, so what's your problem?' I asked.

'But we told you it would be an insult to us as hosts if you went,' they countered.

'Was it ever a pre-condition of you hosting this international conference, that no delegate would go north?' I asked.

'No,' was the reply.

'So, what is your problem?' I persisted.

They had, of course, no answers. They want a Cyprus that is Greek, and are not kindly disposed to those who think that the Turkish Cypriots are entitled to the fulfilment of the promises that were made to them over thirty years ago by the Greeks, that they would be treated properly and would have a proportionate say in government.

The tragedy is that neither the guarantor states nor the United Nations have yet been able to reconcile the two communities. Until they do so, there will have to be a 'green line' separating the potentially warring factions from each side, policed, as it has been these past thirty years, by armed units of the United Nations. It had been hoped that Turkey's application to join Greece as a member of the European Union might serve as a catalyst for unity and peace, but sadly, no such agreement has yet materialised.

The rest of the year

In February 1985 I flew to Moscow with Gloria, for a weekend visit to meet seven families of 'refuseniks'. In July I returned, with the Foreign Affairs Committee, for a ten-day visit to launch our wider enquiry into

Britain's relationship with the Soviet Union. Apart from a one-day meeting in Amsterdam of the European Parliamentary Committee for Soviet Jewry, the only other trip I made abroad that year was in August, to take a family holiday in Amalfi and Tuscany.

The Security Express robbery and three other cases kept me busy at the Old Bailey for a third of the year, and I sat for a month as a Recorder at Knightsbridge and the Inner London Crown Courts. Eleven speeches in parliament, and forty in Burton and for Conservative Associations at fund-raising dinners around the country, with one at the Cambridge Union, made 1985 another full and exciting year.

The proudest day for Gloria and me that year was when Rachel celebrated her coming of age as a seventeen-year-old Jewish girl, by conducting her own Sabbath morning 'batmitzvah' service in Hebrew, at the North West Surrey Synagogue, in the company of many friends and relations. The day could have been spoilt when the chef at the restaurant by Shepperton Lock, at which we afterwards celebrated the event, swept into the dining room holding proudly aloft his exotic salmon dish – decorated with religiously forbidden prawns and shrimps! The speed with which I managed to turn him round back into the kitchen, before the rabbi and orthodox Jewish guests could see what was about to be served up to them, was not only straight Fawlty Towers, but was just about the single most constructively useful action I can claim to have really achieved on my own all year.

17

1986: Brinks Mat

'Whatsoever thy hand findeth to do, do it with thy might; for there is no work, nor device, nor knowledge, nor wisdom, in the grave, whither thou goest.'

(Ecclesiastes, 9.10)

The year 1986 began with seventeen visits to organisations and businesses in Burton, my Saturday morning surgery, and two busy weeks of parliamentary activity. On several nights we voted well after midnight. I spoke three times in the Commons – on compulsory seat-belts, the rate support grant and Hong Kong – and I was a guest speaker at the Hendon South constituency annual lunch, and at the centenary meeting of the Burton branch of the Salvation Army. Gloria and I were invited to Number Ten for dinner, when Mrs Thatcher entertained Shimon Perez, the Israeli prime minister. I met up with him later at his hotel, and he said, in his deep, thickly accented voice, that he had been told that she was the 'Iron lady' but that he had felt only the lady. I advised a reformulation of his description of that memorable event!

At the end of the month, I was a delegate to the World Jewish Congress in Jerusalem, where I spoke on East-West relations. After my return home, my diary is full of evening meetings of the various committees in the House, two more parliamentary speeches on the Drug Trafficking Bill and the Roskill Commission's proposals for the reform of criminal trials, and speeches to Harrow Conservative Association and the Oxford University Jewish Society. Then I began my defence of Patrick Reilly at the Old Bailey, for the murder of little Leonie Darnley – for the second time.

Patrick Reilly

Leonie Darnley was a mischievous little nine-year-old West Indian girl, four feet tall, with curly hair and a cheeky look on her pretty face. She

255

lived with her mother and sisters on the sixth floor of Atkinson House, a tower block on the large Battersea Park council estate in south London. Sunday 24 July 1984 was a sunny day, so after lunch, at around 2.30pm, Leonie went off to find some friends to play with on the estate. When she failed to return by tea-time, her worried mother went looking for her, and friends joined the search.

At 9.20 in the evening her father was called, and he telephoned the police. Someone had found Leonie's sandals at the top of the stairs leading to the basement of Atkinson House. The searchers went down and, in an empty, dark, filthy and rubbish-filled basement room, found the little girl's body. Her throat had been cut and she had been the victim of a sexual assault. After she had died, her back had been slashed into a pattern of ten incisions with a sharp blade, like that of a Stanley knife, by someone who was either mad or under the influence of drugs. It was fashionable, at that time, for glue-sniffers to use Evo-stik as a stimulant, and an Evo-stik wrapping was found underneath Leonie's body. Also after death, her vagina had been entered with a sharp pointed stick. There was seminal staining on a blanket that had been wrapped around her, and also on the carpet upon which she was lying. A wave of deep horror swept through the housing estate, and millions of readers of the tabloid press and television viewers throughout Britain felt sick.

In those days, the Battersea Park estate was so lawless, that when the police set up an investigation centre in its midst, practically half the crime in south London stopped. The police took hundreds of statements. No fewer than twelve suspicious-looking men, who had either been seen recently in her company or with or near Leonie on the day that she died, were taken into custody and questioned for days.

On 17 October the police arrested Patrick Reilly, a ginger-haired 'down and out', who lived on the other side of London. After his arrest, he admitted to committing four rapes and indecent assaults upon women in a north London park. It is not clear why he was questioned about the murder in south London, but he was asked if he had ever been to the Battersea Park estate. The interviewing police officers said that he had helpfully told them that he had been there several times, and had even gone so far as to say that he may have been in another basement on the estate on the very day that Leonie was murdered. Furthermore, he told his interrogators, he might even have been sitting on a wall rolling a cigarette and watching the women and children playing. He denied, however, that he had had anything to do with Leonie's death or that he had ever met her.

'I think I was there,' he was reported as saying, 'but I'm not going to get stitched up for a murder I never done.'

The police and forensic scientists searched for evidence that might link Reilly to the killing. Lo and behold, nestling within the curly black hair on her head, a sharp-eyed police officer found one ginger hair, which he removed. Miraculously too, amidst the mass of filthy hair, fibre and detritus on the blanket, three golden brown armpit hairs were discovered, which happened to be microscopically similar to Reilly's hairs, and could have come from him. On Leonie's dress were found three blue acrylic fibres that were not dissimilar in colour, material texture and dye to those of a jacket that was found at Reilly's home. That evidence turned out to be much weaker than at first sight, for just such a jacket could be found on sale in countless markets all over Britain. Anyway the experts could not say that either the hair or the fibres were certainly Reilly's; only that it was a strong coincidence that both items should have roughly matched.

I was instructed, by the solicitors firm Cohen and Naicker, to lead my friend in chambers, Cedric Joseph (later to become the Senior Judge at Croydon Crown Court), in Reilly's defence at the Old Bailey. There were two trials. At the first trial, in December 1985, before the Recorder of London James Miskin, and prosecuted by Ann Goddard QC (later to become an Old Bailey judge), the jury disagreed. The judge afterwards told me that he had very nearly stopped the case at half time, for lack of reliable evidence.

At the first trial, although we had more or less succeeded in discrediting the prosecution witnesses, we had failed to secure an acquittal. We had to do better at the re-trial two months later, before Mr Justice Pain. Could we find a possible alternative killer? We decided to take the risky step of subpoenaing Leon Van Brown, who had been one of the early suspects interviewed for Leonie's murder. He would obviously be a reluctant witness, but he certainly fitted the bill, and the circumstantial evidence against him began to look much stronger than the evidence against Reilly.

He had been living at the time in the next block of flats to Atkinson House, and would have been able to see children playing outside it from his window. He was a drug addict, and an Evo-stik glue-sniffer in particular. Regularly engaged in 'do-it-yourself' activities, he usually had a Stanley knife to hand. More chillingly, he was in the habit of taking his girlfriend, Debbie, into the very cellar where the murder had taken place, to have sex – and amongst his perversions had been sticking a knife inside her vagina. Debbie, perhaps unaware of the significance of what she was describing, made a statement to Reilly's solicitors, and then gave evidence in court confirming all this. Furthermore, Van Brown, at the time of the trial, was serving a prison sentence of four years – for a violent attack on a man. His alibi for Leonie's death was that he had been elsewhere at the time, in the company of a man – with ginger hair! The police had decided to charge the man who was unable to provide them with an alibi. Had they got the wrong man?

The jury was out for over a day. Both Cedric Joseph and I were sure that they must have been agonising, less over the strength of the evidence against Reilly, than over the possibility that, if Reilly was truly the killer, as the police gave every appearance of believing, an acquittal would mean releasing into the community a homicidal maniac who might kill yet more children. The jury of eight women and four men returned to the jury box in a state of obvious anguish. The foreman delivered the verdict in a trembling voice: 'Not guilty.'

The jury's emotional state confirmed our apprehensions. On the judge's direction, they had not been told at the trial about Reilly's guilty pleas or of his previous convictions, because then he would have stood little chance of being acquitted of a murder of which he might well have been completely innocent. I suggested to the judge that if he considered it appropriate to do so, he might, in these particular circumstances, tell the jury that Reilly had pleaded guilty to three rapes, an attempted rape, and two indecent assaults on a child, in Totteridge, Hampstead and Notting Hill, for which the maximum sentence was life imprisonment, and that he would be sentenced on the following day. The jury could then be reassured, whether their verdict was right or wrong, that Reilly would not be roaming the streets again for some time. The judge agreed with me, and told the jury. Some of them burst into tears with relief, and sank back into their seats.

The tabloids, as usual, got it quite wrong. 'A Jury's shame' screamed the front page of the *Sun*; 'Jurors weep as they clear sex beast' said the front page of the *Mirror*; 'Did the jurors weep for shame?' demanded the front page of the *Daily Mail*. Only the *Star* got it right. Its leading article said: 'The most fundamental principle of English law is that a defendant is innocent until proven guilty ... for the jury system to work properly, their verdict must be arrived at without passion or prejudice – which means without gruesome details of past crimes or confessions to other offences.'

Next day, the judge sentenced Reilly to imprisonment for life for the rapes, and told the jury, all of whom had come back to court, that he had agreed with their verdict. He said of the press reports: 'Let it be said that this sort of ridiculous nonsense should be consigned to the waste paper basket where it belongs, and you should leave court holding your heads high, having done your public duty with no sense of shame.'

Reilly, without any hint of sarcasm in his voice, thanked the judge for the sentence.

Some months later one member of the jury, recognising me as I got off a train at Waterloo station, came up and introduced himself. He said that if I had been wondering what had kept them deliberating for so long, when there was so little positive evidence against Reilly, it had been the fear that, acquitting him because of the weakness of the evidence, they might be setting free a maniac who would strike again. When the judge had more or less told them that Reilly would be facing life imprisonment for the offences to which he had pleaded guilty, it had lifted an almost unbearable load from them all – hence their fears.

The Far East

On 7 April 1986, only six weeks after President Marcos and his wife Imelda had been swept away in an American helicopter from a very large crowd in Manilla thirsting for their blood, I joined the Foreign Affairs Committee on its visit to the Phillipine capital.

Our hosts, the new government, took us round the exotic Marcos Malacanyang Palace, which had been left exactly as it was when they were living there. Despite the public fury there had been no looting, and the people had been allowed to walk round the palace rooms to see what had been happening to their money. The daily queue was very long, but as VIPs we were taken straight inside. The basement of the palace had been converted into a hospital, the sole purpose of which, with its rows of oxygen cylinders stacked high, seemed to have been to keep the president alive indefinitely. We also saw the hundreds of pairs of Imelda Marcos's expensive shoes, which, someone explained to us, she had kept not because she was a hoarder, but because she believed in voodoo, and the power that any woman possessing her shoes might be able to wield over her as their former owner.

The new government, under President Corazon ('Cory') Aquino, the widow of the murdered opposition leader, had barely got itself together by the time we arrived. Cory effervesced to us about her plans for her country. Her reputation was that she was a living dynamo who left her ministers and staff tired out by the wayside. I asked her to what she attributed her amazing vitality and drive. She produced from her handbag a small bottle of '10 in 1' vitamin pills!

The committee met the Archbishop of Santiago, named, incredibly, Cardinal Sin. A hero of the revolution, he had personally gone into the middle of the angry crowd when Marcos had shown no sign of leaving, and had pacified them. I asked the great man, in the smattering of Spanish I had learnt in the Barcelona part of my misspent youth, if he had not been embarrassed (*embarazada*) by accusations that as the senior cleric he had allowed himself to become too friendly with the country's military junta. This enormous, utterly charming and charismatic man, more Friar Tuck than Cardinal Archbishop, smiled sweetly at me, patted his portly stomach and replied in a beautifully deep resonant voice, 'Oh no, I am always like this!'

Only later did I discover the meaning of the word *embarazada* in Spanish – pregnant!

We next met Fidel Ramos, the West Point educated general in command of the Phillipine Armed Defence Force. I asked him, without bothering to deploy my miserable Spanish a second time, how long the army would be giving the hastily put together Aquino government to find stability.

'Six months,' he replied.

His aide-de-camp quickly explained that what the general had meant to say, had his English been better, was that the army would support the new regime for as long as it was necessary to do so. General Fidel Ramos gave each of us a box of Phillipine half-corona cigars, inscribed with his name. These became even more valuable when, after Mrs Acquino stepped down as president six years later, he assumed the presidency himself, and ruled the country for a further six years. He is thought to have been an excellent president; which is more than I can say for his cigars, probably because they have been drying out over the past twenty years, but which I still offer to dinner guests, who sometimes accept them and assure me they can still enjoy them!

After the Phillipines, the committee went on to Vietnam. There the approved hotel turned out to be rat-infested so we had to be put up in government barracks, where we slept, without air conditioning, under mosquito nets. The best restaurant in Ho Chi Minh city (Saigon) was accessible only after stepping across an open sewer at the entrance. The rice dish I was given with the main course on my only visit to this gastronomic haven was so covered with flies that I had to remove the outer crust and put out of my mind the near certainty that the flies had settled in the sewer before they had landed on my food. Our British Embassy hosts assured us that there was no better restaurant in the entire city, and that ambassadors from the other European countries regularly ate there. The French Ambassador, I was assured, was actually eating there that night. He would have been thrilled by the cuisine and the hygiene. Anyway, I lived!

I was not certain about the food even at official dinners. One charming and beautiful hostess tried to reassure me that lamb would be the next course – when the menu clearly read '*chien*' (dog)! Had I been a diplomat I would not have risked causing offence: as a mere backbench politician I took the risk and declined.

We had a formal meeting with Pham Van Dong, the 85-year-old prime minister of Vietnam. He was wheeled out in his carpet slippers to welcome us, and looked as though he had been dragged through a room full of cobwebs for the engagement. A heroic relic of Ho Chi Minh's trail and of Mau Tse Tung's long march, he had also been the Vietnamese leader during the war that had cost 58,000 American lives and the lives of 3.5 million of his own people. His prescient forecast of the war is famous:

'Americans do not like long, inconclusive, wars, and this is going to be a long inconclusive war. Thus we are sure to win in the end.'

While we were in Vietnam, our party whips inconsiderately called us to return to Westminster for a free vote on the issue of whether shops in Britain should be allowed to open on Sundays. We were not overly keen to abort our far more exciting adventure in the Far East. A quick survey of our respective views on Sunday trading happily revealed that the committee were equally divided on the subject. There was therefore no point in aborting our mission, because we could pair with each other. And so we did. This spared us the embarrassment of having to explain to our constituents why we had failed to vote on so important a measure.

The Brinks Mat Gold Bullion Robbery

What was then considered to be the biggest, most audacious, meticulous and ferocious robbery in British history had taken place at Heathrow airport shortly after 6.30am on Saturday 26 November 1983. Five men in balaclava helmets, brandishing revolvers, burst into the Brinks Mat warehouse at Unit 7 on the International Trading Estate at Hatton Cross, and managed to get past no fewer than eleven locks, five alarms, and six security guards. After pouring petrol over one of the guards, the attackers threatened to set him alight if he did not surrender the combinations. This repeated a successful technique employed by the robbers in the £6 million Security Express robbery in the East End of London's Curtain Street at Easter a few months earlier, at which trial I had defended Billy Hickson. But the haul at Heathrow was very much greater: the robbers made off with 76 boxes containing 6800 bars of pure gold weighing 3.5 tons and valued at £26 million.

At the time the gang had no idea how much they were stealing, but the hunt for the gold, and the money it realised, kept New Scotland Yard busy for the next twenty years. Little of the gold has been found, but its proceeds are said to have triggered the 1980s property boom. The heist altered the face of organised crime in Britain and led to important changes in the law.

Catching the robbers turned out to be surprisingly simple. One of them, Brian Robinson, lived with the sister of Tony Black, who was one of the security guards. Once that connection was discovered, the police had little difficulty in unravelling the other links. Black identified Micky McAvoy and Tony White as accomplices. Both were arrested, tried at the Old Bailey and convicted. Robinson and Micky McAvoy received sentences of 25 years imprisonment. The runner, Brian Reader (friend and former colleague in crime of my former client John Goodwin), received a nine-year prison sentence. But the gold, having been immediately melted down and disguised with impurities, proved to be much more difficult to find.

I was not in the robbery trial, but I was in the two later trials of those who were accused of receiving the Brinks Mat gold and laundering the proceeds. Of these, the trial of Terry Patch was the more interesting. Terry Patch worked at Scadlyns, a secondhand coin-dealing business, in the village of Bedminster, outside Bristol. The prosecution case was that some of the gold, and much of the money which was the proceeds of the gold bullion robbery, passed through that company.

'Patch,' prosecuting counsel Michael Corkery QC alleged, 'was so closely involved in virtually everything, that he must have known the true situation, and since he was running the business, must have been participating in the crime.'

There was no dispute that he had collected considerable amounts of gold from a Post House hotel, from Bristol Temple Meads and Swindon railway stations, and from Membury service station on the M4. Nor was it disputed that he had dispatched gold to John Palmer for smelting, and recorded the transactions: nor that he had communicated with, and then had sent the gold to, the national assay company in Sheffield. He had also collected the money from Barclays Bank. The prosecution asked the jury to assume that Patch must have known that he was dealing with Brinks Mat gold. But why must this man of more or less good character have known? Was it impossible for him to have been an innocent person who had been caught up in the net? Unless he had been in the conspiracy at the start, would they have run the risks of telling him he was involved in such a crime?

The facts were much in his favour. It was never suggested that he had been one of the robbers, or that he knew any of them. There was no evidence that he had had anything to do with the gold for eleven of the months following the robbery. There was no evidence that he knew Kenny Noye, Brian Reader, or anyone else alleged to have been at the first stage of the money-laundering process. Everything Patch did, with the gold and the money, was open for everyone to see. There was no evidence that he had said anything to anyone indicating guilty knowledge, or had used a false name or had held a bank account under an assumed name, or had been hiding anything. When questioned by the police, he had given an unhesitating and coherent explanation; and although he did not give evidence at his trial, it seemed doubtful that he could have added anything further. Several prosecution witnesses said that the main operators of Scadlyns were Garth Chappell and John Palmer, and they agreed that since Patch did not actually run the business, he might not have known what was going on. There was no evidence that when he had joined Scadlyns it had looked like a suspicious company. On the contrary, the most reputable bullion-handling companies, Engleharts, Johnson Matthey, and Soldens, had checked Scadlyns out before dealing with them. Furthermore, Patch's Barclays Bank manager confirmed that he was always open with his accounts, and that the transactions, although many in number, always appeared to be legitimate. The only evidence that might have suggested any dubious activity concerned Patch's presence during a conversation about false VAT invoices. However that evidence came from a highly suspect and unreliable source, and also had nothing whatever to do with the Brinks Mat gold. In the circumstances the acquittal of Terry Patch came as no great surprise. The other defendants were less fortunate.

Kenny Noye, under whose floorboards some of the gold was found, was convicted of receiving the bullion, and was sentenced to 14 years imprisonment. Patch's superior at Scadlyns, Garth Chappell, received a 10-year sentence. The smelter, John Palmer, known as 'Goldfinger', escaped to Spain. When he was eventually brought back and tried in 1987, he was acquitted – and blew kisses to the detectives from the Old Bailey dock. Ten years later he was even ranked 105 in the 'Sunday Times Rich List', with a fortune of £300 million, in line with the Queen, Duke of Devonshire and Michael Heseltine. But in 2001, he was less fortunate, and was jailed for 8 years for a conspiracy to defraud timeshare investors of £30 million. Noye, some years after his release from prison, was arrested again in 2004, for a road rage murder at the Swanley roundabout off the M25, and he was tried, convicted and this time sent to prison for life.

If I were to guess what the jury might have thought was the most telling point in Patch's favour, it would be this: that if a respectable high-street bank saw nothing wrong with large sums of money being entered into an account on a regular basis from a small coin business, and the national assay company saw nothing wrong with this sudden burst of gold bullion activity in which that business was involved, then why should a part-time businessman of good character have necessarily noticed anything wrong?

But no one could say that it was not suspicious, and if we were to take money-laundering seriously in this country, should we not have been placing financial institutions like banks under some sort of obligation to report suspicious transactions to the police for their investigation?

The officers of the Conservative backbench Home Affairs Committee used to meet the Conservative home secretary of the day, and his ministers, every week after our Monday evening party meetings, to tell him what issues were worrying backbenchers, and to hear the latest government thinking on issues of law and order. At one of those meetings I raised with Douglas Hurd what had happened in the Brinks Mat case, and suggested that we might start requiring financial institutions to report suspicious transactions to the police. Later that year, the Drug Trafficking Offences Bill was introduced and passed into law. It obliged financial institutions to report suspicious transactions and protected them from actions for breach of the duty of confidence that they owed to their clients. Seven years later, in 1993, the Criminal Justice Act established a new criminal offence of failing to report suspicious transactions. In the following years, the law against money laundering, which had simply not existed as a crime in my early years at the Bar, has been continuously tightened and has introduced effective restriction on the mushrooming of this evasive crime of the internet age.

The Brinks Mat gold bullion robbery helped to bring about one such important improvement in our laws in the fight against organised crime, and provides an example of how useful the interlink could be between the work of an MP and the work of a practising barrister.

18

Babes in the Wood

'I have supped full with horrors'
(Shakespeare, *Macbeth*)

In May 1987 the Conservatives, led by Councillor Erl Thornewell, regained control of East Staffordshire District Council, and made my victory in the general election the next month a more or less foregone conclusion. I won Burton for the fifth time with a majority of 9830 – almost the same as I had had in 1979. The Conservative victory was not surprising, for under Margaret Thatcher Britain had become the fastest-growing economy in the Western world.

In this year I was one of the UK's representatives at the Commonwealth Parliamentary Association Conference in Malaysia, and I addressed two hundred and fifty other parliamentary representatives of a quarter of the world's population from sixty nations, in an attempt to correct the utterly false impression that the British government supported apartheid in South Africa. The British team joined in discussions about the world problems of population growth, protectionism in world trade, colonialism, human rights and AIDs, and we laid wreaths to the Second World War's fallen, at the most beautifully maintained Commonwealth War Graves site at Kranji, in Singapore.

In parliament (and in the letter columns of *The Times*), I supported the government in their attempt to stop publication of Peter Wright's book *Spycatcher*, because those whom we entrust with the nation's secrets should never be permitted to betray our country for money. I supported the reform of the absurd laws against Sunday trading. I also supported the introduction of the poll tax. It was so unpopular that there were riots in the streets. But we have forgotten how unpopular and unjust the rating system was that it replaced. Seventeen million users of local services made no contribution to their cost, and widows and the elderly living alone had to pay more for those services, while houses with four

267

wage earners living next door could avoid paying anything! When the poll tax became law, those who were genuinely poor did not have to pay it. Most of us considered that the poll tax was the least worst of the alternatives, and that was why it was in the manifesto upon which the Thatcher government was returned to power in 1987. I think the truth was that those who rioted, demonstrated, or campaigned against the poll tax were really using it as an excuse to attack Thatcherism and the government generally.

In this year also, I was sworn in as a Recorder, to try cases as a part-time judge in the Crown Courts, and I led for the defence in another of the most sensational cases of the decade.

Russell Bishop

On Friday 10 October 1986 the bodies of two little nine-year-old girls, Karen Hadaway and Nicola Fellows, were discovered in the bushes on the hillside of the Wild Park recreation ground, at Moulscoomb, two miles north-east of Brighton. They had both been sexually assaulted and strangled. It was one of the most horrifying cases of modern times. There were lurid tabloid headlines for weeks. In a hate campaign, houses were daubed with red paint, and the house of a potential witness was burnt down. There was a street march. There were undercurrents of video pornography and child abuse. The case became known to readers of the tabloid newspapers as the 'Babes in the Wood Murders', and the man accused of committing them, Russell Bishop, was acquitted 14 months later, by a Lewes Crown Court jury. That verdict was greeted by a cheering crowd in the High Street outside the court.

The large 7000-resident council housing estate on which the girls lived, enjoyed a reputation for squalor, neighbour disputes and crime. It was a 'sink' estate, where problem families were sent from all over Brighton. Karen and Nicola, who were friends, lived a few doors away from each other in Newick Road, and went to separate schools on the estate – Karen to Coldean Junior School, Nicola to Moulscoomb Middle School. A fortnight before the murders, the police had circulated a letter to parents warning them that a ginger-haired man, driving a blue car, had been seen prowling outside the schools and trying to get girls into his car.

On Thursday 9 October, Karen and Nicola met up after school and played together in the street. They were seen buying fish and chips and then playing in the park as darkness fell. They were never seen alive again.

When the little girls failed to return home an alert went out, and a hundred policemen, together with residents of the Moulscoomb estate, searched the park, the railway line, the schools and the gardens of the houses. Some of the neighbours and friends were 'citizen-band' radio enthusiasts, and they were enlisted in the search. Someone using the radio user name 'Whispering Willie' called in to say that he had killed the girls. Another man, searching the railway area with two friends, at 12.45am the next morning, radioed the police to say that someone had just run past him out of the park bushes, and that, shortly afterwards, he had found what he thought was a recently discarded blue sweat-shirt with a 40-inch chest size and the words 'Pinto' picked out in white lettering on the front. He was told that neither girl was wearing such a shirt, so he left it draped over a fence and resumed his search. By the following morning the search had become more extensive, with hundreds of policemen engaged in door-to-door enquiries, tracker dogs, a helicopter, and heat-seeking equipment.

At the time of the disappearance, Karen's father was delivering furniture in Cambridge with a man called Stephen Judd. Nicola's father had not yet arrived home from a job he had had with Duggie Judd, Stephen's brother, cleaning out a swimming pool in Hove: he arrived home at 7.30pm, two hours after Duggie Judd. Their original statements said that they had arrived back by bus together: why there was this difference was never explained. There was some delay before the disappearances were reported to the police.

Russell Bishop, was a 20-year-old local unemployed man who earned some money mending cars. He lived on the Moulscoomb estate, and was known to both girls. He did not have ginger hair. His mother, Sylvia, was a well-known international dog trainer, and was the author of a best-selling training handbook, *It's Magic*. Russell had a common-law wife, Jennie Johnson, and a girlfriend, Marion Stephenson, also living on the estate. He joined in the search the next day with Misty, one of his mother's tracker dogs, and carried with him a jumper belonging to Karen that her mother had given him for the dog to scent. He chatted to a policeman and went off with Duggie Judd to Stanmer Park and the golf course, walking back towards the cricket pavilion at Wild Park, where he had arranged to meet Karen's mother and another friend. He was back near the entrance to Wild Park, talking to a uniformed police officer at 4.20pm, when the bodies of the two little girls were found by two youths. They were lying in a makeshift 'den' of brambles in the thick undergrowth, just behind the cricket pavilion. One of the youths ran out of the bushes shouting and waving to attract the attention of other searchers. The officer sent Bishop ahead, because he could run faster, to tell the youths not to touch anything.

Over the next two months, the police took hundreds of statements from possible witnesses: several people became suspects. Russell Bishop, being one of the last people to see the little girls alive, became the principal suspect; and he had certainly been in the park, and therefore near them, when their bodies were found. The statements he made to the police contained discrepancies. The Pinto sweatshirt, which had been found and then discarded, was retrieved; it was thought to have been worn by the killer, and was identified by Bishop's common-law wife as his. He was arrested on 31 October, and held for interrogation for three days before being released on police bail. On 3 December 1986 he was arrested again, and charged with the murders. He now had Ralph Haeems acting for him. Ralph instructed Charles Conway, as junior counsel, who submitted before the justices at Hove Magistrates Court that there was not sufficient evidence to send Bishop for trial. That submission was unsuccessful and, after the committal proceedings, I was taken in to lead for the defence.

The trial opened at Lewes Crown Court on 11 November 1987, before Mr Justice Schiemann. It was his first murder trial as a High Court judge, and his conduct of the month-long proceedings could not have been fairer. He is now the British judge in the European Court of Justice. After Brian Leary QC had opened the prosecution case, we all went to the park to inspect the 'den' and its approaches, so that the jury might have some idea what the witnesses would be talking about. I had earlier been to the area with Conway – and recognised the park as the place where, 35 years earlier, I had had a trial for the Brighton and Hove Albion boys soccer team.

The jury, having been directed that they could only convict Bishop of the murders if the prosecution were able to satisfy them beyond any reasonable doubt that Bishop had committed the crimes, must either have believed him to be innocent, or have come to the conclusion that the police and the forensic scientists had together made such a mess of the evidence that they could not be sure of his guilt. Either way, their verdict was the only one possible on the evidence – not guilty.

It is necessary to say this because, three years later, Bishop was arrested, charged, convicted and sentenced to life imprisonment at Lewes Crown

Court, for attempting to murder, and indecently assaulting and kidnapping, a seven-year-old girl. While she was roller-skating on her own in Moulscoomb, he had snatched her off the street, bundled her into the boot of his car, and taken her to Devils Dyke, a local beauty spot, where he assaulted her, strangled her and left her for dead. Confronted with the evidence of the little girl's positive identification of him, the indisputable presence of his car at the scene of the assault, and his semen both on the attacker's discarded tracksuit bottoms and on his victim's vest, the verdict of guilty and the sentence of life imprisonment, were inevitable. Equally inevitable was the claim that, although Russell Bishop had been acquitted of the murder of Karen and Nicola four years earlier, he had obviously been their murderer. But had he?

Bishop always denied the Babes in the Wood murders, despite over 50 hours of questioning, at which he did not ask for a solicitor to be present. He told lies at the interviews, but then he was a petty criminal with convictions for dishonesty and drugs possession, and he frequently lied – he was that afternoon, on his own admission, on his way to steal a car. Even so, most of his lies were not told when he was being treated as a suspect, and they were about such irrelevant matters as the insurance value of his dog. He boasted untruthfully of being an ambulance driver, and of once, imaginatively, being defended by an American lawyer. He also claimed to have gone into a newsagents shop on the evening of the killings, but then admitted that he had lied to protect a woman from whom he was going to buy some cannabis: the prosecution attached no importance to that lie.

They did, however, attach importance to the lie he told about what he had seen when he had run to where the bodies had been found. He reported that Nicola had 'blood-flecked froth' coming out of her mouth. Later, when he realised that he had become suspect number one, he said that he had lied about that detail in order to make himself look important to the police and the media. Mr Leary dramatically told the jury that Bishop had not gone inside the 'den' when the bodies had been found, so he could only have known about that detail if he had been the murderer.

There was nothing in that point. He had gone up to the entrance to the den and had got within seven or eight feet of the girls, and from that distance he could certainly have seen something: a doctor had noted the injuries to the girls' faces and neck in precise detail from a distance of four to five feet. Bishop may perhaps have been repeating what the youths had told him when he had arrived on the scene, for they certainly went right up to the girls when they first saw them, to see if they were alive: one of them was a hospital porter used to seeing dead bodies. The police photographer, quickly on the scene, put an end to the point: he said that there was no 'blood-flecked froth' coming from either girl's mouth, although there was a reddish tint caused by blood. Pure invention seemed the most likely explanation.

Bishop told another lie: he pretended that he had felt for a pulse, when he could have done no such thing. He was not the only one lying. The youths had also lied about what they had seen: their first account was that the little girls were cuddling. The truth probably was that they were all pretending to be important to the press and to the police, and that no particular significance could sensibly be attached to anything that anyone said about those very traumatic moments.

More important than evidence of ambiguous lies was the need for the prosecution to establish the time of the killings, in order to negate any alibi Bishop might present. On that matter, the prosecution were in total confusion.

At the start of the trial, in the presence of the jury, I asked Brian Leary what time he was alleging that the murders had actually taken place.

'I do not propose to respond,' was his lame and surprising reply.

That underlined early on the fundamental and enduring weakness of the prosecution's case. They did not know the answer, although they should have done. Usually the time of death is established by a pathologist taking the body temperature of the victim when it is found. In this case, the first pathologist called by the police had failed to do so with either girl. Later, Leary told the jury that the murders must have taken place between 6.15pm and 6.30pm. But although that was the time the girls were seen to go across to the park, there was no other evidence to support that timing. If that was the correct time, then there was no observation evidence that Bishop was involved. None of the several people in the vicinity saw Bishop going to, or coming from, the place where the bodies were found.

On the contrary, there was the clearest evidence that Bishop had not followed the girls. The park keeper told the jury that Bishop had come up and stopped to speak to him minutes before 6.15pm. It was quite a lengthy conversation about his broken-down car, and football. He had even shown him some scars that he had on his body. At that time, the little girls were nearby and swinging from a tree. Bishop took no interest in them, said the park keeper. After this conversation Bishop walked off

– in the opposite direction to the little girls and the 'den'. Two other witnesses also saw Bishop walking away, along the busy main road, past a police box several hundred yards from where he had been speaking to the park keeper, and he waved to another acquaintance across the road.

If Bishop had been on his way to sexually interfere with the little girls and then to kill them, at the time alleged, would he have stopped for a long chat with the park keeper? And then walk away in the opposite direction? He cannot have just killed them, for they were alive and playing while he was talking. But if the park keeper was mistaken about that detail, if he had just come from killing them, why was he not bloodstained from struggling with the girls, with torn or dishevelled clothes and bleeding from bramble scratches? Again, would he have drawn close attention to himself by stopping to chat? Or wave to acquaintances as he walked past a police post? How could he have got the two children into the bushes, sexually assaulted them, and killed one while the other was there watching and neither struggling, nor screaming, nor tearing at Bishop's clothes? And how could he, in a few moments, have destroyed all traces of the evidence that would have linked him to the crime? If the prosecution had the time right, then Bishop could certainly not have been the killer.

The police identified Bishop as a suspect and at 2.30am they went to his home and found him in bed with Jennie. He was unlikely to have killed the girls after he had gone home. So if he had killed the girls, it would have had to have been between the time he left the park and his arrest. It all began to look rather unlikely.

There was other evidence about the timing. A young friend of the two young girls, Miss Brown, gave clear evidence to the jury. She, and two adult ladies (who happened, by odd coincidence, to be called Miss Black and Miss White), swore that they had seen the little girls, whom they all knew, at a newsagent shop on the council estate eating fish and chips, and alive as late as 6.30pm. They could not be shaken by Leary in cross-examination. Most importantly, what they described the girls to have been doing, destroyed the prosecution theory as to the time of the deaths completely.

Dr West, one of the pathologists, had given evidence that there were the remains of a chip meal in Nicola's stomach. This would put her time of death at least one and a half hours later than 6.30pm. Karen had completely digested her chips by the time she died, and Dr West said that the time of death might even have been as late as 3am. He admitted that it was impossible to ascertain with certainty the time of death. They may even have had more chips later, which would have moved the time of death later still.

There were other witnesses who put the likely time of the killing very much later. A search party of three men had heard screams, from what sounded like little girls, at about 6.20am. The screams had come from the area of the wood in which the bodies were to be found nine hours later.

One thing was clear: the prosecution case about the time of the killings, and the connection to Bishop as he went home, had been shot to pieces by their own evidence, and by the evidence of witnesses whose statements they had taken, and who were tendered to the defence for us to call – and we did so. There was no evidence at all to suggest that Bishop had left his home in the middle of the night to kill the girls. They had after all, on the prosecution's allegation, gone missing the evening before.

There were yet other serious flaws in the prosecution case. They said that Bishop had been alone in killing the girls. Was that likely? Nicola was assaulted from the front while alive and from the back when dead: her pants were taken off and put back on and taken off again. What was Karen doing: just watching? Not even screaming? If Karen, who also had her pants removed, was attacked first, what was Nicola doing? Was any of this likely to have happened in a space in the bushes so small, and so sloping, on the steep side of the hill that the pathologist said that he did not have room to take the body temperatures? It was surely impossible for one person to have carried out the indecent assaults and killings alone – with two struggling little girls. Yet it would also have been quite impossible for two men to have got themselves into the tiny space of the 'den' with the two girls. If anything like that had happened with one man, there would have to have been evidence of a struggle: yet there was none. No scratches from the brambles or evidence of what must have been a struggle were found on Bishop. If two men had been involved, where had the bodies been brought from, and in whose car? There was evidence that Bishop's car had broken down earlier that day and could not have been driven.

DNA testing was not yet available to the police in 1987, but that does not excuse the forensic failures and omissions, which were many, and which in a murder trial of this nature were inexcusable. Apart from the absence of body temperatures, no one had bothered to measure the hand-marks on Nicola's neck, or take the fingerprints left there by the strangler. No one had tried to match the blood found on Nicola's pants, which, from its position, was unlikely to have been hers. The police never tested the body fluids of anyone else for the murders, although there were no fewer than nine suspects. These were people from the area, people with criminal convictions for violence or who had been sex-offenders. Others had made statements to the police, when interviewed, which contained serious discrepancies and lies. No one suggested that the ginger-haired prowler in a blue car stalking pupils after school, about whom parents had been warned, could have been Bishop.

Dr Ian West, the pathologist, found and carefully removed from Nicola's private parts three human hairs and a fibre which could not have been hers, and were therefore likely to be the killer's: these, we were told, had been unfortunately mislaid and so could not be produced at the trial. When one of the forensic experts later produced the numbered exhibit, which was supposed to have been those items, and the judge called for them to be examined because no one had yet bothered to do so, they turned out to be a dog hair and some totally different mineral matter! I was able to say to the jury that there were three possible explanations for this exhibit: either that vital evidence had been changed into something else by magic, or that the distinguished Home Office pathologist, Dr West, was so incompetent that he could neither tell a human hair from a fibre nor could he count, or that the forensic experts had falsified the exhibit. Whatever the explanation, the exhibit was equally worthless as evidence against Bishop. Even Brian Leary was driven to admit that 'somewhere something had gone wrong'. If any of that evidence had been properly dealt with, it might have eliminated Bishop from the enquiry at an early stage.

Then there was the evidence of the Pinto sweatshirt, discarded on Bishop's route home: it was the strongest piece of evidence that the prosecution thought they could offer. But first they must prove both that it had been worn at the murders and that it did in fact belong to Bishop. They fell a long way short of proving either.

To begin with, the shirt was not found near the murder scene. Nor was it found at Bishop's home. Although it was covered in ivy hairs similar to those found at the 'den', it transpired that all the ivy in Britain emanated from the same species, and therefore had the same hairs; that thousands of hairs are produced from only one or two sprigs of ivy; and that the ground of the lane in which the sweatshirt was found was covered in ivy. There were some pink fibres on the sweatshirt, which might have come from Nicola's jumper, but they were very common.

There were also some green fibres on it, which could have come from Karen's jumper. At first Mr Peabody, the forensic scientist, suggested that they were not very common, there being only a 1 in 5339 chance that they could have come from anyone else. But when I pointed out that it was a Coldean School standard jumper, worn by hundreds of girls in the same area, he agreed that he could not be certain about that either. There were some blue acryllic fibres found on the jumper of one of the girls that might have come from the Pinto sweatshirt, but the material was in such wide circulation that no one had even tried to trace its source. There were thousands of foreign fibres on the sweatshirt. 170 of them were removed for examination, and they turned out to be a large number of pink, green, purple, brown and other colours that certainly could not have come from the girls. Since fibres are not identifiable with the accuracy of fingerprints, Mr Peabody could not say that the Pinto sweatshirt had been worn at the murder scene – only that it could have been. There were many other reasons why even that possibility was no help to the prosecution.

The sweatshirt had been contaminated, by contact with other pink and green garments. Apart from the contamination which might have occurred before it was found, and after it had been kicked 32 metres down the lane from where it had been dropped, it had later been poked about with a stick by an inquisitive passer-by, and no fewer than fifteen police officers and others had handled it before it was 'sanitised'. It had been placed on an electricity sub-station table, on a police officer's car seat, it had been held close to the chest of another officer wearing a jumper with pink fibres in it, and it had even been examined on the same table in a police station as the garments in which the little girls had died. The 'scenes of crime' officer admitted in evidence that he might well have accidentally contaminated the sweatshirt.

That was not all. No fibres from the sweatshirt had snagged onto branches or twigs in the 'den' although, on the prosecution's case, there must have been a struggle. No hairs, vomit, saliva or blood from the girls were found on it although, if worn by the killer, it could not have avoided contact with the girls in the 'den'. There were hairs on it that might have come from Bishop, but Mr Peabody could not be sure. There were some dog hairs on it which might conceivably have come from Bishop's dog, but Mr Peabody had unfortunately missed seeing those when he had first looked for hairs a year earlier, and dog hairs were an even less reliable identifier than human hairs. There was very common red paint on it, which another forensic scientist was unable to say had come from any of the cars connected with Bishop. The only time a witness saw Bishop spraying red paint on a car, he had certainly not been wearing the Pinto sweatshirt.

There were still further problems with the Pinto sweatshirt. It was large, but Bishop was small; and there was no evidence that it could have fitted him. It was found not just on Bishop's way home; it was found on the way home for hundreds of people living on the large Hollingdean estate, who went to the railway station to take a train or bus to and from Brighton. The time of the deaths, as alleged by the prosecution, was nearly six hours before the witness saw a man jump out of the bushes and had assumed, because it was raining and the sweatshirt was dry, that he must have discarded it. The likelihood that Bishop would have left home to deliberately drop the sweatshirt on what he told the police was his route home would be absurd, unless he was mad, which a psychiatrist said he was not. Bishop had washed the clothes he was wearing on that night: he would have had to have deliberately decided not to wash the one garment that might give him away, and to have then slipped out later to throw it away on the path he would later be telling the police he took home!

What had led the prosecution to place so much reliance on the shirt being Bishop's, was what had happened when his common-law wife, Jennie, had been shown it by the police. She had told them it was his, although she had refused to sign her statement to that effect. When she gave evidence in court for the prosecution, she denied it was his shirt. Brian Leary, who was allowed to treat her as a hostile witness and to cross-examine her, asked her why she had said that it was when it was not. She said that she had snapped under the pressure of the moment. What had happened, she explained, was that the policeman had come in and had informed her that Bishop had resumed his sexual relationship with her rival, Marion, up the road, and by the way, did she recognise this sweatshirt as Bishop's? What, she asked the jury, do you think my angry and jealous reaction would be? The prosecution had no alternative but to treat their prize witness as thoroughly unreliable. Mr Leary told the jury in his final speech: 'I don't invite you to rely on her evidence at all, unless what she said could assist Bishop.' So the jury could place no reliance on what she had told the police, but they could place reliance on what she said in the witness box about the sweatshirt not being Bishop's!

The prosecution searched high and low for any evidence that the sweatshirt was Bishop's, but all they could come up with was witness after witness, people who worked with him, drank with him, saw him round the estate, who all said that they had never seen him wearing that shirt. There were no fibres from it in his car, which he had been driving that day before it broke down. Nicola and Karen's mothers said he was not wearing it that night. The park keeper, to whom Bishop spoke minutes before the little girls would have met him, according to the prosecution's case, and lifted his shirt to show him his scars, gave evidence that he was certainly not wearing that shirt. In fact that witness identified another shirt as the one Bishop was probably wearing; the mothers of the little girls agreed that that one looked like the one Bishop had been wearing that evening, and Jennie confirmed that that shirt certainly was the one. That shirt had, of course, no hairs, fibres, ivy or anything else to connect it to the murders.

I did not call Bishop to give evidence. There was no need to do so. There was now no evidence to link him with any of the garments. There was no evidence to connect him with the 'den'. There was the clearest and strongest evidence that he went home – in the opposite direction to that of the little girls. The prosecution had no idea what time the killings had taken place. Their case was a complete mess. Bishop had by his plea denied his guilt, he had already given 50 hours of interviews and explanation, and in any event he was a normally dishonest man, who often said anything that came into his head. There were more reliable witnesses than Bishop who were called to give evidence establishing his innocence.

Mr Justice Schiemann summed up concisely, accurately and fairly. The jury returned after two hours – a relatively speedy return in a case with so much evidence to consider. The not guilty verdict was greeted by loud shouts of relief and joy in the court. Bishop's brother jumped over a high rail into the dock to embrace him, and he was promptly felled by the prison officers and disappeared down the steep steps leading to the cells. Seeing this, Bishop's mother let out a scream – and his father had a heart attack. The judge called for order, and threatened to clear the court if there was any more disturbance. Silence fell momentarily, then we in court heard a cheer going up from the crowd that had gathered in Lewes High Street for the verdict – just as used to happen in the days before television.

Massive as the volume of evidence presented to the jury had been, the case had come away in the prosecution's hands: there could have been no other verdict. The same could not be said of the kidnapping and attempted murder five years later. I was not available to defend

Bishop at that trial in 1992, because it took place at the time of the general election.

19

Europe: Margaret Thatcher and John Major

'Europe, the fault-line that runs through the bed-rock of the Conservative Party.'

(Michael Heseltine, *Life in the Jungle*)

Although an island nation, Great Britain has been part of Europe for most of our history. Our monarchs have been Danish Vikings, French, Dutch and German. We have fought European wars. To unite Europe against any more such wars, and to help to create a common market that would guarantee a high standard of living for Europe's people, was the cause for which I campaigned in the referendum in 1975: to ratify Britain's entry into the European Economic Community.

But I certainly did not want my country to surrender its power to govern itself through its own democratically elected parliament, or to sacrifice the independence of its courts. Nor, I believed, did the British people. If I had ever fought an election in Burton on a mandate to surrender powers of the Westminster parliament to an un-elected bureaucracy in Brussels, as a step on the way to Britain becoming part of a federated European super state, I would not have got many votes. Yes, I wanted to be part of Europe, but not that kind of Europe, thank you! That is still my view.

As the confidence and economic strength of France (paranoid about being at the mercy of a German nation state), and of Germany (paranoid about being hated as a nation by the French), grew through the 1970s and 1980s, the European power base strengthened. Other nations of the European continent, big and small, wanted a piece of the action, and joined the club. The true meaning of what we had signed up to – an 'ever closer union' – became ever clearer. But the European institutions all argued that they were being held back, in competition with the expanding markets of the United States and south-east Asia, by not having the powers of a truly united Europe. Even Mrs Thatcher, intensely

281

nationalistic in every fibre of her body though she was, was persuaded by the strength of that argument.

Prior to our debates in parliament in 1986 on the Single European Act, which required us to surrender more powers to Europe, the Foreign Affairs Select Committee investigated Britain's position. We visited the European capitals, and listened to their political leaders explaining why it was so necessary to them that Britain should be there, in the centre of things – not actually leading, of course, but influencing and guiding, with our greatly admired wisdom and experience, the future of this great world power. We were all flattered and some of us, who should have known better, were momentarily blinded to the true extent of the sacrifice being demanded of the British people and our national institutions.

Word got out that I was going to be awkward, and that I was contemplating a dissenting report that might well sour the unanimity of the committee's support for the Single European Act – though why anyone should be concerned about one unimportant Conservative MP's disagreement with the majority was beyond me. But no pressure was put upon me, no threats were made, no enticements were offered. The decision makers knew that such action would be counterproductive. I did not want office, and I resented threats. Someone did come and suggest that if Mrs Thatcher herself believed that it was in Britain's interests to sign up to the agreement, and that the surrender of sovereignty would be minimal, perhaps she was right and I was wrong. I am ashamed to say that I found that argument persuasive enough to change my mind. After all, who was I, and what did I know? Nor was I particularly interested in drawing attention to myself as an extremist, when I was not. To my regret ever since, I pulled my dissenting version, and signed up to everyone else's text. I should have had more self-confidence. Events proved me right to have had such doubts.

For the Single European Act was just the start of the slippery slope. No sooner had this package of powers been transferred to Brussels than Nigel Lawson, in 1987, began shadowing the German deutschmark, and interest rates in Britain started rising. When the Berlin Wall came down in November 1989 – a people's revolution overwhelming the wishes of Europe's political leaders, led by Margaret Thatcher, who had no wish to see either a more powerful Germany or the inevitable rise in European interest rates that would follow the inevitable reunification of Germany – British interest rates rose even further. Everyone could see that the German government was not going to let this monumental development be funded by higher German domestic taxation: Chancellor Kohl said as much to the Foreign Affairs Committee, and removed the head of the Bundesbank, Karl Otto Pohl, who had told us, the day before, that it would only be financed by higher interest rates over his dead body! Reunification took place in October 1990. Mrs Thatcher was persuaded by the leaders of British industry and the Cabinet that we must join the Exchange Rate Mechanism to stabilise our economy. But interest rates went on rising even further. As a result, the many small businesses, created in Britain by the Thatcher revolution, became unable to afford to borrow money at rates of over 15%. They went into bankruptcy, unemployment spread rapidly, mortgages failed and homes were repossessed on a large scale. This was not just something that I read about in the newspapers and heard discussed on the radio and television: it was something I was told about at first hand at my constituency surgeries every Saturday morning, in my constituents' letters, at constituency meetings, and when I knocked on doors in my constituency. It was only after we left the ERM on 'Black Wednesday', 16th September 1992, that the British economy began to recover.

From the signing of the Single European Act, and at every further diminution of Britain's sovereign power since then, at Maastricht, Nice, Brussels, Rome, and Lisbon, the pro-Europeans have needled anti-Euro-statists with the mantra: 'Thatcher gave more of Britain away with the Single European Act than any prime minister since.'

The fall of Margaret Thatcher

Margaret Thatcher regretted her earlier weakness, and blamed Nigel Lawson, Douglas Hurd and Geoffrey Howe for the wrong advice. She became more autocratic, imperious and contemptuous towards them, though they had laboured long, hard and loyally in the nation's cause. She used to irritate some of her closest colleagues by her arrogant ego, her use of 'we' or 'one' when she meant herself, her sometimes strident fish-wife manner, and also her total lack of any obvious sense of humour. But these were all trivial reasons besides her strengths: how could they be weighed in the scales against her immense courage, her personal political power and her magnificently successful achievements for Britain?

She was surely the outstanding peacetime prime minister of this century. She did not inspire the winning of a world war, which will always be Churchill's greatness. But she cast her magic over the motley crew of Conservative ministers and diplomats who served her: she dipped them in the bubbling cauldron of Thatcherism, inspiring them to awesome tasks, which, she had been repeatedly assured by many of them, were totally impossible. In 1979, many of the most senior Conservatives had believed that the best that could be achieved by any prime minister was, in the words of the distinguished political journalist Bruce Anderson, 'the orderly management of national decline'. She would have none of it. She reversed the ratchet of socialism. She stemmed the abuse of trade union power. She constructed a beacon of economic success, which lit the way to political freedom for countries too long in the thrall of the Soviet empire. She breathed new life into the corpse of what had been Great Britain, and made us great again. I will never forget attending European human rights conferences, where ambassadors from Eastern European states would say with gusto and excitement, and for all to hear: 'The British are back.' Nor will I forget the obvious respect, and even admiration, in which she was held in the Soviet Union. She was undeniably Reagan's backbone and therefore jointly responsible for the demise of Communist power in the world. Sadly for the Conservative Party, so totally did she destroy Socialism in this country that when Labour took over in government, they could only do so by becoming Conservatives – which is why it has, until David Cameron's succession, proved so difficult, despite New Labour's seemingly endless catalogue of failures, for the Conservative Party to be seen as an alternative government. We seemed to no longer have a real enemy to fight!

And yet, in November 1988, all this remarkable achievement, and all the support she had from Conservatives and others throughout the country, counted for nothing to most of the ministers who had owed their positions to her, and who therefore owed her their loyalty. Was it just ingratitude and irritation? I think not. I am sure that the most powerful single element in her demise was Europe. The most powerful of her cabinet ministers were against her on Europe. The depth and strength of feeling on both sides became obvious to us all when Michael Heseltine walked out of the cabinet over Westland. His support for the helicopter company was a European matter: that company had rejected the American Black Hawk in favour of the product of a European consortium. She, on the other hand, was suspicious of the European plan, and wanted to repay the debt to the United States we had incurred at the time of the Falklands war. The Europhiles had no doubt that if Britain was ever to become part of a super state, she would have to go, and the sooner she went, the better. I believe that for some of them, the ends justified the means.

She resigned because she was assured by her cabinet that having won the first ballot of Conservative MPs, by 204 votes to Michael Heseltine's 152 with 16 abstentions – which was just less than the 15% lead she had needed to put her leadership beyond doubt – she stood no chance of winning on a second ballot. A succession of cabinet ministers trooped into her room. They told her that she stood no chance, while undertaking to stand by her loyally if she decided to stay in the race. Not unreasonably, in the circumstances, she believed that she could not win and was finished. So she resigned. But had any of them seen the polling which had been done by backbenchers of backbenchers, and which was more likely to have got truthful answers than any minister's questioning of cronies? Reluctant as I am to think that any of my friends and colleagues were capable of deliberate misrepresentation, there certainly was a great deal of wishful thinking.

Michael Neubert (MP for Romford), my Whip, had given me a list of over fifty names to canvas for the first round. Michael Colvin, whose secretary shared a room in the House with mine, and with whom I was daily in touch, was given another fifty. Others were similarly tasked. I had certainly done enough canvassing, in the thirty-five years of my political life, not to be taken in very easily by people who gave me assurances that they would be voting in a certain way when they had no intention of so doing. What I can say of a certainty, is that from the quarter of Tory backbenchers that we re-canvassed for the second poll, the information passed on to Margaret Thatcher that she was losing support, and would be bound to fail, was false. A number of my fifty, who had not voted for her first time round, were clearly shocked at what they had done, and convinced me that they wanted her to stand in a second round, and that they would certainly be voting for her at the next vote. Michael Colvin reported exactly the same experience to me and to the Whip. Of course, it was always possible that one or two who had voted for her on the first ballot might have changed their minds and voted against her on the second ballot, when they saw that she could after all be beaten by Michael Heseltine; but since he lost twenty-one votes between the first and the later ballot – won by John Major who was not even in the reckoning at the time of the Thatcher ballot – I think this would not have affected many, if any. I passed my information on to Michael Neubert, and I assumed that he would be passing it on to Peter Morrison, her PPS. The tragedy is that it was obviously not passed on to her. Only Michael Portillo, it seems, told her that the cabinet had got it wrong.

History may decide it was a good thing for the party that she did go when she did, and that she was wrong to have stayed on past her tenth year in office. That may be so. But it is not the point. I am sure that those who told her she could not possibly win had no basis for making such a confident assertion. I am equally sure that, although John Major won the next general election brilliantly, the disloyalty shown at the top of the party helped to unglue the support of grass-root party members in the years that followed, and greatly contributed to our wipe-out seven years later.

Gloria and I were really distressed at what happened. In 1994, when my constituency honoured me with a banquet attended by two hundred and fifty friends and supporters, to celebrate my twentieth anniversary as MP for Burton, with guest speakers Norman Tebbit and Bernard Ingham, Margaret Thatcher and Denis drove for two and a half hours up the motorways to attend the event. Unfortunately there remains no record of the splendid speeches that were given by Margaret, Norman Tebbit and Bernard Ingham, because Stan Clarke sacked the video photographer who had been booked to tape the wonderful evening. I recall Norman, in his speech, asking Margaret why I had not been made Home Secretary. In my speech, I said it was because of what Ronald Kray had said to me before they took him away. I think Margaret may have missed the joke!

Margaret Thatcher, though deeply hurt by her treatment, recovered and demonstrated that she had lost little of her fire and skill. On one occasion, a few years after her fall, she spoke to a packed Inner Temple after-dinner audience, giving a brilliant *tour d'horizon* of the political scene for forty-five minutes without once looking down at her notes or hesitating – then went on to savage several unfriendly questioners. On another occasion, in the twilight of the Major government, she was the guest of the Treasurer of the Inner Temple at his Grand Night Dinner. I was supposed to be looking after Ted Dexter, the former England cricket captain, who was speaking to her after the main course. Unfortunately I had to make my excuses and rush off to the Commons to vote at the end of a debate on the NHS. I explained that we had a three-line whip and only had a majority of three over the other parties.

'In my day, Ivan,' the great Lady quipped, 'we had a majority of 103.' Yes. Quite!

The rise and fall of John Major

Margaret Thatcher passed the baton to John Major whom, we were led to believe, she had chosen, not just to stop Heseltine, but because of his Euroscepticism. Once again, she seems to have misjudged the person.

From the moment he won the leadership contest, the rush towards ever closer union with Europe gained pace, and a systematic attack was launched upon those within the parliamentary party who were prepared to put their opposition to a federated superstate ahead of their political careers. No better, or more readable account, of these times and pressures is to be found than in Teresa Gorman's book, *The Bastards*.

It may, of course, have been entirely my fault, but I am ashamed to say that I had no idea who John Major was, until he became a whip. He had kept his head well down behind every parapet. But he must have impressed Margaret Thatcher, whose disciple, we were assured, he was. It is difficult not to feel great sympathy for John. From relatively nowhere, he awoke one morning to find himself Foreign Secretary, awoke next morning to find that he had become Chancellor of the Exchequer, and awoke the following morning to find that he had become Prime Minister! He must have been as amazed as anyone in the land.

In time I got to know him a little better. He was always most charming, engaging, considerate, and he had absolutely no side. He would join backbenchers at lunch or dinner, chat with us in the voting lobby and, if we had an issue to raise with him privately, he would always be happy to meet us in his room to discuss it. When prime minister, he came to meetings of the 1922 Committee, and invited the executive, of which I was a member, to discuss almost any issue of importance when it arose. He was also delightful to our wives, and knew everyone by first name. He was so much nicer than some important people I have known – and some Prime Ministers. Gloria and I were thrilled to be invited, on New Years Day 1995, to Chequers for a lunch and tea with his family and a very few friends such as Jeffrey and Mary Archer, Shirley and Leslie Porter and the lovely black singer, Patti Boulaye, and her husband.

I think everyone was amazed to learn, from the newspaper serialisation of her book years later, of John Major's relationship with Edwina Currie; they seemed such an unlikely couple. Nor did John ever appear to be the sort of person to take such incredibly dangerous risks. That their liaison was not discovered while it was taking place can only have been because nobody, not even the ever-foraging and cynical media, was looking in that direction. That she, having seduced him, was capable of betraying him in the end because he had not mentioned her in his autobiography, will have surprised no one who knew her. She nearly always behaved as though she was the only one on the planet who really mattered. Who but Edwina, immediately after the 1992 election, could have had the brass nerve (and lack of judgement) to announce to her thousands of loyal voters, and hundreds of her South Derbyshire party workers – some of whom will have given up their summer holidays to help her to win – that she did not really want to be a Westminster MP after all. The future, her future, would be in Europe, she announced. She was promptly rejected by the voters of Bedfordshire, in her attempt to become a European MP at the next European elections. To the surprise of many, she was forgiven by her South Derbyshire Association, and re-adopted to fight the 1997 general election. Although she had, undoubtedly, been a most hard-working, dynamic and popular MP, this must be some evidence that party activists put loyalty to the party ahead of their own feelings.

For John Major to have risked all – his future, his family's happiness, his party's future – for Edwina Currie, is truly mystifying. One can only imagine how terrified he must have been, having decided that it was not in the national interest to have her in the government, that she might betray their relationship before the next election. That he should have refused to take the easy way out and silence her with the high position in government she craved, shows how politically principled he was.

Courage was also the last quality that he lacked. With, it is true, a little help from Neil Kinnock (and Kinnock's 'experts' in public relations), he fought and won the 1992 general election unexpectedly, and almost single-handedly, as he took his soapbox and charmed the nation on many of its street corners. Then he kept the party in power until 1997: by no means a small achievement in all the circumstances.

The media, cheated of a Labour victory, were mercilessly unkind to him. He must have been both hurt and hardened. In truth he was neither grey nor wooden off the public stage. When he felt that his authority as leader was being undermined, he challenged his opponents to 'put up or shut up.' That was another act of courage. But sadly for his reputation and for the Conservative Party, he was stubborn, devious and wrong about some of the most vital issues of the day. These defects, because they destroyed the party, have inevitably, but very sadly, put his virtues into the shade.

In December 1991, John Major signed the Maastricht Treaty. He did this after a parliamentary debate in which Margaret Thatcher spoke for the first time from the backbenches for two decades. She did so with enormous conviction and authority.

'The fundamental issue that will confront the government at Maastricht,' she said, 'is that the draft treaties propose an enormous, and to me unacceptable, transfer of responsibility from this House, which is clearly accountable to the British people, to the European Community and its institutions, which are not accountable to the British people. Our authority comes from the ballot box and we are talking about the rights of the British people to govern themselves under their own laws, made by their own parliament. It is the character of the people which determines the institutions which govern them, and not the institutions which give people their character. It is about being British and what we feel for our country, our parliament, our traditions and our liberties. Because of that history, that feeling is perhaps stronger here than anywhere else in Europe.' She went on to call for a referendum on this next stage of European advance. 'Anyone who does not consider a referendum is necessary must explain how the voice of the people shall be heard,' she said. 'We should not deprive the people of their say on rights which we are taking away not only from them but from future generations... We should not make a massive transfer of power to the Community which is not accountable to our electorate.' Although, as her critics never fail to point out, she had not thought much of a referendum over the Single European Act!

At every stage of the drive towards European unification, the British people have been assured that the moves were desirable, necessary and involved no serious removal of power to Europe. Yet the Maastricht Treaty was described by one of its progenitors, Chancellor Kohl of Germany, as 'the foundation stone for the completion of the European Union. The European Union Treaty introduces a new and decisive stage in the process of European union which within a few years will lead to the creation of what the founder fathers of modern Europe dreamed of following the last war: the United States of Europe.' That was surely clear enough, from its promoter in chief.

John Major had undeniably achieved success in securing opt-outs to the agreement, with his refusal to accept the social chapter and a single currency, but there was no guarantee that these could or would be maintained, or that the European Court of Justice, which was extending its own powers as if there was no tomorrow, would not find some way around those particular obstacles to European power. Feeling about the Conservative Party's position on Europe was growing, and those of us who were most concerned about the government's pro-European policy, started meeting to get our views and actions together.

With Michael Lord, Christopher Gill and Chris Butler, I went to see the Prime Minister after his return from Maastricht. We urged him to have a referendum before he decided upon further integration into Europe. He told us he would have no truck with a referendum. We implored him not to rule one out, because it seemed to us inevitable that there would have to be one, whether he liked it or not, if only because the opportunistic Tony Blair would promise one as soon as the going got rough. John ignored our opinion and went public in ruling out a referendum. When Blair decided there should after all be a referendum, as we had said he would, John Major had to change his mind, and he too conceded the promise of a referendum. He had been totally wrong-footed. How could he have not seen that coming? The irony is that Tony Blair, having promised a referendum in his manifesto at the 2005 election, reneged on that clear pledge as part of his swansong, as did his successor Gordon Brown. The new version of the constitution, now accepted in the Lisbon Treaty by the Labour government and all our EC partners, is almost identical to the original version. To assert that the removal of our right of veto in sixty situations, the removal of the right of Parliament to vote on future amendments, the creation of such features of a super-state as an elected president, a foreign and defence minister with a large diplomatic corps, the imposition of a charter of rights with an 'opt-out' which is unlikely to be recognised by the European Court, are not changes justifying a referendum, is too absurd for words! What is it with referenda?

Many accuse John Major of weakness over Europe. He was not just weak: he was also a dissembler on the subject. He used to meet the Eurosceptics (or Euro-realists, as Bill Cash, the staunchest and most heroic among us, prefers to be called), and say, or at least give the strong impression, that he was more Eurosceptical than any of us. He would meet the Europhiles and say, or at least give the strong impression, that he was more Europhile than any of them. To those in the middle, he would say that his only concern was to keep the party on an even keel. Once, as I escorted John from a lunchtime meeting with Michael Spicer's eurosceptic European Research Group, after we had been discussing the party's future policy on Europe, he said that he wished that they had had discussions like that in cabinet. Why on earth had they not?

He certainly reacted badly to the pressure that was put on him by the eurosceptics who were, of course, the overwhelming majority of the parliamentary party – a fact I am not sure that he ever appreciated. At the now famous 'Fresh Start' Group meeting on 13 June 1995, which was chaired by Michael Spicer, and held in a basement conference room of the House of Commons not far from where Guy Fawkes had once prepared to raise parliamentary debate to a higher level, he seemed not to realise how strong the feeling really was, not just on his own backbenches, but also in the country. In his autobiography, he discloses a touch of paranoia on the issue: 'the meeting was as rigged as a scaffold'. It was no such thing. He was invited to come and hear what the majority backbench view on the single currency and the European issue was, and to respond to us.

Over 50 backbenchers crammed into the room. He told us that he did not know whether there would ever be a single currency, but that if there was, he wanted to be part of the negotiations. When he told John Townend (Chairman of the Backbench Finance Committee and a member of the 1922 Executive) that he did not think the voters were interested in Europe, the temperature rose, for the feeling of the meeting was that this was utter nonsense. Norman Lamont (ex-chancellor of the exchequer), said that if a single currency had been unacceptable in principle in 1991, it was still unacceptable now, and that it represented more of a loss of sovereignty than the devolution issue which John had felt strongly about. George Gardiner (the MP for Reigate and Chairman of the 1992 Group within the parliamentary party, who later lost the party whip and who stood, unsuccessfully, as an independent at the 1997 election), said that we could not go into the next election on a 'wait and see' ticket. I added my two-pennyworth. I said that if Europe was not top of the voter's agenda, it was up to us to put it there, and, because people felt so strongly about it, if we did not give a strong lead we might find that we were not in government after the next election. Many spoke in similar vein. The strength of numbers and the seniority of some of the speakers might well have alarmed John Major. But a prime minister, sure of his ground, should have been able to calm us, if not actually to persuade us: he should not have allowed himself to be savaged, and then to storm out of the room in a rage – as he did.

The next time I saw him mauled was when he came to speak at a regional rally that Shirley Stotter had efficiently organised at the impressive JCB factory at Rocester in my constituency, during the 1997 election campaign. The rally had been very successful, although John was preaching to the converted. Afterwards he joined Sir Anthony Bamford, and his father Joe Bamford, the founder of the company, in the chairman's office. Between them, they gave the prime minister such a verbal pasting over his weakness on Europe that even I felt sorry for him.

When the Maastricht legislation went through parliament, I took my place alongside the opponents to the European sell-out. I rebelled 37 times on the European Communities (Amendment) Bill; and I could not bring myself to vote for the Paving Motion or the Second and Third Readings of the Maastricht Treaty ratification bill, so I abstained. I have no doubt whatsoever that the Major government's position on Europe, so contrary to the sentiments of most of the British people, was a substantial reason for the Conservative government's wipe-out in the 1997 general election.

Contrary to the general perception, there was no massive defection of Conservatives to New Labour at that election. Tony Blair received half a million fewer votes than John Major had received in 1992, although the electorate had grown. The Liberal Democrat vote also fell by a quarter of a million. With the reduced vote representing only 43.2% of the poll, New Labour secured a majority of 178 seats. With the Conservative vote falling from 14.1 million in 1992 to 9.6 million in 1997, and the turnout falling from 77.7% to 71.5%, there can surely only be one conclusion: that 4.5 million former Conservative voters stayed at home. I have little doubt that this was mainly due to John Major's failure to stand up against further surrender of sovereignty to Europe without a referendum.

Some of our Conservative leaders still insist that the man and woman in the street consider our place in Europe to be a relatively unimportant matter. I am sure they are wrong: the issue matters a great deal to people. Whether we continue to surrender large chunks of our sovereignty, constitutional, parliamentary, legal or monetary, to un-elected bureaucrats in Brussels or anywhere else in Europe, is a country thing: the issue becomes one of patriotism. If we ask ourselves what people would still be prepared to go to war and to die for, if it ever became necessary, the answer would surely be family of course, and then country. Britain's right to control Britain is still a very important matter in the hearts of people: even if that feeling does not always manifest itself in a tick against the word Europe on a polling list.

In October 1999 I visited, for the first time, the Normandy beaches, which had seen the awesome Allied landings in June 1944. I went again in April 2001. Those visits – and those I have more recently made to the Flanders fields and trenches – moved me more than I can say. Yes, we are now united in Europe, and God willing there will never be another European war because of that unity. But the sacrifices made by those tens of thousands of men were for the freedom of their country, and what was then the British Commonwealth. Would we ever be able to mobilise troops like that for a European Union of the kind being urged upon us?

It is a very great pity that the last Labour Government refused to let this nation vote in a referendum on whether to sign up to the Lisbon Treaty which was, in all but name, a European constitution, and which stage by stage will whittle away and finally dismantle British sovereignty as we have known it. Had they done so, we would surely have found out who was right!

20

1991: The National Lottery

'Remember that you are an Englishman, and have consequently won first prize in the lottery of life.'

(Cecil Rhodes)

In almost every week of 1991, an event occurred which touched on the political causes and legal activities I have recounted in this memoir. It was the year in which the Soviet Union finally collapsed; when Solidarity won a free election in Poland; when Yugoslavia broke up and ethnic cleansing followed; when Israel bombed the Iraqi reactor, and the war liberated Kuwait; when a major step in dismantling apartheid took place with the passing of the Racial Classification Act in South Africa. It was the year of the European Community's Maastricht Treaty; of the acquittal of the Birmingham Six because of fabricated police evidence; of the IRA bombing of 10 Downing Street and Paddington and Victoria railway stations; and of my Brinks Mat trials. In all of these events my avid reader will recognise my interests but, my criminal trials apart, I have to confess that the role I played was totally unimportant. Save for two preoccupations.

I had a walk-on part in the passing of the War Crimes Act which, important though it was, could never have been expected to have substantial long-term consequences. I took a much more active part in the establishment of the National Lottery, the beneficial results of which were immediate, substantial, widespread and, hopefully, will long continue.

The War Crimes Act

The War Crimes Act was the product of the Parliamentary War Crimes Group, whose chairman was the highly respected Lord Merlyn Rees (the former Labour home secretary), and its secretary, and the dynamic force behind the measure, was Greville Janner, who had been a war crimes investigator during his national service. The group reflected the outrage felt by many people at the hundreds of Nazi war criminals who had been allowed to settle in this country as displaced persons, with no questions asked, and who could not, as the law stood, be prosecuted for the appalling crimes they had committed nearly fifty years earlier. The legal problem was that the British courts did not have jurisdiction to prosecute foreigners who had become British citizens living in Britain for crimes committed in foreign lands against other foreigners, however heinous. I was a member of the group that persuaded the Conservative government to set up an enquiry into whether a change in the law would be justified.

When Douglas Hurd (Home Secretary and former diplomat) agreed to an enquiry, and commissioned Sir Thomas Hetherington (the former Director of Public Prosecutions and first head of the Crown Prosecution Service) and William Chalmers (the former Scottish Crown Agent), to conduct it, I am sure he thought it would report against taking any such further action. Indeed Sir Thomas was frank enough to tell the Conservative backbench Legal Committee, when I was chairman, that he had so thought when he started the enquiry. It says much for the strength of character of these two servants of the state, that by the time they had investigated several possible cases, in July 1989 they had come to the conclusion that 'The crimes committed are so monstrous that they cannot be condoned' and that to 'take no action would taint the United Kingdom with the slur of being a haven for war criminals'. They recommended that the law be changed, so that prosecutions could be brought in this country for foreign war crimes where those alleged to have perpetrated them had since become British citizens. Although most of the suspects had either died, or were too old to face trial, or the witnesses against them were unable to give evidence, they concluded that there was sufficient admissible evidence against four men to justify prosecutions.

Despite the cogency of the report, there was very considerable opposition to any new law – particularly from those still in positions of influence, some of whom were prominent in the Jewish community. They had long ago decided to let bygones be bygones. This became clear when the report was debated in the House of Lords in December, and former lord chancellor Lord Hailsham, former prime minister Lord Callaghan, the former leader of the Liberal Party Lord Grimmond, various Lord Bishops and Lords Longford and Soper declared that they wished to see no further action being taken. The vote was 207 against, and only 74 in favour. On the other hand, opinion in the House of Commons was strongly in favour of a change in the law, and the debate there, after some very powerful speeches, was 340 votes in favour, and 123 against.

David Waddington, a supporter of the recommendation, replaced Douglas Hurd as Home Secretary, and with Prime Minister Margaret Thatcher also a supporter, legislation was drafted, and the War Crimes Bill, of which I was a sponsor, had its Second Reading in the Commons in March 1990. This time the vote for the Bill, again following very powerful speeches in favour, was 273 to 60. The Lords rejected the Bill again, this time by 137 votes to 62.

I could understand the argument that, since there were only four suspects strong enough to face trial, it was not sensible to expend time and money on bringing such old men to trial. I could also understand the position of those who, whether as junior officials after the war who had been party to the decision that a line should be drawn under the whole horrible affair, or had come to that decision now for the first time, were against any change in the law. What I could not understand, was how some great legal minds could be confusing 'retrospective' legislation with the quite different concept of 'retroactive' legislation.

It is 'retrospective', and Parliament and the courts have hardly ever approved of it, when someone is to be later criminalised for an act that was not only not a crime at the time it was committed, but which no one had any reason for thinking involved criminal acts. On the other hand, it is 'retroactive', and hardly subject to the same objection, when an activity which was obviously criminal to everyone at the time, including the perpetrator, is only later put onto the criminal register for some reason. There surely could not be the same objection to criminalising mass murder, for the perpetrator must always have realised that what he was doing was legally wrong, even though this country had not taken jurisdiction previously to prosecute foreigners for murdering foreigners on foreign soil. Some of their lordships, who could not understand the difference, branded the War Crimes Act 'retrospective' legislation, and therefore objected to it as a constitutional abuse. It was surely no such thing!

There was, nevertheless, a serious constitutional problem. The Lords had rejected a Bill from the Commons. Until the twentieth century, the House of Lords could stop legislation, because an act of parliament had to have the approval of both Houses. The Parliament Acts of 1911 and 1949, removed this power, and allowed the House of Lords to do no more than delay a Bill for one year, provided the House of Lords was given two opportunities to consider the issue. But since 1949 that power had never been used. Would the government use that power for the first time to force the War Crimes Act onto the statute book? Margaret Thatcher had had enough of the Lords on this matter: they were given one more opportunity to reconsider the matter and refused again to change their minds. The Parliament Acts were duly invoked. The War Crimes Act received Royal Assent in 1991.

Meanwhile, a special War Crimes unit had been set up by the Metropolitan Police, which investigated 367 cases. Prosecutions were brought against only two men. Andreas Sawoniuk was tried, convicted on two counts of murder, sentenced to life imprisonment, and died in prison. Szymon Serafinowicz was committed for trial on murder charges in 1996, but was held to be mentally unfit to stand trial by an Old Bailey jury. He died shortly after.

Had the whole business been worthwhile? I am sure it had. This country could no longer be tainted with the slur of being a haven for mass-murdering war criminals: that by itself must surely have justified the campaign. To that can be added the fact that the publicity given to the campaign, and to the horrifying evidence exposed by the enquiry and the trials, has helped to silence the Holocaust deniers, and to make sure that the Holocaust will not be forgotten.

I am now privileged to be a trustee of the Holocaust Educational Trust, which, with the help of both private and public funds, takes British schoolchildren from every secondary school in the country to Auschwitz, so that they can learn that these horrors were indeed true and become more determined that they should never happen again anywhere in the world.

The National Lottery

As a lawyer I had to advise clients, from time to time, that their money-making schemes were a 'lottery', and therefore illegal gaming under the law. I also had political interest enough in the subject to have supported Simon Burns (MP for Chelmsford) in 1988, and Ken Hargreaves (MP for Hindburn) in 1990, with their 10-Minute Rule Bills for a National Lottery. But I cannot put my hand on my heart and say that the introduction of a National Lottery had ever been one of my burning causes in parliament. Not until shortly after midday, one Thursday in October 1991, when I learnt that I had miraculously come top in the House of Commons' own lottery – for a Private Member's Bill.

The Speaker annually presides over the formal ballot for such Bills, and whoever comes in the top half dozen of the draw, stands a real chance of getting a Bill onto the statute book, provided he chooses a subject that the government of the day supports. Governments even have their own pet subjects, for which they may have been unable to find sufficient parliamentary time, ready to hand to any sympathetic but unimaginative backbencher. Although I always put my name into the ballot, I had never bothered to attend the draw. I only knew of my good fortune when the media swamped my office with telephone calls, demanding to be told what I had selected for my subject. I felt rather foolish when I had to tell a succession of lobby correspondents that I had not yet chosen a Bill. I should have realised that if I did well in the ballot, and my subject was interesting enough, I could get maximum media coverage on the lunchtime news that day. But then the odds against me winning the ballot seemed as long as, well, winning a lottery.

Within two minutes of being given the news, my phone was jammed both by lobby correspondents and applicants for my parliamentary favours. The first bid came from Richard Luce (Conservative MP for Arundel, ex-minister of state at the Foreign Office, and now Lord Chamberlain), who asked if I had thought about running with a national lottery? If I did, he would be delighted to brief me, as would Denis Vaughan of the Lottery Promotion Society, whose telephone number he happened to have to hand. Wow! Something as sexy as a national lottery: why had I not thought of that myself? Cautiously, I said that I would consider it.

The next call was from no less an eminence than the Lord MacKay of Clashfern, the Lord Chancellor himself. He told me, in his soft Scottish lilt, that the government would consider it a very considerable favour if I would take up a Bill that he, personally, was most anxious should become law. It would, he felt able to assure me, provide but a modest challenge to my widely admired legal abilities, and, by implementing the recommendations of the Law Commission, about which he knew I had always been most enthusiastic and, being vital to the future of the entire British commercial shipping industry, a cause he anticipated would be close to my heart, it would undoubtedly earn me the gratitude and admiration of the entire nation to the end of my days. It is very difficult to say no to such a person pressing such a cause with such irresistible charm. What was this extraordinary Bill that had moved so great a personage to so anxiously (and flatteringly) seek my assistance? Why, it was nothing less than The Bills of Lading and Carriage of Goods

(Miscellaneous Provisions) Bill, and was concerned to repeal an Act of 1855, and to modernise the right of suit in relation to important shipping documents! Should I leap at this chance that might never come again in my lifetime?

I am ashamed to have to disappoint my reader. After eighteen more or less anonymous years in the House, I did think that it might be time for me to make some kind of an impact, and immense though the persuasive powers of Lord MacKay usually were, his Bill struck me as an unlikely way for me to achieve that goal. 'Don't call me, James, I'll call you,' I thought, but did not, of course, say. Instead I thanked the great man, and asked if I might take time to consider his generous offer.

Over the next few days, dozens of campaigners for dozens of the most worthy causes swamped me with suggestions. But after the first few minutes, there was never much doubt in my mind: I had to go with a national lottery. I was, however, totally unprepared for the task, so there could be no sitting back to let it happen. First, I had to learn all I could about the subject. Then I had to draft a Bill. Then I had to canvas support in the country and in parliament. Then I had to get the thing onto the statute book.

My first surprise, and disappointment, was that my own Conservative government ('Freedom for the individual!'; 'Trust the people' etc.) was so strongly opposed to it. Reading the memoirs of the great Conservative leaders of the day, one would be forgiven for thinking that they had nearly all been madly in favour of a national lottery. Memories, I fear, are short! The Treasury was strongly against it, and Norman Lamont (and his junior minister, David Mellor), had just done a deal with the Pools companies, who would be guaranteeing 5% of their income (or £60 millions) for sport and the arts, in return, of course, for a tax concession of 2.5%. I never quite understood why the Treasury preferred to reduce their tax-take in order that only a few millions could be raised for good causes, when, by supporting a national lottery, they could increase their tax-take by hundreds of millions, at the same time providing hundreds of millions a year for good causes. I could more easily understand why the social welfare ministers were against it: they naturally tended to be paternalists and feared, as Mrs Thatcher herself had done, that social security benefits would be frittered away on feckless gambling. It may be that John Major was avidly in favour of a national lottery, but if so it is surprising that he never told me so nor gave me any encouragement, although I saw him often.

Fortunately for us all, there were strong supporters in the government: Chris Patten at Environment, Tim Renton at Culture and the Arts, above all, Kenneth Baker at the Home Office. There were many supporters on the backbenches – from both sides of the House. There were supporters in business and industry. There were supporters in the arts and sport. There were supporters in the media. There was massive support from the public. And there was Denis Vaughan. Denis, a well-known international orchestral conductor, who had seen the Sydney Opera House built with lottery money in the 1960s, could not have been more helpful to me. He was dedicated, determined, and inspirational. He nearly bankrupted himself in the service of the cause. When I think of those who sometimes get honoured for comparatively modest services to the community, I am amazed, and a little ashamed, that Denis, who has done so much for the good of our society by the work he did in establishing our national lottery, should still have been given no recognition of any kind.

From the moment of my decision, it was Denis who set about organising meetings, introducing me to helpful people, drafting a Bill and providing strong secretarial support in the form of Andrew Yale, a young and very enthusiastic lawyer. Much work in preparing for a national lottery had already been done by the Lottery Promotion Society, under the joint chairmanship of Lord Birkett (the former deputy director of the National Theatre), and the impresario Sir Eddie Kalukundis (head of the Ambassador's Theatre Group and chairman of the Sports Aid Foundation). At least since the celebrated broadcaster Robin Day had argued for such a lottery before the Rothschild Royal Commission on Gambling, and they in turn had recommended it in their report in 1978, elements of big business, sport and the arts had been gearing up organisationally for it. Little work needed to be done from scratch. But what was undoubtedly needed, in the face of such powerful opposition to the idea, was a surge of public feeling in favour so strong that the government would feel driven to adopt it – if not through my own Bill, through its own. And that is just what we achieved.

Doubtless there would have been a national lottery sooner or later, because by 1992 every other European country had one – even Albania! What my Bill did was to concentrate attention on the idea, work it up into a parliamentary issue, galvanise public enthusiasm through the media, bring together all those who had an interest in making a national lottery work, and stimulate the production of a package which John Major would be driven to adopt as a manifesto commitment for the 1992 general election.

I had meetings with sports, arts and charity organisations, all eager to reap the benefits of a national lottery; with lottery operators worldwide, to demonstrate how we could make the thing work; with businessmen and industrialists, anxious to get in at the start of what seemed likely to be a profitable enterprise for all concerned. I had daily newspaper and broadcasting interviews. Sam Wanamaker, the film star and film director, needed lottery money to build the Globe Shakespeare Theatre on the south bank. Lord 'Dickie' Attenborough, wanted the lottery to resuscitate the dying cinema industry and the arts. To my surprise, amidst all this fervour, Bass the brewers, one of my Burton constituency's great companies, and itself part of a syndicate that had been particularly eager to win the franchise, for some reason never explained to me, backed out and completely missed the boat. We had only a short time to make a big impact. Denis Vaughan's draft Bill was modified, with the assistance of the always helpful and wise clerks in the House of Commons Bills office.

On Friday 17 January 1992 I launched the National Lottery Bill with its Second Reading Debate.

'I hope that the House will think it appropriate', I said in my opening speech, 'that having won the lottery of the Private Member's ballot, I should devote the proceeds of my good fortune to a more glorious lottery. I look forward to the time – very soon I hope – when a national lottery, so big that it will attract millions of players and tens of millions of pounds every week, will breathe considerable new resources into areas of British life which the taxpayer's money barely reaches – into the arts, to sport, to our national heritage, to charities and, of course, into the pockets of the lucky winners. The aim of this Bill is nothing less than to raise the quality of life in Britain to even higher levels.' I pointed out that no fewer than 116 countries now had such lotteries; that unless we had one of our own, British money would continue to go to lotteries that produced no benefit to the people of Britain generally; that an endless list of sport and arts councils supported the lottery; and that, since 72% of the adult population told pollsters that they would play it, we could raise £3 billion a year from 25 to 30 million players. We could divide the proceeds three ways – a third to charities and good causes, a third to the prize-winners, and a third to operating costs and the relief of the taxpayer. I pointed out that France had 20 times as many covered tennis courts as we had, and that Germany had 20 times more swimming pools and 96 more opera houses. But in Britain, our 50,000 competitive swimmers had to share 12 Olympic pools in the country.

Then there was crime. Teenagers had become the main perpetrators. Bored by television and the absence of sporting facilities, their boredom was leading too many to crime. 'If we give them better swimming pools, more and better football pitches, more and better athletic grounds and gymnasia, more local theatres and musical instruments to engage their interest and vitality, there is likely to be a reduction in juvenile crime.' I gave examples of lotteries working well in other countries and I addressed the main objections being raised. Finally, I explained that what was before parliament was only an enabling Bill, which deliberately did not go into too much detail, providing but a framework within which government and a regulatory authority would work out such matters as the kind of games to be played, the proportion of prizes, the granting of operators licences, the selection of operator's and the policing of the institution.

There were no fewer than 35 contributions to the debate from speeches and interventions, as well as from Peter Lloyd (the Home Office minister), and the Speaker had to impose a ten-minute limit on speeches. Most speeches were in support: a few raised objections. The football pools were convinced that they would lose business. Some charities feared that their income would be diverted to the lottery. There was concern that the poor and feckless would overspend. Some believed that we had already allowed too much gambling.

The Bill in fact failed to get a second reading, and there was tremendous disappointment. Turnout was usually low on Fridays, because MPs always had engagements in their constituencies, and getting 84 MPs into the 'aye' lobby was actually quite an achievement. But it was 16 too few. We needed, but did not get, a hundred. This was entirely because John Major's government, being opposed to a national lottery, had ordered the 'pay-roll' vote, of about 100 ministers and their parliamentary aides, to stay away. Michael White of the *Guardian* greeted me in the lobby, informed me that that was now the end of the bold venture, and invited my comments.

'Why do you say it is the end?' I asked him.

'Because Number Ten has told me so,' he replied. 'They do not want a National Lottery.' Well, well, well, here was indeed another challenge! My hackles thus raised, I prepared myself for battle.

In the event, the vote did not matter, and the battle never took place. We had done enough, with the powerful assistance of the tabloid media, to get the issue firmly into the public arena. National interest had been well and truly aroused in the run up to the debate. The *Daily Telegraph* had described the lottery as 'A winner the nation could safely put its money on.' Within weeks the government was persuaded by the media and public reaction, that the lottery's popularity could indeed be a vote-winner. John Major, desperate for popularity, made it a centrepiece of the 1992 Conservative general election manifesto. During the course of the campaign, he now felt able to agree that 'it was the only way to fund a rebirth of cultural and sporting life in Britain.'

The rest, as they say, is history. John Major surprised everyone with not only an electoral victory, but the largest vote any prime minister in this country had ever received and, a considerably larger vote than Tony Blair was to receive in his landslide victory five years later. How much of that victory was due to my Bill and the promise of a National Lottery I will, alas, never know!

After winning the election, the government introduced its own improved Bill, which swept through parliament. Nearly all of the fears expressed turned out to be baseless. In fact the success and the benefits of the National Lottery have far exceeded our early expectations.

Camelot, who won the franchise and has run the National Lottery for sixteen years since its launch on 14 November 1994, has extended the concept into many different games, and has succeeded in providing enormous benefits for British society. To date £24 billion has been raised for 240,000 good causes and charitable projects. This country has never seen so much patronage of the arts and sport: the Royal Opera House has been saved for the nation; the Tate Modern art gallery has been established; there is the new Wembley Stadium; the Eden Project for the Environment; the upgrading of the British Museum, the improvements to the Natural History Museum and to the Tower of London; British medal successes at the Beijing Olympic Games have been substantially attributed to lottery money; and thousands of local sports stadia, cricket pitches, football fields and theatres which have been built or improved throughout the United Kingdom. If only it had not coincided with the enormous and frightening increase in drug taking by young people, the National Lottery would have been even more successful in achieving one of my main aims – to take potential young offenders off the streets and away from a life of crime.

Medical research has also benefited. Tens of thousands of jobs have been created. Over £2 billion in commissions have gone to 36,000 retailers enabling thousands of small shops, many of them in village post offices, to remain in existence. Over £35 billion has been paid out in prize money to the 60% of the population who regularly play the lottery, helping to raise their standard of living and enjoyment of life. Even with only a 1 in 14 million chance of winning the national lottery, no fewer than 2400 people have managed to beat those odds to become millionaires. There have been 11,000 jackpot winners – over half of whom return to work after their win. There have been over 15,000 second prize-winners, averaging over £100,000 each. The government and taxpayer have benefited from the £9.3 billion of duty paid by the National Lottery. I am very proud to have played a part in producing what has become the most successful lottery in the world, and has now become an accepted part of the British way of life.

Even so, one cannot be entirely happy with the way the National Lottery has developed. To begin with, it is surely unfair and short-sighted for governments to have allowed those organisations which only distribute the money to take the public credit: while Camelot, the franchise company which has the problem of actually raising the money from us, gets little thanks. If the credit went where it properly belongs, and Camelot's name were, for example, to appear on England sports shirts, instead of Sports Aid or Sport UK, who have done little to encourage us to spend our money on the twice weekly bet, more people might want to play the lottery. For then the point would be driven home that even if the punter loses, 28p of his £1 bet will go to boost Britain's sport and other charitable causes, and the rest will go to boost employment and to reduce taxes.

Then there have been the inevitable problems and some drama. Richard Branson's Virgin empire was a disappointed party in bidding for the franchise, and a libel action against the chairman of G-Tec, the operational brains behind the lottery, ended in the High Court with victory for Branson, resignation for Snowden of G-Tec and then of Peter Davies, the highly regarded head of Oflot, the lottery regulator. The government's Millennium Dome, built from lottery money, was a financial disaster. Large sums of money have been lost on a National Jazz Centre, Sadlers' Wells Ballet, the Earth Centre Leisure Park in Doncaster; and in 1999 the Commons Public Accounts Committee reported that most of the fifteen schemes sponsored by the Arts Council had overrun their projected costs by nearly £100 million. A Big Lottery Fund, set up to hand out half the money raised by the National Lottery for good causes, somehow manages to spend nearly £80 million a year or 10% of income on over a thousand employees, while other major charities can distribute their money with a fraction of the staff and at a fraction of the cost.

Some of the money has gone to ridiculous causes. The Community

Fund, one of the organisations set up to direct the money to good causes, donated £723,000 to the National Coalition of Anti-Deportation Campaigns, helping failed and therefore bogus asylum seekers and Palestinian bombers to fight their cases. Money has gone to help Peruvian farmers to breed more guinea pigs for eating. Aromatherapy massages have been provided through the Scottish Prostitutes Education Project to sex workers; £20,000 has been granted to an artist to explore cultural attitudes towards women's bottoms – something that I have no doubt many researchers would have done for nothing! Yet money has been refused to manifestly deserving causes, like the Caister Volunteer Rescue Service in Norfolk, which, having saved 150 lives over the last 25 years, was only asking for a new lifeboat. These public blunders are sad, because when publicity is given to them, it turns off many would-be lottery players, and deprives the genuine good causes of funds.

The worst development has been the way that the Labour government treated the National Lottery as its own. Despite loud protestations when in opposition, and the promise that when it came to power Labour would not siphon off National Lottery money to pay for the education, health and environmental programmes that should come from the Treasury, the two later National Lottery Acts of 1998 and 2006 have done the opposite. It is the National Health Service that should be providing hospital body scanners, and the Department of Education that should be providing the right food for children in schools: National Lottery money should only go to good causes that the Treasury cannot be expected to fund.

Instead of stealing from the National Lottery, government should be ensuring that no further political interference can deter the public from contributing towards the cultural, sporting and social life of the nation. Perhaps the new coalition government will ensure that this happens.

21

A Knighthood

'Is not life a hundred times too short for us to be bored in?'
(Nietzsche, *Beyond Good and Evil*)

As usual, 1992 began with a week in the constituency. I visited seventeen
factories and businesses, spent a day inspecting new homes in Burton
upon Trent, took time strengthening my links with the local media, and
I held five weekend surgeries. Back in London, the Brinks Mat trial
started at the Old Bailey, I launched the National Lottery Bill in the
Commons, made thirty-five radio and television broadcasts, delivered
nine speeches (including one at the Oxford Union in favour of capital
punishment), and visited Paris and Bonn for two days, engaged with
the Foreign Affairs Committee's enquiry into Britain's European future.
On Sundays, when there was no Board of Deputies or other meeting, I
played squash and tried to improve my pitiful butterfly stroke at a leisure
centre pool in the morning, and went down to Brighton to see my
mother and take her out to dinner in the evening.

During February the Brinks Mat trial continued almost daily at the
Old Bailey, and every evening that the House was sitting, I attended
committee meetings. I also made short speeches to gatherings of the
faithful, appeared on *Newsnight*, BBC *Breakfast News*, *World at One*,
Central Television *Weekend* and various other programmes, and had my
usual weekend constituency surgeries and calls. The Foreign Affairs
Committee completed its European visits with a return to Bonn to meet
Chancellor Helmut Kohl and other German ministers. Rachel went into
hospital for a few days for intravenous antibiotic treatment, and Gloria
and I took turns to be with her.

On Thursday 21 February, a family tragedy occurred. My dear mother,
aged 85 years, lit a cigarette and settled down to watch *Home and Away* on
television. The cigarette must have fallen from her hand, and she and the
room went up in flames. The firemen arrived very quickly, but found my

mother dead. They successfully stopped the fire from spreading to other parts of the flat and building. I was told that it was unnecessary for me to identify the body, and was advised not even to see her, as she had been so badly burnt. The pathologist was able to determine that she must have died of a heart attack before the fire started, for the autopsy revealed that there was no smoke in her lungs. Thank God she had not been burnt to death! The thought of it had horrified us. Her death was totally unexpected, for she had all her wits about her, needed no stick to move about, climbed the stairs without assistance, and went out shopping on her own. She was fiercely independent and had no wish to move nearer to us and leave what had been her home for fifty-six years. Her death was a tragic loss for me and the family. I had seen quite a lot of her after my father had died in 1989, and we spoke often on the phone, chatting about our day-to-day lives. She came on holiday with us to Guernsey and Greece. Looking back, I am sad that I never thought to ask her, and she never told me, whether she had had a happy life.

Within a month of my mother's death the 1992 general election campaign started, and ended on 9 April, with the surprising Conservative win. My own majority was reduced to 4127. Our national success was widely attributed to the personal failure of Neil Kinnock to engage with the floating voter, and his misplaced triumphalism at his party's national rally in Sheffield. Or it might have been John Major's personal achievement in successfully engaging with the floating voter from his soapbox on the nation's street corners. Perhaps, as Mort Sahl said of Ronald Reagan, he won because of who he ran against [Jimmy Carter]. 'Had he run unopposed, he would have lost!'

I like to think that the victory might even have had something to do with the popularity of the National Lottery.

A knighthood

For all its achievements, the new Major administration often seemed to have some element of muddle about it. I can point to one particular example that affected me directly. On Saturday 11 April, two days after our election victory, and as I sat talking with two constituents at my surgery in the Burton office, the phone rang. The prime minister's private secretary introduced himself, and asked whether I would be prepared to answer a call to Number 10 on Monday, to accept the offer from the prime minister of a position in the government.

Left: Rachel and me
– two members of
Chambers in conference.

Below: With my mother
and father, 1985.

Bottom: Prime Minister Margaret
Thatcher and some of the
Burton team during the General
Election campaign of 1987.

Top Left: Rachel, London University, LLB. *Top Right:* Rachel, star of ITV's hit show *Blind Date.*
Below: With my leader, Rachel, after the Quinten Hann case.

Left: With Ethiopian Jewish children in Jerusalem, 1985.

Below: Painting by Ronald Kray, a gift after his murder convictions.

Above: On the House of Commons terrace with left, Sue Dennis (my secretary) and Samantha (Sam) Walker (my researcher).

Below: In full flow on Europe in the Commons.

Above: With Princess Diana at a national Relate reception. *Below:* As Visiting Professor of Law at the University of Buckingham with (L–R) Dean Charlotte Walsh, Vice-Chancellor Terence Kealey, Chancellor Sir Martin Jacomb and Dean of Law Professor Susan Edwards.

Above left: With Prime Minister John Major.

Above right: With Soviet Union President Mikhail Gorbachev.

Left: With Pope John Paul II.

Above: With King Juan Carlos of Spain and the Foreign Affairs Committee.

Left: My Armorial Knight Bachelor crest: representing Burton upon Trent (fleurs de lis and brewery barrel); Member of Parliament (portcullises); Queens Counsel (silk tents); Gloria (her Ogle family half moon crest on the tents); Rachel - the shepherdess (the ermine collar on the hierocosphinx); Judaism (the pointer used to read the bible in synagogue (yad) held by the hierocosphinx); and the motto in Latin ('How glorious (pun) to serve mankind').

GLORIA SERVIRE · HOMINUM ·

Left: With my wife Gloria and daughter Rachel after Investiture.

Below: Being knighted by Her Majesty The Queen in 1992.

This was a complete surprise to me. I had never wanted to become a minister – in the early days because it had simply never occurred to me that I had the ability, and in the latter days, when I had become less impressed with the ability of others, because it seemed too late to start out on a ministerial career. Also, I had a future at the Bar – which meant, of course, that I would have been delighted to be asked to become Solicitor-General. But I had certainly never told whips or ministers that I would be interested in joining the government, as I think is necessary unless one's ambition is apparent and one's potential is outstanding and obvious. Since I had been chairman of the Conservative Home Affairs Committee, as well as of its Legal Committee, it occurred to me that I might be being offered the post of Minister of State at the Home Office. Whichever it was to be, I must admit that I was thrilled, and I told the private secretary that I would be delighted to accept the invitation. I knew that I had no need to consult Gloria before I gave my answer.

But there was a problem. I was in the middle of the Brinks Mat gold bullion money-laundering trial, and I was not sure that I could just walk away from it. I telephoned my friend, Sir Robert Johnson (the High Court judge and former chairman of the Bar Council), for his advice. He said that becoming a government minister had always been accepted as a valid reason for withdrawing from a case: Gerald Gardner had done it, at considerable inconvenience to everyone, when he was appointed Harold Wilson's Lord Chancellor. I also consulted the Bar Council on Monday morning, and they confirmed that view. However, I needed the permission of my client, my instructing solicitor, my junior in the trial, and the judge. I secured these without problem over the weekend: Ralph Haeems was a good friend, as was Robert Flach, my junior in the trial who, being older and more experienced than me, was a very safe pair of hands in which to leave a case. Both my client and the judge were also supportive. On Monday morning I had to tell other members of the Bar, appearing with me for co-defendants in the trial, as a matter of courtesy, and anyone else whom I might, however remotely, be leaving in the lurch. My clerk had to be told, other members of my chambers, other solicitors who had booked me for future cases, my wife, daughter, bank manager, accountant and Uncle Tom Cobley of course. Goodness knows how many friends and relations Gloria also proudly informed of my promotion. Late afternoon television showed the comings and goings of the lucky and the unlucky – but for me, the call never came.

Next day I telephoned Richard Rider, the Chief Whip, and asked what was happening.

'All the new ministers have been appointed,' he told me.

'What about me?' I asked.

'What about you?' he replied.

I told him about my summons from Number 10. He said he knew nothing of it. Besides, he informed me, Derek Spencer, the new MP for Brighton Pavilion, had been appointed Solicitor-General. I did not find that much consolation. Charming and able as Derek was, he had been out of parliament for five years, having served for only four years until he had lost his Leicester seat in 1987.

I was not just disappointed – I was livid! Never to seek a position is one thing: to be told that you are to be appointed, and then, after making the many necessary arrangements, be made to look foolish, was another thing entirely. I wrote an angry letter to the prime minister. He scribbled a reply on my letter inviting me to go and see him in his office in parliament.

He was almost unbearably charming. He apologised disarmingly, saying that he was very sorry that there had been such a muddle. He did not explain how or why it had happened. He did say that the least he could do was to promise to bear me in mind for a ministerial position next time, and to offer me the knighthood that I would have automatically received as Solicitor-General. Then, knowing that I would be opposing him and the government over European integration, he said, with the thoughtfulness that was typical of him, that if I considered that it was the wrong time to accept, he would quite understand: the honour would be mine whenever I wanted it. I am ashamed to report that I had a most unworthy thought in response to his very decent gesture. I was not at all sure how long John would remain prime minister, if he did not get Europe right for the party very quickly: so I said that it would not embarrass me at all to accept the knighthood immediately!

Some political commentators have been flattering enough to say that I must have refused the offer of such relatively lowly positions in the hierarchy as Solicitor-General or other junior ministerial appointments. The internet even tells me that I was about to become Minister for Defence Procurement when Jonathan Aitken beat me to the post, because he had useful connections with Arab countries and I did not. Such generous conjectures are, sadly, wide of the mark. This was the only offer of a government appointment ever made to me during my entire parliamentary career. I was obviously judged to be either unworthy (which I may well have been), or uninterested (which I certainly was). By the time John Major made his next ministerial appointments, he had either forgotten about me or considered that I would not fit into a government that he had purged entirely of eurosceptics. While I do not blame him, I can only say that it would have been nice to have been asked.

So I resumed normal service at the Old Bailey on the Brinks Mat case, which had been going on since 1991 and continued until August 1992. Things went so well for my client, Mr Clarke, and so badly for the prosecution's case against him, that I was able to open my final speech to the jury thus:

'Today is the five-hundredth anniversary of the day that Christopher Columbus discovered America. What has that to do with this case? Only this, that when Columbus set out he did not know where he was going, when he arrived he did not know where he was, and when he got back, he had no idea where he had been. Does not that accurately sum up the prosecution case against my client in this trial?'

As I spoke these words, another unkind thought passed through my mind about John Major's government. My client was acquitted; very sadly, the government was not.

My life began to be even more hectic. The month of July, in which the trial moved towards its close, presents my hopefully loyal reader with a further snapshot of the preoccupations of my daily life.

I took part in a sponsored charity swim at the RAC Club in London's Pall Mall. Burton Conservatives were so successful in helping me to raise money, that I was awarded the magnificent Wilkinson Sword prize, and became Parliamentary Swimmer of the Year. I spoke in one debate in the chamber (on prisons and the probation service) before the House rose for the summer recess That month I appeared in fifteen radio and television broadcasts for the BBC, ITN, Sky and Radio 4's *The Moral Maze*. I held three surgeries in the constituency, attended a speech day at St Mary and St Anne's (a girls' public school in Abbotts Bromley, then in my constituency), a school fete at Anglesey Primary School in Burton, a church restoration service at Barton under Needwood, a crime prevention display in Burton precinct, and a public meeting in historic Tutbury. Then the rural part of me went walkabout to meet my farmers at Uttoxeter cattle market, and into the adjoining street market, where a truly great man of letters, Dr Samuel Johnson, two hundred and twelve years earlier, had done penance, hatless in the rain, in memory of his father whom he had, when a young man, refused to help to sell books from his market bookstall.

On Tuesday 21 July, Gloria and I took Rachel for her last time to the annual garden party at Buckingham Palace. As a single daughter of an MP, she had been able to attend these occasions after her sixteenth birthday, but the invitations had to stop when she was twenty-five. I had asked my friend David Lightbown (MP for Tamworth, who, as a senior government whip, also held the post of the Queen's Treasurer) if it were possible for him to arrange for Rachel to be introduced to the Queen, as debutantes used to be in days of yore. This kindness was duly arranged with great efficiency by courtiers, and the three of us were positioned at the foot of the steps leading down from the palace into the gardens, to be the first to be introduced to the Queen. When Her Majesty arrived, she stopped for much longer than was necessary for Rachel to execute a curtsey; she stayed for several minutes for a good old chat about Rachel's achievements, dreams and aspirations. Then Her Majesty turned to talk to Gloria and me. I felt that she was being too generous to the Lawrence family with her time, and I told her that we would be meeting again the following day.

'Oh, really?' Her Majesty asked, 'Where?'

'Here, Ma'am,' I replied, 'when, hopefully, you will be doing me the very great honour of conferring a knighthood upon me.'

The following day, all those to be honoured gathered in the ballroom at Buckingham Palace, in an atmosphere of excited expectation, with the two members of the family we were allowed to invite. Looking around I saw a number of famous people, such as the film star Michael Caine, there with his beautiful wife Shakira, to be honoured with a CBE. Years later he also received a knighthood. While Home Secretary Kenneth Clarke called out names, and a succession of men and women moved forward to receive their awards from the Queen, soft music wafted down from a military band in the elegant minstrel's gallery.

'Sir Ivan Lawrence, for political service,' announced the Home Secretary.

I stood up, Gloria squeezed my hand, Rachel beamed at me, and I walked rather self-consciously to where Her Majesty stood, sword in hand. I knelt before her on an ornate stool. She dubbed me once on each shoulder. Then I stood before her as she placed the knight's medal and ribbon round my neck.

'Hallo, again!' said my beloved monarch.

I had been invested, by Her Majesty, Queen of Great Britain and the Commonwealth, with the dignity of Knight Bachelor. The honour, stretching back to its creation in the Saxon Middle Ages, is the oldest non-royal title that can be conferred upon a British citizen. If only my dear parents had been alive to share my pride.

Americans, in particular, find it almost impossible to address me as they should – by my first name: 'Sir Ivan'. They always say 'Sir Lawrence', because the correct address sounds too intimate for someone they do not really know. At about the same time as me, our national poet Stephen Spender was knighted. He observed, on television, 'I suppose it won't be long before some fool American calls me Sir Spender!'

Select committees

The select committee system, which cynics believe was invented to keep troublesome MPs busy and out of the chamber of the House of Commons, was becoming a more important part of our parliamentary democracy. By its operation, government is held publicly to account by backbench members of parliament, over detail of its actions as well as the broad issues of policy.

Governmental proposals (of whatever party) for the improvement of the nation's welfare are often opposed when they are first announced. This may be because too many people would have their lives adversely affected by the change. Often it is because vested industrial interests are involved. There is also Her Majesty's Opposition, whose leader is actually paid by the state to oppose the government. This is seldom opposition for opposition's sake: its purpose is to put proposals to the test of challenge, to discover before it is too late whether the proposed legislation is really necessary, whether it says what it means, and whether it may have unintended consequences which would make the proposal counterproductive. The tabloid media often take a strong view for or against a government proposal, and strongly influence millions of readers. But if the evidence supporting their line comes only from people interviewed in the street, who may never have considered the question before, or who are ignorant of the facts, a wrong conclusion might result.

So, in a perfect world, knowledge of all the relevant facts should guide the legislator, and he must discuss, and be prepared to argue through, such proposals. As much as I had read widely, had many interests, and had experienced life vicariously as a criminal lawyer, I was always surprised to find how little I knew about so many of the matters upon which I was always being called on to express an instant opinion. I found that, listen as I would to colleagues explaining and airing their views in the chamber, in the committee rooms, at meal times and in the tea room, and necessary as this was to my learning process, it seldom provided me with enough to form a sound basis for judgement.

The parliamentary activity that more than any other I found to be vital for my own knowledge and understanding of events and issues, was membership of a select committee. Here we received thorough analytical briefings on each subject from civil servants and from independent experts. We could follow up that information with fact-finding visits, and the opportunity to put informed questions to those most knowledgeable or most likely to be affected by the proposals being made. We had the power to call for any documents, and to question anyone we thought might be helpful. We could usually, although not always, take time to consider the issues. One particular advantage of the system is that it tends to break down party political differences: those who do not want to be seen to be against their own party's policy in the chamber, can afford to be more objective in select committee deliberations in a room upstairs, away from the direct attentions of the press.

A particularly important feature of the system is that the government has to give a reasoned reply to select committee recommendations within four weeks, and can often be forced to debate subjects they are reluctant to address. Unlike the United States congressional committees, our select committees, with no control over the purse strings, cannot oblige governments to adopt recommendations against their wishes. But, less in my time and more so now, government has to face the challenge of intense media attention, and it is more difficult to deny a well-researched and reasoned select committee report. The aspect of my political life that I have most missed, since 1997, has been the knowledge that I used to gain from my membership of select committees.

I had been serving on select committees almost since I entered parliament in 1974. My first venture had been with the Social Services and Employment Sub-Committee of the Expenditure Committee, under 'Red' Renée Short, the veteran MP for Wolverhampton North-East. The work of that committee had prepared the ground for what was to become the very important Childrens Act of 1989, and for extensive reform of the social services. So wide was the committee's remit that we were able to investigate and report on the high incidence of perinatal and neonatal mortality, as well as juvenile crime and unemployment. In 1979, on the recommendation of parliamentarians led by Sir Norman St John Stevas, select committees were reorganised to monitor individual government departments, so their scope was narrowed and deepened, and their influence increased.

I was also, for many years, a member of the Joint Committee (with the House of Lords) on the Consolidation of Statutes. This was presided over by a succession of brilliant Law Lords. As governments increased the size of the statute book, our task was the happy one of reducing it – by consolidating several acts of parliament into one, and weeding out altogether old acts of parliament from the Middle Ages which had become obsolete – a hopeless and mostly rather tedious task! We still managed to leave on the statute book many old laws dealing with bows and arrows, debasing the coinage and seducing a member of the royal family. The real work was nearly all done by a specialist breed of lawyer called the parliamentary draughtsman – even when he was a woman! They were perfectionists who seldom made mistakes, or none that we, as mere committee members, were able to spot. But they were not infallible. On one occasion, in the 1970s, we accidentally abolished the right of pensioners in Scotland to enjoy subsidised bus and train fares. When this was discovered, panic set in with the Wilson government, and a new statute had to be passed very quickly to correct our error. It was surprising how quickly such things could be done if the politicians set their minds to it: the passage of the Bill took one hour of parliamentary time one Friday afternoon, and I am not sure even that was a record.

In 1983 I was appointed to the Commons Foreign Affairs Committee, under Sir Anthony Kershaw (MP for Stroud) and then David Howells (the ex-Cabinet Minister and MP for Guildford). I have already described in earlier chapters, some of our work, which was exciting for its contemporary relevance and importance. Sometimes we considered urgent issues of the moment – such as the abuse of diplomatic bags and whether demonstrations outside embassies should be restricted following the murder of WPC Yvonne Fletcher outside the Iranian Embassy in April 1984. But mostly we reported on the wider aspects of Britain's relations with other countries and world events.

What a privilege it was to have been a member of that committee at a time when the new world order began to be created. We visited Eastern Europe in the months of 1989, following Gorbachev's introduction of Peristroika (reconstruction) and Glasnost (transparency) which led momentously to the collapse of the Soviet Union and the Eastern bloc. I have notes of our meetings with leaders of some of those countries that reconstructed in that year. Horst Sindermann, the 73 year old

President of the East German Volkskammer (Parliament) and member of the Politburo, assured us that Communism was about to spread around the world. Within the year, he had to resign all his posts, was expelled from the East German Communist Party, imprisoned and was released only shortly before he died.

In Warsaw Peter Shore and I met members of General Jaruzelski's government, several leaders of the banned Solidarity movement and one of the church leaders. Poland, together with Hungary, Czechoslovakia, and then East Germany, was about to lead the way, with its revolution and reforms, to the free elections in Europe that would bring about the total disintegration of the mighty Soviet Union. The Cardinal Archbishop at the time was unable to meet us himself, but a meeting was arranged with his deputy, Bishop Davroski. I asked him, quietly and courteously, questions which had arisen from our meetings with the Solidarity activists. What was the church doing to help Solidarity? Why did he think they were not being given a seat in government? Would that not have made it less likely that they would scupper reforms when the economic going 'got hot' and shipyards had to be closed? I do not remember all the answers, but I do recall the astonishing reaction of this religious dignatory. Blood seemed to drain from his face, his hair seemed to stand on end, and he stood in front of me with his fists so clenched that I feared that he was about to do me an injury. We hurriedly left the august presence, Peter observing that I had seemed to have found and touched a nerve! We conjectured that the church had probably been helping Solidarity secretly, that the Bishop thought I had stumbled upon some information I should not have had, and this might have explained his angry reaction. Now we know, from the surprise resignation of Archbishop Wielgus minutes before his inauguration as Archbishop of Warsaw as recently as 7 January 2007, that Wielgus had admitted to spying for the secret police in Jaruzelski's time! Whatever role the church might have played, talks between the Communist government and Lech Wallensa, soon to become the leader of Poland's Solidarity government, began within weeks of our visit.

When the collapse of the Eastern Empire began, it took members of the German Bundestag completely by surprise. At a cocktail party on 25 October, at the German Embassy in Strasbourg, two West German MPs assured me that the wall could not conceivably come down within the foreseeable future. It fell on the night of Thursday 9 November 1989, two weeks later. On a visit to Bonn at the end of November (when I took the opportunity to collect a piece of the Berlin Wall as a memento for our living room), several members of the Bundestag laughed when I asked whether it was possible that the capital of the new Germany might return to Berlin. That, I was assured, would be quite impossible, for there was nowhere for the Bundestag to be sited in Berlin and besides, a new Bundestag chamber had recently been constructed in Bonn. Within twelve months Berlin had become the new German capital, and ten years later the new parliament opened in the new capital on the site of the pre-war Bundestag. Did I say that one of the great virtues of being an MP was early access to information?

We were always excellently briefed by the Foreign Office on our foreign visits, so I was usually able to hide my ignorance about world affairs. But I was not always able to do so. On one visit to Rome, I boldly asked the seven-times Italian Prime Minister, Giulio Andreotti, whether the reason why he, the leader of a proudly independent nation, was so keen to surrender Italian sovereignty to a European super-state, was that it was the only way to curb the all-embracing power of the Mafia. He laughed so merrily that his short neck all but disappeared into his shoulders. Perhaps I could not really have been expected to know that he was, at that very moment, being investigated as a suspected member of the Mafia! In fact, some time later, he was convicted of involvement in a Mafia-related killing, and sentenced to twenty-four years imprisonment. In due course he was acquitted on appeal, but later still was tried and acquitted again, on a technicality, for having ties with the Mafia.

On another occasion, in Paris, I was sitting on the platform at a meeting, listening with rapt attention to the attractive, impressive and soon-to-be Swedish European Commissioner, Anita Gradin, and preparing to follow her with my own brief contribution. I did not recognise the short, balding man in his late fifties who took the seat beside me. I glanced at him and held out my hand, pretending the briefest of interest.

'Lawrence,' I muttered. He took my hand firmly.

'Mitterand,' he replied.

I knew the 80-year-old United States Supreme Court Justice William Brennan Junior from visits that he used to make to London. He had an awesome reputation over forty years, as the leading proponent of civil liberties, human rights and all things then considered to be left-wing. When I was in Washington he invited me to sit in on one of the Supreme Court sessions, and then introduced me to the other incredibly distinguished Justices. Bill had been unwell for some time, so I asked him why he did not retire from the fray.

'Because Reagan will appoint a right-winger to replace me,' he replied.

'But weren't you appointed by Eisenhower?' I asked.

'Oh, yes,' he replied, 'but I wasn't a left-winger then!'

When my own stupidities got the better of me, I could always console myself with the thought that far greater politicians than me have had similar moments. Did not President Kennedy stand on the Berlin Wall in 1962 and announce, '*Ich bin ein Berliner*', which correctly translated means 'I am a doughnut'? Did not Margaret Thatcher, praising her deputy Willie Whitelaw on television, announce that 'Every prime minister needs a Willie'? And when I was part of a delegation of British MPs lobbying against Noraid collections for the IRA, in the Pentagon, General Colin Powell (then chief of the United States Armed Forces and later Secretary of State), admitted ignorance of the British army when he said to us, 'We have a problem at the moment with gays in the army. I expect you have the same problem in the UK?'

'Certainly not,' I felt able to assure him. 'That's what we have the navy for!'

He thought that was funny, and asked if he could use it in a speech he was giving that evening.

The Home Affairs Select Committee

It was in October 1992 that I joined the Home Affairs Select Committee, which always had to deal with what the media call 'breaking' issues. Over my next five years, the Home Affairs Committee studied, took evidence, visited, reported, and made recommendations on twenty-one different subjects. These were all matters of contemporary public interest, and the government, under pressure to legislate, would usually value our work as an all-party examination before it did so. We covered a wide range of topics: the delay in processing immigration applications, domestic violence, video violence, juvenile offenders, computer pornography, organised crime, murder, legal aid, racial attacks and harassment, identity cards, the private security industry, the private management of prisons, the possession of handguns, freemasonry in the police and judiciary, judicial appointments, dangerous dogs, and the funding of political parties.

It is interesting how many of these topics are still being urgently debated. We said, for example, in our computer pornography report, that we were 'particularly concerned by suggestions that some paedophiles have attempted to lure children into sex by passing pornography via bulletin boards.' Few of us had any idea, in February 1994, just how widespread and horrific child pornography through the internet was to become, and the subject is haunting society today.

The committee had meetings with all the decision makers – commissioners of police, senior judges, directors-general of the prison service, civil servants and ministers. For our crime enquiries, we visited penal institutions in England and Northern Ireland, a boot-camp in Massachusetts, prisons in Texas and California, areas of racial trouble in Manchester, Liverpool and London, young offender institutions in Denmark and Germany, and refuges for battered women in London. Although we were an all-party committee, and our recommendations often cut across party lines, many of our recommendations were accepted and implemented by the Conservative government. Some, like the offence of racial attack and harassment, had to wait for New Labour. Others, like identity cards, while still generating heat, remain unimplemented because of advances in technology, the escalation of costs, the proliferation of security breakdowns and the antipathy of new Conservative and old Liberal united now in the coalition government.

Our remit was generally to monitor the work of the Home Secretary and the Home Office (also the Lord Chancellor's and the Law Officer's departments), but there was one area of the Home Office portfolio that was forbidden to us – national security. In January 1993 the committee felt that the time had come to do something about this ban, particularly when we discovered that some newspapers had been allowed access to MI5 (the Home Security Service). We told the Home Secretary, Kenneth Clarke, that we would like to have a meeting, in private if necessary, with Stella Rimington, the head of MI5. He refused to let us do so. We argued that some journalists had just had a meeting with her, and it was constitutionally wrong that the media could have access, but the parliamentary committee, with oversight of his department, could not. He found this to be a convincing argument and relented. One or two of us could have lunch with Mrs Rimington, provided we only discussed matters of policy and administration with her – not day-to-day operations. In fact, seven of us attended the lunch. This being a major breakthrough in parliamentary control over the executive, the detailed arrangements were inevitably leaked to the media. Indeed, it became quite a media event.

Cars collected in New Palace Yard to whisk us to the then unknown MI5 headquarters, and as soon as we passed through the iron gates into and round Parliament Square, paparazzi in large numbers attached themselves to us. We had not been told the address of our destination, so they pursued us like Mack Sennett's Keystone Cops, north across London. Motorcyclists sped along, contemptuous of other traffic, with cameramen and film crew hanging over the side lest they miss some dramatic photo opportunity. Mrs Rimington says in her memoirs that there was no particular reason for keeping the address secret. Of course there was: the last thing the secretive MI5 ever wanted outside its front door – which turned out to be just off Gower Street – was a media circus generated by MPs. Well, they certainly got one with our select committee! But on our arrival, none of us said anything to the media, either because we were rushed unceremoniously inside or because, unusually for MPs, we had nothing to say.

Mrs Rimington welcomed us politely, if a little awkwardly, since she was unaccustomed to an experience like this. She briefed us, in a soft voice, about the size of MI5 (about 2000), its organisation (half women), and its functions (counter-terrorism and subversion). Although we were also supposed to be monitoring Home Office expenditure, we heard nothing about the organisation's cost to the taxpayer. I told her how much we appreciated the new openness, appropriate to a modern democracy. Tony Benn, in his excellent *Diaries*, writes that it was 'outrageous' that a committee of the House, with the power to summon people, papers and records, should have allowed themselves to be summoned by someone of the rank of permanent secretary. (Tony could be quite elitist, couldn't he!) I think we just felt that we were making a breakthrough and anyway, we had not been summoned – we had invited ourselves. We settled down to a pleasant lunch.

Civil service humour is seldom very funny: it reported only that we had been served 'Reform chops'. *Private Eye*, which is mostly much funnier, described the menu thus:

Snoop of the day;
Fresh Leaks; Scrambled Eggs; Grilled Mullin or
Code Fillets; Steak Out (not Well Done) or Bugged Hare with
Shredded Vegetables and Spilt Beans;
Mince Spies with Cold War Custard or Double-Agent Cream.
To Drink: Lager Stella Rimington;
Wine: Red (Under the Bed). Water: Tapped.
Undercover Charge: 10%. Surveillance not included.

Thus did my committee strike a blow for parliamentary control of the executive. Once we had nudged over the first domino, there inevitably followed a Parliamentary Intelligence Committee (not us), to monitor some of MI5's functions; legislation to subject the work of the secret intelligence services to better supervision and less vulnerability to abuse of power; an annual debate in parliament; a magnificent new publicly identifiable headquarters on Millbank; and autobiographies sailing suspiciously close to breaches of the Official Secrets Act.

Whenever the committee discussed law and order matters, I noticed the beginnings of a change of political attitude among its members. It used to be that the Conservatives were the ones who favoured tough measures against criminals, and the Labour Party was decidedly less interested in toughness and more liberal in its approach. Harold Wilson's anti-terrorism legislation had been a bitter pill for Labour supporters to swallow. But as time went on, and the line of mostly liberal-minded Tory home secretaries gave way to the more authoritarian Michael Howard (whom I strongly supported), the Labour members of the Home Affairs Committee (Donald Anderson, Mike O'Brien, John Hutton, Stephen Byers, Barbara Roche, Jim Cunningham, Gerry Bermingham and even Chris Mullen), appeared to grow less opposed and more supportive, of the hard line.

What was happening was obvious enough. Labour, defeated even in 1992 when they had been well ahead in the polls, was coming to realise that rising crime was an issue so important to the electorate that unless they did something about their image, they might never get power again. Tony Blair got the slogan just right: 'Tough on crime' (for the majority of the voters): 'Tough on the causes of crime' (for the Old Labour supporters)! Under Home Secretary Michael Howard, crime began to fall, and the slogan 'prison works' struck a strong chord with an over-burgled and over-street-robbed electorate, because removing offenders from circulation obviously stopped them offending. But it came too late for the Conservative government, and judicial opposition to minimum sentences hardly helped. By the time David Blunkett became home secretary, followed by John Reid, the political law and order circle had reversed polarity. Labour seemed to be taking over the title of the law and order party, and the Conservatives, while calling for more prisons and attacking Blair's failed promises, were talking more and more about human rights, civil liberties and the lack of social responsibility that is at the root of the causes of crime.

One of the consequences of being chairman of a high-profile parliamentary committee, was that I was always being invited to appear on television and radio current-affairs programmes. When the media asked for the Home Secretary or other minister in the department, and they would not or could not make themselves available, I was often asked to go along as the least worst substitute. I have lost count of the number of times in any month that someone seems surprised to learn that I am no longer an MP – thirteen years after my last speech! In Burton people often come up to me and say: 'Excuse me, are you who I think you used to be?' I assure them that I still am! A taxi driver recently looked hard at me, seemed puzzled, and said, 'Help me out'. I told him that I had appeared frequently on television and in the courts. 'No,' he said, 'which airport terminal do you want?' Sometimes avid television watchers would write to me, commenting upon both my performance and my appearance. A gentleman from Gloucestershire wrote:

Dear Sir Ivan,
I often see you on TV as being a senior MP and an expert on the law. However, with all kindliness, I think you should know that recently you have become so bottled-looking, untidy and baggy round the eyes, that I am sure that you are only asked to appear or to speak as a joke. Nobody could take you seriously as a Conservative spokesman. As a long serving member I wish you would not appear on TV etc. until you have smartened yourself up. I am sorry to say, you let down the Party and I hope you take this criticism seriously,
Best Wishes...

A vicar wrote to take me to task for 'always wearing a coloured shirt with a white collar'. I felt able to reply that he being a man of the cloth, the phrase about the pot calling the kettle black leapt to mind! I wondered what Anthony Henley would have made of all this.

One evening in May I returned to the House from the Old Bailey for voting duty, and meandered aimlessly through the Aye lobby, during a vote on an obscure clause in the Finance Bill. Nicholas Winterton (MP for Macclesfield, and a member of the Speaker's Panel), approached me.

'Doing anything important after the vote?' he asked.

'I am always doing something important after the vote, you must know that I am an extremely busy man,' I replied portentously.

'What a pity,' he continued, 'because Betty is giving an important dinner in Speaker's House, and the pianist she booked to provide background music thought the occasion was tomorrow and hasn't turned up. Betty hoped you might help her out, if you're not too busy, and might tinkle some ivories for her.'

I discovered that I was not too busy after all, and hurried along the corridor to sit at the Steinway piano in Speaker's House. After a little thumping (tinkling being foreign to me) of this and that, Betty Boothroyd came over, thanked me profusely, and asked what I thought of her piano. I said that it was OK, but needed tuning, and some of the keys were rather stiff.

'That's interesting,' she said, in the greatest put-down I can remember receiving, 'Moura Lympany was playing it yesterday, and she made no complaint!'

Betty cannot have been too put out by my obtuseness, for next morning I received a charming note from her, on the back of a postcard photograph of demonstrating suffragettes. It read:

You were wonderful last evening to come and tend to this woman's suffering! Everybody was thrilled: you provided such pleasure. I hope you had a good supper and caught up on the work-load – though I doubt the latter. Affectionately, Betty.

I have kept tight custody of that note – the press could so easily misinterpret it!

In September 1992 we moved from Grove Farm into Marchbank, our charming new riverside house in Burton, detached, modern, three minutes drive from the centre of the town, and by a weir where herons meet at meal-time, on the banks of the River Trent.

In October, as a Bencher of the Inner Temple, I had the joy of calling Rachel to the Bar. Earlier the same day, as Chairman of the East Staffordshire Branch of 'Relate' (formerly the Marriage Guidance Council), I had had the honour and the pleasure of being introduced to Princess Diana, the national president. Sad to report, she showed far less interest in talking to the Lawrences than her charming mother-in-law had done so recently.

In November I was made a Freeman of the City of London. Henceforth I could herd my sheep over London Bridge, go about the City with a drawn sword, be drunk and disorderly without fear of arrest, have the right not to be press-ganged into service with the Royal Navy and, if I should be convicted of a capital offence, be hanged with a silken rope. A man would sacrifice much to avail himself of such privileges. I have never been offered the freedom of the town of Burton upon Trent. Perhaps they have never forgiven me for losing the seat!

I was quite often invited to take part in debates at the Cambridge or Oxford Unions and at other universities, defending the government's law and order policies, attacking those who wanted to see Israel driven into the sea, arguing for the restoration of capital punishment, and, on one memorable occasion at Cambridge, preferring censorship to pornography with Mrs Mary Whitehouse – a debate in which we astonishingly swept to victory because she was so charismatic and brilliant! On another occasion, in late 1995 I debated on BBC's *Panorama* with the prominent left-wing barrister, Michael Mansfield QC, the justice of Private Lee Clegg's sentence of life imprisonment for murder. David Dimbleby presided.

Private Lee Clegg

Paratrooper Lee Clegg had been convicted, in June 1993, of murdering Karen Reilly, an 18-year old joyrider, and wounding her driving companion. He was sentenced to imprisonment for life. He had been on foot patrol duty on the night of 30 September 1990, at a road block in the Upper Glen Road in West Belfast. Karen had been a passenger in a stolen Vauxhall Astra which, failing to stop at the obstacle, had crashed through it and continued on down the road. Private Clegg, and others on his foot patrol, had shot 18 bullets at the car as it passed by them in the dark. One of four shots from Clegg's gun had, allegedly, gone through the back window of the speeding car, killing Karen in the back seat. The driver was also killed, and another passenger escaped with minor injuries.

The prosecution had argued that as the car had already passed Clegg, and no longer presented an immediate threat when he had shot at it, the fatal shooting of Karen must have been both intentional and unlawful, since it could not be said to have been a shot in self-defence. The Criminal Court in Belfast found the allegations to be true, and Clegg was convicted of murder. The only penalty for murder, prescribed by law, was life imprisonment. The motion for the television debate was whether such a sentence could be called just, in such circumstances.

I argued that, having served two and a half years in prison, Clegg should be released. He was a 21-year-old inexperienced, but otherwise honourable, soldier on active duty, at a guard post on a road where soldiers were at constant risk from terrorists, faced in a split second with a high-stress situation not of his own making, and he was being threatened with immediate injury by a car hurtling towards him. Holding a loaded rifle in anticipation of a life threatening attack, he had shot at the driver to stop the car once it had passed, because it might contain terrorists. He had missed, and had accidentally hit a passenger. His action, though deliberate, was far from what anyone would call premeditated murder. Had there been a lesser sentence than life available, there could be no doubt that the judge would have imposed one.

After very brief opening speeches, each side called witnesses. I called three: a soldier who was with Clegg that night on his patrol, to describe the situation as it actually had been; General Sir Anthony Farrar-Hockley (a former army commander in Northern Ireland) to speak about the pressures faced by soldiers on active service; and finally, Lady Olga Maitland (my colleague and Conservative MP for Sutton) who was strong on defence. Michael Mansfield called a driver who had stopped when ordered; John Ware, the *Guardian* journalist, who spoke of an aggressive macho cult among Clegg's army group; and Joe Hendron (the SDLP MP for West Belfast). After cross-examination and final speeches there was a vote. I won the debate handsomely both before the studio audience and in a national poll taken after the debate. I could hardly have lost with a case as strong as Clegg's. But this was just a televised debate. The process of the law was an entirely different matter.

Clegg's first appeal went right up to the House of Lords, the highest court in the land. Their Lordships said that while the law was undoubtedly unfair to require the same sentence for such a killing as it required for calculating murderers, in our legal system it was for parliament, not the judges, to change the law if it so wished. It was particularly for parliament to decide whether there should be degrees of murder rather than one statutory sentence for such a wide range of wrongdoing. As far as the appeal was concerned, the sentence must stand. They were right of course.

Clegg was released on licence in 1995, and returned to army duties. There were riots from the nationalists in Belfast. Some months later it was discovered that the bullet that had killed the young girl had been fired from the side of the car, not from the back. This meant that the car had not yet passed Clegg when he shot at it, and that he had, after all, a defence of self-defence. An expert, yet again, had made a mistake. A retrial was ordered in 1998, and this time Clegg was acquitted.

The sentence for murder, not needing so urgently to be changed once Clegg was free, remains today as it was then.

I was recently involved in the defence of a young girl of seventeen who stabbed her lover, the father of her two-year-old son, with a kitchen knife, after a great deal of provocation. The partial defence of provocation to murder is undoubtedly in a mess: the Law Commission has said so, and has recommended changes, some of which have been introduced in the Coroners and Justice Act 2009. Perhaps it will not be too long before the entire law of murder is brought up to date by Parliament, and judges will no longer be obliged to pass inappropriate sentences. Sadly, I will not be there to play any part!

22

South Africa

'The time for the healing of wounds has come. The moment to bridge the chasms that divide us has come... We have triumphed in the effort to implant hope in the breasts of the millions of our people. We enter into a covenant that we shall build the society in which all South Africans, both black and white, will be able to walk tall, without any fear in their hearts, assured of their inalienable right to human dignity – a rainbow nation at peace with itself and the world.'

(President Nelson Mandela's Inaugural Address, 10 May 1994)

Although not a particularly good year for the Conservative government, 1994 was a year of hope for the wider world, with the ballot replacing the bullet in the Middle East and Northern Ireland, and 'peace with reconciliation' looking set to follow the extended democracy of South Africa. South Africa must be one of my favourite causes.

I had visited the country under apartheid on four occasions during the 1980s, and I had met its leaders in government and non-governmental organisations, as well as many opinion formers. Like slavery, apartheid is contrary to all we now stand for in today's world. But dreadful as the oppression of the majority black population was, by minority white policemen, soldiers and others in authority, to say nothing of particularly horrifying events like the Sharpeville massacre, Britain, once South Africa had left the Commonwealth, had neither the power nor the authority to intervene. In the 1960s, 70s and 80s, few really believed that the blacks would ever gain majority rule without bloodshed on an enormous scale. The whites could claim that they had always governed South Africa, had planned and invested heavily in the country's infrastructure and industry, and had, despite economic and political sanctions, enjoyed a very high standard of living in a land of sun and outstanding natural beauty. The idea that white authority would ever be surrendered without armed resistance, seemed too unlikely to contemplate.

In 1985 the Foreign Affairs Committee examined the political situation in South Africa, in order to provide up-to-date information to parliament and anyone else who might have an interest in the country. For although the kind of constitutional settlement South Africa might achieve, with no models to follow, could only be a matter for South Africans, the future of that nation was obviously still of great concern to the United Kingdom. We had a mutual colonial legacy. We were important trading partners. South Africa was a major non-Soviet supplier of strategic minerals like platinum, and it was vital for Western security that the country, stayed outside the Soviet sphere of influence. Furthermore, there were nearly two million people of British descent in that country with a million having the right to settle in Britain if things went wrong.

The committee took evidence from the South African government, and the opposition parties. The ANC leader in exile, Oliver Tambo, came to see us, as did Thabo Mbeki (the future president of South Africa), Chief Mangosuthu Gatscha Buthelezi (the Zulu leader), President Mangope of the Boputhatswana homeland, and a number of trade, cultural, political and diplomatic leaders.

We came to the conclusion that time was running out for a peaceful solution to what was becoming the South African crisis. Despite resistance from extreme whites (and some Afrikaaners), even the Botha government was coming to regard apartheid as an outmoded policy, and some steps were taken towards the release of Nelson Mandela. But there were still few signs that it was actually prepared to accept majority rule: it would share power, but not transfer it. But if the South African government continued to resist pressure from the Commonwealth and United States to release political prisoners like Nelson Mandela, to unban the ANC, and to negotiate a new constitution, it seemed inevitable that the 'carrot' of substantial aid to arrest economic decline would be replaced by the 'stick' of ever-increasing sanctions. Still, I do not recall that at the end of our enquiry any of us believed that a bloodbath would or could be avoided.

In the years that followed, I attended Commonwealth Parliamentary Association conferences where the British government was pilloried, by black and anti-Western governments, for being sympathetic to apartheid. The accusation was ridiculous, although it was certainly true that the Thatcher government did not believe that all aspects of apartheid could be removed overnight – still less that white rule could be replaced by black rule in the immediate future. Most of us believed that violence could only be avoided by education and steady but slow progress. Britain was actually giving help to the dismantling process but this was either unknown, underestimated or just wilfully ignored by most of the delegates to such gatherings. Yet we were training and supporting the military of South Africa's front-line states. We were honouring sanctions as far as humanly possible. We gave encouragement – financial as well as verbal – to the opposition minorities, particularly the churches, inside South Africa.

Nor was it true that all the blacks in South Africa wanted all the whites out. I asked the Chief Justice of South Africa why there were hardly any black judges. He said that it was because there were hardly any black lawyers from whom judges could be chosen. Strong as hatred of the whites might be in certain quarters, he explained, the problem of inter-tribal hatreds was no less. Black litigants and defendants frequently refused to answer questions in court put to them by advocates from another tribe. Often a white judge was asked to try cases by both black parties to a court action, because they did not trust black judges to be independent. Tragically, in the years since apartheid has gone from South Africa, we have seen bitter and murderous tribal conflicts in the rest of Africa, in the Congo, in Rwanda, in Sierra Leone, in Mozambique and Angola and even between the Zulus and the Xhosas in South Africa itself.

On one of my visits, a black anglican bishop assured me that he was the representative of a much larger proportion of South African anglicans than Archbishop Tutu, and that he and his followers even supported some of the apartheid laws that limited inter-racial contact. 'There is no other way,' he told me, 'to protect the exploitation of black women by white men.'

When, amazingly, the swift and total transfer of power came, with comparatively little bloodshed from white extremists and some Zulus, there had been more to it than the unquestionably strong and magnificent leadership of Nelson Mandela and his supporters. The world seems to have given little credit to the leadership of F.W. de Klerk, whom I have met on three occasions, and his National Party: for their achievement was also remarkable in persuading the deeply entrenched and determined white majority to surrender power without a fight.

In April 1994 I was privileged to be one of the hundreds of international parliamentarians, government officials, retired diplomats and policemen, from Western Europe in particular, who went to South Africa as observers and monitors, to ensure that the first ever non-racial elections were free and fair. By our very presence trouble was contained, and the new democratic process was established, acknowledged and rendered more effective and peaceful.

Nevertheless, there were some dreadful moments, which filled me with foreboding at the time. Half an hour after I had booked into the Johannesburg Holiday Inn, a terrifying explosion threw me off my bathroom seat onto the floor. For a few moments I thought that they had dynamited my hotel room and had come to get me! When nothing more happened, I picked myself up and went to the window. I could see that, a hundred yards away, a bomb had destroyed the offices of the African Nationalist Party. It killed 10 people, injured 95, and laid waste a large area in the centre of the city. That night two more bombs went off, right outside my hotel window. Next morning I woke to news that another bomb had gone off in South Johannesburg, killing 9 people, and injuring another 45. The following day the Jan Smuts International airport, through which most of the international observers had entered the country, was blown up. Later a bomb went off in one of the largest towns in the North Transvaal, and another was defused, we were told, outside the municipal hall of Warmbaths, in the Orange Free State, the town in which the electoral commission directing my activities was situated. When thirty-two right-wing white extremist AWB members were arrested, the terrorism stopped. Thereafter, apart from some tribal violence in KwaZulu-Natal, the worst that happened was some electoral fraud. The election was reported, by the ever-observant British press, to have been peaceful.

The election

Three days had been set aside for voting. The first was for the elderly, the disabled, mothers with young children and government workers. The next two days were for everyone else. Everything in our district was organised so efficiently that only two days of voting were actually needed, because by then everyone had voted. So on the third day, our team rested – and some of us went off to the Mabula Lodge Safari Park to track, on horseback, a white rhinoceros and its young. I had never ridden a horse before in my life. Had my charge realised that and thrown me, my reader might have been spared these recollections!

Neil Kinnock (the former Labour leader, future British European Commissioner and member of the House of Lords) was the team leader of my small group. His aide-de-camp was the very amiable Sir David Mitchell (Tory MP for Basingstoke), and there was also Jacqui Lait (the no-nonsense Tory MP for Eastbourne), Glenys Kinnock (the no-nonsense wife of Neil, who later became an MEP for Wales and a minister in Gordon Brown's government), a charming lady who had been an Irish Senator, a local driver, and myself. We were responsible for fifteen polling stations, and we were part of a larger group consisting of other MPs from Belgium, Portugal, Ireland, and Mozambique. We wore baseball hats, armbands and identifiable t-shirts to show that we were international observers. Apart from being useful to the peace process, our task was also enormous fun.

We had to watch for, and report, any intimidation of queuing voters, and ensure that the registration process was being fairly conducted. There was no electoral register, and every South African citizen over the age of 18 could vote at any polling station, in both the national and the provincial elections – for both were taking place at the same time. Every voter had to have a hand stamped with an invisible number, to ensure that they did not go to the end of the queue and vote again. We had to be satisfied that all the ballot papers contained the name and picture of Chief Buthelezi, the Zulu leader, because he had been late in deciding to put his party into the election, and many ballot papers had already been printed without him. All the ballot boxes had to be correctly sealed, and we had to see that there were enough of them, as well as sufficient voting booths and native language speakers available to provide assistance. No one knew how many people were eligible to vote, how many would be likely to vote, or where exactly they would decide to cast their vote. A large number of voters in the black townships of Northern Transvaal, and the former homeland of Boputhatswana, could neither read nor write. Some had never seen a pencil, let alone knew how to use one. Some were scared; most were very apprehensive. Here was a recipe for chaos. That the election turned out to be so relatively well ordered was certainly surprising – and must have been to a large extent due to the presence of so many international observers and monitors.

Thousands of voters in our district, overwhelmingly black, queued patiently in the heat of the burning sun for hours. Could we speed the process? It became obvious, after a while, that many could read and write. So I went up the line asking: '*Kan jy skryf?*', which I was told meant 'Can you write?' Those who said they could were directed off to a separate booth where they were able to vote quickly and without assistance. We had to help the others to vote in the booths.

We opened for them the incredibly long voting paper, with its confusing collection of names, pictures, and party symbols. Then the simplest course was to ask these first-time peasant voters who they had come to vote for and, since nearly everyone in our station had come to vote for Mandela and the ANC, point to the picture of Mandela for confirmation, place a pencil between their fingers, show them where and how to put a cross, avert our eyes so that we could not see who they were actually voting for, fold the paper for them, and direct them over to the ballot box, where someone else would show them how to push it into the box. This fell a little short of being a secret ballot, but had we done it any other way, they would still be voting! Then, to cut down the queues and the waiting time, we arranged for more booths to be placed inside the polling stations.

I went outside, and noticed a number of young women queuing with babies strapped to their backs, in the burning sun. So, with a black official, I went along the queues, asking these women if they would like to step out of the sun and come with me to the head of the queue and into the polling station. This was a most popular move and I had many takers. After a while, I noticed much giggling down the line.

'What's causing the amusement?' I asked the official. His face lit up with a broad grin, and he explained.

'It's because the same baby is being passed down the line to girls without babies. The same baby keeps being re-used time and time again, and you can't tell the difference!'

In one country area in our district there was a polling station being used by the mainly white residents, and no queue, while at a nearby black polling station there was a queue over two miles long. I descended upon a couple of enormous white Boer farmers, election observers for the National Party, who were standing with their arms crossed in what appeared to be silent defiance coupled with incredulity at what they were witnessing. I asked them if they had any trucks; they said they had. I asked if they would mind helping us by going to get them, loading them up with black voters from the long queue, then trucking them a mile down the road to the empty white polling station. I did not really expect any cooperation, but to my great surprise they agreed and went off to get their vehicles. Literally hundreds of men, women and children in relays, climbed onto the backs of the trucks. I wondered whether any of these farmers would have offered their trucks six months earlier to hurry the end of white rule. And if they had, how many of these people would actually have got onto the white man's trucks?

'We were so wrong,' one white farmer, built like an oak tree, who had lived all his life in the area, admitted to me that day. 'We should have done this years ago.'

Another white South African official told me, 'The AWB (the right-wing extremist party that had placed the bombs that greeted our arrival) should be shot without trial, because they have been ruining everything with their violence.'

I noticed one old black woman, who must have been waiting for several hours in the queue in the burning sun. I went up to her and offered to take her straight into the polling station. With tears in her eyes (mine too) she said, 'I've waited 70 years for this. Do you think another five hours matters to me?'

I was disturbed, at first, to see how many children there were in the queues: then I realised that their parents had brought them along to be witnesses to history being made. It was indeed a privilege – a very moving privilege indeed – to be in South Africa at such a time.

Nelson Mandela and the ANC swept to victory, of course, on a landslide. The world rejoiced. Some considered it fortunate (and rather surprising) that they did not achieve the two-thirds majority that would have allowed the ANC to draft the new constitution on its own, without input from the other parties. Because of this, full power was not given immediately to the blacks, and the whites with British passports did not become, in the main, too terrified to stay. Another important consequence was that the economy did not collapse. Shortly after the election, the new South Africa was warmly welcomed back into the Commonwealth. In time it was decided that previous wrong-doing should be dealt with, not by putting the perpetrators on trial, but by setting up a 'truth and reconciliation' process, headed by Archbishop Tutu, and bringing them 'voluntarily' before it. Undoubtedly more truth came to light, and it seems that there has been reconciliation on a large scale. But was that justice?

Thabo Mbeki continued after Mandela for nine years to steer the new South Africa on a more or less even keel, despite serious problems, and then was replaced by the new ANC leader, Jacob Zuma. Both Mbeki and Mandela looked for guidance from other black nations in Africa and beyond, to which they had also been an inspiration. When the dreadful problem of Mugabe's destruction of Zimbabwe is solved, and the three million Zimbabwean refugees who have poured into South Africa and put pressure on its resources begin to decline, the standard of living of the black people will hopefully continue its rise. Then with the level of education improving, and democracy and the rule of law enduring, we can be confident that never again will British parliamentarians need to attend as observers at a South African general election, to ask voters: 'Kan jy skryf?'

Modern South Africa

Nevertheless, terrible problems face South Africa today. The biggest of these is AIDS. It was estimated, by those who understood the full extent of the problem, that as many as one sixth of the population of the country (7.5 million), will have died of AIDS by 2010. Education must become the vital tool for controlling the epidemic, for a third of the population apparently believes that close proximity to a sufferer is enough to pass on the disease, and witch-doctors spread the fantasy, which has led to a massive increase in child rape, that sex with a virgin will cure it. The international community must do all it can to help to spread education about this horror.

Violent crime has become another tragically escalating problem in South Africa: an average of 50 murders and 150 rapes a day. Street attacks, killings and violent burglary have reached such frightening proportions that in some urban parts of the country, traffic lights have become a frequent site of attacks, and drivers are advised by the police not to stop at them. Nearly everyone you meet has a story about such attacks. A few years ago, former President De Klerk's first wife was raped and murdered by a security guard in her own flat in Cape Town.

For several years now, my family have spent Christmas in beautiful Cape Town, where we meet up with friends from England. At the beginning of 2000, having just returned from a Christmas visit, Michael Howard, then the Conservative Shadow Foreign Secretary, asked me if I could join him in South Africa on a speaking tour. We were to support the South African National Party, which, like the Conservative Party in the UK, had lost the confidence of most of the population. I had just unpacked, but could hardly refuse such a challenging invitation, so I re-packed. Michael spoke, with me in a supporting role, at several very well-attended meetings in Johannesburg and Durban. We also met up to discuss ideas with a number of people concerned with law and order, and with prominent individuals. Then we went to Richmond near Durban where, shortly before our arrival, a local 'war lord' had been assassinated.

Retaliation from his supporters had been swift: they had massacred nine members from the village of the suspected killers. The army took us on a tour of the area, in a heavily armoured truck. To the consternation of the army commander, Michael insisted on stopping to talk about the recent events to villagers sitting outside in the street playing chess. I am not sure he realised at the time that he was, in fact, speaking to some of the very people thought to have carried out the massacre!

Two days earlier, we had been guests for lunch at the parliament building in Cape Town, of Marthinus van Schalkwyk (de Klerk's successor as leader of the National Party, who has since joined the ANC). As we chatted outside, there was a loud rumble in the distance.

'That's a bomb,' I said, knowingly, for I was fast becoming an expert.

'Nonsense,' I was politely told, by both Michael and Marthinus, and we went inside to take our seats at the lunch table. Then someone ran in to announce that a bomb had just gone off in the nearby police station. The media were particularly interested in asking Michael, as a former home secretary responsible for dealing with terrorism, what the South Africans might do about this problem. So we all hurried to the scene, to be greeted by television cameras and reporters. Fortunately, no one had been killed in the explosion, although there had been minor injuries, and the damage to the inside of the police station and street was quite extensive.

I treasure a certificate hanging on a wall in my room in chambers, given to me after one of my speeches by the Johannesburg Central Community Policing Forum. It reads, flatteringly:

Certificate of Appreciation, awarded to Sir Ivan Lawrence QC. In recognition of his assistance in bringing about a reduction in crime in Johannesburg by sharing his knowledge and experience.

If only it was that easy!

The Commonwealth

South Africa's return to the Commonwealth was a tremendous moment for all of us who believe in the importance of this unity of nations. I felt very honoured, as Chairman of the United Kingdom Branch of the Commonwealth Parliamentary Association, to welcome Vice-President Thabo Mbeki to Westminster, before he became Nelson Mandela's successor as South Africa's president, and honoured also to have hosted Pakistan's tragic prime minister, the late Benazir Bhutto, in the week following her country's return to the Commonwealth.

The British parliament traditionally plays host to delegations from all over the Commonwealth, who seek to find out more about our democratic traditions and to meet our parliamentarians. In their turn, Commonwealth countries continually invite British MPs to be their guests, and I have very happy memories of visits that I was privileged to make in the years before I became chairman.

Perhaps I might mention one – the most memorable. In 1978 I was part of a delegation to India of six MPs led by Lord Listowel, a trim and lively near-octogenarian, who had been the Secretary of State for India before independence in 1947. Can my intrepid reader imagine how impressed modern Indians were with him, thirty years down the line? 'No! Not *the* Lord Listowel? Friend of Gandhi and Nehru? Oh my goodness...' This in a country still governed by law and democratic institutions established by us; where steam locomotives, made in Sheffield, still pulled goods wagons; where statues of Queen Victoria, Empress of India, still presided over public squares; and a shopping emporium we passed on our way to Agra still displayed a sign proudly declaring: 'By Appointment to Queen Mary'.

Here old habits died hard. At lunch, in a hotel in Delhi, we were most apologetically denied wine, because it was a 'dry' day on which alcohol was not permitted. But the waiter appeared moments later with a tray of delicate china cups and saucers and hoped that we would not mind this drink too much – as he poured white wine from the teapot!

Everywhere we British parliamentarians went, we were royally and lavishly welcomed: by the president of India, by Prime Minister Maraji Desai, by the speakers of the two houses of parliament in Delhi, by the governors and chief ministers in the six states we visited all over that wonderful country, and by the ordinary people who welcomed us to their villages, their factories and even their weddings. The last (and next) prime minister Mrs Indira Gandhi was released from 'prison' to attend a reception being given for us. The sights to which we were taken were mind-blowing: the Taj Mahal, the Red Fort, four Maharaja's palaces, the Golden Temple at Amritsar, the Elephanta caves – as well as the dreadful slums and the self-mutilating beggars of Bombay.

The Indians we met spoke proudly of their British history. Governors spoke of their years of imprisonment by the British without rancour: 'in fact,' we were told more than once, 'those years made me!' Their credibility as politicians had been established by their imprisonment.

'Here I stood on a soapbox and repeatedly courted arrest,' our MP guide in the Punjab complained, 'but no one arrested me!'

We saw film sets in Bollywood, preparing productions shortly to be seen in Southall. We visited a half-empty village – half-empty because its population had been resettled in the Birmingham constituency of John Sever, one of our team. We attended sessions of federal and provincial parliaments, and everywhere we were garlanded with flowers and showered with gifts. The progress that India has made over the generation since 1978 in becoming one of the leading industrial (and sporting) nations in the world is phenomenal.

Such channels, of friendship and exchange of democratic ideas and practice, must continue forever. We have only to remember the sacrifices Commonwealth countries made in the world wars, to be determined to maintain that unity. Meeting those who, although not British, were prepared to lay down their lives for Britain, is one of the most humbling experiences I know. It happened to me in 1995.

I did not have a ticket for the celebration ceremony, in Hyde Park, of the fiftieth anniversary of the end of the war with Japan, so I went to see if I could get into the venue without one. Security was very tight, and the security guards refused me entrance. Not wanting to cause a fuss, I walked back around the perimeter of the enclosure to where my car was parked. On the way I passed an old man in a white turban who was desperately looking for the entrance. I asked if I could help. He told me that he had come from India, especially for the occasion as an invited guest, but he had been unable to find his hosts, and had no ticket. He was very upset. I asked, scarcely believing him, why he had been invited as a guest to come all the way from India. He fumbled in his pocket, and produced a Victoria Cross that had been presented to him by King George VI in 1945.

He was, I found out later, Captain Umrao Singh VC, one of the bravest soldiers of the Second World War, who had won this greatest award for gallantry fighting for Britain against the Japanese in Burma. Then a non-commissioned field gun commander, he had held off wave after wave of Japanese attacks for 90 minutes with a Bren gun and, when the bullets ran out, had picked up an iron rod in hand to hand fighting, taking the lives of several assailants until succumbing to a rain of blows that left him barely alive. I took him to the nearest entrance, and explained to the security official that this man was a very important guest of honour, with a seat on the platform with the prime minister and the royal family. He hurried off with the valiant man. I felt so privileged to have met him, and as I walked back to my car thinking of the sacrifices these men had made for a country that was not theirs, I had to struggle with tears.

Umrao Singh died in 2005 at the age of 85 years. It is surely a disgrace that we should have refused for so many years to offer the heroes of the old Empire the right to come and settle in Great Britain. After all, they had been prepared to lay down their lives for us: what greater generosity could there have been?

23

Life After Parliament

Never go back. Never go back.
Never surrender the future you've earned.
Keep to the track, to the beaten track.
Never return to the bridges you burned.

(Felix Dennis, *Never look back*)

My parliamentary career came to an end, as I knew it would, at the general election, on 1 May 1997. The Conservative Party was wiped out, and me with it. This time I achieved only 39.4% of the Burton poll and 21,480 votes, while Mrs Janet Dean, a 48-year-old Labour Borough Councillor, widow of a former East Staffordshire Council chairman, former mayor herself, and a compulsory woman candidate in accordance with Labour Party regulations then obtaining, won 51% of the poll with 27,810 votes. This proved what I had always believed: that while a bad MP could lose thousands of votes even when the political outlook was quite steady, a good MP is only worth five or six hundred votes when the tide is going out for the Party. Albert Costain, the former MP for Folkestone, had a different slant on the subject. He told me that the less he took part in an election campaign, the more his majority increased!

I cleared my office just behind Big Ben, said goodbye to secretaries, messengers, policemen, clerks and waitresses, and started to ferry sixty boxes of my parliamentary papers to my garage at Shepperton, for sorting out and shredding. Sadly, many of these have still to receive my attention. It is possible that there could be further revelations. When anyone asks me why I left parliament, I tell them that it was for medical reasons: my constituents got sick of me!

A more difficult question is: 'Do you miss parliament?' Of course I do. I miss not being where the political action is, and not really knowing what is going on in the world. I miss no longer belonging to a historic institution which is at the heart of British life. I miss my friends, and the free Commons car park! But I do not feel any pang of loss each time I drive past Big Ben and parliament, as I know some of my former colleagues do. I really have been able to move on, and that is because I had the immense good fortune of having another full-time job to go to.

I must confess to a further sadness and a considerable concern: the diminishing number of practising lawyers in the House of Commons. I know it is generally believed that the House is full of lawyers, but that is quite untrue – and has been getting more untrue over the past two decades. There are now no more than half a dozen MPs who have any experience of how the criminal laws they pass are actually operating daily in our courts. It surely matters a great deal if there are no practising lawyers in the House of Commons who could warn that laws will be unworkable or a waste of time. It must matter even more, in a nation founded on the 'rule of law', that the legality of proposed government action in the nation's interest should at least be considered even if it is not decisive in the end – a situation that has not been helped by the removal of the Law Lords from Parliament into the new detached Supreme Court.

Two recent examples illustrate my point. The invasion of Iraq may have been in the national interest but before making the decision should not its legality at least have been considered and discussed in Parliament by practising lawyer MPs? In 2008 the Serious Fraud Office decided to drop the prosecution of British Aerospace for the way in which it had won the arms deal contract with the Saudi Arabians. It was said to be in the national interest to do so because the Saudis had threatened not only to withdraw at the cost of thousands of British jobs but to end cooperation on international terrorism. Was the British government condoning corruption on a large scale in breach of our laws? If so, could that be justified? Or should justice be done though the heavens fall ('*fiat justiciam ruat caelum*')? The highest court in the land, then the House of Lords, held that this was a political question which should be decided by government acting on the advice of its pre-eminent lawyer politician, the Attorney-General. The matter was resolved by a partial guilty plea and a very substantial fine.

My point is that if such decisions are to be taken on the advice of an Attorney-General who is no longer in the House of Commons, and the decision cannot be challenged in that House because there are no longer any practising lawyer MPs, the temptation of a government to place consideration of the legality of its actions lower down the order of priorities will be considerable: and will that serve the 'rule of law'? The coalition government, with its law officers back in the House of Commons, will have improved the situation, but it has become nearly impossible for an MP to be any longer a practising lawyer in the courts.

The Bar full-time again

After my defeat I was able to return to full-time practice at the Bar. Almost immediately I was invited by my good friend Paul Norris, the head of my chambers at 1 Essex Court, to take over the headship from him. Chris Doe, my clerk, now had to get me into court – no easy task since nearly all of my loyal solicitors had died, retired, or sold their practices to those who had never heard of me. But I was certainly entering a new and exciting phase in my life.

I was prepared to do any work that came my way, and shortly afterwards I acted in a defamation case for a Turkish newspaper, circulating in Britain. It was being sued for publishing an article accusing a firm of solicitors of offering legal assistance (and legal aid), over the telephone, to people they knew to be illegal asylum seekers. An undercover Serbian reporter, working for *The Sunday Times*, had caught out one of the firm's lawyers on tape, and the Turkish newspaper had picked up the story. As I explained to the jury, the solicitor had not dared to sue *The Sunday Times*, which had first published the story, because they would have retained the services of the brilliant George Carman. They had gone for this small Turkish newspaper with a limited readership, because they could only afford to retain – me!

This was my first civil case for forty years. I suggested to my instructing solicitor that she go to the libel Bar. She said that she had no wish to do so because they always wanted to settle their cases, and that if they had to go to court, she found that they had often forgotten how to cross-examine. So she explained, convincingly enough for me, that in cases requiring a fight before a jury, she always went to criminal barristers who knew how to cross-examine and to speak to a jury, because they were doing it all the time. I said that I would be delighted to take the case (which had the added attraction of being privately paid), but I had to have with me a good junior, experienced in libel cases. So I led Bitu Bhalla, a leading junior in my chambers, who undertook all the preliminary paperwork.

Although our case seemed strong, and despite my knowing how to cross-examine and how to speak to them, the jury found for the solicitor. She was a woman who had built up a small practice on her own over many years. Breaking down in tears in the witness box, she explained that she knew nothing about what was going on, and that if the verdict went against her she would be ruined and her life's work destroyed. Nevertheless, some weeks later I was able to successfully apply to the Court of Appeal for leave to appeal on a strong point of law, and when that leave was granted, the solicitor decided to accept a settlement from the newspaper out of court. Mr Justice Morland, the trial judge, told me after this half-success, that I could expect much defamation work. He was wrong: I have not received any. And I had to wait nearly seven years to be paid. So much for civil cases!

But so great was my hunger for work that shortly afterwards I took on another civil case. This time my client was suing the Home Secretary for wrongful imprisonment in a detention centre for more than a year. The client was a black Nigerian by birth. The Immigration Department had insisted that he was falsely pretending to be a British citizen. In fact, he really was a British citizen, and the Home Secretary eventually had to concede the fact. Although the Home Office had earlier made a substantial offer in settlement of the claim, the lawyers acting for the man, before I came upon the scene, had advised him to turn it down as being inadequate. The case must serve as a dreadful warning to the greedy, for unfortunately it fell apart in my hands. As the trial progressed in the High court, before Mrs Justice Hallett, a series of falsified documents and lying explanations seemed to indicate that my client, although a British citizen, had been up to no good. It emerged that he had been involved in possible passport irregularities, and that he could have left his British detention for Nigeria at any time had he wished to do so, and so was the author of his own misfortune. He lost the case before the jury, and recovered nothing. My civil career was not going too well.

I found myself on safer ground back in the criminal courts. However, one criminal court to which I turned for employment at this stage in my career was not in England or Wales, but in Holland. There I learnt, in sickening detail, about man's inhumanity to man.

Yugoslavia

My interest in Yugoslavia had begun long before, in the summer of 1971, when Gloria and I had taken a driving holiday through Eastern Europe in our Daimler Sovereign. Our visit to East Germany had not started well. I had asked a border guard, while we were being processed through Checkpoint Charlie, whether I was allowed to use my cine camera in East Germany. He told me that I could film anything because they had nothing to hide. I suppose, on reflection, that it was a little naïve of me to photograph the guard towers on the inside of the Berlin Wall, even from some distance. But I was taken aback when a soldier, breaking all the rules of international hospitality, shouted rudely at me, pointed a gun in our direction, and then began to shoot. Perhaps less taken aback, more terrified out of my wits! In a panic I threw the film away, drove off into the centre of East Berlin, and Gloria and I hid as fugitives on the run for three hours in a supermarket in the shopping centre of Alexanderplatz. When the coast seemed clear, we hurried back to Checkpoint Charlie, and exited as surreptitiously as it was possible to do while driving a white Daimler in an impoverished Communist country. Having escaped the tyranny of East Germany, and our thirst for excitement not yet fully slaked, we journeyed southwards via Austria, through to the tyrannies of Hungary, Czechoslovakia and Bulgaria and into another part of the Communist empire of tyrannies – Tito's Yugoslavia.

Gloria and I drove slowly through the streets of Belgrade. I caught sight of the name of the road along which we were passing. It read 'Dalmatinska', written in Cyrillic script. The name rang a bell. Thinking hard, I remembered that, when I was fourteen years old, I had had a Yugoslav pen friend called Svetozar Makerov – who lived at, yes, Dalmatinska 101. We decided to try to find him.

I stopped the car and looked for the house number. By good chance, we found ourselves almost outside number 101, a block of exceedingly dreary-looking flats. I looked down the faded and grubby list of names by the door, but there was no Makerov. I thought the bottom bell might bring me a caretaker, so I rang it. Time passed, and then a wizened and stooping old lady, dressed shabbily, appeared at the door.

'*Da?*' she requested.

'Makerov? Makerova?' I asked, hopefully.

She thought for a moment and then shook her head slowly. I apologised as best I could, not knowing the language, for bothering her, and Gloria and I turned to leave. As we were walking away, she called and waved us back. She led us into her flat. There, in a dark and dingy room, she pulled out a deep drawer, rifled through an untidy pile of papers, and triumphantly held one up. She showed us the crumpled extract, with the name 'Makerova' and an address written on it. She took us back to the front door, and mimed and gestured that the address was three blocks back to the right, two blocks down to the left, over a bridge, past a traffic light, round a roundabout, past a church and a cinema,

343

another right turn and there would be the block of flats, facing us. We blew grateful kisses and left.

The old lady's directions were impeccable. It took us only five minutes to find the new address. There, at the entrance, was another column of bell-pushes and names. This time one did read 'Makerova'. I rang. A pause. A whirr. Then the catch released itself. We went inside, got into a tiny lift, and ascended to the fourth floor. The front door of one of the flats opened, and a smart, grey-haired, middle-aged woman greeted us as if we had been friends for a thousand years. She said, unbelievably, and in perfect English, 'I am Svetozar's mother. You must be Ivan from Brighton.'

I had never met or spoken to her before in all my life. I had only corresponded with Svetozar for about a year – and that had been 21 years earlier. I doubt that the little old caretaker lady had had a telephone number to warn Mme Makerova of our coming, or she would have given it to us. Even if she had telephoned the news of our imminent arrival, she could not have known that I was Ivan from Brighton. Inside the small flat, on the dresser, there was something even more amazing – a photograph of me, in school uniform, wearing short trousers. That really was uncanny!

Svetozar, we learnt, now married with a family, lived nearby in Belgrade. He was working for a tobacco company and he was out of town that day. He would be mortified to learn that such an old friend, from another world, had called and that we had missed each other.

We chatted with Mme Makerova about our lives. She was an English teacher in Belgrade. Her husband had worked for the government, and he had stopped the letter writing when it seemed that I had begun to grow too inquisitive. They decided to divorce when he had insisted, against his wife's wishes, on returning to live in another part of Yugoslavia where he had been born. We asked her to join us for lunch, and she took us to a pleasant-looking restaurant, at which we ate, drank wine, and discussed the state of Yugoslavia. Mme Makerova told us that her country was nothing less than a seething cauldron of ethnic and cultural differences: a pressure-cooker, the lid of which was being firmly held down by President Tito, of whose Communist Party, she assured us, she was not a member, or she would certainly have had much larger living accommodation. When he died, she forecast with considerable prescience, there would be the most almighty explosion. There was talk of a possible joint succession of ethnic leaders, but that was to be a few years down the line.

And so it did indeed come to pass that, when Tito died in 1980, a joint leadership was set up in Yugoslavia. Later in that decade, the ethnic explosion, which Mme Makerova had foretold, also took place. In 1991

Croatia and Slovenia wanted to break away from the Yugoslav Republic. They were encouraged to do so by our European partner Germany, whose irresponsible foreign policy in a coaliton government was controlled by a minority party, and afterwards by a compliant and errant European Community, which recognised their independence. The break-up of the rest of Yugoslavia began. Milosevic and the Serbian majority resisted. The mainly Muslim Bosnia and Herzegovina was the next province to demand its independence and, as that became inevitable, the Bosnian Serb minority decided to create a separate Serbian enclave within the territory. Since there would still be a substantial number of Muslims and Croats living in the new Serb region, the Serbs set about their permanent removal by 'ethnic cleansing'. Some Muslims armed themselves and took to the hills. Others stayed in the towns and villages awaiting developments with resignation.

The Serb army swept through the Bosnian countryside, and in the early hours of 30 April 1992 entered and seized control of Prijedor, a town of some 112,000 inhabitants, situated on the road south from Croatia to Banja Luca. It occupied a strategic position linking the Serb-controlled Croatian Krajina in the west, with the Republic of Serbia in the east. The army immediately imposed restrictions upon the movement of the inhabitants, and there was strong resistance, which was brutally crushed by Serb troops. Those who remained and were thought to be a threat to the occupiers – over 7000 in number – were rounded up between May and August, and detained in camps called Omarska, Trnopolje and Keraterm. At those camps, war crimes and other sickening atrocities began to be perpetrated.

The Hague Tribunal

The International Criminal Tribunal for Yugoslavia (ICTY) was set up by the United Nations in The Hague, to bring justice, after the war, to the victims and their families. In 1998, on the recommendation of my soon-to-be next head of chambers, Desmond de Silva, I was invited by the tribunal to defend Dr Kovacevic, who had been both the Director of Prijedor Hospital and head of the local authority. Unfortunately, shortly after he was informed that I was to defend him, he died of heart failure. Early in 2001 I was invited, again by the tribunal, to represent another Serb, Dragan Kolundzija, a shift guard leader at Keraterm camp, who stood accused, with Dusko Sikirica and Damir Dosen, of responsibility for numerous atrocities. He was also alleged to have ordered, on the night of 24 July 1992, the horrific machine gunning to death of 200 Muslims and Croats in a hut on the camp. He had pleaded not guilty to everything.

I was to lead an American Serbian-speaking trial lawyer from Chicago, whose preferred tactic was to re-open the entire history of the conflict between Muslims and Serbs from the fourteenth century onwards. My view was that such an approach, being largely irrelevant to any issue the court would be addressing, would not assist our client. Our tribunal consisted of three judges, two of whom, Judge Richard May QC (an English circuit judge) and Judge Patrick Robinson (a West Indian judge, who was president of the court) had been trained in the English common law where such evidence, if more than merely touched upon, would be certain to be rejected. The third judge, Judge Mohamed El Habib Fassi Fihri, was Moroccan. My preferred approach would be, quite simply, to test and challenge any evidence there might be that our client had taken part in the activities alleged. Since my American co-counsel and I were not seeing eye-to-eye about this most fundamental of tactics, he was no longer happy for me to lead him. He told me so, in a form of anglo-saxon commonly used in colonial Chicago. I therefore withdrew from the case before the trial started, and returned to my law practice in London.

The Kolundzija trial began in March and continued over the next eight months, but with several breaks in between. In May, Kolundzija succumbed to medical depression, and sacked the aforementioned American lawyer whom he considered had brought about his affliction. He asked the court if I could be asked to return. The Hague authorities telephoned me in London, and were very keen that I should come back into the case and help them out. I said that I would certainly be prepared to come back for a day to see how much evidence I had missed, and to consider whether, so many witnesses having already given evidence, it was really practicable for me to carry on with Kolundzija's defence.

I arrived to find that the court actually expected me to go straight back into the trial, and to start cross-examining witnesses that day! This was quite absurd. As politely as I could, I told them so. I could not seriously be expected to take over the reins until I had caught up with all of the evidence that had already been given, and which neither myself, nor my newly appointed co-counsel, John Ostojik, had heard. Justice looked as though it might be difficult to come by in such a court.

John was another Serbian-speaking American trial lawyer from Chicago, a giant of a man in his late thirties, overflowing with joking asides and good humour. He charmed everyone in sight and was a delightful companion and colleague. Michael Greaves, another British barrister, was being led by a Serb lawyer, Veselin Londrovic, for Sikirica; and two other Serbs, Vladimir Petrovic and Goran Rodic represented Dosen. I asked the court for four weeks adjournment so that I could catch up with all the evidence and take instructions from my client. Everyone thought this was both sensible and necessary – except the court! The president told me I could have ten days. That seemed outrageous. I was about to withdraw from the case on the spot, and let the court get on with it without me. But then, I thought, here was a challenge (my Achilles heel), and to reject it would be defeatist. To accept might even raise Great Britain's standing at the tribunal. So I accepted. But John and I had to work 18 hours a day for the next month to get up to speed.

At the end, after all that work, I had difficulty getting the United Nations to pay me the modest fee and costs I had been promised for taking the case. Frank Sinatra's daughter-in-law, who was one of the lawyers in another court, later told me that the tribunal had a real problem finding the money to pay anyone their fees. I was surprised that the Americans put up with it. It was hardly a satisfactory way to run an international criminal justice system.

Dragan Kolundzija

Dirk Ryneveld QC, the Canadian lead prosecutor, had begun his opening speech in March, in my absence, declaring: 'The purveyors of Serbian nationalistic fanaticism unleashed an orchestrated rampage of persecution and terror throughout the non-Serb dominated parts of Opstina Prijedor."

He and his two diligent and charming Australian junior counsel, Daryl Mundis and Julia Baly, called forty-five witnesses to give evidence of what had taken place at Keraterm, in a former ceramics factory on the edge of the town. Murders, torture, beatings, rapes, other sexual assaults, harassment, humiliation, psychological abuse and confinement in inhumane conditions, had undoubtedly all been perpetrated over a period of three months.

Although not charged with genocide, my client was facing a charge of mass murder of the 200 in the hut at Keraterm, and charges of persecution on ethnic grounds as a crime against humanity, perpetrating inhumane acts, and violation of the laws and customs of war as a party to outrages upon personal dignity. The indictment was horrifying and the challenge I had accepted was enormous.

Dragan Kolundzija, nicknamed 'Kole', had been seized by the British SAS, acting on behalf of the multinational stabilisation force (SFOR), and had been imprisoned in The Hague for two years to await his trial. He was a shyly good-looking 41-year-old, married and with a young family. When the war started he had been a one-man road haulage firm, and he had been conscripted into the army with the rank of private. To me he was always polite and charming, and we got on so well that he and the prison medical team decided, after a few days, that he was no longer suffering from depression. Indeed, his reputation in the prison among the staff could hardly have been better. The Dutch detention unit commander, later told the court that Kole had behaved like a gentleman, always complied with the rules, had been helpful to other detainees to whom he showed respect, and so made life more tolerable for everyone in the unit. The prison officers did not believe that he should have been there at all.

I spent many hours in conference with him, learning his story through interpreters. With no instructing solicitors (as I would have had in Britain) to do all the preparatory work, I had to type up these interviews either on the word processors in the defence counsel room, or in my hotel, or, when there were breakdowns in the technology, in a nearby 'internet café'. It was quite an experience for a British barrister. All the administrative work, billing, telephone calls, organisational arrangements, preparation of affidavits, the serving of documents as well as interviewing of witnesses, had to be done by John Ostojik and me, when the court was not actually sitting. John, as an American trial lawyer, was used to combining the roles of advocate and solicitor; I was not – and I have no wish to do so again.

It became obvious that we would have to go to Prijedor to view the scene, take photographs for the trial, and interview anyone in sight who could help, but the UN would not pay for both of us to go. I would have loved to have gone, since by all accounts the area was beautiful, and particularly so when bathed in the summer sun. But, as a non-Serbo-Croat-speaking English barrister, I would have seemed remote and perhaps treated with suspicion by the locals. John, on the other hand, who had been brought up speaking Serbo-Croat, would make a much better impression. He also had Serbian-born staff in his Chicago office who spoke the language and would be able to investigate more directly and therefore effectively. So I agreed that John and his team should go.

Their visit yielded very positive results for Kole.

Much of the evidence presented by the prosecution concerned the co-accused Sikirica, who was a camp commander, and who, at the start of the trial, faced a genocide count; and Dosen who was, like Kolundzija, a shift leader. The evidence was imperfect to a degree. The events had, after all, happened nine years earlier, and the trauma suffered by the victims was bound to have affected their memories. Statements had not been taken from witnesses until many years after the events they described, and only after much discussion had taken place between those who had actually been involved and those who had merely heard others talking about it. No surprise, then, that the statements were often contradictory, as well as merely hearsay, and uncorroborated. There had been no identity parades, so even identification became problematic. To add to all that, there were difficulties of interpretation and translation.

There were two main allegations against Kolundzija. First, that he had committed persecutions for political, racial or religious reasons, and had committed inhumane acts, outraging personal dignity. Second, that he had been responsible for mass murder in what was known as Room Number 3.

As far as the first allegations were concerned, the evidence of Kole's alleged wrongdoing was given by witnesses who were inaccurate, untruthful and on identification, in serious conflict with other witnesses.

One witness, N, gave evidence of violent incidents occurring, he said, on Kole's watch. Kole's shift had arrived on 23 July and had set about beating him and other detainees. Kole had called a man out of his room, at night, who was later shot with fourteen others. On another day, as N was being beaten, Kole had asked him why he was screaming. But there were substantial inconsistencies between the statements witness N had made some time before he gave evidence, and his actual evidence in court. Then he admitted in cross-examination that he did not know what Kole looked like; that at the time of the offending incidents, he had not known the name of the person he was talking about; and that no-one present at any of the incidents had ever told him that the guard was called Kole. The only reason he had said that the offender's name was Kole, was because some days later he had overheard a conversation between two people who had mentioned Kole by name, but he did not think that either of them had been present at any of the incidents he was describing, nor could he even be sure that they were talking about the same occasions! We could not question the people who had mentioned

Kole's name because N had no idea who those people were. How could such evidence be effectively held against Kole?

Another detainee gave a detailed account of the appalling behaviour of Kole on 23 July – but then pointed to Dosen in the dock, as the man he was talking about! A third detainee contradicted that identification, saying that it was a third man, called Cupo Banovic, who had carried out the beating on 23 July, that Kole had never been on the same shift as Banovic, and that the attacks had anyway occurred on Dosen's shift. Yet another detainee, who had been present when the man had been called out for the beating, contradicted the other two: he said that he was sure that the calling-out had been done by another guard called Faca – who was not even on Kole's shift. There was other evidence that Kole had been nowhere near Keraterm camp on that day.

Only one witness of any reliability was produced against Kole on the first of the allegations, but her evidence fell short of proving Kole's involvement. Witness O was a woman whose sister, she said, had been particularly kindly treated by Kole. She gave evidence that Kole was standing with her at the camp entrance when a bus full of new detainees arrived who were then hit by the guards as they got off. But she agreed that she had been standing with Kole 50 metres away from the violence, and that in order to spare her the pain of witnessing this behaviour he had advised her to leave the scene, which she immediately did. She conceded that she was therefore in no position to deny that Kole had tried to stop the beatings after she had left. In fact, she had to agree that from his considerate behaviour towards her sister and herself, that he might very well have done so.

It was clear from the evidence these witnesses actually gave to the court, that the prosecution had proved nothing against Kole. All they had proved was what we had never disputed, that Kole was a conscripted shift leader at the dreadful Keraterm camp. The prosecution would need more evidence than that to bring home any specific charge of abuse against him.

The allegation that Kole was the mass murderer at Room Number 3 also fell apart. He was undeniably the shift leader of about a dozen men who had been on duty guarding several hundred detainees that night. But there was clear evidence that at the time of the killing, he was no longer in control. Witnesses said that a large number of soldiers, a disciplined unit, had swept into the camp and had taken over, totally ignoring the guards already on duty. They had set up a machine gun facing Room 3, and sometime later, when it had looked as though some detainees were trying to break out, they had opened fire.

Not one witness suggested that Kole had manned the machine gun, or had played any part in its emplacement. The gun had been placed in position before Kole's guard had even come on duty. There was no evidence that Kole had prior knowledge that a machine gun was going to be brought onto the camp, or that once it had been, he must have foreseen how it was to be used. Even if he had known that a gun was going to be used in that terrible way, he could not have done anything about it, witnesses said, because he had not been in control of the army unit and would have been powerless to intervene. There was no evidence that, as a mere shift leader without any rank, he had any authority over the incoming soldiers who had clearly been given orders, by those of more senior rank, to shoot if necessary. There was certainly no evidence that Kole had told anyone to shoot at Room Number 3, or that he had encouraged, condoned, aided, abetted, or approved of the shooting. In fact there was evidence that when the shooting started, he had bravely run in front of the huts to try to stop it. Immediately after the massacre, Kole left the camp in disgust, and did not return for several days. So much for the mass slaughter charge.

Nor was there any evidence that anyone had been mistreated on Kole's shifts, and it was clear that he did not have the power to discipline anyone, even if he had seen abuse. He could only go to the senior camp commander and complain – and there was evidence that he had done just that, courageously, several times. Nor, as an unranked shift leader, had he any authority to change the bad camp conditions of overcrowding, food and water shortage, or lack of sanitary or hygienic care in Keraterm. But could he have run away? As an enlisted soldier he would have been sent to the front line or been shot, said one witness. He could clearly do more good by staying and trying to help the detainees, some of whom were actually his neighbours and friends in the town of Prijedor.

Prosecution witnesses also gave evidence that Kole was without racial or religious bias against Muslims, with whom he daily worked and lived. He had once tried to stop a Serb burning a Muslim flag: 'Leave the flag alone,' he had said, 'it represents someone's symbol.' On another occasion he had said, 'All this will pass, and if we survive, we'll all work together again.' 'He never differentiated between Serbs, Muslims and Croats,' said yet another prosecution witness.

It was a surprising feature of the trial that nearly all of the forty-one Muslim or Croat prosecution witness who had correctly identified or recognised Kole, had something good to say about him. They spoke of his attempts to make life better for the detainees – at considerable risk to himself. They said that if Kole saw any violence, he would intervene and stop it. Abused detainees would call out to him to come to their aid and he would go to them.

I asked Witness DM, 'Did he also try to help detainees to reduce the level of their misery?'

'So far as he could he helped us ... he couldn't have done anything more in the circumstances.'

Witness A said, 'Kole's shift was one of the best shifts ... we were never forbidden to go to the toilet ... he found a driver and they went and they brought this food to the camp and distributed it to the inmates ... we had enough time to eat decently ... he did not allow men to harm the prisoners ... we could wash ourselves, wash what little clothes we had ... spend a lot of time in the open air, breathing fresh air during Kole's shifts ... Kole would sometimes bring food, call out those men under age who were hungry, and tell them "come out and take this" ... I want to tell the truth about Kole, and I want to thank him for helping me and many other prisoners to survive ... I said "Could my father bring some extra food during your shift?" And he said, "You can bring as much as you like". Kole had allowed water to be brought into the camp and to be distributed among the detainees ... a hose was brought in ...'

'He disagreed with the things that went on in Keraterm?'

'Yes. Of that I'm quite positive.'

This kind of evidence was repeated by prosecution witness after prosecution witness. Kole had tried to alter the camp conditions when he was on duty. His was the best shift. Detainees felt safe.

With evidence like this, John Ostojic and I thought it would be unthinkable for any court of common law, where the burden of proof lies with the prosecution to make the tribunal sure of guilt, to say that Kolundzija had any kind of a case to answer. So on 15 June we filed a motion for acquittal, and I addressed the court on 21 June. We were quite wrong. When the court pronounced its decision six days later, it rejected every one of my submissions, and said that it would give reasons in writing later. Sikirica did succeed in his plea to have the genocide charge against him alone, dropped. Dosen partly succeeded in one of his submissions. The trial continued with Sikirica's defence, followed, when that was concluded, by Dosen's.

When Kolundzija's turn came to start his defence, a month later on

30 July, I told the court that I was neither ready nor prepared to do so. We had been waiting for six weeks to receive the court's promised reasons for dismissing my submission that there was no case to answer, and we had still not received them. We surely could not be expected to start our defence without knowing what witnesses we needed to call to deal with evidence the court had found to be reliable against Kolundzija, or what witnesses we no longer needed to call because the court had accepted that part of our submission. Besides, it was Kolundzija's right, under the European Convention of Human Rights, to see those reasons in writing. Why the court had to wait for my submissions before it realised that what it was inviting me to do was quite ridiculous, was beyond me. My submission this time was accepted, and the court adjourned. It took a further month to produce those reasons.

They turned out to be short and, frankly, nonsensical. The court said that there was sufficient evidence that Kolundzija bore responsibility for the inhumane conditions at Keraterm. As far as the Room Number 3 massacre was concerned, there was some evidence that Kolundzija knew that the shooting was about to start, that he had talked to the soldiers beforehand, that he had asked the soldiers not to shoot without his order, that he was present for part of the shooting, and that he had only ordered the soldiers who had obeyed him not to shoot at another two rooms. There was also evidence, the response stated, that Kolundzija was involved in the beating of twenty detainees before the massacre, and of detainees being beaten or mistreated during his shift or in his presence. The president said that the court was not at that stage saying whether it was satisfied beyond reasonable doubt, only that there was evidence upon which a reasonable court might convict.

John and I were flabbergasted. Had no one been listening to the evidence? The reasoning was a travesty of that evidence. Most of what was said by the court to justify their conclusion had been in statements that witnesses had made some time before trial, but was not the evidence that had actually been given in court. Even where such evidence had been given, it had been discredited, as I have described. I could not believe that any court could produce that response to our submissions.

We were then given, no doubt begrudgingly, a further few days to prepare the defence in the light of these reasons. John's visit to Prijedor, and other witnesses statements which had been disclosed to us, had brought to light another twenty Muslim witnesses who would only speak well of Kole.

What then happened was quite bizarre. Kole told us, when we returned from the August recess, that the prosecution had passed word to him – without consulting us, if you please – that they would be prepared to accept a plea of guilty to the least serious of the allegations against him. They would withdraw the serious charges, and particularly the charge of mass murder! He said the prosecution had told him that if he pleaded guilty to having some responsibility for the conditions at Keraterm, they would ask for a low sentence of three or four years; and since he had already served two years and three months in custody, and would receive a further reduction for a plea of guilty, he would be released and could return home. What advice, he asked, did John and I have for him?

Advice? I was almost beside myself with anger! I told Kole that although the court had said that they had found *some* evidence, I could not believe that they could be satisfied *beyond reasonable doubt* about anything. When that test was applied, as it would have to be at the end of the trial, he would be bound to be acquitted. He asked me if I could guarantee that. Alas, I could only answer that since the court's written reasons for rejecting my 'no case' submissions were such a travesty of the evidence, anything might happen, and I could not give him the guarantees he asked for. Indeed it looked, from their written reasons, as though the court might even have been capable of convicting Kole of mass murder.

Kole was very upset. He said that his wife had been to see him and they had discussed the matter. She and the children wanted him home.

'What about your reputation as a convicted war criminal? Do you want to live with that?' I asked him.

'All I am is a lorry driver,' he replied. 'I have always lived and worked in the small town of Prijedor, from where everyone concerned in this case has come. They were all prepared to speak for me. So are all the witnesses still to come. They all know that I am guilty of nothing. What reputation have I got to be worried about? My only worry is about getting back to my family. They cannot take any more pain.'

I was not too sure about my ethical position as Kole's counsel. My client continued to deny his guilt to anything, and in my view there had been no evidence of any guilt. Yet he was prepared to pretend that he was guilty of something in order to be freed to return to his family. I was not sure that, in those circumstances, I could continue to represent him. John told me that this sort of thing happened all the time in the United States, where 'plea-bargaining' was the norm. I told him that we were not allowed to 'plea-bargain' like that in Britain. I was so worried about the situation that I contacted several of my legal friends in London to ask their advice. In the end I was persuaded that I did have a duty to continue to act for Kole, if he insisted on pleading guilty: the alternative was that John and I would be walking out on him while he was still in peril, and that would certainly not be right. I told Kole that we would continue to act for him, and that we would do our best to persuade the court that he ought to be released immediately.

We went to see Dirk Ryneveld, to see whether we could cobble together an agreed basis for the plea of guilty to offer the court, so that they might be persuaded to impose the least possible sentence. We were greatly helped by my colleagues, acting for Sikirica and Dosen, who said that if Kole pleaded guilty to something, their clients would do likewise. Dirk now said that the least sentence he could ask for, on fresh instructions from those above, would be five years imprisonment; more than the three to four years Kole had reported that he had originally been offered. Dirk's superiors had obviously decided to squeeze more out of him. I considered this to be an abuse, and said that I would go to see the Chief Prosecutor, Carla del Ponte. But Kole stopped me. He was worried that if I put them under pressure, they might change their minds and that if, at five years, he would not be covered fully by the time he had already served, he would be content to serve a little longer.

So it was that on 4 October 2001 I delivered a 41-page written mitigation brief on behalf of Dragon Kolundzija. When the court hearing came, I called Kolundzija into the witness box to say that he felt that he could have done more to help the detainees at Keraterm, and how sorry he was that he had not done so – the nearest he could come to an admission of guilt, though it patently was no such thing. I addressed the court for over an hour. I pointed out that my client was a man of excellent character, whose behaviour had been exemplary while in custody. He could not have deserted his post without risk to his life. He had no power to control guards who were not on his shift, and he had prevented abuse on his shift. He had no authority to change camp conditions, but had done what he could: he had complained to his superiors. Despite being a Serb at a time of acute secular conflict, he had nevertheless done so much to relieve the misery of Muslim and Croat detainees, even refusing to obey orders at very considerable risk to himself. No fewer than forty-one victims had spoken up for him. No man could show more remorse than to plead guilty when he had every reasonable chance of being acquitted. He had suffered greatly in physical and mental health from his imprisonment, and the level of mitigation must be at the highest end of the scale. 'For all the harm he did to anyone on the camp, has he not suffered enough?' I asked the court. I invited the judges to pass such a sentence as would enable Kole to return to his family immediately. To allow that to happen, they would have to pass a sentence of four and a half years imprisonment.

What sentence did they pass? Three years imprisonment – telling Kole, in effect, that he had already served well over the time required by his guilty plea! Still, believe it or not, the system would not release him. I had to make further representations to the court, some days later, about the meaning of habeas corpus. After some more days in custody, a tearful Kole at last went home to Prijedor.

The judges who had tried Kolundzija went on to try Slobodan Milosevic in the same courtroom. I was not sure, after what I had seen, what kind of justice Milosevic, who had been arrested and brought to The Hague during Kole's trial, would receive for the crimes of genocide alleged against him. Two years into that trial Judge Richard May, the English judge to whom the presidency of the court had rotated, was tragically taken ill with cancer, retired from the trial, and died shortly after his return to England. Four years into his trial, at which Milosevic insisted on defending himself, and which at times became little more than a farce, Milosevic was found dead in his cell. He had died of natural causes. Fifteen other defendants at The Hague also died during the tribunal's proceedings.

Fascinating and stimulating as much of my own six months in The Hague had been, and despite having helped to achieve one of the best results yet secured in that tribunal, I was unhappy with my experience. No man should have to plead guilty to crimes he did not commit in order to avoid the risk of a greater injustice. I do not know whether to blame the system, or that particular tribunal. Either way, the new International Criminal court will have to do a lot better if it is to be credible.

Tragically, the carnage in what was Yugoslavia did not stop with Prijedor and Keraterm. It went on for a further four years. There followed the war in Kosovo, the horrifying massacre of 8000 in Srebrenica and the slaughter in Sarajevo. The killing was only brought to an end when the Clinton government of the United States was persuaded, it is said by Tony Blair, to join the Coalition of Europe, and to bomb Belgrade. Milosevic gave in. It has to be said that however horrific this slaughter was, it hardly registers on the Richter scale compared with the one million who died in only a hundred days in 1994 in Rwanda.

In the past decade there have been hopeful developments for the future of a world riven by ethnic divisions and abuses of human rights.

NATO has found a post cold-war role, being prepared to intervene in the internal affairs of a sovereign state, by warfare if necessary, in order to protect their peoples from the most flagrant abuses of human rights. Hopefully, despite the comparative failures of Iraq and Afghanistan, the principle will endure. And for all its faults, the fact that there has been an international tribunal at The Hague (and in Rwanda, Sierra Leone and Phnom Penh) has demonstrated that those countries whose own political systems cannot accommodate prosecutions can see the point of bringing to justice those responsible for the most serious human rights abuses. Even if, like Milosevic with his thousands, or Charles Taylor of Liberia with his hundreds of thousands, they are heads of state. The believers among us should pray!

24

Back to the English Courts

Wouldn't it be better to stay peacefully at home, and not roam about the world seeking better bread than is made of wheat, never considering that many go for wool and come back shorn?

(Cervantes, *Don Quixote*)

I certainly felt happier engaged in criminal rather than in civil trials, and after my Hague experience I felt much happier pursuing my life of crime in the English courts. So in 1998 I returned to the Old Bailey, and wherever work was to be found round the country.

British crime has been getting more international. The prisons of England and Wales now hold inmates from 174 of the 192 countries in the world and members of 47 religions. In one Old Bailey murder trial my client was a Colombian who had stabbed an Afghan to death, following a clash of ethnic cultures in an asylum seekers' hostel in Islington. Our open door for the world's troubled masses certainly makes work for our police, courts and prison service. My client was convicted of manslaughter. One Afghan witness informed the jury that every man and boy in his country carries a Kalashnikov, and it seems that they sometimes bring them with them to the UK when they come as asylum seekers.

In another Old Bailey murder trial I defended a man who, having enticed a tramp off the street in south-east London, had strangled him, set light to his body and the flat, and had gone to Australia, from where he had tried to claim insurance taken out against his own death.

At St Albans Crown Court I defended a Sri Lankan taxi driver who had been provoked, beyond endurance, by a young hooligan who had tried to attack him with a baseball bat. The jury found that he had deliberately run the man down in his taxi, but because he had been so provoked they acquitted him of murder but convicted him of manslaughter.

Then, at Winchester Crown Court, I led Ali Mohammad Azhar (one of the leading Bangladeshi barristers practising in Britain) in defence of

359

Khalilur Rahman, the owner of a take-away food shop in Southsea, who had allegedly bludgeoned his wife to death in the basement of his shop. What was fascinating about that case was that he could hardly have had a more impressive-looking alibi. Covering the period of time over which the prosecution's pathologist said the killing must have taken place, Rahman was able to produce a timed receipt from a Southsea clothing store, a mechanic at a garage outside the town who recognised him as having been the man whose car he had repaired that afternoon, CCTV film of him filling his car with petrol at Fleet Service Station on the M3, and more CCTV film showing him driving down London's Oxford Street an hour later. Unhappily for him, this otherwise near-perfect alibi was destroyed by the fact that his finger, palm and shoe prints had been left, according to another prosecution forensic scientist, actually in the newly spilt blood. These were not the prints one might find from anyone working in the food preparation room: these were prints which the expert said had been left within a minute of Rahman's wife being attacked, and while she was still pouring blood. He simply had to have been there at that time; there was no other possible explanation. The only way this fact could be reconciled with the near-perfect alibi was if the pathologist had got the time of the wife's death wrong – which the jury must have found to be the case. So much for the reliability of forensic experts – yet again!

In recent years international drug trafficking on a very large scale has replaced bank robbery, which, in the 1960s and 1970s, had been the organised crime of choice of professional gangsters. The criminal lawyer has increasingly become involved in trials concerning drug conspiracies: defending or prosecuting foreigners (or British truck drivers) caught bringing heroin, cocaine and cannabis into Britain, and those manufacturing, processing, delivering and money-laundering the proceeds of the drugs. Horrifyingly, the police estimate that 60% of all crime is now drug related – either drug crimes, or crimes of burglary, violence, and fraud, committed to raise money to pay for the offender's drug addiction. It is estimated that there are now over a third of a million users of heroin and cocaine alone in this country.

Rene Pedro Black

Rene was the champion show-jumper of Peru. He had come to Britain, with his brother Rudolfo, to establish a European show-jumping base in what was fast becoming one of the great world equestrian centres. Unfortunately, he became distracted. He set up a factory, near Heathrow airport, specialising in the manufacture and supply of a vast quantity of crack-cocaine processed from imported cocaine, and was caught. So serious was his crime, so massive was the amount involved, and so dangerous was he thought to be, that he was brought to Southwark Crown court for his trial by helicopter. He then had to sit in the dock behind the first bullet-proof glass screen our courts had seen. He did not pretend that he was innocent.

There was certainly mitigation, and my task, with Charles Conway as my Junior again, was to persuade the court that it was substantial. The evidence clearly showed that his brother Rudolfo, and a man called Alverado, had been the brains behind the operation, and having invested lavishly in the drug factory they had returned to their native country with the substantial proceeds of their enterprise, leaving Rene Pedro holding the baby. A man of hitherto blameless character, he had a high reputation in his sport, and money enough to buy a house, grounds and stables large enough to indulge his love of all things equine. But he found it hard to get sponsorship, his marriage had fallen apart, and Rudolfo had exploited his vulnerability. The company had been formed, and the building had been set up, as a warehouse for fruit import and export – the family business back in Peru.

In long hours of interviews Rene Pedro told the police everything they wanted to know. He offered to turn Queen's evidence, and demonstrated remorse by his 'guilty' plea, which would save the taxpayer the not inconsiderable expense of a trial. From then on, he would always have the fear of possible attacks on his life and, worse still, on the lives of his family. He could not have been more frank about the crime and its proceeds, and he had nearly £1.5 million of criminal profit to hand over to the court. He had been awaiting trial for thirteen and a half months, seven of them in solitary confinement, and had spent two and a half months in hospital, depressed and contemplating suicide. Despite the dramatic use of the helicopter to transfer him to and from court, neither the police nor the customs officers suggested that there had been any violence, threats, physical attacks or the use of guns connected with the case – unusual for a crime of this magnitude.

I pleaded that this amount of mitigation must surely justify some leniency. The judge disagreed. Pedro was sentenced to imprisonment for 25 years, was ordered to hand over the £1.5 million, and was subsequently to be deported to Peru. Charles Conway and I last saw him as the helicopter lifted him away over Tower Bridge to a secure prison. How long he actually had to remain imprisoned in this country no one has ever told me.

The changing face of serious crime

Serious drug crime continued to expand throughout the 1990s. Sitting as a Recorder at Isleworth Crown Court, many of my trials involved young girls who had been stopped on their arrival at Heathrow airport, carrying large quantities of the forbidden substances heroin and cocaine. Back in their own country, usually the Carribean, they were persuaded to act as couriers on the promise that the risk of arrest was small, and that the financial reward was great. They did not know that customs officers in Britain would receive information from their counterparts in the originating and transit countries, and that the 'greeters' would be watched, followed and arrested – together with these so-called 'mules'. Sometimes the girls had swallowed condoms filled with the drugs that they expected to pass through their digestive systems unnoticed. But Customs and Excise have a transparent toilet at Heathrow, where the passing of the packets from the body can be observed! Sadly and tragically, from time to time the packets would burst open inside the mule, who would die from the rapidly spreading poison.

Recently I was instructed by the north London solicitor, Tom Egole, to lead David Martin in defence of an alleged member of what the media had christened the 'Bling-Bling' gang. They were so-called because, while the principal drug traffickers invested their very substantial ill-gotten gains in large-scale commercial and residential property developments, those involved at lower levels could only afford, or choose, to spend their profit on Gucci and Rolex watches, designer clothes and extravagant jewellery. The operation was enormous, flooding the streets of the UK with 160 kilos of crack-cocaine. This is much in demand because it produces such a 'high', although it also quickly induces dependence. The 'mules' in the case were mostly young girls who were ferrying cocaine to Britain from St Marten, in the French West Indies, via France and Holland, to be manufactured into crack. Starting off as a kilo of coca leaves costing little more than £1, it becomes cocaine costing £1000, and finally it is turned into crack-cocaine, worth £100,000. The sixteen 'mules' were caught with cocaine valued at £50 million, an extremely successful international policing operation. No fewer than sixty-five people were imprisoned, in the UK, United States, France and Guyana. The judge, at Snaresbrook Crown Court, sentenced the principal offender to 27 years imprisonment, and the others to sentences of 18 years downwards, according to the extent of their involvement. The Court of Appeal rejected all appeals against the sentences.

There is another sickeningly substantial area of modern crime, which was hardly ever before the courts when I began at the Bar – that of sexual offences with children. Not just offences being committed today, when sexual activity screams out at us from every medium, but sexual offences now being recalled and complained about twenty, thirty and even forty years after they took place. Unlike civil actions, there is no time limit on criminal prosecutions. In pursuit of these criminals, even if there has been no complaint, the police have been contacting former residents of children's institutions to ask if they had been interfered with. Organisations now exist to bring together former victims and advise them of the substantial sums of compensation available. I recently appeared for two weeks in the Court of Appeal, representing a former schoolmaster at two Approved Schools in Wales who had been convicted of 17 of the 35 acts of gross indecency and buggery of pupils with which he had been charged – all offences committed thirty to forty years ago. There is no longer a legal requirement for a sexual assault to be corroborated before a prosecution is brought, so it is not surprising, in view of the compensation, that there has been an increase in the number of these trials, known as 'historic child abuse'.

Today schools constantly remind children to report inappropriate adult behaviour towards them, and schoolgirls from dysfunctional families have been known to gather in the playground to swap stories about the behaviour of their step-fathers and even their natural fathers. Now that one person's word – even a child's – may be enough to carry conviction against another, child psychology, as an area of medical expertise, has also become a growth area. Some juries and judges find these complaints more difficult to be certain about than others. I have sadly found myself being instructed in an increasing number of child sex cases. I have just finished defending a father charged with twenty rapes against his daughter, then aged four to nine years old. It is the least enjoyable area of my work.

Another area of lawlessness, much in vogue at the present time and creating considerable work for criminal lawyers, is 'white-collar' crime. Large-scale international fraud received a big boost when Britain became part of the Single European Market – an effect little contemplated when we signed up! Value Added Tax does not have to be paid, and if paid can be recovered, upon goods commercially bought from other members of the European Union, or upon goods commercially sold to those countries. There is now a massive international market in mobile phones and computer chips. So one increasingly common type of multi-million-pound fraud takes place when companies, having received VAT from the purchasers of their phones or computer chips, and which they ought to pay over to the Customs and Excise, fail to do so and then disappear. Another version of the fraud occurs when companies pretend to have purchased such goods, and to have paid VAT on them, and then falsely reclaim the money from Customs and Excise. It is said that such frauds, which sometimes involve solicitors and accountants, are now costing the British taxpayer as much as £8 billion a year in lost tax. Altogether, it is officially estimated that VAT fraud is costing the British economy £14 billion a year.

Since the purpose of white-collar crime, and large-scale drug trafficking, is to make very large sums of money, the criminal Bar is now finding itself increasingly engaged in 'confiscation' proceedings calculated to remove the ill-gotten gains once the offender has been convicted. Of course, where possible the taxpayer's stolen money should be recovered, and those contemplating crime might be deterred by the fear that, if caught, they will lose both their liberty for a long period and the enjoyment of the proceeds of their crime when the sentence is served. I used to make speeches, during the 1970s and 1980s, calling on governments to introduce legislation to deprive the criminal of his money, and later I was a sponsor of Michael Colvin's Private Member's Bill that extended confiscation proceedings in fraud and drugs cases to all crimes involving financial activity. But I hardly expected the parliament I had left to introduce a law that so shamefully betrayed every principle of our Common Law, as the Proceeds of Crime Act 2002 has done.

Under this law, if someone is convicted of certain crimes he has now to forfeit not only what he gained from that crime (which is as it should be), but also the financial value of everything he has bought or invested in or given away for six years before that crime, if he cannot prove it to have been innocently obtained. The trouble with this new law is that certain assumptions as to his guilt have to be made whether sensible or not, little or no discretion is given to the judge, and the burden of proof of innocence passes from the prosecution to the already-convicted man. If he is an international trader it may be quite impossible for him to call on the support of any foreign witness with whom he may have been dealing legitimately, but who has no wish to put himself at risk of arrest by coming to Britain. So he has to persuade a judge, without any supporting evidence, that he is giving honest evidence about how he came by that property – although a jury has just convicted him of being a dishonest thief in relation to the main crime! Worse, if he is unsuccessful before the judge, and the value of the property he handled is £1 million – not an unusual amount in the mobile phone or computer trades – and he no longer has such money, he must go to prison for an additional 10 years on top of the sentence he has received for the crime of which he was convicted! Worse still, if he and several others have deprived the tax-man of £5 million in total, each of the gang has to find £5 million, so in theory the tax-man, in our interests, will be making many times more than he has lost. Although it is difficult to feel sympathy for any villain who has deprived honest people of their savings, it is nevertheless important that we uphold our British tradition of fairness and justice in the operation of our laws. And the parliament of 2002, with few practising lawyer MPs, seemed to be unaware of that principle – or least had no idea what it was doing!

Whether my work involved these 'new' crimes, or the old ones of murder, robbery and rape, Gloria and I certainly expected that I would be able to earn a reasonably good living at the Bar for a few years after parliament until I retired. We hoped that we could afford to upgrade our two homes and tour the world at leisure whenever we so wished. But we reckoned without the government's determination to slash the fees of self-employed barristers engaged in publicly funded criminal cases by an astonishing forty to fifty per cent. Since I wanted to carry on doing this work, I needed to increase its volume. So I moved to Clarendon chambers (then in Lincoln's Inn, and now back in the Temple), headed by Mrs Gay Martin, a strikingly elegant and very senior family law practitioner. The chambers did not just attract work in London and the south-east but also had a criminal section operating in the Midlands out of Northampton, and a very energetic and efficient chief clerk in Russell Burton.

Recorder of the Crown Courts

I also continued to sit, for a while, as a Recorder – a temporary judge trying criminal cases in the Crown Courts. The retirement date for

Recorders had always been 70 years, but as I reached my sixty-fifth birthday, the government decided to retire us at 65 years to make room for youngsters in the judicial system ambitious to become full-time judges. Five years later, the government accepted that they had breached their own rules against ageism by retiring Recorders too early, and the earlier retirement age was restored. But by that time I had reached my seventieth year, and so I was too old even under the old rule.

I had sat as a Recorder for nineteen years and I have to confess that I had made little impression upon the Law Reports. But that was hardly my fault: practically every time one of my cases presented me with the opportunity to decide an important point of law, and to make my mark as a judge, the defendant was acquitted by the jury. This meant that there would be no appeal against conviction to the higher court, and there would be no compliments from appeal court judges on the brilliance of my interpretation of the criminal law!

What right had I to sit in judgement over my fellow man? Well someone has to do it, and by the time I was appointed an assistant Recorder in 1983, I had been practising as a criminal lawyer for over twenty years, and I had been a member of parliament dealing with the problems of ordinary people for nine years. I had not been brought up, nor had I lived in, an ivory tower, and although my knowledge of television soaps and boy-bands may have left something to be desired, I did have a pretty wide experience of life. There were, of course, times when I had to agonise over the correct sentence to pass and, being human, I had to recognise my own prejudices and master them. A judge also has to remember that he represents the law-abiding members of society, and so must be independent, firm and fearless as well as humane. I can only say that I tried very hard to be all these things.

But it has to be said that such discretion as I was able to exercise as a judge was mostly confined to sentencing, and that could always be reassessed by a superior court. For in the Crown Courts, unless a defendant admits his guilt, judgement of a citizen's guilt or innocence is made by a jury of ordinary people from ordinary walks of life. The judge does, of course, have to decide whether certain evidence shall or shall not be admitted for a jury to consider, and he can rule that there is not enough evidence for the jury to convict a defendant. But such guidance on the law that he may have to give to the jury in his summing-up is laid down by statute, precedent, and guidelines, from which he is not permitted to stray.

I do not think, looking back, that I perpetrated too much injustice.

In fact, throughout my nineteen years as a judge I was appealed against on no more than half a dozen occasions. On at least two of them, the Court of Appeal observed that they had some difficulty in understanding why I had imposed such a short prison sentence – and I was teased for being too 'merciful' in Commons debates, by political adversaries like Alex Carlile, the Liberal QC MP, who liked to think of me as a 'hanger and flogger'. At Gloucester prison, which I visited with the Home Affairs Committee, a prisoner greeted me like an old friend. He said I had given him his two and a half years. I said I was sorry that it had been necessary. 'Oh no,' he said, 'that was fine. I expected you to give me five!'

Did my position as a Recorder ever conflict with my duties as a member of parliament? The only occasion I can recollect that it might have done, but in fact it did not, was when a defendant objected, through his counsel, to me trying his case. My opinion about burglars who invaded people's houses while their elderly victims were actually at home was apparently well known to him from my television appearances. He preferred not be tried by me. I told him that whether he was the burglar or not would be decided by a jury, not by me, and that in the event of his conviction any sentence I might pass, if thought to be excessive, could be appealed against to a higher court. In those circumstances I did not consider that there was any justification for postponing his trial, re-arranging the lives of witnesses, and having to wait for possibly weeks until another court could be found. My summing-up to the jury must have been fair, for they acquitted him!

Stimulating as this supplementary work was, I still had to earn a living. So, happily settled into my new chambers, I went off to do battle on battlefields new to me, all over England. A case at Northampton Crown Court lasted three months. A feud between two large families, one of Scots the other of Irish background, both of whom had settled in the steel town of Corby, had resulted in a conspiracy to murder trial. The inter-family violence had culminated in a horrific attack outside a nightclub, leaving one of the troublemakers in a lifetime vegetative state. Another Corby murder case followed, at which my client pleaded guilty. There were murder trials in Leicester, Nottingham and Winchester. Seven months was taken up with a VAT fraud and money-laundering trial at Canterbury Crown Court, the tedium of which was greatly relieved by early evening swims in the sea at Whitstable where I was staying, and with magnificent dinners at that town's renowned fish restaurants. This was followed by four weeks of the confiscation proceedings in London.

Then three weeks of rape in Coventry, and two weeks in the Court of Appeal in London.

During my post-parliamentary days, three cases – two of murder and one of rape – stand out for their human and legal interest from the others.

Serena Kayretli and the concrete coffin

Serena was a tall and strikingly good-looking nineteen-year-old redhead, born in the United States but brought up in Essex. She was charged, with her Turkish husband Vedat Kayretli, with the murder of her former lover Fevsi Demir, another young Turk, for whom Vedat had worked. The trial contained so many twists and turns that it was almost too incredible for fiction, let alone real life. If ever a case justified Sir Walter Scott's words – 'Oh! what a tangled web we weave, when first we practise to deceive!' – this was it. Serena's eventual acquittal was a stroke of good fortune, exposing, believe it or not, the incompetence of another expert – a Home Office pathologist.

Vedat's case, although he did not give evidence, was that it had been his wife, not he, who had killed Fevsi, although in self-defence. Serena's case, and she did give evidence, was that her husband had told her he had been provoked to kill Fevsi, after Fevsi had attacked her honour. At the trial the jury acquitted both of them of murder, convicting them of manslaughter by majority verdicts of ten to two. They received sentences of six years imprisonment. Eighteen months later the Court of Appeal acquitted them both.

Vedat's body, or what was left of it, had been discovered on the morning of Monday 21 April 1997. Two workmen, clearing up a building site at the back of a take-away kebab shop in the High Street at Maldon in Essex, were burning their rubbish. They were using a concrete slab they had found on site as a fire-break. The slab began crumbling at the edges because of the heat, and the foreman, noticing something odd, called his men over. They pulled the slab from the fire to examine it. Chipping away at the crumbling part with hammer and shovels they saw, to their horror, that they were uncovering a human skull and parts of a badly burned and decaying human body. The fire-break was a concrete coffin!

The decomposed body was identified as Fevsi's. In June the previous year he had gone on holiday to Turkey, leaving the shop to be run by

Vedat, with the help of Serena, Fevsi's then girlfriend of three months. On his return to Maldon, Fevsi considered the shop had been so badly run in his absence that he sacked Vedat, who now had neither a job nor anywhere to live. Serena offered him a room in her flat, and Vedat moved in. A close relationship developed, she became pregnant, and they married in November. Their son Kerim was born on 20 March 1997.

Fevsi disappeared in September 1996. Vedat and Serena gave differing explanations for this to their circle of Turkish friends, and to her parents, a medical doctor and his wife. Fevsi had gone back to Turkey temporarily, because his mother was sick; or he had died; or he had left Britain permanently, for no particular reason, having sold the lease of the shop to Vedat. Fevsi had certainly not been seen alive after 17 September.

On 18 September Vedat visited a Turkish friend to borrow a shovel. Then he sought the advice of the builders working on the roof of the kebab shop, about how best to mix concrete. He went to a local builder's merchants where he bought bags of cement that were duly delivered to the shop. Vedat and Serena ran the shop erratically until the end of October 1996, when they closed it up, and sold off some of the equipment. Meanwhile, Vedat was seen driving Fevsi's BMW, using Fevsi's credit card and forging a cheque in Fevsi's name. Six months later, on the day before Serena gave birth to Kerim, Vedat suddenly left the country. The prosecution said that he must have realised that the builders were likely to discover the body, which in fact they did a month later. Surprisingly, Vedat returned to England on 7 May 1997, using a false passport. He may have wanted to collect his son and take him away to Turkey, but he was arrested and charged with Fevsi's murder. He denied the charge but was remanded in custody.

After the body had been discovered back in April, Serena had of course been interviewed by the police. At first she had denied all knowledge of Fevsi's death, and there was no evidence to suggest otherwise. She was interviewed again in May (after Vedat's return), and again in June. On both occasions she stuck to her original story. But after Vedat had returned, was arrested and interviewed, he had given the police a different account. He told them that he had witnessed Fevsi being killed by Serena in self-defence, he admitted disposing of the body in concrete, and also that he had continued running the shop, had driven Fevsi's car, and had forged one of Fevsi's cheques.

On the day before her husband was due to appear at the magistrates court to be sent for trial, Serena's solicitor told the police that her client wanted to be interviewed again. In that interview she completely changed her story. She admitted that she had in fact played an active part in Fevsi's death. She had gone to the shop on the evening of Monday 15 September, with Vedat, to collect some money that Fevsi had owed them. There had been an argument. Fevsi had abused her, lost his temper, come at her with a knife and then kicked her savagely in the stomach. She was seven months pregnant. Vedat had grabbed Fevsi to stop him, and Fevsi had dropped the knife. Fevsi had broken free and had gone for Serena again. She said that she must have picked up the knife in terror and Fevsi, in his rage, ran onto it, stabbing himself once, accidentally, under the left ribcage. He slumped against the wall and collapsed onto the floor. Serena was distraught and wanted to call an ambulance, but Vedat told her it was too late, Fevsi was dead. Vedat had taken her home and had gone back to the shop alone to clean up and dispose of the body. The first that she knew of the concrete was when bags of cement were delivered to her home. She had guessed what Vedat intended to do with it.

The police did not believe a word of her story. They thought that she had made it up to take the blame away from her husband for the killing, and then to protect herself by pleading self-defence. She was allowed to go home. But she kept insisting to the police that what she had told them was the truth. She made such a nuisance of herself, raging at the police inside and outside the police station, that they eventually charged her, not with murder, but with conspiring to pervert the course of justice – to which, in due course, she pleaded guilty. She continued to make a nuisance of herself, so she was rearrested and taken into custody – where she remained until and during her trial.

On 6 October 1997 the police interviewed Vedat again. This time he more or less confirmed Serena's account. Fevsi had been cutting meat when they went to get the money he owed them. Fevsi told Vedat that he had spent it all. Vedat argued with him. Fevsi insulted Serena. She swore back at him. He said he would kill her. The premises were small, and there was little room for the three of them to be fighting. The next thing Vedat saw was Serena in the next room on the floor, with Fevsi laying into her. He pulled Fevsi off and saw that he must have been stabbed with the knife. He did not see how it had happened.

But Serena's account was full of serious discrepancies. To begin with, the date she gave for the killing was not the same as the date Vedat had given. The time she gave was certainly wrong, both because the take-away would have been still open and because there was evidence that Fevsi had phoned a friend seven hours later. Her description of the clothes Fevsi was wearing when he had died did not conform to the partial remains of the clothing found on the body. Her description of the state of the room in which Fevsi had died was inconsistent with the forensic evidence: if she had stabbed Fevsi only once, why were the walls covered with blood-splatter marks? Notwithstanding all this, the police (and the Crown Prosecution Service) seemed to have lost patience with her, changed their minds about her role and, on 30 September 1997, she was also charged with murder.

Three months later, and eleven months before the trial started, Serena changed her story yet again. She now said that the statement she had made, admitting that she had killed Fevsi, was untrue. She had *not* been present at the killing. She had known nothing about it until Vedat told her what had happened when he returned from Turkey in May 1997. They had thought up the previous story together, when she visited Vedat in prison. She had done this because he was having a nervous breakdown and wanted to commit suicide. She was worried that if he took the blame, he would kill himself. At the trial she said in evidence that Vedat had told her Fevsi had insulted her, and he had confessed to stabbing Fevsi three times.

The trial of both husband and wife began at Chelmsford Crown Court on 3 December 1998 before Mr Justice Keane (now Lord Justice Keane) and a jury. Patrick Mullen and myself had been instructed to represent Serena by Christine Plampin, an experienced and highly regarded Essex solicitor. Stephen Kamlish and Anne Shamash defended Vedat. Graham Parkins QC and Andrew Williams (who tragically died shortly after the trial) were for the prosecution. The trial lasted 43 days and there were 100 witnesses. There were hours of tape-recorded conversations, some recorded at police interviews, and some, which were all but unintelligible, recorded by a Turkish friend who had volunteered to be a police informer, and had had a wire-tap attached to his body.

As the days passed, the issues got even more complicated. There were so many possible variations by which the complicated facts might come within the complicated law, that at the end the judge had to provide the jury with a five page flow-chart which he hoped might assist them: 'If you are sure about question 1 in Part A then go to question 2. If you are sure about question 2 then go to question 3. If yes, then go to question 5 and ignore question 4. Then try question 6. If you are not sure about Part A, then go to Part B and answer another 7 questions…'

There was a great deal that was odd about this case, even before any evidence was given. Fevsi had a large number of friends in Maldon, and family in Turkey, yet no one seemed to have been in the least concerned about his total disappearance for six months. Why did Vedat, instead of burying the body in a wood where it might not be found for ages, leave it in a slab of concrete in the yard, where it was bound to be found before long by the workmen? Why did he use Fevsi's property, leaving a trail of evidence pointing directly at him? Having fled the country, why did he return knowing that he would be arrested and charged? Why did Serena, against whom there was no evidence at all, suddenly admit to killing Fevsi, albeit in self-defence? Why did she then retract her story? How did Fevsi actually die? And who actually killed him?

When the trial got under way, the puzzling features multiplied. Vedat, through his counsel, mounted a vicious attack upon his wife, but refused to go into the witness box to substantiate his allegations. The pathologist called by the prosecution had thoroughly examined the body for the cause of death and yet had failed to notice a large hole in the dead man's head! How had that happened if he had died from a stab wound? There had been a walk-in freezer in the room where the blood was found, and around the lock on the inside were gouge marks, as if someone had been locked in and had been trying unsuccessfully to escape. Had a wounded Fevsi been locked in and died trying to get out?

The prosecution faced serious problems in trying to prove murder against either defendant: there were too many possible explanations for Fevsi's death. He could have been murdered in cold blood, by one or other or both of the defendants. He could have provoked Vedat into killing him, which would have been manslaughter. He could have been killed in self-defence, by either Serena or Vedat, which would have been no crime at all. He could have died accidentally, with Vedat disposing of the body because he was frightened that he would not be believed. One of the defendants could have killed him alone, without the other being present or a party to the killing. The jury could certainly not be expected to guess which possibility was true. Where was the hard evidence? And who was to blame?

No forensic evidence linked Serena to the killing. No independent witness saw Fevsi being killed, so there was no reliable direct evidence about when he died, how he died, why he died, who killed him or who was present at his death. If one of the defendants had deliberately killed Fevsi, which one was it? And where was the evidence that the other defendant had agreed to, and therefore was a party to, the killing? That they may have gone to Fevsi together to ask him to repay money owed, was not proof of any murderous intent. Serena had dumped Fevsi, but there was no evidence that she had been angry because he had dumped her – and she did have the consolation of marrying Vedat instead. At one point it was suggested that her motive might have been anger because Fevsi had infected her with AIDs, but there was nothing in that, since she did not receive the medical report – which had cleared her of infection – until some time after Fevsi's death. Without any hard and reliable evidence, the prosecution tried to argue that there was enough circumstantial (indirect) evidence of Serena's guilt. But the jury would be told that circumstantial evidence could only be relied upon in the absence of any other reasonable explanation for the death – which was certainly not the case here.

All the prosecution had to rely on was Serena's account, in only one statement, made in the course of no less than eleven interviews over three months, that she had killed Fevsi in self-defence. If that was true, she would not be guilty of either murder or manslaughter.

Serena had an interesting background. She had a conviction for perverting the course of justice, having retracted a story in court to save a previous lover whom she had alleged to the police had beaten her up. She was also neurotic, with a history of depression, attempted suicide, self-mutilation, drugs use, and a tendency, according to the psychiatrist we called on her behalf, to allow herself to be manipulated by anyone who could show her love. Even when she had admitted her involvement in the killing, the police had not at first believed her. The explanation she gave latterly for trying to take the blame from her husband, as he was about to be sent for trial, was certainly credible on the evidence, for his letters to her showed that he was suicidal. It cannot have done her any good to have gone back on this explanation when she gave evidence on oath.

The prosecution, on the other hand, were in the unhappy position of having to rely on the somewhat incredible argument that although Serena was a liar when she said she had killed Fevsi in self-defence, she could be relied upon to be telling the truth about that part of her statement which suited their case – that she was present at the killing by Vedat. In reality it was obvious that no reliance could be placed on anything she said at any time about anything.

The prosecution's case was that Fevsi had been stabbed to death, there being no evidence of any other cause. Blood had splattered over the walls of the room where meat was prepared for cooking, although there was no evidence that it was Fevsi's, and it might even have been animal blood – as one might expect in a meat shop. Both defendants had talked about a knife and there seemed to be no other obvious explanation. Yet, several days into the trial, a vital piece of forensic evidence emerged which completely devastated the prosecution's case on the cause of death. It appeared that Fevsi might have had his brains blown out with a gun. If so, there was no evidence of any kind to link either of the defendants with that cause of death.

The first pathologist to examine the body was Dr Paula Lannas, an expert called by the prosecution whom Mr Justice Keane in his summing-up described as 'very experienced'. But experienced though she was, she had not taken an x-ray of the skull, nor had she examined the body very thoroughly – or she could hardly have missed seeing a large hole in the side of Fevsi's head! That there was such a hole was the evidence of the second pathologist, Dr Jerreat, who had examined the body on behalf of Vedat. When I cross-examined Dr Lammas on this, she insisted that she could not have missed seeing a hole had one been there, because there had been no hair, flesh or tissue on the skull to hide it. The neat hole must have been caused, she explained, as though it was the most obvious explanation in the world, on the journey by road from one laboratory to another as bone banged against bone. We called the two technicians who had transported the body to give evidence. They said that no damage could have been caused in transit, because the bones had been properly wrapped and they had travelled at normal speed along a well-maintained main road. Dr Jerreat, in his evidence, said that the hole in the head was quite obvious to any examiner, although he had had to remove hair and tissue from the skull to see it. It was upon the unsatisfactory nature of Dr Lannas's evidence, in the face of Dr Jerreat's, that the prosecution case eventually foundered in the Court of Appeal.

At the end of the prosecution's case at Chelmsford, I submitted that there was no case to answer against Serena. There had been no direct or indirect evidence against her, save her one admission of innocent involvement in the killing, and if that statement was true, she was not guilty at law. Even if it was a lie, it could not be sufficient proof, on its own, of either murder or manslaughter. Moreover, the prosecution had the duty of producing evidence to satisfy a jury that there was no self-defence, and they had been unable to produce any. If the part upon which the prosecution wished to rely had been true, Serena would surely not have got the day of the attack, the time, or the clothing being worn so wrong. If she had been kicked in the stomach, being pregnant, she would surely have called an ambulance. There being a hole in the dead man's skull, which another medical expert had said in evidence was the most likely cause of death, how could a jury be certain that Fevsi had been stabbed to death? Furthermore, since the prosecution could not prove which of the two defendants had actually killed Fevsi, they had to produce cogent evidence that they had acted together as part of a joint enterprise: again there was no such evidence, only a possibility.

Apart from the doubtful elements of the prosecution's case, there was a good deal of inferential evidence in Serena's favour. She had played no part in the disposal of Fevsi's body. Two men were seen clearing up the next day; not Serena, nor anyone who looked like a woman. No real motive had been established for the murder. Her behaviour to her mother and doctor step-father, after the body was discovered (both of whom were called to give evidence by the prosecution) was more consistent with her innocence than with guilty knowledge, for she had been so shocked when she discovered that Vedat had suddenly left the country that she had called the police herself – an unlikely act if she had been a party to the killing. When Vedat had telephoned Serena from Turkey he had lied to Serena about his reason for leaving Britain – which would have been unnecessary if Serena already knew the real reason. Serena had even called the police, shortly after Fevsi's death, to remove a drunk from the shop: would she have done that if she had known that Fevsi had been murdered at the shop? The false statement she had undoubtedly made, for which she had been charged, had pleaded guilty and which the prosecution had originally accepted, was to prevent her husband being charged with murder. I submitted at the end of the prosecution case that there was no evidence of murder or manslaughter fit to be left to the jury. Mr Justice Keane disagreed. The trial continued.

Serena insisted on giving evidence. In part she was a good witness; in part she was very bad. She was undoubtedly attractive, and she was persuasive about her devotion to Vedat, the first man in her life to have shown her love. Unfortunately, she had somehow managed to get hold of some drugs while she was in prison during the trial, and she was clearly under their influence when she was giving her evidence. The trial had to be held up for a day so that she could be examined, and she was declared fit to continue. Worse than the bad impression that gave to the jury, she had forgotten to tell her defence lawyers that she had written many letters to Vedat in prison – in which she had actually admitted that she had killed Fevsi! Vedat's counsel produced those letters in court, his client having kept them, and Serena was cross-examined about them. She explained to the jury that since she knew her letters were being read by the prison officers and the police, she was deliberately repeating her lying account in those letters, in order to strengthen the credibility of the story. True though this might have been, it hardly helped her defence (or Vedat's) that Mr Kamlish had obviously been instructed to attack her story, and to brand her a liar.

The saga developed a new twist when Serena raised the issue of the walk-in freezer. The prosecution had been totally silent about that matter, presumably because they could not fit it into their tidy theory. But Serena, in the course of her evidence-in-chief, explained why she had retracted her self-defence account of being present at the killing. She said that she had been shown colour photographs that the police had taken of the walk-in freezer in which kebabs were stored. From marks that she could see on the inside of it, it looked as though someone had been locked in and had tried to get out. The appalling thought had dawned on her, she explained, that Vedat had locked Fevsi in the freezer, and that he had then frozen to death. She had felt sick at the thought. In fact the police had obviously had the same suspicions, which is why photographs had been taken of the inside of the freezer and the unusual marks around the door release mechanism. Although the freezer door locked itself when it shut, it could have been opened by a release mechanism from the inside, unless there was something preventing it, like a heavy chopping table that could have been wedged against the door. The evidence was that there had indeed been such a table close by. Serena told the jury that she had asked Vedat if that had been what happened, and he had said yes. So Mr Kamlish had to address the matter.

He suggested in cross-examination that Serena had made the gouging marks herself; that she had taken a loaded gun from Fevsi's car, and had accidentally shot into the door; then she had tried to gouge the bullet out so that it would not be found. The trouble with that suggestion was that it was both manifestly absurd and contrary to the evidence.

For both defendants had sent scientific experts to Malta to examine the freezer, which had since been sold to a Maltese company. Travelling together, they had discussed the case. There had been no mention of any bullet, understandably since the expert Vedat's team had sent to examine the freezer had not been a ballistics expert but a paint specialist. In fact, there was not the slightest scientific evidence that a bullet had ever been fired: no bullet could have broken through the outer skin of the freezer leaving no track and no residue. Even if Serena had decided to use a gun in the confined space of that room, dangerous to her pregnant self and to Vedat, how could she have managed to get the heavy door off its hinges on her own, and lay it down to gouge out a bullet? And why would the gouge marks have been on the inside if she was gouging out a bullet accidentally entering from the outside? If so fired, and if it had coincidentally just happened to hit the inside release mechanism without leaving any mark on the outside, why had it been necessary for Serena to gouge out an area as wide as two feet, if she was just trying to remove a single bullet?

The unlikelihood of the allegation may have been the reason why Vedat refused to go into the witness box to substantiate his account, and thus to provide the only evidence there would have been that Serena, and not the dead man, had been responsible for the marks on the freezer. Yet if the allegation that Serena was responsible for the marks in the freezer was so ridiculous, what did that say about the truthfulness of Vedat, on whose behalf the fanciful allegations were being made? Important an issue as the freezer had clearly become in the case, both because it might have explained how Fevsi had died, and because it exposed the untruthfulness of Vedat's account, Mr Justice Keane surprisingly directed the jury that the freezer had nothing to do with the case. As surprisingly, the Court of Appeal, at one of the hearings, seemed to agree with him. So much for my advocacy!

Serena was cross-examined by Mr Parkins on another issue, her suggestion that Vedat had been suicidal – her reason for inventing the story of her killing Fevsi in self-defence. The prison authorities, it was put to her, had stopped treating Vedat as a suicide risk long before she had made that statement. She insisted that they were wrong: he was still suicidal in September and she had received a letter from him to that effect.

'Where is it?' Mr Parkins asked.

'I hid it in the rafters of my attic,' she answered.

A police officer was sent to find it and reported that, after a thorough search, he had not found it: it was not there. Serena seemed to have been caught out in a big lie on oath before the jury, and they obviously did not believe her explanation. The judge reminded the jury of this in his summing-up.

But, in another of the amazing twists in this case, the letter was discovered some months after the trial, by the next tenant of the flat – in the attic where Serena had said she had put it, and to which she could have had no later access. That finding formed the basis of one of our grounds of appeal. Although the letter did not actually mention the word suicide, suicide was its clear meaning. Furthermore, a photograph of her son Kerim, which Serena had forgotten about when she gave evidence, and which had been written on after she had made her 'admission' statement, was also found. On the back of the picture the word 'suicide' did appear, and it had been written after she had made her 'admission' statement – by Vedat.

Even without that evidence at the trial to support her account, the rest of the evidence remained insubstantial, conflicting and complex enough in its inconsistencies for the jury to have been justified in acquitting both defendants of murder. They did so: after deliberating for nearly twenty-one hours. But they convicted both Serena and Vedat of manslaughter. She was sentenced to six years imprisonment: he to a total of eight years imprisonment because he had pleaded guilty to concealing Fevsi's body, thus preventing a lawful burial.

We will never know why the jury convicted both of manslaughter. They told the judge that they had ruled out provocation as the reason for their manslaughter verdict. Serena had given such a poor account of herself in the witness box that they may have been driven to the conclusion that she was lying when she had put forward self-defence, and lying when she said what Fevsi had told her. But, lies or no lies, the prosecution still had to prove that Serena was responsible for Fevsi's death. A hint came, perhaps, from a question the jury had asked the judge after they had been deliberating for many hours: would it amount to manslaughter if the defendants had failed to take a dying man to hospital? In theory yes, Mr Justice Keane had told them, but since that issue had never been mentioned in the case, they should not consider it. Perhaps they did.

We appealed the jury's verdict, although Vedat's team decided not to do so. A single appeal court judge decided that there was no valid ground for appeal. We did not accept that ruling, and persisted in our appeal to the full court, as the system allows, as long as the barrister does not expect to be paid out of public funds for so doing. The court agreed to listen to my argument on the matter and set a date for the hearing. I was not too optimistic that they would think any more of our grounds of appeal than had the single judge. But before the case was heard there was yet another surprising turn – an enormous stroke of good luck for Serena.

Patrick Mullen, my very experienced and senior junior, happened by chance to see a report, in *The Times*, of another murder trial in which Dr Lannas, the prosecution's pathologist, had given such unsatisfactory evidence that the prosecution had felt obliged to withdraw its case. The senior Home Office pathologist Dr Iain West had given evidence in that case that Dr Lannas had probably been responsible herself for a bruise that she had said had been caused by strangulation. Patrick thought it possible that there might be a file at the Home Office concerning Dr Lannas: if so, it ought to have been disclosed to the defence. I asked Lord Justice Rose, the vice-president of the Criminal Appeal Court, if the matter could be investigated. He agreed, and it was. I suggested that Vedat might want to be joined in any appeal, and the court agreed to allow that too – and we told his astonished solicitors.

Reports then emerged that Dr Lannas's work had been found to be below standard in 1996, and that in 1997 the Essex coroners had refused to allow her to undertake any more post-mortems in their area. They had submitted three further cases – one being Serena Kayretli's – which showed that she had missed injuries, had inaccurately diagnosed symptoms, and had failed to attend post-mortems. All this had occurred before Serena's trial, and the Essex Crown Prosecution Service and the Essex police said they were unaware of it. They should have been, of course. In June 1999 the Home Office Committee found that Dr Lannas's work remained consistently below that to be expected of a forensic pathologist on their register. This information also was not conveyed to Serena's defence team until after we had asked for access to such a file if it existed.

On Tuesday 4 July 2000, Lord Justice Henry, sitting with Mr Justice Gibbs and Mr Justice Henriques, said that, had that information been available to the jury, they might have concluded that Dr Lannas's evidence had been unreliable, and that there had in fact been a hole in the head when she examined the body. It followed that no jury could ever be sure that Serena's 'admission', upon which the prosecution had relied for a conviction, was the truth: for she had described a stabbing, not a shooting or any other blow to the head which could have accounted for the large hole. The other grounds of appeal did not have to be addressed and remained unresolved. The convictions had to be quashed. The prosecution did not ask for a retrial.

So, eighteen months after their trial, Serena and Vedat were freed. He was deported back to Turkey. She rejoined her two young children, who had been in her mother's care. She owed her freedom to the alertness of Patrick Mullen. Very sadly, the ordeal of the death, the trial and her imprisonment must have been too much for Serena, for she has since taken her own life.

Quinten Hann

Over Christmas 1997 I went with my family to Australia for a holiday. At Melbourne airport Rachel recognised from television, introduced herself, and got into conversation with Quinten Hann, the twenty-year-old Australian snooker champion, who was hitting the international scene as world pool champion and as the leading snooker player in his country. In 2001 he reached sixteenth ranking in the world and nearly beat Mark Williams, the world champion, at the Embassy Championship in Sheffield. In November 2002 he was in London being charged with rape.

The girl making the allegation was a very pretty, fair-haired South African student in her early twenties. The scene of the alleged crime was, of all places, an apartment at the Savoy Hotel in the Strand. Quinten asked Rachel to represent him. She decided that the case, being high profile, required a leader. As a dutiful daughter she asked for me, and I was duly appointed by the court. Although quite a wealthy young man, and a foreign national, our over-generous laws entitled him, if he so chose – and he did – to have us both representing him on legal aid.

Late one Saturday evening in October, having just been knocked out of the British Snooker Championship in Preston, Quinten returned to the Savoy apartment he was sharing with a male friend. He was tired, and about to retire to bed when his friend telephoned him from the Roadhouse nightclub in Covent Garden, very close to the hotel. There were, said his friend, some pretty girls there having fun with some other of his friends, why not join them? Feeling the need to be cheered up, Quinten agreed to go, and minutes later appeared in the bar.

One of the girls, enjoying a night out on the town with her best friend and in search of a good time, was Miss S. She was introduced to Quinten. They chatted, drank a little and danced. A little while later, Quinten and his flat-mate invited the two girls back to the Savoy apartment, and they accepted. The four sat for a while in the living room having coffee and non-alcoholic drinks, then the other couple, being as they later said embarrassed by the intimate interest being shown in each other by Quinten and Miss S, went into the next room. Quinten and Miss S were left alone together. Miss S said she was raped.

It has to be said that rape, in the circumstances, seemed a little unlikely. Miss S had lost no time getting acquainted with Quinten, whom she had only heard of as a snooker player, when they were intimately engaged on the dance floor together. She had been happy enough to go back to his apartment, and to stay with him alone when the friends had gone off to bed. She had no physical injuries and no torn clothing.

During Miss S's cross-examination and the evidence given by her girlfriend and the police officer, a number of facts came to light that made the rape allegation more unlikely.

Miss S had been kissing and cuddling Quinten on the dance floor of the club. She had told her girlfriend that she fancied him, and wanted to go back with him to the flat. She agreed that she had allowed Quinten to take all her clothes off. There was even a time when she sat astride him, his penis erect, as they laughed together. In an earlier statement to the police, not disclosed to the defence until after she had left the court – although very properly admitted in evidence by Prosecuting Counsel Miss Irena Ray-Crosby as soon as she knew of its existence – Miss S had said that her body 'was not acting in synchronisation' with her mind. She tried to excuse her behaviour by saying that she was too drunk to know what she was doing, but the prosecution's own forensic evidence showed that she would have been only just over the lower drink-driving limit, and certainly could not have been said to be drunk. But, she insisted, she had said no to Hann and had meant it. His evidence was that she did say no, but not until after he had actually entered her, and he then immediately withdrew. She agreed that he had, in fact, only penetrated her for a second.

Even if her evidence were accepted, what young man intending rape would withdraw after only a second? Was it so unreasonable, in such circumstances, for him to think that she was actually consenting, and that even if she did say no, she did not really mean it? My comment to the jury on that point produced the main headline in most of the tabloids and broadsheets that were avidly reporting the case in their columns day by day.

That evidence, so helpful to Quinten's denial of rape, did not stop there. When Miss S decided to leave, she went into the bedroom to say goodbye to her best friend, omitting to tell her that she had just been raped, and the friend told the court that she saw nothing about Miss S's manner that gave her any cause for concern. Miss S kissed the man she alleged had just raped her goodbye, on the cheek, and even gave him her mobile phone number so that he could call her the next day to arrange a meeting over lunch. She went down in the lift, past the porter on the desk of the small entrance to the apartments, hailed a passing taxi and directed the driver to her own flat, without telling either of them that she had just been raped, or asking them to call or take her to the police. During the taxi journey she spoke to Quinten for four minutes on her mobile phone – a fact about which she had to be reminded. When she arrived at her flat she did not bother to wake her flat-mate to tell her she had just been raped. Her friend was only told that anything untoward had happened when, being unable to sleep, she had got up and gone into the kitchen to ask Miss S how she had enjoyed her night out. Even then Miss S's words were only, 'I think I have been raped.'

The flat-mate decided to tell Miss S's boyfriend, who had given Miss S the night off. It was the boyfriend who called the police. They went immediately to Quinten's apartment. There they discovered him in bed with another girl. The police must have thought they had a sexual predator. But this other girl, a former acquaintance, had telephoned Quinten out of the blue shortly after Miss S had left and asked, with sex on her mind, if she could come round. He had not discouraged her.

What jury was likely to convict of the dreadful crime of rape, with its promise of a very long prison sentence, on evidence like this? Quinten, who had always denied any wrongdoing, and who had shown shocked surprise when the allegation had been made, went into the witness box. He not only presented himself as a very charming young man, but he could not be shown to be lying about anything. After his evidence, the case was all but over. The jury unanimously acquitted him after a short retirement.

The interesting question was why such an apparently sweet and gentle-looking young lady had pursued such a terrible accusation in the first place. She said in evidence that she was in love with her boyfriend, and he always stopped immediately before penetration when she asked him to. She was upset because Quinten had not done that, although he had done so after a second or so. She volunteered the information that she had deliberately hurt her boyfriend on an occasion the previous year: to teach him a lesson, she had had a one-night sexual stand with a stranger she had picked up – in the same Roadhouse club in Covent Garden! Then it emerged, when I was cross-examining the police sergeant in charge of the case – another fact not disclosed to the defence before the trial – that Miss S had actually tried to stop the prosecution. She had faxed the officer to that effect from South Africa.

I asked the officer if he knew why, having not wanted to pursue the allegation, she had changed her mind and decided to come to Britain to continue with it after all. Had he, perhaps, said something to stop her withdrawing the allegation?

'Certainly not,' he assured the court with some feeling. 'That would have been quite wrong.'

'But did she not ask you what would happen to her if she withdrew her accusation?' I asked.

'Oh, yes,' he replied, 'she did ask me that.'

'What did you tell her?' I persisted.

'Only that the matter would have to be placed before a judge to decide' – whether any action should be taken against *her*, of course!

Poor confused young lady! If she decided to continue with the allegation, she could expect to be asked embarrassing questions in the Old Bailey about her own behaviour that night, and perhaps have to suffer ridicule for the absurdity of it. If she decided not to continue, she would have to come and explain herself to a judge, who might not be best pleased about the waste of time and money and the misery she had caused. Perhaps she chose to continue with the allegation because of her boyfriend. Or perhaps it was because, however embarrassed she might be by the questions, she was at least protected by the rule of anonymity, and no one could give her name to the newspapers or take a photograph of her face.

Quinten Hann, on the other hand, was not protected by any anonymity rule. His name and face were all over the newspapers every day of the trial. He will always be remembered, as long as he remains in the public eye, as the snooker star accused of rape in the Savoy.

The time has surely come when a rule, which did exist for some years, should be reinstated: that a defendant, like the complainant, should be able to claim anonymity until such time as he is convicted of rape. A high proportion of those charged with rape are acquitted yet continue to bear the stigma of the accusation throughout their lives. In some cases complainants later plead guilty to having made a totally false allegation which ruins the lives of their victims. The argument that is always deployed, that rape should not be treated differently from any other serious offence where the defendant has no anonymity, has now been seriously weakened. The law has been changed so that it is no longer necessary for the jury to have heard evidence that corroborates the allegation – injuries, torn clothing or DNA. That will make it easier to get a conviction for rape – and easier to perpetrate an injustice.

After the trial Rachel and I appeared on a television programme to discuss the crime of rape. One of the other participants, a leading anti-rape spokeswoman in the country, told viewers that whenever a woman cries rape she has to be believed whether or not there is any other evidence to support her claim!

With such women on a jury what chance would any man, charged with rape, have of being acquitted? And what chance would Quinten Hann have had of an acquittal – however strong the evidence was in his favour?

The 'Bin-bag beasts' murder

This murder trial, headlined by the media as the 'Bin-bag beasts killing', took place on 5 November 2003 at Nottingham Crown Court, before Mr Justice Morland. Although high on the 'gruesome' scale so important for tabloid circulation, it received little national attention at the time, for it was taking place while the nation's attention was focused on the trial of Ian Huntley, for the Soham child murders in Cambridgeshire.

A year earlier, charity walkers taking part in a pleasant Sunday morning activity along the Grand Union Canal tow-path between Loughborough and Zouch, noticed a full black bin-bag bobbing about in the water. They thought nothing of it until, on their return journey some hours later, they saw the same bundle, tied round with silver tape, still bobbing at the water's edge. One public-spirited walker decided to pick the unsightly object out of the water, and find a refuse bin for it. Curiosity got the better of him, and he opened the bag at one end to see what was in it. What he saw, to his horror, was a human arm and a hand.

Later that day, two human legs were found in another bin-bag, by a woman walking her dog. In the following days other body parts and discarded clothing were discovered in bin-bags and carrier bags in streets across Loughborough. Under a canal bridge, a team of specialist divers found yet another black bin bag sealed with silver tape, containing a large, heavy, rounded object. It was a human head.

The dismembered body, first thought to be that of a girl, turned out to be that of 14-year-old schoolboy Adam Morrell. He was the son of mixed-race Loughborough parents who were no longer living together. Forensic scientists established that, before he had died, Adam had been brutally tortured: boiling water and sugar had been poured over him, and he had been subjected to a sustained assault over a day or two, suffering more than 280 injuries from punches and kicks that had left him almost unrecognisable. Then he had been strangled and finally dismembered.

A few days later, Nathan Barnett, a 27-year-old man, walked into a police station and gave himself up. He admitted sole responsibility for the killing. He gave the police a bag containing a saw, which he said he had used to dismember the body. At his later court appearance he pleaded guilty to manslaughter on the ground of diminished responsibility, four psychiatrists having agreed that he was suffering from the mental condition called Asperger's syndrome. Two of his friends, who lived with him at a two-up two-down house at 72 Havelock Street in Loughborough, Matthew Welsh aged 19, and Sarah Morris aged 17, were interviewed and physically examined. They were later charged with Adam's murder, as was Daniel Biggs aged 19, a friend who had been visiting the house over the period of Adam's death. I was instructed, by the Midlands solicitors Dodds and Partners, to lead Phillip Gibbs, for the defence of Biggs.

Mr John Milmo QC (now His Honour Judge Milmo), opened the case for the prosecution and said, 'These defendants will seek to place as much blame as possible on Barnett. It will become your task to determine the extent to which he was alone to blame for Adam's death, and the extent to which each defendant, if at all, played his or her own part in causing it ... The Crown's case is that each of the defendants joined in the prolonged and sadistic attack on Adam ... each of them encouraged the continuation of the attack so that whether Adam's death was caused by head injuries resulting from the nature and extent of the attack to which he was subjected, or by the ultimate strangulation, or by both, they all went along with it and are guilty of murder.'

The trial lasted seventeen days, and the jury heard what had happened mainly from the defendants themselves, for they had been interviewed over many hours by the police, and later gave evidence in court. Their accounts conflicted, and the jury had to sort out the lies from the truth. The hundred other witnesses, police officers, scientists, neighbours and acquaintances of those in the dock could only describe the terrible injuries they eventually found to have been suffered by Adam, or fill in some of the evidential links.

Adam, a friendly, cheeky and jolly youngster, enjoyed 'hanging out' with this older group, and had struck up a friendship with Matthew Welsh, whom he used to visit at the Havelock Street address, the home Matthew shared with his girlfriend Sarah Morris and Nathan Barnett. There, Adam would meet another friend of theirs, Daniel Biggs, who lived at a hostel nearby. They would gather and smoke cannabis and take 'uppers' (called 'Bin Ladens'), which they bought from local drug dealers. During the evening of Friday 15 November 2002 Adam was seen by a policeman, and other youngsters who knew him, larking around and in good spirits, in the company of some young girls and boys near the dodgem cars at Loughborough Fair. He spent that night at Matthew's house. During the course of the evening, Barnett and Biggs went to Sainsbury's and bought £11-worth of drinks. But at some time during the night, Adam seems to have begun to annoy the older ones, who were probably high on drink and drugs. Sarah told the police that he had started moaning that he didn't feel well.

'He was told to shut up because the drugs were making us feel happy and he was bringing us down,' she said.

Which of them then did what to Adam thereafter, was the subject of considerable dispute. He was mercilessly kicked and punched, intermittently throughout the night. Sarah said that he kept being kicked off a bed, and would curl up into a ball to ward off the attacks. She admitted to the police that she had been one of his attackers, and had kicked him in the head, chest and legs herself, before punching him in the face. Matthew also admitted taking part in the attack, but both said that they had no intention of doing the boy any serious injury. Barnett had decided to scald him by pouring boiling water mixed with sugar over him, but they had played no part in that. Barnett, when he gave evidence, admitted causing that awful injury. Next morning, when Sarah saw Adam, she said his face looked 'like an alien. He wasn't recognisable.' It was clear that, rather than take Adam to hospital and get into serious trouble for the terrible harm they had done to him, they decided to strangle and murder him. That done, they had dismembered his body, and had scattered his clothes and body parts all over Loughborough.

Once parts of Adam were discovered, and the media hue and cry had started, it was agreed that Nathan Barnett, the oldest member of the group and suffering from serious mental illness, would give himself up and take the blame for everything. He was the one who had earlier gone shopping for the saws, bin-bags and tape that had been used. He was the one who had led the police on a wild goose chase, pretending that he had assaulted Adam, and had cut him up in areas of Loughborough well away from Havelock Road. All four defendants went along with this story at first, but when it became obvious that it was nonsense they all admitted the lie, and pleaded guilty to conspiring to pervert the course of justice.

As the trial developed it became clear that the issue was not simply, as the prosecution had alleged, that Barnett would be blamed for causing the serious injuries, the murder and the dismemberment, so that the part played by Sarah, Matthew and Daniel would be diminished. What

Matthew, Sarah, and Barnett did, during the trial, was to put the blame on Daniel Biggs for initiating the attack, and then both provoking and assisting Barnett in the killing. Sarah told the police that Biggs had wanted to carry on the beating. She explained that Biggs had said, 'Let's kill him. It will be fun. Let's kill him ... Matt and I said that we wanted nothing to do with it. We wanted it all to end.'

Barnett was not in the dock because he had pleaded guilty to the murder, but Rex Tedd QC, who was defending Welsh, called him to give evidence. Barnett told the jury that it was Biggs who had put the idea of killing Adam into his head. He said that they had agreed that Adam's fate should be determined by the child's game 'rock, paper, scissors', to decide which of them would kill Adam. That was Biggs's idea as well. The loser was to be the killer. He said, 'I don't remember what I came up with but I was the loser.' He explained how he had started to strangle Adam, but his victim was flailing his arms about and struggling. Biggs had come into the room and helped. He had said, 'Kill, kill, kill!' He had stood with his left foot across Barnett's hands to add pressure while he was squeezing Adam's throat. When he realised that Adam was dead, Biggs had kicked him to make sure of it. Neither Matthew Welsh nor Sarah Morris had anything to do with the scalding of Adam with the boiling water and sugar, the decision to kill him, his murder, the dismemberment of his body, or its disposal around the town. That was the account given by Barnett, Welsh and Morris, three of the four eye-witnesses to the attack upon Adam.

We called Biggs to give his account of what had happened. He told the jury that he had not attacked Adam. But he did admit that he had stayed in the room while Adam was being attacked, and had done nothing to stop it, of which he was thoroughly ashamed. The reason was that he had been terrified of what Welsh would do to him. He had neither suggested the killing, nor taken any part in it. He was not even at the house when it must have happened. Nor had he played any part in either the dismemberment of the body or its disposal. He had joined with the others in the lying story they first gave to the police, only because he was frightened to do otherwise. He had accepted his guilt by pleading guilty to conspiracy to pervert the course of justice.

When I first read my instructions, containing Biggs's account, I believed that I was about to be defending a guilty man with a hopeless case. Yet by the end of the trial the jury could not be satisfied that Biggs had either been a party to the attack on Adam or had actually been his killer, and they returned not guilty verdicts.

They must have concluded that Biggs's friends had turned on him and blamed him, untruthfully, for everything. Why? Probably because when he had broken down, at his eighth interview, and had told the police that the story his co-accused had all been giving had been untrue, he had betrayed them. Mr Milmo conceded to the jury that Barnett's confession, and the original story, might well have stopped the truth coming out, because the police would have accepted that explanation. It was Biggs, therefore, who had put Matthew and Sarah in the dock. As for Barnett, he had admitted in evidence that Matthew was his best friend, so he too had developed 'a very strong dislike' of Biggs.

Since the prosecution's case against Biggs rested entirely on the evidence of the three co-defendants, if they were all liars, all with an interest in blaming Biggs and getting themselves out of trouble, and Barnett, the principal witness, was a self-confessed murderer with a serious mental problem, there was no reliable evidence that Biggs was guilty. There were certainly no independent eye-witnesses; no CCTV, or fingerprint evidence on the saws or bags or receipts, to show that Biggs had bought the disposal items; no mobile phone evidence against him; and no DNA evidence or blood on him to show that he played any part in the dismemberment of Adam's body or its disposal. His fingerprints did not even appear on the Loughborough street map found at the house and which the murderers must have pored over to decide where they could deposit the remains.

But what of the attacks on Adam before he was murdered? Did Welsh have a personality so dominating that Biggs was too terrified to do anything to stop those attacks, or to tell the police about the murder when he had discovered it? Biggs had been in the army, it is true, but only for a year, and the evidence was that he had left because he was not strong enough to take army life. There was no evidence that he had ever been violent to anyone: he had no convictions for violence (or of any kind), although he had been cautioned for shoplifting when he was 15 years old. Welsh, on the other hand, had several convictions for violence: he had violently attacked a man on one occasion, just because he was black, and he had admitted to the police that he had been the first to land a punch on his young friend Adam. Certainly, the prosecution considered Welsh to be so dominant a personality that he might well have put Barnett up to the killing, and he had undoubtedly been able to talk the mentally unstable Barnett into giving himself up to the police and taking all the blame. Welsh even agreed in evidence that he was 'probably' the dominant personality of the four. He was also caught out lying to the jury about Biggs. He told them that Biggs had been at 72 Havelock Road before going to buy the bin-bags, tape and rope. But if Biggs had been in the house, why had Welsh needed to call him on his mobile phone from the Havelock Road land-line? He could not explain that to the jury.

What of Barnett's evidence about the killing? That depended on whether he was a remotely credible witness. Apart from being a self-confessed killer with a serious mental problem, he had told a number of lies on oath to the jury. He had insisted he was as dominant as Welsh, but Welsh had already agreed that that was untrue. He had said he had been the first to hit Adam, but Welsh had already admitted that he had been the one who had started the attack. He had said Welsh could not have known that Adam was being strangled; but Sarah, who said she was with Welsh at the time, had told the police that she had to turn the music up, to drown out the sound of Adam choking. Barnett had said that Welsh knew nothing of the dismemberment of Adam's body, but Welsh had admitted in a police interview that he did know all about it. Barnett insisted that he had been alone when he had dumped everything after the murder, but a police house-to-house enquiry had unearthed a witness who had given evidence of seeing two men and a girl dump what turned out to be Adam's clothing, behind a clothes factory at 1 am on the Sunday morning. Besides, it was clearly impossible for Barnett to have dismembered the body in the bath, bagged the parts and dumped them all, by himself, with no assistance from his friends. Furthermore, Barnett had completely forgotten to mention to the police in his interviews that Biggs had urged him to 'kill, kill, kill', or that they had played the game of 'scissors, paper, rock' to decide who should kill Adam, or that Biggs had helped him by putting his foot on his hands to increase the pressure to Adam's neck.

Even more significantly, letters were produced in court that had been written three months after their arrests, in which Barnett and Welsh made it quite clear that they indeed intended to put the blame on Biggs, because he had betrayed them. They had been together at Wakefield prison before the trial, and had had every opportunity to concoct a story and make sure that their story was agreed. Other letters also showed that Barnett was infatuated with Welsh – a fact confirmed by two psychiatrists – and that Welsh felt maliciously inclined towards Biggs.

Sarah Morris, who was defended by Frances Oldham QC, also gave evidence. She too seemed to have forgotten that she had given a different account to the police. In evidence she said that Biggs had gone out of the room in which they were, to see Adam, while he was still alive: to the police, she had said that had not happened. She was Welsh's lover, and infatuated by him. The more the accounts of the three unwound, and their hatred of Biggs became evident, the more probable it became that, if Barnett had to be encouraged to kill Adam, and needed to be helped to do the deed and to dismember and dispose of the body, it was Welsh not Biggs who was responsible. Witnesses to the aftermath spoke of seeing only three people – one of them a woman – shouting, arguing and disposing of the clothing. It was most unlikely that Biggs had been one of them.

The jury delivered their verdicts after deliberating for eight and a half hours. They found Welsh guilty of both the murder and deliberately inflicting grievous bodily harm upon Adam. He was sentenced to life imprisonment, with an order to serve at least 20 years. Nathan Barnett was to be detained indefinitely. Sarah Morris was found not guilty of the murder, but guilty of causing grievous bodily harm with intent, and she was sentenced to prison for four years. Daniel Biggs was acquitted of both the murder and the grievous bodily harm inflicted on Adam, although he was sentenced to two and a half years in a young offenders institution, for conspiracy to pervert the course of justice – a sentence which he had, in effect, already entirely completed while awaiting trial.

The trial was yet another vindication, if any was needed, of the thoroughness of the British criminal justice system and the good sense of a British jury.

25

To the Present Day

'Work expands so as to fill the time available for its completion.'
(*Parkinson's Law*, Ch. 1)

Free of my commitments as a Member of Parliament, I had more time to devote not just to earning a living at the law, but to other activities related to my two loves of politics and the law.

I started delivering 'after-dinner' speeches, at business conferences and charity functions. I began lecturing on cruise liners, to audiences that seem to be made up almost entirely of former constituents, Conservative officials, distant members of my family, childhood sweethearts, solicitors, judges, magistrates, and even former clients – now spending their ill-gotten gains on world travel! From time to time I have written articles for *The Times* the *Guardian* and the *Daily Express*, and I have broadcast on affairs of the day on television (terrestrial and digital) and Radios 4 and 5, whenever the invitation coincides with my happening to know something about the subject. I even started writing this memoir!

Out of the blue in 2003, I received an invitation from Dr Susan Edwards, the Professor of Law (and now Dean of the Law Faculty) at the University of Buckingham, to become a Visiting Professor of Law at the University. Since I had on several occasions been ranged in television interviews against Susan, an academic expert on women's rights and gender issues, I was as surprised at the invitation as my law tutors at Oxford would have been. But to be offered this prestigious, if unpaid, post, at such an internationally renowned and student-popular independent university, two of whose Chancellors, since its foundation in 1976, had been Lord Hailsham and Baroness Thatcher, and whose Principals and Vice-Chancellors had numbered amongst them such academic charismatics as Professor Max (later Lord) Beloff, Professor Sir Alan Peacock, Professor Chris Woodhead and Dr Terence Kealey, was as flattering as it was undeserved. I accepted the offer with joy and delivered my inaugural lecture – 'Politics and other Crimes: reflections of a QC/MP' – to a packed audience. I could not understand why my lectures continued to be so well attended until, passing a student notice-board on my way out after one lecture, I noticed that stamped across the lecture announcement were the words: 'Attendance **compulsory** for all Law Students'!

I also kept up my interest in international human rights, which began when I first became a Member of Parliament, developed with my membership of the Foreign Affairs Committee and the Commonwealth Parliamentary Association, and which had taken more practical form with Soviet Jewry and during the Kolundzija war crimes trial. It is impossible to be active in public and political life these days, especially if you are a lawyer, and not be concerned about the serious breaches of human rights occurring throughout the world. After all, our very purpose as lawyers is to stand up for the rights of individuals against the abuse of those rights by Governments and other powerful institutions. But how often do we have the opportunity (and time) to do anything about these concerns?

Sometimes we do. The old attitude, that what happens in some far country is no concern of ours, has passed away, and lawyers can these days expect to be allowed into another country thought to be failing to honour their international obligations to uphold human rights. We have, of course, to show respect for those countries and their heads of state, and never forget that it is the democratic right of sovereign nations to decide their own laws without interference from foreigners. So we must go with no particular political axe to grind, and normally only get involved in any individual's guilt or innocence, if we are professionally instructed to do so.

Even so, when I look back, it is often difficult to see that my efforts have made much difference, and when something has been achieved, it is usually impossible to say that I was more than just another 'do-gooder'. Which is why the Maldives visit by a small group of English barristers, which I was asked to join and lead in 2005, and which led to the release of a political prisoner and his election as that country's President, is remarkable.

Human Rights in the Maldives

To hundreds of thousands of the world's tourists, the Maldives is a Paradise on Earth. Like jewels floating in the Indian Ocean, this country consists of 1100 coral-reefed small islands, only 34 of which are inhabited, and 12 of them are beautiful hotel resorts, with crystal clear waters, pure white sand, golden sun by day, and bright star-laden skies by night. It also has mouth-watering food, and charming people whose only wish is to make your stay so delightful that you will want to return. The capital of the Maldives is Male, 45 minutes' flying time south-west of Sri Lanka. Sadly, an ecological cloud hangs over the Maldives and its population of a quarter of a million people. Since 90 per cent of its land surface is no more than one metre above sea level, it is not merely threatened by tsunamis (the 2004 waves took 84 lives), but also by the seemingly inevitable effects of global warming. Sadly, it was not just ecology that was threatening the citizens of the Maldives: for many of them the country's legal system was more Hell than Paradise.

In 2005, the Maldives was a one-party state. In response to international pressure, the Majlis (Parliament) passed a law permitting the existence of political parties. But when Mohamed Nasheed, the leader of the newly permitted Maldivian Democratic Party (the main opposition party), called for the replacement of President Gayoom (who was the Head not only of Government, but also of the Armed Forces, the Police, the Judiciary and the State Islamic religion), he was thrown into prison, where he was long to await his trial for crimes against the state and terrorism. Since no one who had ever been tried for such political offences in the Maldives had ever been acquitted, his fate seemed unlikely to be any improvement upon that which has befallen Jennifer Latheef, the 32-year-old daughter of the exiled founder of the MDP. She had been arrested on a charge arising from allegedly throwing a stone at a policeman during a political rally – an allegation she vehemently denied. She had been released and told that there was no evidence against her, then, when her father had printed a pamphlet against the all-powerful President, she had been rearrested, charged again, convicted, and sentenced to imprisonment for ten years.

In September 2005, Ali Mohammad Azhar, amongst whose virtues is a profound knowledge of Sharia law, asked me to accompany him, and two other English barristers, his daughter Rubeena and Abdurahman Jafar, to the Maldives, to see if we might be able to help the political opponents of the President at least to receive fair trials. The United Nations High Commissioner for Human Rights, the European Union, the Commonwealth Secretariat, the Association of South Asian States, Amnesty International, the International Commission of Jurists, the British Foreign Office, and the United States had all been concerned about abuses of human rights in the Maldives. The Maldives needed international humanitarian support following the tsunami, and some senior politicians and lawyers thought that a visit by members of the respected British Bar might be opportune and helpful – particularly if they could meet Government leaders. President Gayoom would not see us, but the Maldive Government did arrange meetings for us with the most important relevant Ministers, the Attorney-General, the Minister of Justice, the Home Affairs Minister, the Foreign Affairs Minister and the Chief of Police. We also had discussions, over five days, with Nasheed's defence lawyers, Jennifer Latheef, the Head of the Maldivian Law Society, representatives of the press, the Human Rights Commissioner, and we also had meetings in Male, and in Colombo, Sri Lanka, with Jennifer's father, other members of the MDP who had been imprisoned, the British High Commissioner Adrian Evans, and representatives of the United States Foreign Service and other governments: thirty meetings in all.

We explained to the ministers and state officials, that we were not an official delegation representing any organisation, but had come as unofficial friends of the Maldives. Great Britain having enjoyed a long and peaceful history with this fellow member of the Commonwealth, we felt that, without embarrassing the President, we might help the country to become more international human rights compliant if, as we had been told, human rights abuses were making their criminal trials unfair. Our hosts assured us that they were keen to be doing everything in accordance with international standards, that they had, in fact, already begun an intensive programme of reform, and would indeed welcome our helpful advice and assistance.

We identified at least twenty serious breaches of internationally accepted standards. Mohamed Nasheed had not been alone in calling for the resignation of the President and organising public gatherings for the purpose of peaceful demonstration. Excuses had been found for branding these activities crimes against the State and there had been many arbitrary arrests. Men and women had been held in custody without charge for weeks, with no access to a lawyer, and with no right to be brought speedily before a court of law. There were few criminal lawyers in the Maldives, who, since they had to be licensed by the Government, ran the risk of having their right to practise withheld or withdrawn arbitrarily. There was no legal aid for the indigent, and so there was little opportunity for legal advice and representation. If a lawyer could be found, he had no automatic right to challenge witnesses against his client by cross-examination at the trial. Judges had to be brought in from other Sharia law countries, and were not always adequately trained. There being no text-books of Maldivian law or procedure and no legal precedents to follow, the law was what the judge in a case thought it ought to be. Judges were hardly independent, since they were selected, employed, paid and dismissed by the President, to whom an appeal would have to be addressed even though he was a party to the prosecution of alleged crimes against the state. Both the Commissioner and the Chairman of the Maldivian Human Rights Commission, set up after the shooting of prisoners by the security services two years earlier, had resigned because their organisation was powerless and no attention had been paid to its findings. As for the press, the trial reporters of the main newspaper had been arrested, and its printers threatened if they printed reports of any trials.

Would Mohamed Nasheed, and the others, receive a fair trial? The system was not reassuring. Evidence was sometimes obtained under torture and duress, and since the courts could convict on confession evidence alone, that particular abuse was bound to continue. Charges were disproportionate to the wrong-doing: alleged stone throwing and assault being crimes against the State yielding disproportionately long prison sentences. There seemed to be no presumption of innocence: before his trial, government officials had announced to the media that Nasheed was guilty, and would be sentenced. He and his lawyers would only be told which day the trial would be started on the day itself! With two weeks to go, he had not been informed of allegations he had to face, who the witnesses would be, what evidence there was against him, and so he had little opportunity to prepare his defence.

The Attorney-General seemed genuinely surprised at our concern! He explained that he was under pressure to have the proceedings brought quickly. But Jennifer Latheef, although on bail, had been tried for her alleged crime against the State fourteen months earlier, and had still not been told whether she had been convicted or acquitted! She insisted that we raise her case with the Minister of Justice and the Attorney-General, even though it was likely to result in her prompt re-arrest, conviction and a long sentence. We did as she wished and the inevitable happened: she received a ten-year sentence for terrorism.

Clearly, there was much wrong with the Maldives legal system, and our team was not convinced that everyone we met in the Government even understood what was meant by such concepts as 'fair trial', 'presumption of innocence', 'burden of proof' or 'full disclosure'. To be fair, the ministers did accept that all was not well, attributing failings to the limited resources of the tiny state, the inadequacy of its laws and procedures and the absence of qualified lawyers. For the future, they welcomed our help – British judges and professors of law, and anyone else's – to improve the legal system, and they assured us that they were committed to reform. Whether any of that would ensure that Mohammed Nasheed's trial would be fair, was another matter.

We reported our findings to every organisation that had shown interest – the British Government, the Inter-Parliamentary Union, British MPs, the International and Human Rights Committees of the English Bar, the Commonwealth Secretariat, the United Nations High Commissioner for Human Rights, Amnesty International, and 'Justice', and our report was circulated widely, receiving particularly wide coverage on the Internet. Azhar and I were interviewed on international radio and television.

At first, we seemed to have achieved no success, but shortly after Jennifer Latheef received her sentence, she was released – and came to London to thank us. She was followed by the Maldivian Attorney-General and the Minister of Justice, both of whom came to London to tell us of the improvements they were introducing. Then two and a half years after our visit, Nasheed himself, having been tried and sentenced to ten years imprisonment, was released. President Gayoom, apparently fearful of the continuing street demonstrations on Nasheed's behalf, called a Presidential election. Nasheed stood against the incumbent of thirty years, and to everyone's amazement – especially President Gayoom's – he emerged victorious with 54 per cent of the vote against Gayoom's 46 per cent. On 29 October 2008, Mohamed Nasheed became President of the Republic of the Maldives.

Five months later, President Nasheed, on a diplomatic visit to London, invited our team to breakfast at his hotel. He said that he wished to thank us all personally for what we had helped him to achieve. He assured us that he would still have been in prison without our help. By throwing such a bright international light upon his country's human rights abuses we had done something that governments had been unable to do: we had empowered his people. Our report, and the international response, had given them the confidence to rise up and take to the streets so that the regime was shamed into releasing him and calling the election. He told us that our activities should be a model for other necessary human rights activities around the world.

Whether or not our little group of English barristers was entirely worthy of such a generous tribute, it is certainly good to know that our intervention in the world of international politics was not, as it might have been, a total waste of time. Perhaps it will encourage others from the British Bar who are engaged in similar activities. More immediately, we are confident that President Nasheed's own suffering of torture and six years of imprisonment will ensure that his success will have been a major victory for human rights.

Egypt and Bangladesh

I cannot say 'flushed with success', because I did not then know how successful our visit to the Maldives had been, but certainly feeling that something useful might have been achieved, I saw every reason for trying to help with another human rights problem, when I was invited to do so by Justice International. There were, I was told, serious human rights breaches occurring in Egypt.

I am no admirer of the Moslem Brotherhood. They have never seemed over anxious to guarantee peace with Israel and that nation's survival: indeed in the past, they have encouraged violence. So my visit to Egypt had nothing to do with the fact that the alleged human rights abuses of the Egyptian Government were being visited upon members of the Moslem Brotherhood. My only interest was human rights when I was invited, again with my friend Ali Mohammad Azhar, and Dr Sayyed Mohyeddeen, another British barrister, by relatives of members of the Brotherhood, to assess whether the impending trial before a military tribunal of 32 civilians (numbering amongst them university professors, medical doctors, teachers, accountants, journalists, businessmen and politicians), was in accordance with the international standards of human rights which Egypt had agreed to honour.

Our arrival in Cairo on 15 July 2007 was not uneventful. Ali Azhar was refused entry at the airport. The driver of the car sent to collect me thought he was Lewis Hamilton, lost control of the car at high speed on the airport road complex, and I was lucky to reach the hotel alive and uninjured – and able to write this memoir! Briefings began early next day.

Abuses of basic human rights certainly seemed to have occurred, for the defendants, all civilians, having been acquitted by the criminal court, were now about to be re-tried on the same matters, before a military tribunal. There access to lawyers would be limited and the public and press would be excluded. There had also been failures, we were told, to disclose evidence, and defence documents had been seized and interfered with by the police, who had forcibly entered the defendant's homes and destroyed property without a lawful warrant. There seemed to be no law of *habeus corpus*, so these men, having been acquitted by a properly constituted court of law, had been kept in custody for over seven months. The erstwhile United States Attorney-General, Ramsey Clark had arrived ahead of our British delegation, had been refused entry to the military tribunal, and had taken a very dim view of the situation.

We held press conferences and broadcast our visit and concerns. No-one expected success on the Maldives scale, but our team has since been assured by a spokesman for the 32 that 'because your press conferences had made the authorities aware that the international world was watching, some of the defendants were not convicted, sentences on those who were convicted were many years less than everyone had expected, and human rights activists have been galvanised into greater activity'. Another worthwhile international human rights activity, it seems.

Shortly afterwards, I was invited to represent, this time in a professional capacity, Begum Khalida Zia, a former Prime Minister of Bangladesh, at her trial on corruption charges in Dhaka. The Bangladesh Government had cancelled elections, had imposed emergency rule and had installed a caretaker government. They also refused my application for a visa to enter the country and take instructions. Then they relented and a visa was granted. But just as her British solicitor, Richard Cornthwaite of the London city firm of Garstangs, and I prepared to fly out to meet our client, Begum Khalida was released from house arrest, the charges against her were dropped, and she stood again for election as Prime Minister of Bangladesh. She was opposed by Sheikh Hasina Wazed – also a former Prime Minister lately subject to corruption and murder charges and also released for the election. When this took place, on 29 December 2008, Sheikh Hasina was the victor by a landslide. We are obviously living in interesting times!

May I end this account of my political and legal lives with a plea for another of my 'causes'- the strangulation of the self-employed Criminal Bar and the importance of its survival?

The self-employed Criminal Bar: has it a future?

The English Bar having nurtured me, provided me with a living, and given me so much satisfaction during my working life, I felt that I must contribute something to its future. So on leaving Parliament I signed up to the excellent Inner Temple advocacy training scheme to help new barristers to improve their advocacy; for the Bar's existence is predicated on our skill as advocates in the courts and in the analysis and presentation of legal argument. That, as they say, is what we do! But more immediately urgent, and a far greater challenge, has been the very survival of the self-employed Criminal Bar – being throttled over the past decade by a Government seemingly oblivious of its importance in maintaining the high standard of British criminal justice.

Most of the 14,000 barristers undertake criminal cases, and that work is almost entirely legally-aided, that is, funded by the taxpayer. This has to be so, for half the criminal work is prosecuting, and obviously the state must pay for that: the other half is defence work, and as most people cannot afford to pay for their own health care and medicine, most alleged offenders cannot afford to pay for their legal defence. Even those charged with financially rewarding crimes will have their assets frozen by the courts soon after arrest, so that nothing is available to pay for long trials, and the taxpayer, at least in the first instance, has to pay. Private insurance is not the answer to the problem of funding criminal cases, for unlike sickness insurance, when everyone at some time or other in their lives is going to need medical assistance, and the sheer volume of subscribers makes medical insurance worthwhile, the comparatively limited number of potential law-breakers is never going to make legal defence insurance viable. Besides, those who will most need legal defence will be criminals who usually repeat their offending, and insurance is unavailable by law to those whose trade is breaking the law. So if there is to be an effective criminal justice system, lawyers have to be paid by the state: and if they do not earn a reasonable living they will just not take on criminal cases.

Unlike the solicitor who runs a multi-activity business, and can spread his income and expenses across the firm's activities, the barrister does not have such a business across which he can spread the outlay and the losses. He is the consultant and the trial lawyer in the higher courts, an independent contractor working alone: he has no firm that will pay his expenses, and they have to be paid from his gross income from each case. If his or her fees are too low, it will simply not be worthwhile taking years of study, repaying large student loans, not being paid for months after the case has finished, and having to wait, like an actor, for work. Even if work is available, why should anyone want to do it around the clock and at weekends, for returns lower than the average weekly wage – which is surprisingly, too often the position today?

An unsympathetic public, usually misled by a wilful media into believing that publically-funded barristers have their snouts in a feeding trough, seems to have no idea how absurdly low legally-aided fees for criminal work have become. Until very recently, there were days in every trial which paid both the defence and prosecution barrister only £46.50, and most days in a trial lasting a week still only average out at £100 per day: that is before expenses have to be met for the fee to the barrister's clerk, his chambers rent, his travel, car parking, hotel, equipment, books, insurance, paid holiday, and contribution towards a pension. These expenses more than halve the value of the barrister's fee. There cannot be many highly trained professionals who take home, like the criminal barrister, only £25 to £50 a day before tax!

So, far from having their noses in the trough of a very high-income profession, thousands of busy practitioners at the Criminal Bar have an annual income, before tax, of less than £20,000. This is ridiculously below the average income in England and Wales of £34,000 (£46,000 in London). It is also much less than that of the most junior police officer engaged in a criminal case (£32,000), or of a qualified teacher (£31,000) or even of an underpaid nurse (£24,000). Furthermore, there has been no increase in the standard fees for well over ten years, and with its dying breath the Labour government ordained a further reduction of 13.5 per cent over the next three years! Since barrister's work does not usually provide a regular daily income, most of the Bar are not earning anything like a living wage. So much for snouts in the trough!

One result of this failure of the state to properly fund legal-aid has been that there are now hardly any pupillages (apprenticeships) being offered to youngsters wishing to come to the Criminal Bar. Another is that criminal practitioners are leaving for other work and formerly healthy sets of criminal chambers are collapsing at an alarming rate. If many of the best people are leaving what chance is there of maintaining high standards?

Of course the self-employed barrister can double his income if he surrenders his independence to become an employee of the government or of a firm of solicitors: for then his employer will be paying his expenses. But if too many barristers take employment, that means not only that the cost of criminal cases will rise but that we will become a 'fused' profession. 'Fusion'- making barristers and solicitors into one category of lawyer – is the word no one in government will use, but if we do nothing it will describe what has happened to the profession in the years to come.

My reader may ask: what is wrong with 'fusion'? What is wrong with having just one kind of lawyer, as in continental Europe? Why is it so important to have two parts to the legal profession, with a division between barristers and solicitors, both of which have to be separately paid?

To begin with, it would be quite wrong to assume, as many do, that it would save money. Barristers charge less per hour than solicitors because their overheads are lower. If there is work for two people preparing a case, the cost is not saved by two solicitors doing it rather than a solicitor and a barrister. But the more important answer is that both our system of justice, and the existence of our just society, would lose the enormous asset of a tried and unique system if we amalgamated these independent functions.

For barristers, like surgeons and medical consultants, are trained specialists particularly skilled at performing their tasks. They have not only skill but independence, integrity and professionalism, and an important bond of trust exists between them and our independent judiciary. These elements produce both efficiency and the achievement of justice. Would you not want a brain surgeon to operate on your brain rather than your family doctor? Would you not want a consultant who is independent and particularly skilled in his field of work, to advise you on the prognosis of a complicated illness, not just your GP or someone who works only with his firm? The dual profession provides for everyone charged with crime, however lowly his condition, to have access to the finest defenders practising at the Bar – he does not have to be represented in court by a member of his solicitors firm who may not be up to the task. Furthermore, the independence of the self-employed barrister, owing allegiance to his client, not to an employer telling him what is in the best interests of the firm, is of paramount importance to the integrity of our justice system.

Once all solicitors are permitted to operate as barristers, and barristers are driven by very low legally-aided incomes to become employed by solicitors, or to become solicitors, then the virtues of independence in the present dual system will disappear. What will matter to the employer is the volume of work turned in by what is called the 'fee-earner' in the business, not its quality. The defence advocate will turn up for work at 9 o'clock in the morning to collect his pile of cases to be heard at court that day, and he will expect to be able to go home at 5 o'clock in the evening. The careful preparation 'round the clock' that takes place with an independent Bar will go out of the window.

So too may the traditional independence of judges be weakened. After a lifetime working for someone, will judges have the same independence of spirit which the self-employed Bar has bred into them? Is there not a risk that they may more quickly become ciphers of their employers, the Government? If so, the fearless independence, which has been the outstanding quality of a criminal justice system admired the world over, will be greatly diminished.

At the same time as the attack on barristers, the quality of our system of justice is being attacked on other fronts. The number of solicitors firms in the country available to the citizen accused of crime has been diminishing very fast. By a franchise system introduced by the last Government, the number of solicitors' firms allowed to undertake criminal work has been slashed to a third. And because the state-funded fee allocated to solicitors for a case has been substantially cut, many firms, unable to cover their overheads and unwilling to subsidise their criminal practice out of their privately funded work, are not bothering to apply for a franchise. As a result, there is a fast-reducing supply of country solicitors taking criminal cases, and someone accused of crime has to go to the big town or city if he wants a lawyer. Government services are now the only expanding area of criminal justice activity – the Crown Prosecution Service, the Serious Fraud Office, Her Majesty's Revenue and Customs, the Criminal Defence Service, the Legal Services Commission and the Courts Agency, etc. The newly qualified barrister of the future, if he or she wishes to earn a living, will be driven to securing employment with the Government. The Criminal Bar, independent of government and employed status, will shrivel and die. In my 48 years of practice, the morale at the Criminal Bar has never been so low, nor the quality of service that we provide, so seriously threatened.

I must be honest. The rot began in the last years of Conservative Government, when the move to 'fusion' started with the proposals to allow solicitors the right of audience in the higher courts. It became inevitable that more Crown Prosecution Service work would be done 'in-house' and less would go to the self-employed Bar. The rot spread at an alarming rate under New Labour.

I argued with Mrs Thatcher over her support for these proposals which originated in the so-called Green Papers. I asked her at Prime Minister's questions one Thursday afternoon why, having been steadfastly against such action, she had now changed her mind: particularly since publicly-funded barristers were costing the tax-payer less than publicly-funded solicitors with their substantial overhead expenses. She had not been properly briefed about the matter, and so had not seen the front page of that day's *Times*. It showed Lord Chief Justice Lane laying the foundation stone for a new Court, and reported him as saying: 'As I turn the first sod, I bury the Green Papers.'

When I showed her the article, she was shocked. I pointed out that if this most substantial pillar of the establishment, always so moderate, reasonable, and restrained, was driven to publicly criticise Government policy, it showed how very deep were the feelings not only of the Bar but also of the Judiciary. Surely she ought to take account of it. Her response was:

'James assures me it is all right.'

'Which James is that?' I stupidly asked.

'My Lord Chancellor,' she replied.

'But what experience does he have of the English system,' I persisted. 'He is a Scottish judge, where the system is very different'.

'No, he has been sitting in the Court of Appeal and House of Lords on English cases,' she responded, 'and James assures me it is all right.' Her eyes gazed off to some distant nirvana beyond, of cheaper justice swirling about the personage of her rightly revered Lord Chancellor.

'Is there anything else you have come to see me about?' the Prime Minister asked me sweetly.

'Nothing as important as this,' I mumbled weakly, bowing as I left the presence.

When I first came to the Bar, crimes were both investigated and prosecuted by the police, sometimes through their own prosecuting departments and sometimes through local firms of solicitors. In the following years, and particularly after the Phillips Royal Commission on Criminal Procedure in 1978, the feeling spread that the police should no longer both investigate crime and decide whether and whom to prosecute. There were also too many acquittals, when judges decided that there was not enough evidence to justify leaving the case to the jury. It was agreed, by all Parties, to set up an independent prosecuting authority called the Crown Prosecution Service, with the Director of Public Prosecutions (DPP) at its head. The recommendation of the committee, under the then DPP Sir Thomas Hetherington (of the Nazi War Crimes enquiry, see Chapter 20), which had been set up to consider how best this could be done, had been for a regional service. The Government decided instead to make it a nationally centralised institution.

As Chairman of the Conservative Legal Committee, I suggested to Patrick Mayhew, the Attorney-General, who had overall responsibility for the CPS, that it was taking matters too far for a Conservative

Government under Margaret Thatcher to be nationalising an industry. I warned him that the first thing likely to happen would be the trade unionisation of the new organisation, with demands for better terms and conditions, and a delay in the start of the Service. I was right. The Crown Prosecution Service began operating long after it had been meant to start, and it has been, ever since, an ever-growing inefficient bureaucratic nightmare forever starved of resources. It has been the employer most voraciously swallowing up the independent self-employed Criminal Bar.

In 1997, when Dame Barbara Mills's term of office as Director of Public Prosecutions came to an end, Frances Gibb, the *Times's* legal correspondent, told me that my name was in the frame to become the DPP. I told her that she had been misinformed! I would have had to apply for the job, and I had not done so. The new DPP would be expected to secure for CPS employees who were not barristers, the right of audience in the Crown Courts, and it was known that I was virulently opposed to that break with the traditional position of the self-employed Bar which would be the beginning of 'fusion'. David Calvert-Smith QC, the Chairman of the Criminal Bar Association (now a distinguished High Court Judge), was also mentioned. He too had been virulently opposed to the CPS having rights of audience. He became DPP. My good friend John Morris QC, who had had a most distinguished parliamentary career, and had been Secretary of State for Wales in Harold Wilson's Government, became Attorney-General in the New Labour Government. As my Vice-Chairman in the All-Party Parliamentary Bar Group, he had also been strongly opposed to giving the CPS rights of audience in the higher courts. Rights of audience to the CPS followed shortly after the new appointments. Perhaps things looked different from the other side. Or perhaps it was thought that the time had come to put aside principle – and do what was thought to be right!

So worked up was I getting at this threat to the future existence of the Criminal Bar, that I decided, in 2005, to stand for election to the Bar's governing body, the Bar Council of England and Wales. This august organisation, to which all practising barristers have to subscribe, is responsible for promoting the services that barristers provide, and representing their interests on all matters relating to the profession and the administration of justice including, through the new Bar Standards Board, standards of practice. The self-employed part of the profession that was publicly funded, having been allowed to reach this parlous state, it did not seem to me that the Bar Council had been doing a very effective job as a trade union. I did not expect to be elected to one of the three Queens Counsel places, because never having worked for the Criminal Bar Association, I did not think I could supplant any of their chosen candidates, who would be on their 'slate', and who would naturally attract the support of criminal barristers. I was wrong again. I was elected. I am afraid that I have been a pain ever since, trying to alert the successful end of the commercial and civil Bar to an understanding of the threat to its very existence that the independent Criminal Bar is facing. Of course, I have not been alone, and successive chairmen and their fellow officers have shown concern and have taken action. But as a profession we do not strike, and I am afraid that unless government wakes up to what is happening, and is prepared to stop it, we will be too late.

So has the self-employed Criminal Bar a future? Only if the new Government, faced with a £158 billion deficit, can come up with some totally new method of funding legal aid to the level at which everyone in it can earn a reasonable living. Now there is a challenge!

26

Conclusions

The lyf so short, the craft so long to lerne,
Th' assay so hard, so sharp the conquerynge.

(Geoffrey Chaucer, *The Parliament of Fowls*)

It may be that my most patient and dedicated reader, having read what has been little more than a narrative of the trials in which I have been involved, and the political causes and events in which I took some small part, might now wish to close the pages of this memoir and read no more. My thoughts on the lessons I have learnt may, understandably, be of much less interest than the thoughts of others who have achieved so much more in their lives and who are, or were, better able to teach the lessons of life then me.

But I did say in the Preface that I believed that those who have been fortunate enough to have made something of their lives ought to pass on some of their experiences, and, with them, the message of hope and encouragement to others who will follow down the same path. I have been learning the importance of this from the many university students I have been meeting at the University of Buckingham and the Inner Temple. And so far, I seem to have passed on few messages. So really to complete the task I promised, and in case my patient reader is up for a little more punishment, here are some of the relevant things I believe I have learnt.

Looking back and taking stock, I must first acknowledge my blessings, and their importance in giving me the attitude of mind without which I would have achieved nothing. I can also see that, although I tried to follow certain rules of behaviour, my professional life might have been even more successful had I been able to follow them more perfectly.

Blessings

First and foremost, I have been very fortunate to have been healthy. Bad health, apart from its inherent misery, must be such a distraction

407

from the single-minded application to life's tasks that is so necessary. It eats up valuable time, and inevitably depresses and demoralises the sufferer. When I see Rachel coughing, breathless, sweating, having to plug herself into her nebulizer for an hour when she wakes up in the morning and again before she goes to sleep, injecting herself at mealtimes, giving herself physiotherapy, apportioning a pharmacopeia of pills to a tray of little compartments at night ready for the following day, and then getting on with the stresses and traumas of a young dynamic life of responsibility to other people as though nothing is troubling her, I see a true heroine. She has no self-pity. Her view is that there are others so much worse than herself, and that she is really quite lucky! Those of us who are fortunate enough to suffer no, or few, afflictions, would do well to keep ourselves as fit as we can, by regular exercise, diet and positive thinking – and keep our fingers crossed!

Secondly, I have had the joy of a happy home life for nearly fifty years. For the restless soul in a world of traumas and uncertainties, to have a loving wife or husband to return home to, someone who is always there to provide emotional comfort and stability, is a wonderful boon. A busy politician and a lawyer must have a partner whom he or she knows will provide happiness. For that to happen, each will need to make sure that the other is happy too, with attention to financial security and emotional needs. There ought also to be some understanding at the beginning of the effect that a busy, often preoccupied, life is bound to have on the relationship. The mutual achievement of marital happiness is surely greater then the sum of its parts. We all have to work at it! I have certainly been blessed.

Thirdly, I have had the happiness of having a marvellous daughter. There has been the pain of sharing in some of her suffering, but the joy of having her with us, and being able to encourage her in her achievements, has far outweighed any unhappiness. Gloria feels as I do. Others will have the additional joy of grand-children, but I am not sure that it would be possible for us to have more total joy than we have had with our daughter.

Fourthly, I have been fortunate in my work. I have loved the law, and I have loved politics. I have not risen to the greatest heights, but then by having limited ambitions, I have never been bitterly disappointed or deeply frustrated by failure. I have been comfortable about being moderately laid back, and taking life as it comes. I think it is essential, particularly in politics, to get on well with people and to enjoy helping to solve their problems. Many of the pleasures of my life have come from the unexpected successes. But the most important thing is to have been happy in my work.

So much for my blessings: they have been the bed-rock upon which the rules that I have tried to adopt as a guide have rested. None of them are original, of course. Most of them, in truth, can be found better expressed in well-known aphorisms, slogans and witty comments of the great, the good, and the famous. But the fact that they have been the experience of so many others gives them greater value and importance, and I hope that I will not be judged too harshly for repeating them. Not in any order of importance, here they are.

30 Guiding Rules

1. Develop *self-confidence*. I started off badly. I am sure that I could have achieved more if I had really wanted to achieve more, and I might have wanted to achieve more had I believed that I was capable of it. Looking back, I know now that I could have been an artist. I could have been a better classical piano player or perhaps a jazz pianist. With my life better ordered, I could have learned to play my saxophone and my flute. I could have written books, and more articles and pamphlets, and made a more useful contribution to law and politics. I could have done so much more to help those in need, and to comfort the sick or distressed. One of the most moving film moments for me was when Oscar Schindler, in Spielberg's wonderful film *Schindler's List*, was presented with a gold ring made from the teeth of the Jews in the camp who owed him their lives, as a token of their regard for him and all he had done for them. He broke into tears, muttering that there was so much more he could have done. In a much more insignificant way, I feel the same. I should have had more confidence in my own ability to achieve more or all of what I wanted to achieve.

2. But I have lived a life of little frustration and disappointment. In fact I have always been happy and cheerful. Life being brim-full of problems – like history, one damn thing after another – I have learnt that happiness does not come from the absence of problems, but from finding the ability to deal with them. And there is a difference between success and happiness: success is getting what you want; happiness is liking what you get. *Happiness* is in the mind, so you have to make up your mind to be happy. That is what I have always tried to do.

3. There has been one constant enemy: time. So little time to do so many more things than our parents had to do – so many more books, TV channels, videos, CDs, the internet, music, theatre, art, newspapers, legal publications, statutes, court judgements, rules – and friends. We have to learn to count the hours, for they pass all too quickly. Each day really should be lived as if it is the last – and perhaps every night as if it is the first! One of life's great tragedies is the amount of our human potential we all seem to waste. So we must *organise* our time to achieve the minimum of waste, and the maximum of result. Most of us, with training, could read faster and absorb more knowledge (speed reading), remember things better (memory training), and learn to express ourselves in speech or writing much better than we do (with practice). By planning and programming life a little more, we can manage to get more things done.

4. I have needed and have had *luck*. Although you might think that that is really out of our hands, it is often true that the harder you work, the luckier you get. People sometimes say 'how lucky you are', when the true explanation has been your hard work.

5. I have tried – but have too frequently failed – to *be a doer* rather than just a talker, because it is nice to be remembered, and people remember you longer, for what you did, than for what you said. Anyway, if you really are on the right track, and you just sit there doing nothing, you will get run over by all the others on the same track. And if one cannot do everything, at least try to do something – as much, and as well as, one can.

6. When having something important to do, it is necessary always to *think the matter through*, analyse the pros and cons, and then come to a conclusion. Better schooling and parenting would have got me started sooner, but it is never too late to start doing this.

7. Always *think positive*. To be constantly wracked by doubts and indecision, is to ask for disaster and failure. Once you have come to a conclusion, get on with it! It is what Margaret Thatcher and other great leaders did and do: that is why those of us who have difficulty with positive thinking admire them so much!

8. Whether as lawyer or politician, one has to impress people. The

audience: the jury; clients. First impressions are important, and one never gets a second chance to make a good **first impression**, so putting some effort into the beginning is invaluable.

9. *Welcome challenges*: whether they turn out to be stepping stones to success, or stumbling blocks leading to failure, often depends on how well you address them. Sometimes, to make progress, you have to make compromises. Other times, you have to take big, bold steps, simply because it is impossible to cross a chasm in two or three small jumps. I have never been too keen on walking down the middle of the road, because that is where you are more likely to get knocked down. I suppose I must have been frightened at some time or other – everyone is – but courage is being frightened and conquering that fear. To tell the truth, I suppose I have seldom been that frightened!

10. Often we fail. Then we must pick ourselves up, brush ourselves down and have another go. As one famous High Court Judge, Mr Justice Brabin, once said, 'You will know that you have truly arrived at the Bar of England and Wales when you have dropped a bollock with aplomb!'

Failure can be turned into success if we learn from it. It is not so much how far we fall that matters, it is how soon we can recover, and how high we can bounce back. I usually make excuses for my failures, and my principle excuse is to blame others. Mostly, that is quite wrong. My failure to hit the target is seldom the fault of the target: more often it is my aim that is bad, and I simply must improve my aim. We must always try to do better next time. There are many reasons for failure and there are degrees of failure. Sometimes we fail because we are not taking enough risks: I find it very reassuring to tell myself that. Sometimes it really does not matter if we fail, and it really is better to have travelled hopefully than to have arrived. Sometimes, it is better to have tried and lost, than never to have tried at all. Some goals are so magnificent, it may even be glorious to fail. So although winning is usually better, losing is not always a disaster and so it does also matter how you played the game.

11. We should *not be afraid of pressure*. I work much better when I am under pressure. A lot of people do – particularly in the professions. It concentrates the mind. A diamond, they say, is a chunk of coal that developed under pressure. But I do sometimes have to remind myself not to over-do it!

12. Excellence is never accidental: it only happens with *hard work*. The more excellently we manage to do things, the better the quality of life often turns out to be. By refusing to accept anything but the best, I think we can often surprise ourselves by at least nearly achieving it.

13. It is obvious that if you have a skill you must *use it*, or lose it. More people rust out than wear out. Our skills may be limited, but we should at least try to make the best of them, and use them whenever we can. The people I resent most are those who have a skill, are aware that they have it, and refuse to use it. That really is such an inexcusable waste of a God-given gift.

14. We should try to be *enthusiastic* about the tasks we undertake. Since I enjoy life, I do not have to try too hard to be enthusiastic, and I find that enthusiasm inspires me to greater effort and may even inspire others to follow. Enthusiasm prepares us to seize opportunities. Not, as my Geordie wife might say, 'waiting for the boat to come in', but rowing out to meet it.

15. Does not success often come with *persistence?* Brilliance alone is obviously not enough, because the world is full of brilliant failures.

Persistence is a matter of hanging on when others have let go. In the confrontation between the river and the rock, the rock usually wins, not through strength but through persistence. When you cannot change the direction of the wind, you just have to adjust your sails and persist. I try never to give up – unless, of course it would be madness to continue!

16. I need to believe in something, and that also helps to fire up my enthusiasm. I find that belief in God is best, but not everyone would agree with me. At least one needs *principles*: a person who does not stand for something may fall for anything. In matters of style, we may swim with the current, but in matters of principle, we must stand like a rock. Besides, it is so much easier to make decisions if we have values and principles to guide us. In politics, your principles are your political philosophy, and if you have them as a compass to guide you, you will invariably get closer to your destination.

17. Good character and *reputation* are very important indeed, both in politics and in the law. We must always try to be responsible and hold our standards higher, if possible, than those of the next man. Intellectual dishonesty is bad enough, although for as long as I can remember, the Bar has berated the Court of Appeal, behind its back, for that particular failing. But real dishonesty is another matter entirely, and deserving of the deadly blight upon character and reputation that follows. So a loss which may bring momentary pain, is infinitely better than a dishonest gain which will bring pain for much longer. Politicians, however, should always remember that confession, although undoubtedly good for the soul, is often bad for the reputation.

18. *Judgement* is a necessary element for life in both professions, particularly in the law, for there we are more often alone when we have to form a judgement than we are in the team activity of politics. But we are not born with judgement: it can only come with experience, and one has to learn when it is sensible to do something and when it is not. One important judgement is when to take a chance: we must not be too afraid because, like the turtle, we can make no progress if we are not prepared to stick our neck out.

19. Barristers and politicians always have to make *judgements about other people*, because we need to know whether to follow them, accept their advice or reject it as irrelevant or foolish. We should try to speak well of people rather than speak ill of them, for doing the latter only exposes our own prejudices, does little good, makes people feel worse, and shows us up in a bad light. It is good, not just in the culture of the yob, to show others respect, and not to embarrass them unnecessarily. That means criticising in private, and praising them in public. In politics we are quick to attack an adversary for failing, but the truth is that it may be much better that he should have tried and failed, than that he should have failed to try.

20. We should try to *be kind* to people: and usually a little kinder than necessary. It is better to lift people up, than to knock them down: because everyone is important – and the most important people may be those who can be of no possible use to us. On the other hand, people who may seem to be less important, may actually be on the way up when we are on the way down, so if we are kind to them, they might remember our kindness! Anyway, does it not make you feel better to be kind to others than it does to be nasty?

413

21. When colleagues judge us unfairly, we should try not to carry a grudge. To do so would be wasting our time – while our accuser is out enjoying himself. A poor memory is often the most sensible response. So we should *forgive and forget* if we can, for sour grapes make very bad wine. When we have to defend ourselves against another's attack, we should try not to exaggerate, over-react, or go over the top, because we will only end up by making a fool of ourselves.

22. When under stress, or racked with doubt, that is when we need the comfort of *friendship*, if not of love. To have a friend, you must be a friend. My wife is my best friend, but the lawyer also needs legal friends and the politician needs political friends. I have never searched for them, but I have tried not to drive them away when, from time to time, they have arrived.

23. In politics, success can only come with teamwork, so *loyalty* is very important, to those who support you and to those whom you support. Both must know that they can depend upon you when the chips are down. But loyalty does not have to be blind. If you do not agree with your colleagues, and do not intend to give them the support they will need, then you should give them warning of your position, and give them your reasons. That is not disloyalty, though it may require courage. I have often disagreed with my Party and my friends: I hope no-one could accuse me of disloyalty to either.

24. Both law and politics are thinking professions. Like parachutes, our *minds work best when they are open.* When you do not feel yourself open to argument, it is better not to engage in one. If we are forced into an argument, and have to change position, it would be better if we did it because we have seen the light, not because we have felt the heat. Still less should we want to gain the reputation of being like a cushion that bears the impression of the last person to have sat on us.

25. We do need *courage*, to stand up to judges, Party whips, or even to constituency organisations. If we are sure that we are right, we should be able to argue our way through to success. An MP has no right to argue with the Speaker of the House of Commons, any more than he would have a right to argue with a football referee or cricket umpire: so one has to know when to stop arguing.

26. It is essential to public life, as politician or lawyer, to be *a good speaker*. We must train ourselves so that our audience can hear us, at a level of voice that does not grate on them, and with clarity of reasoning and presentation that requires practice and self-confidence. In my early days, I went to public speaking training classes, I read books on public speaking, and I spoke as often as I could in public, at university debates, political meetings, and moots. Politicians are well-known for intellectual constipation and verbal diarrhoea, so it is very important to try to get your brain into gear before you speak. It is also absolutely vital to any argument that the audience should be interested in it; so we must try to say interesting things or they will not remember very much of what we have said – and that, in a speech to a jury, could be fatal to our client.

27. We must always remind ourselves *not to be boring*. A bore is said to be someone who, when you ask how he is, tells you! The old dictum: stand up, speak up, shut up, is helpful only as a reminder that it is no use speaking at all, if you cannot be heard, and also that you should be as short as you reasonably can to get your message across. But whilst it is undoubtedly true that a speech does not have to be eternal to be immortal, if you are trying to change a jury's mind in your client's favour, you may have to ram your message home. This may mean having to tell them what they are going to hear, then telling it to them, then telling them what they have just heard. Learn about body language, so that you have some idea of whether any of the audience is taking in the message by watching their reaction. Do not be easily put off (except in the Court of Appeal, where the judges make the decisions) by an intemperate judge telling you that you are going on too long before a jury, particularly when they are not looking bored. He may have reasons why he does not want you to be too persuasive!

28. It helps to have a sense of **humour**. We should seldom try to be funny in legal speeches; there humour is usually out of place. But in political speeches, I should use humour to get the attention of the audience and to settle them down to be well disposed to you from the beginning of the speech. Nothing turns away wrath like good humour, so it is a very useful political tool that must be honed by use and kept relevant and up to date with current affairs. Some stand-up comics on television should be watched because they are good at witty topicality – if you can bear their vulgarity.

29. The downside of politics is *spin*: the need to be more preoccupied with how things seem or look than how things are, because popularity is everything and without it there can be no winning of elections in a democracy. In court it is the opposite: when you are defending, you usually have to persuade juries that things are not as they seem. People believe what they want to believe, in the end, so the task of the advocate in politics as well as in the law, is to persuade them that their first impressions may be wrong. That is why developing the advocacy skill of persuasion is so important for both the lawyer and the politician. One lawyer politician says he prefers juries to political audiences, because there are fewer of them and he does not have to see them again! But whilst in politics you have always to believe in the case you are presenting and be sincere: in the courts you have only to put the case that you are being paid to put, whether you believe in your client's innocence or not. In either cause, you have always to do the best you can. I have always tried to do just that. Sadly, that has, too often, not been good enough.

Final thoughts: and my 30th guiding rule

I have been so very fortunate, with all my blessings, to have lived such an interesting and exciting life, and God – and solicitors – willing, I intend to go on doing so.

I might have lived a different life, but my particular satisfaction has come from choosing to be both a QC and an MP, and this has enabled me to do so many different things. I am only too conscious that I have not done many of them well. Mostly that was because of my personal failings. Sometimes, it was because I did not believe that certain courses were possible. RAB Butler called his autobiography of a political life *The Art of the Possible*, and, taking as it were a leaf out of his book, I usually only attempted the possible. If I had my time again, I would attempt more of the impossible, for I think that the enduring lesson I have learnt, and the one I would most want to pass on, is that *what seems to be impossible is often possible, so do not be shy to attempt it: my 30th guiding rule.*

From my 48 years as a lawyer, I have learnt that you can often win a seemingly impossible verdict. From my over 50 years in politics I have learnt that, with strong leadership, the impossible can sometimes be made to happen.

Who would have believed, 40 years ago, when I first became a parliamentary candidate, or even as late as 1979 when I had been an MP for some time, that the ratchet of socialism could ever be reversed? Yet, against the advice of her colleagues, Margaret Thatcher stopped the abuse of trade union power, de-nationalised major industries, introduced a culture of free enterprise and small business, and injected the monetarism concept into public finance, thereby halting and then reversing the ratchet.

Who would have believed, in the 1970s, that the Soviet Union and the Communist bloc would crumble in a generation, and that world communism would be reduced to impotence? Yet Mikhail Gorbachev (reluctantly), Boris Yeltzin, Ronald Reagan and Margaret Thatcher (enthusiastically), achieved that by their leadership.

Who would have thought it possible, as late as the 1980s, that white rule would be replaced by black rule in South Africa, without terrible bloodshed? But Nelson Mandela and FW de Klerk achieved it with their leadership.

Who would have thought, in the 1970s, the 1980s, and the 1990s, that the Reverend Ian Paisley would ever sit down with Martin McGuiness and Gerry Adams to share power in Northern Ireland? But it has happened, and let us hope that the peace endures!

And who would have thought, at the turn of the 1990s, that socialism in this country would or could be so decisively defeated, and that the only way in which Tony Blair's New Labour Party could take and hold onto power from the Tories, would be by taking over our policies and governing as Conservatives – by supporting nuclear defence, privatisation, business enterprise, council house sales, private education, lower income taxation – to name just some of what has endured.

Perhaps I can add a further near-impossibility: who would have thought that we would ever be governed by a coalition government with Liberal Democrats supporting the Conservatives?

So the seemingly impossible does happen and can be made to happen. I am only sorry that I did not realise that when I started!

Now, in the sad knowledge that I myself will never come so close to the perfection I have written about in the final chapter of this book, I think it prudent to take my leave of my very patient reader. For with Andrew Marvell, I hear 'Time's winged chariot hurrying near', and John Milton's call: 'Tomorrow to fresh woods and pastures new' – and I have no time to lose!

Index